TOKYOPOP SHOP

THIS FALL, TOKYOPOP CREATES A FRESH, NEW CHAPTER IN TEEN NOVELS...

For Adventurers...
Witches' Forest:
The Adventures of Duan Surk

By Mishio Fukazawa
Duan Surk is a 16-year-old Level 2 fighter who embarks on the quest of a lifetime—battling mythical creatures and outwitting evil sorceresses, all in an impossible rescue mission in the spooky Witches' Forest!

BASED ON THE FAMOUS
***FORTUNE QUEST* WORLD**

For Dreamers...
Magic Moon

By Wolfgang and Heike Hohlbein
Kim enters the enigmatic realm of Magic Moon, where he battles unthinkable monsters and fantastical creatures—in order to unravel the secret that keeps his sister locked in a coma.

THE WORLDWIDE BESTSELLING FANTASY
***THRILLOGY* ARRIVES IN THE U.S.!**

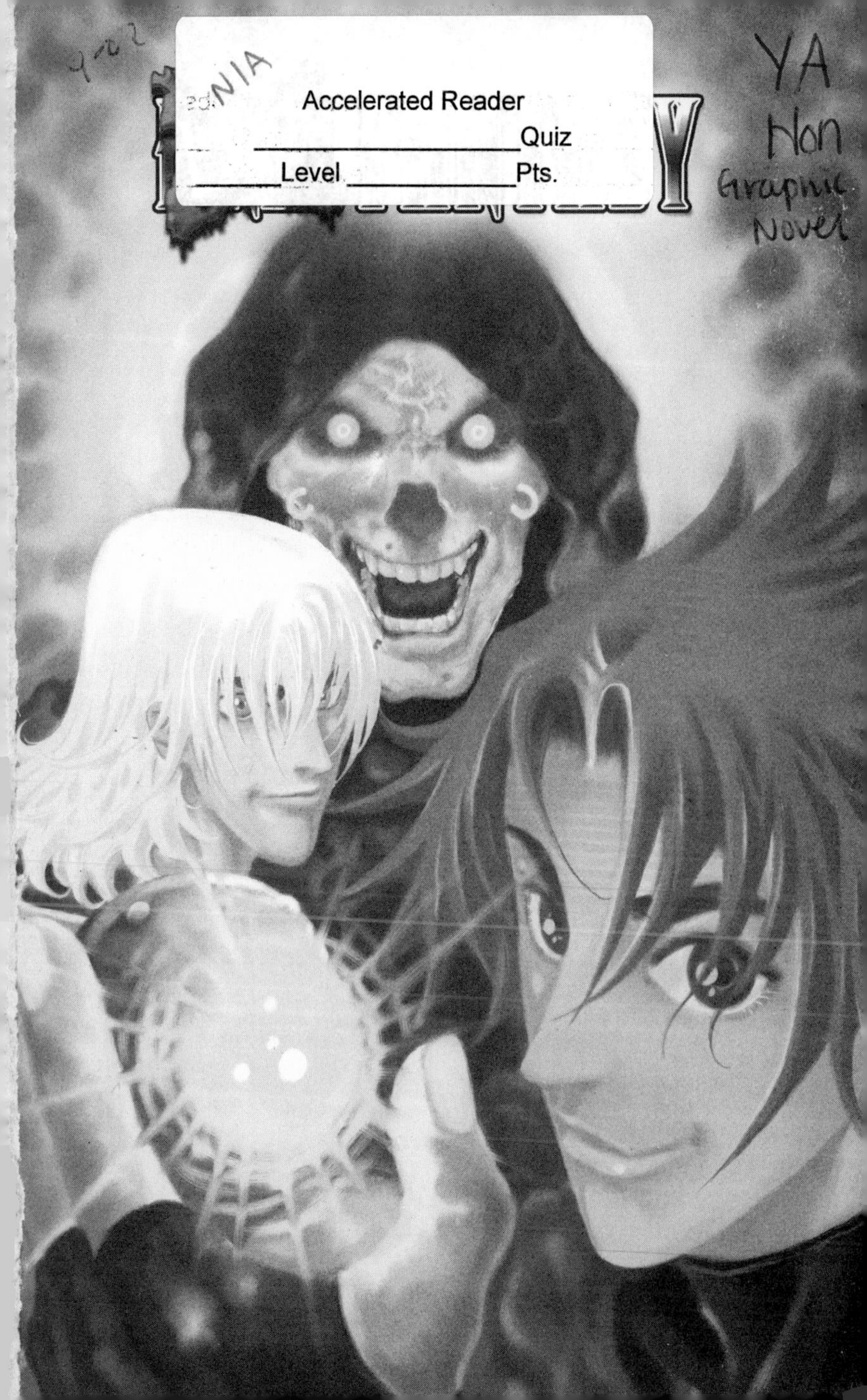

Last Fantasy Vol. 1
Written by Creative Hon
Illustrated by Yong-Wan Kwon

Translation - Sora Han
English Adaptation - Mike Wellman
Copy Editor - Hope Donovan
Retouch and Lettering - Jason Milligan
Production Artist - Erika "Scooter" Terriquez
Cover Design - Kyle Plummer

Editor - Luis Reyes
Digital Imaging Manager - Chris Buford
Production Manager - Jennifer Miller
Managing Editor - Lindsey Johnston
VP of Production - Ron Klamert
Publisher and E.I.C. - Mike Kiley
President and C.O.O. - John Parker
C.E.O. and Chief Creative Officer - Stuart Levy

A  Manga

TOKYOPOP Inc.
5900 Wilshire Blvd. Suite 2000
Los Angeles, CA 90036

E-mail: info@TOKYOPOP.com
Come visit us online at www.TOKYOPOP.com

ISBN: 1-59532-526-3

First TOKYOPOP printing: March 2006
10 9 8 7 6 5 4 3 2
Printed in the USA

VOLUME 1

STORY BY CREATIVE HON
ART BY YONG-WAN KWON

HAMBURG // LONDON // LOS ANGELES // TOKYO

CONTENTS

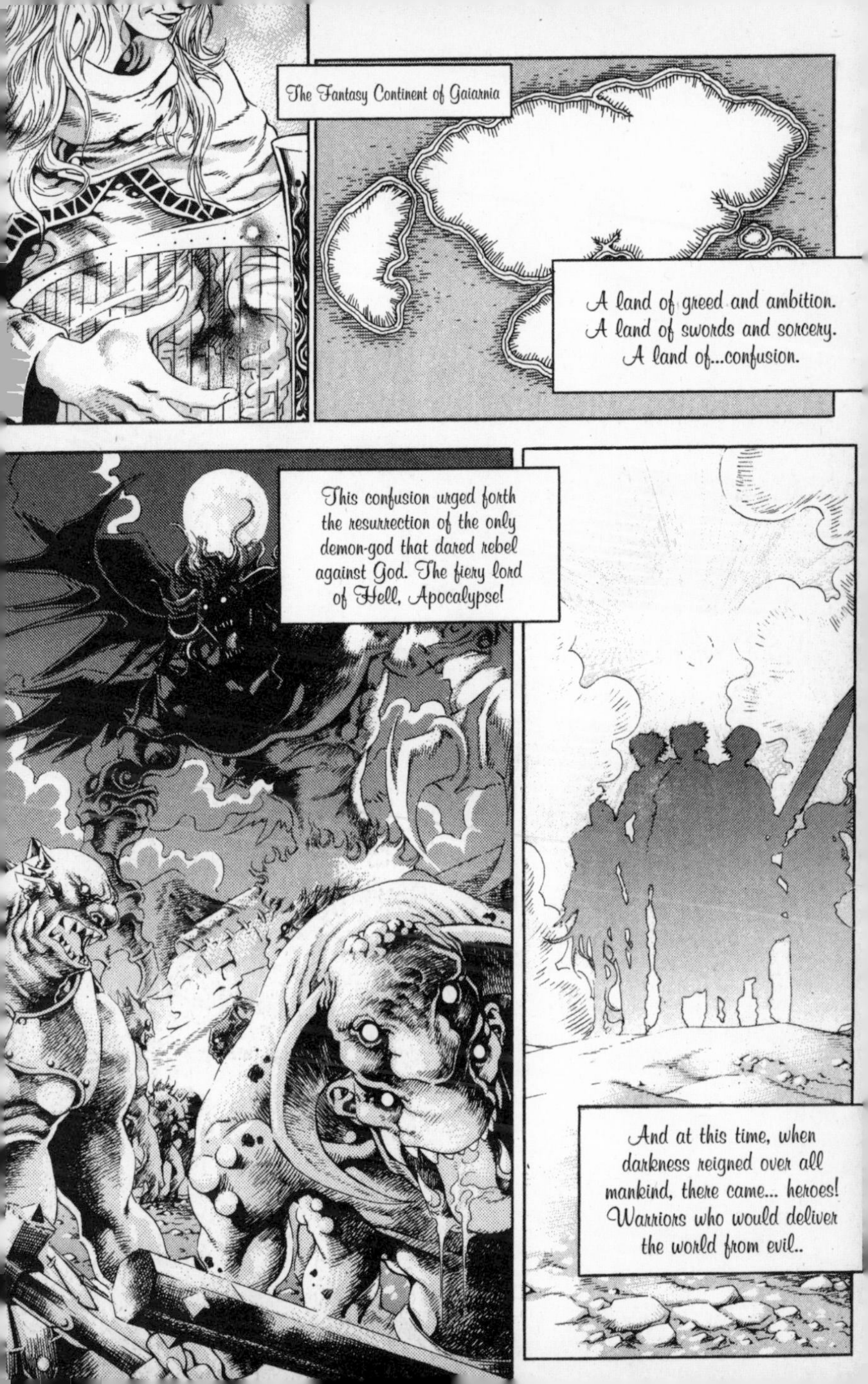
The Fantasy Continent of Gaiarnia
A land of greed and ambition. A land of swords and sorcery. A land of...confusion.
This confusion urged forth the resurrection of the only demon-god that dared rebel against God. The fiery lord of Hell, Apocalypse!
And at this time, when darkness reigned over all mankind, there came... heroes! Warriors who would deliver the world from evil..

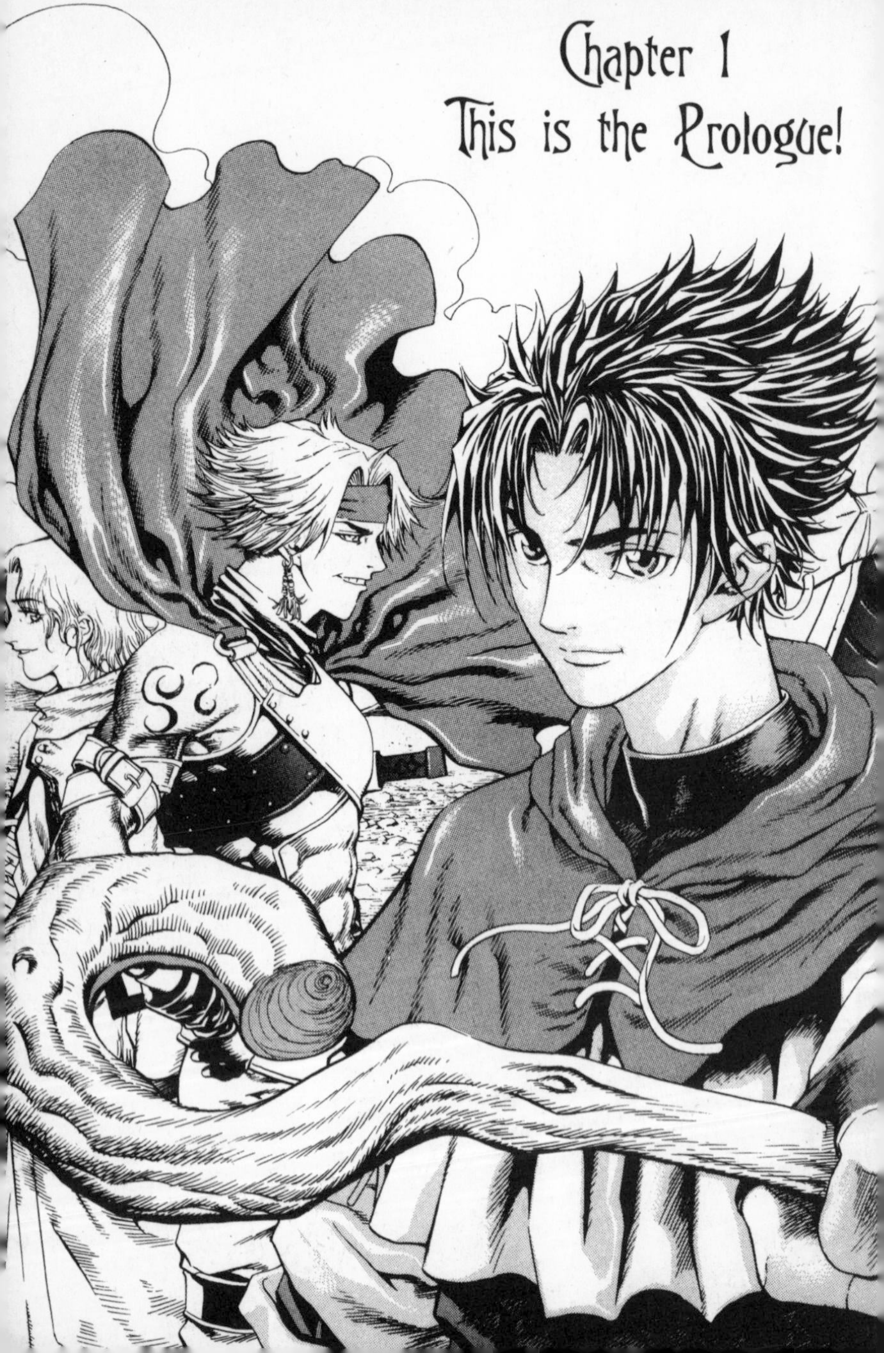
Chapter 1
This is the Prologue!

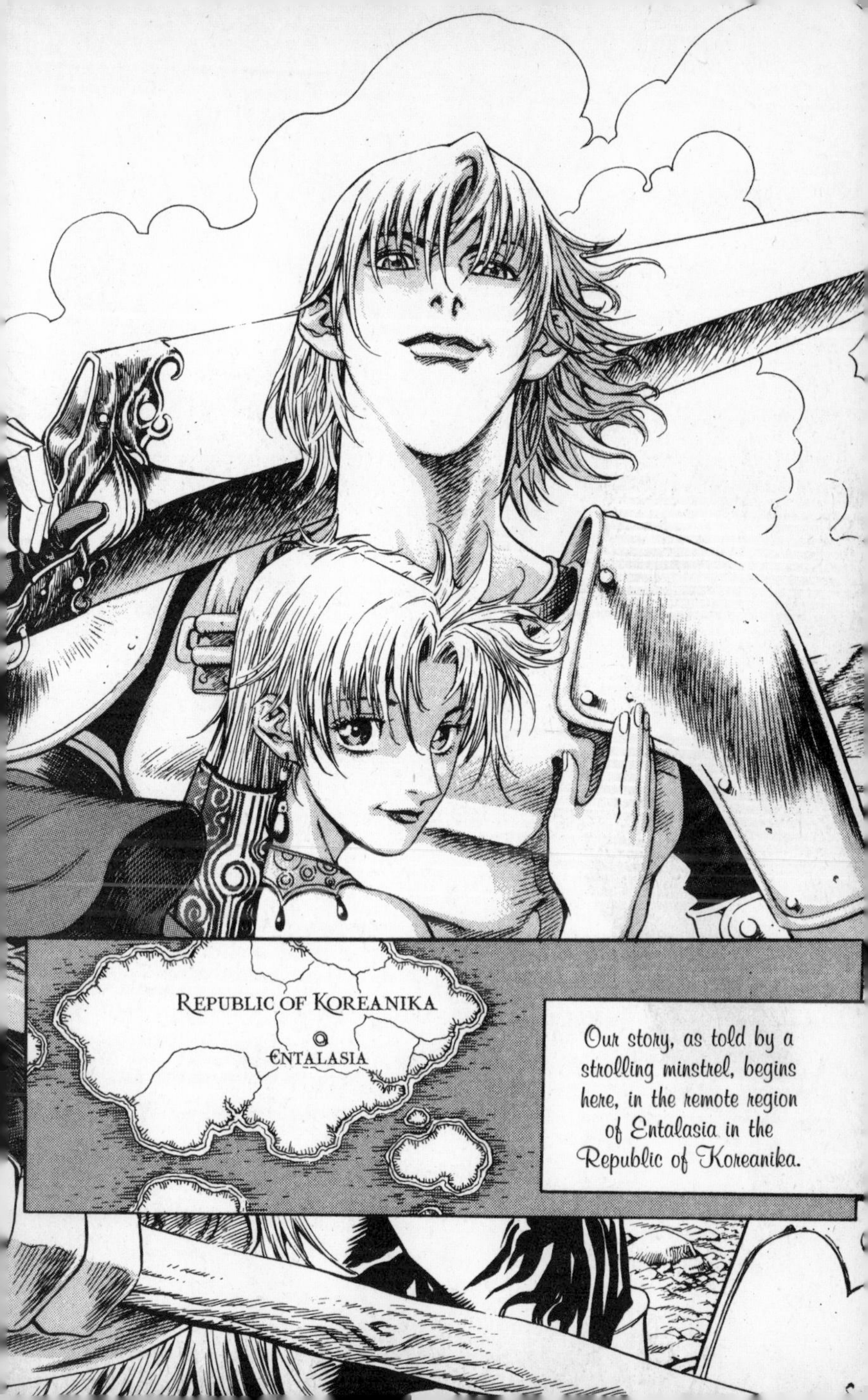
REPUBLIC OF KOREANIKA
ENTALASIA
Our story, as told by a strolling minstrel, begins here, in the remote region of Entalasia in the Republic of Koreanika.

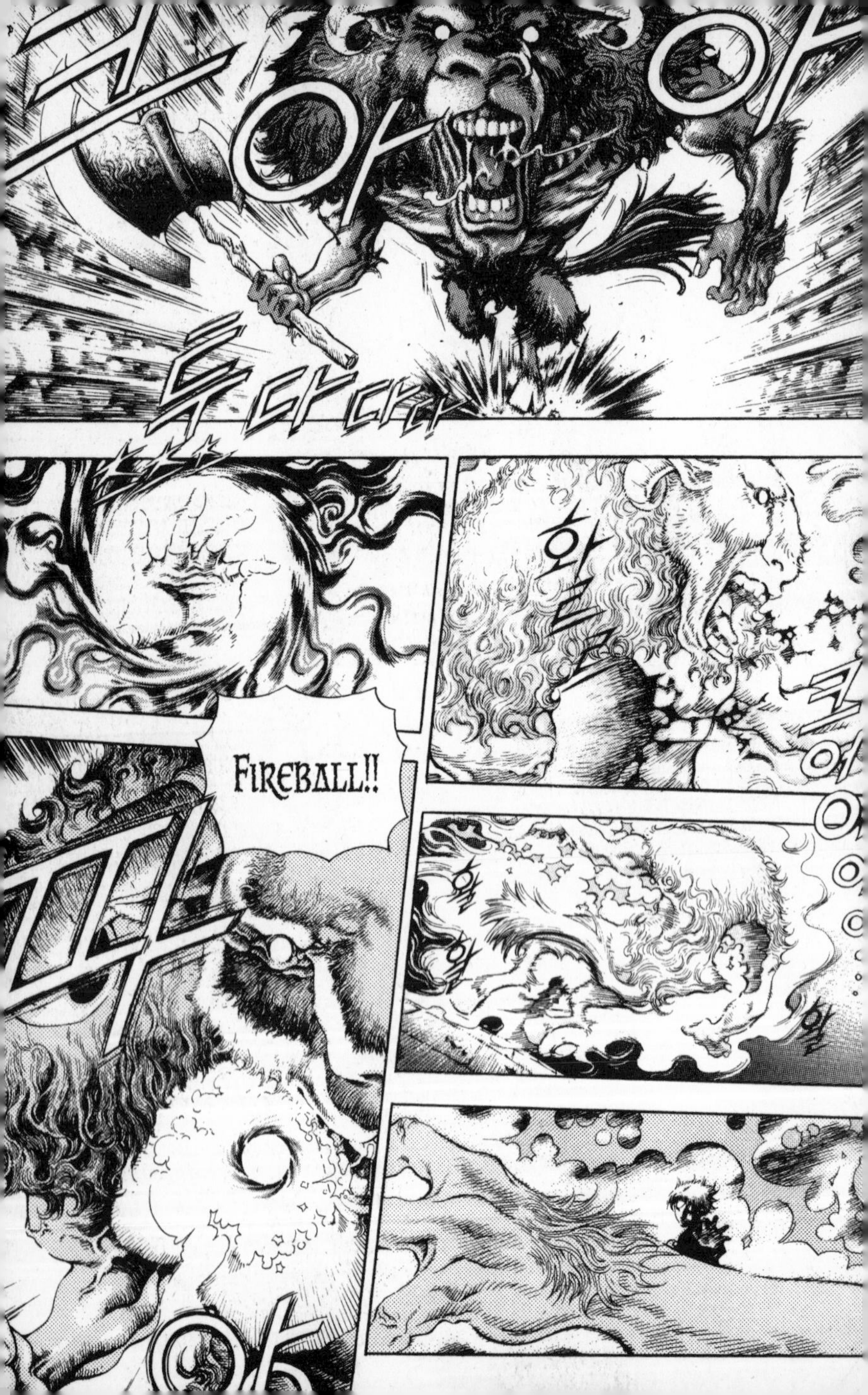
FIREBALL!!

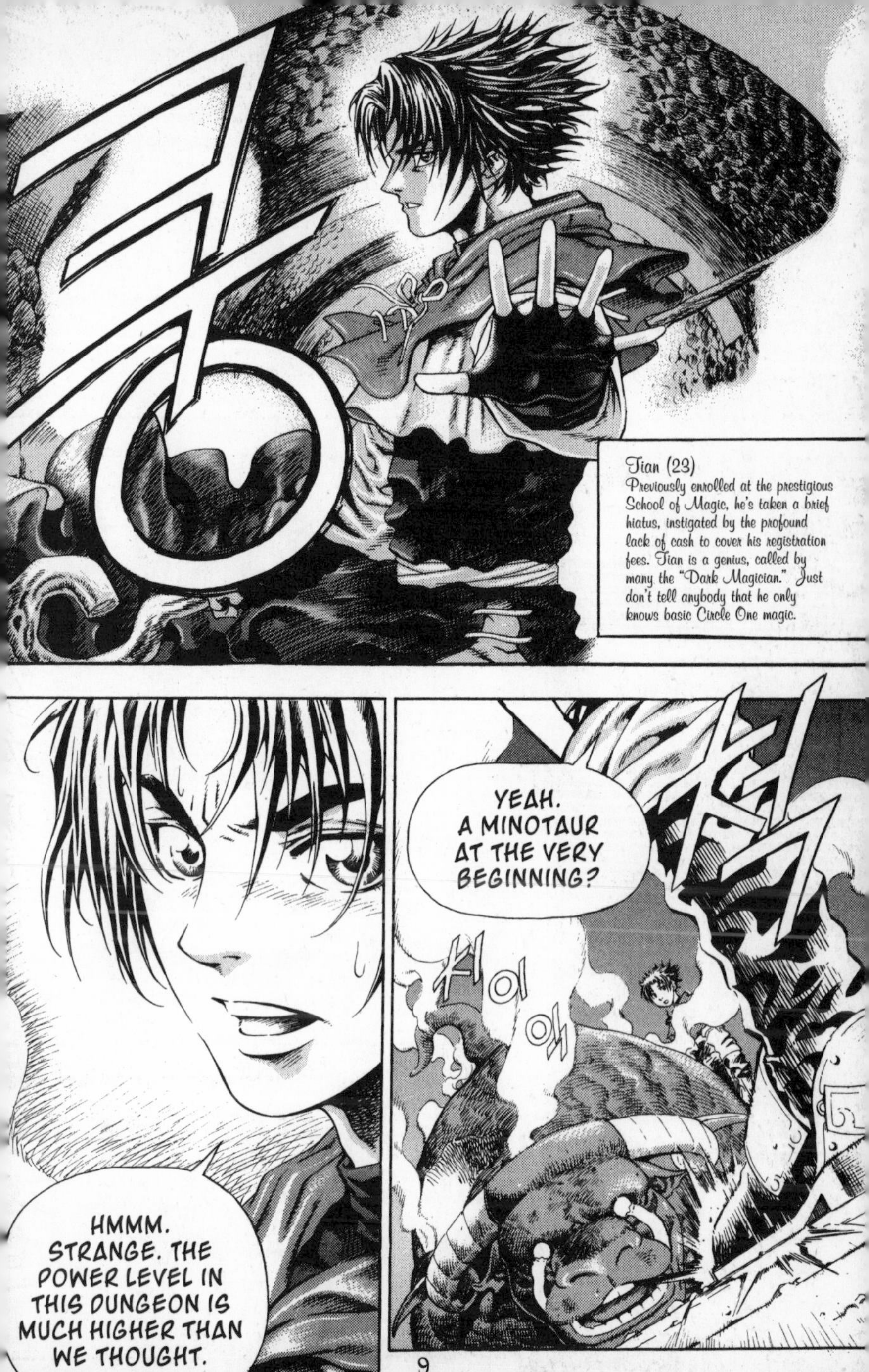
Tian (23)
Previously enrolled at the prestigious School of Magic, he's taken a brief hiatus, instigated by the profound lack of cash to cover his registration fees. Tian is a genius, called by many the "Dark Magician." Just don't tell anybody that he only knows basic Circle One magic.
HMMM. STRANGE. THE POWER LEVEL IN THIS DUNGEON IS MUCH HIGHER THAN WE THOUGHT.
YEAH. A MINOTAUR AT THE VERY BEGINNING?

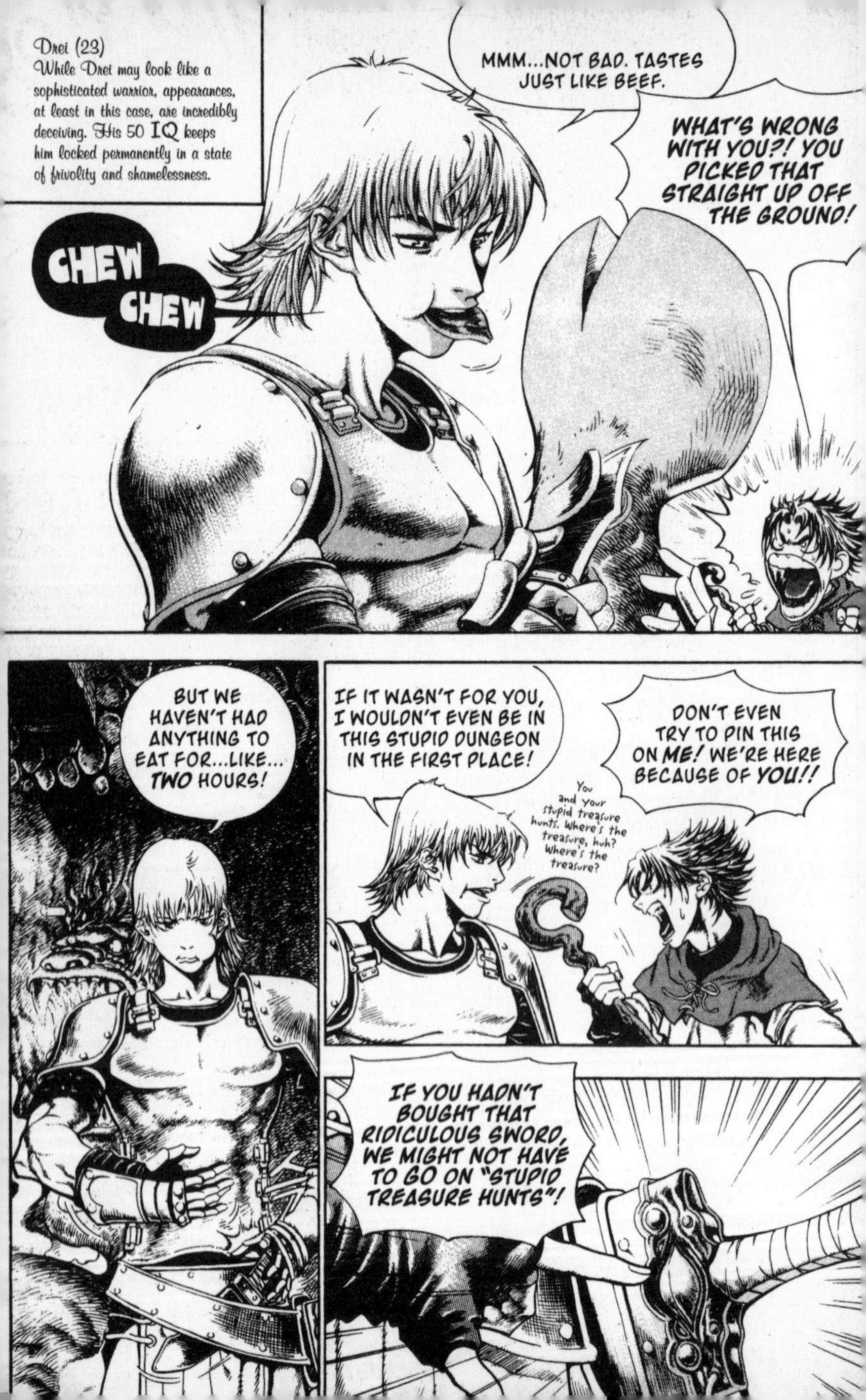
Drei (23)
While Drei may look like a sophisticated warrior, appearances, at least in this case, are incredibly deceiving. His 50 IQ keeps him locked permanently in a state of frivolity and shamelessness.
MMM...NOT BAD. TASTES JUST LIKE BEEF.
WHAT'S WRONG WITH YOU?! YOU PICKED THAT STRAIGHT UP OFF THE GROUND!
CHEW CHEW
BUT WE HAVEN'T HAD ANYTHING TO EAT FOR...LIKE... TWO HOURS!
IF IT WASN'T FOR YOU, I WOULDN'T EVEN BE IN THIS STUPID DUNGEON IN THE FIRST PLACE!
DON'T EVEN TRY TO PIN THIS ON ME! WE'RE HERE BECAUSE OF YOU!!
You and your stupid treasure hunts. Where's the treasure, huh? Where's the treasure?
IF YOU HADN'T BOUGHT THAT RIDICULOUS SWORD, WE MIGHT NOT HAVE TO GO ON "STUPID TREASURE HUNTS"!

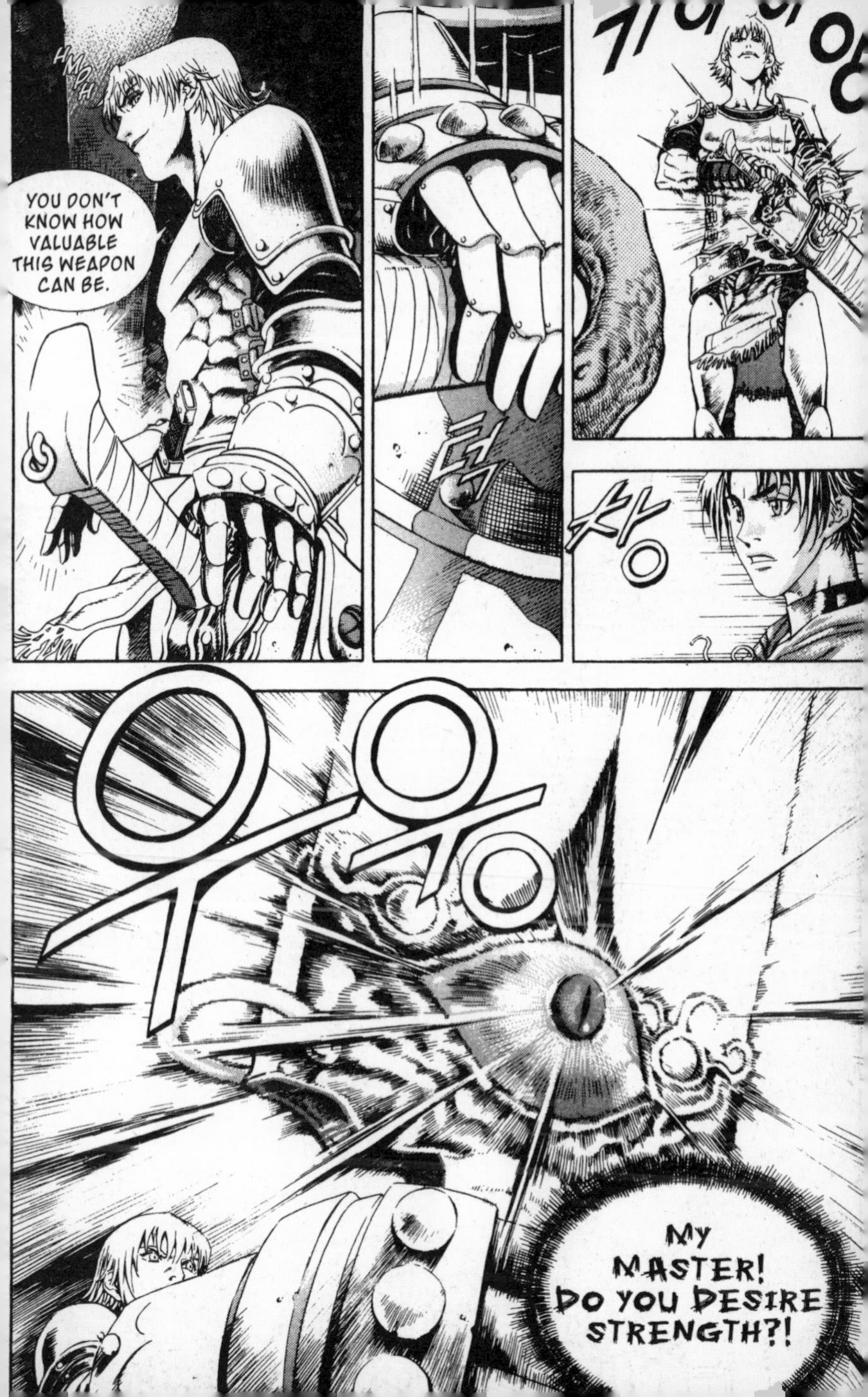
HMPH
YOU DON'T KNOW HOW VALUABLE THIS WEAPON CAN BE.
MY MASTER! DO YOU DESIRE STRENGTH?!

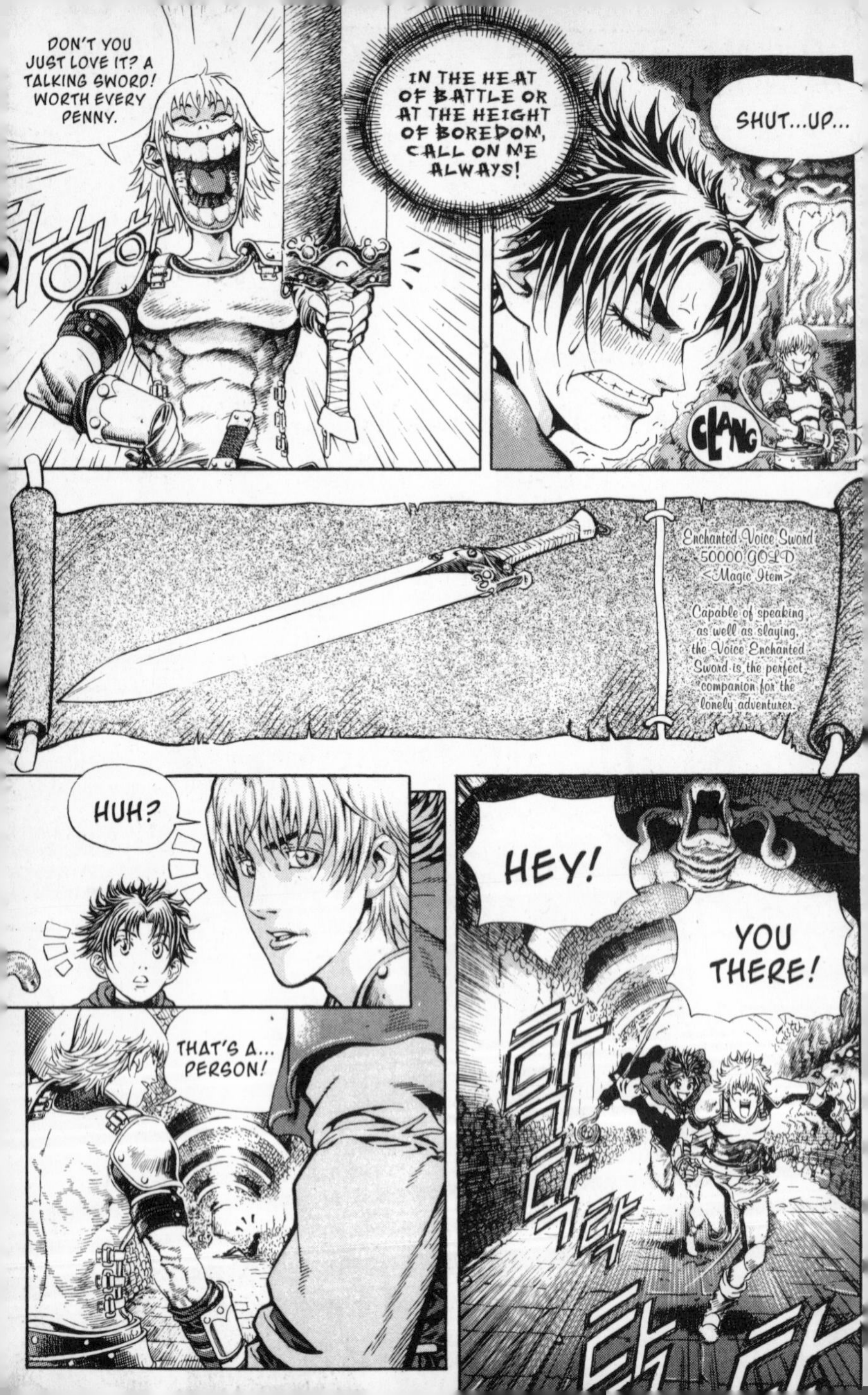

DON'T YOU JUST LOVE IT? A TALKING SWORD! WORTH EVERY PENNY.
IN THE HEAT OF BATTLE OR AT THE HEIGHT OF BOREDOM, CALL ON ME ALWAYS!
SHUT...UP...
CLANG
Enchanted Voice Sword
50000 GOLD
<Magic Item>
Capable of speaking as well as slaying, the Voice Enchanted Sword is the perfect companion for the lonely adventurer.
HUH?
THAT'S A... PERSON!
HEY!
YOU THERE!

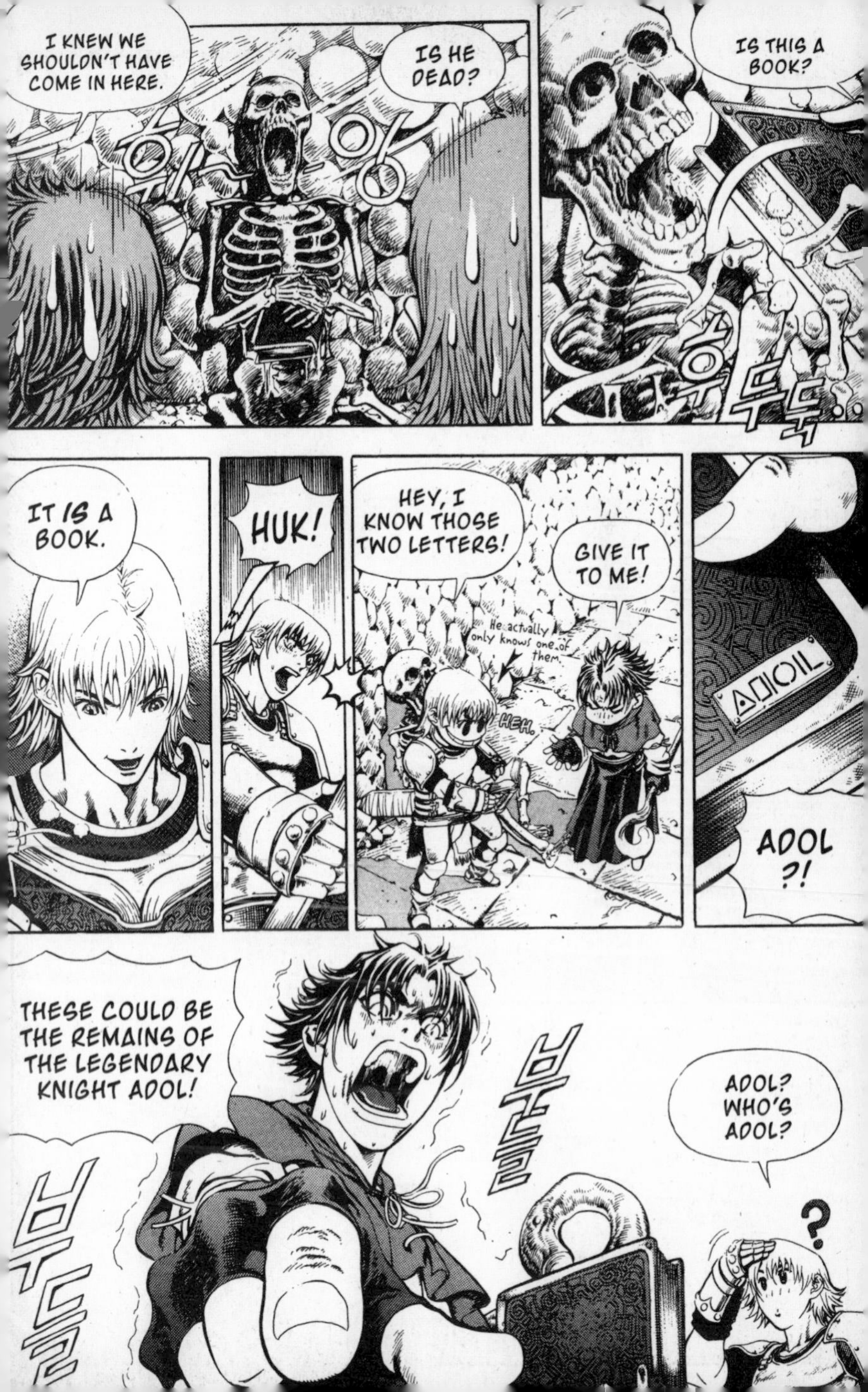
I KNEW WE SHOULDN'T HAVE COME IN HERE.
IS HE DEAD?
IS THIS A BOOK?
IT IS A BOOK.
HUK!
HEY, I KNOW THOSE TWO LETTERS!
GIVE IT TO ME!
He actually only knows one of them.
HEH.
ADOL ?!
THESE COULD BE THE REMAINS OF THE LEGENDARY KNIGHT ADOL!
ADOL? WHO'S ADOL?
?

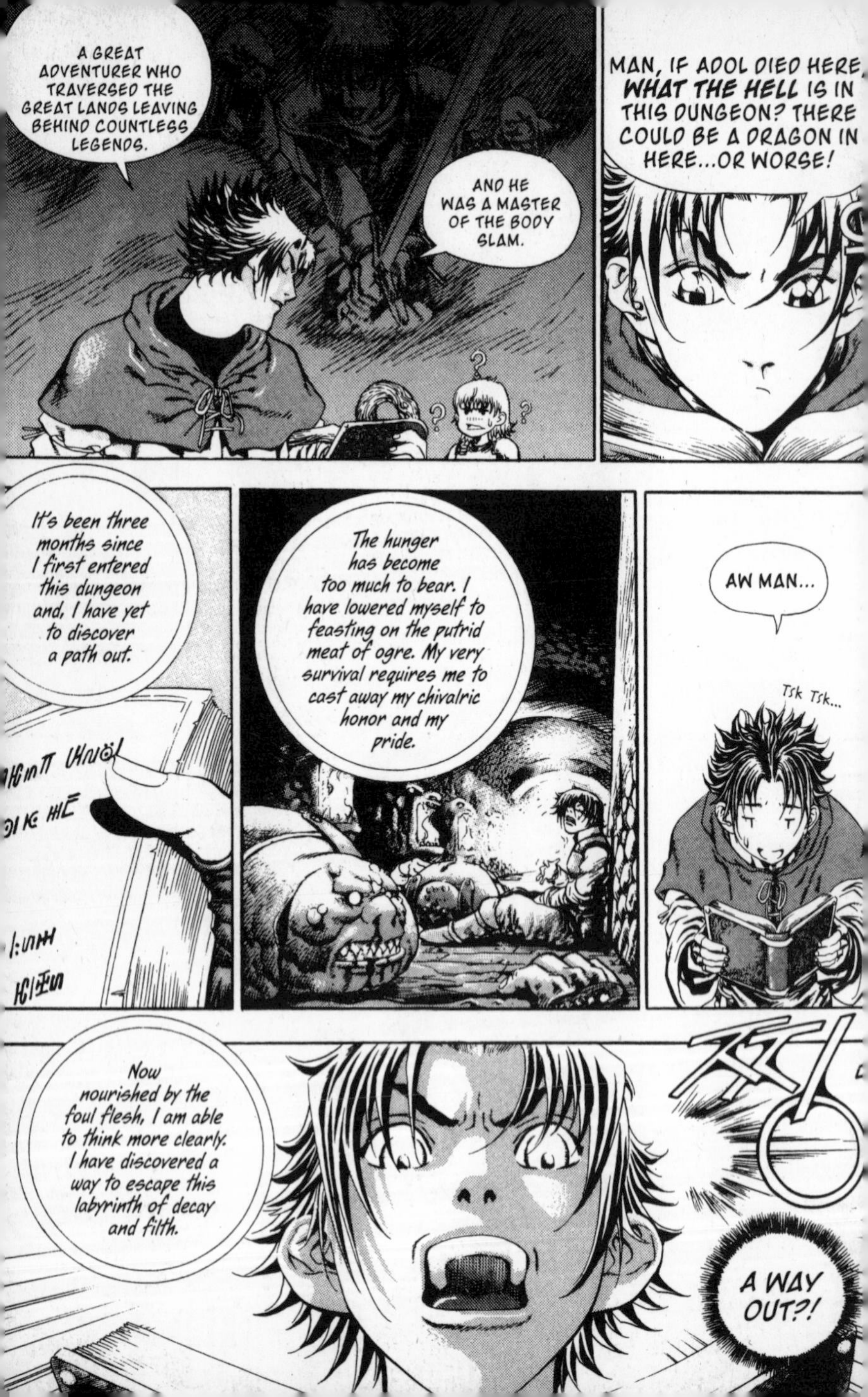

A GREAT ADVENTURER WHO TRAVERSED THE GREAT LANDS LEAVING BEHIND COUNTLESS LEGENDS.
AND HE WAS A MASTER OF THE BODY SLAM.
MAN, IF ADOL DIED HERE, WHAT THE HELL IS IN THIS DUNGEON? THERE COULD BE A DRAGON IN HERE...OR WORSE!
It's been three months since I first entered this dungeon and, I have yet to discover a path out.
The hunger has become too much to bear. I have lowered myself to feasting on the putrid meat of ogre. My very survival requires me to cast away my chivalric honor and my pride.
AW MAN...
Tsk Tsk...
Now nourished by the foul flesh, I am able to think more clearly. I have discovered a way to escape this labyrinth of decay and filth.
A WAY OUT?!

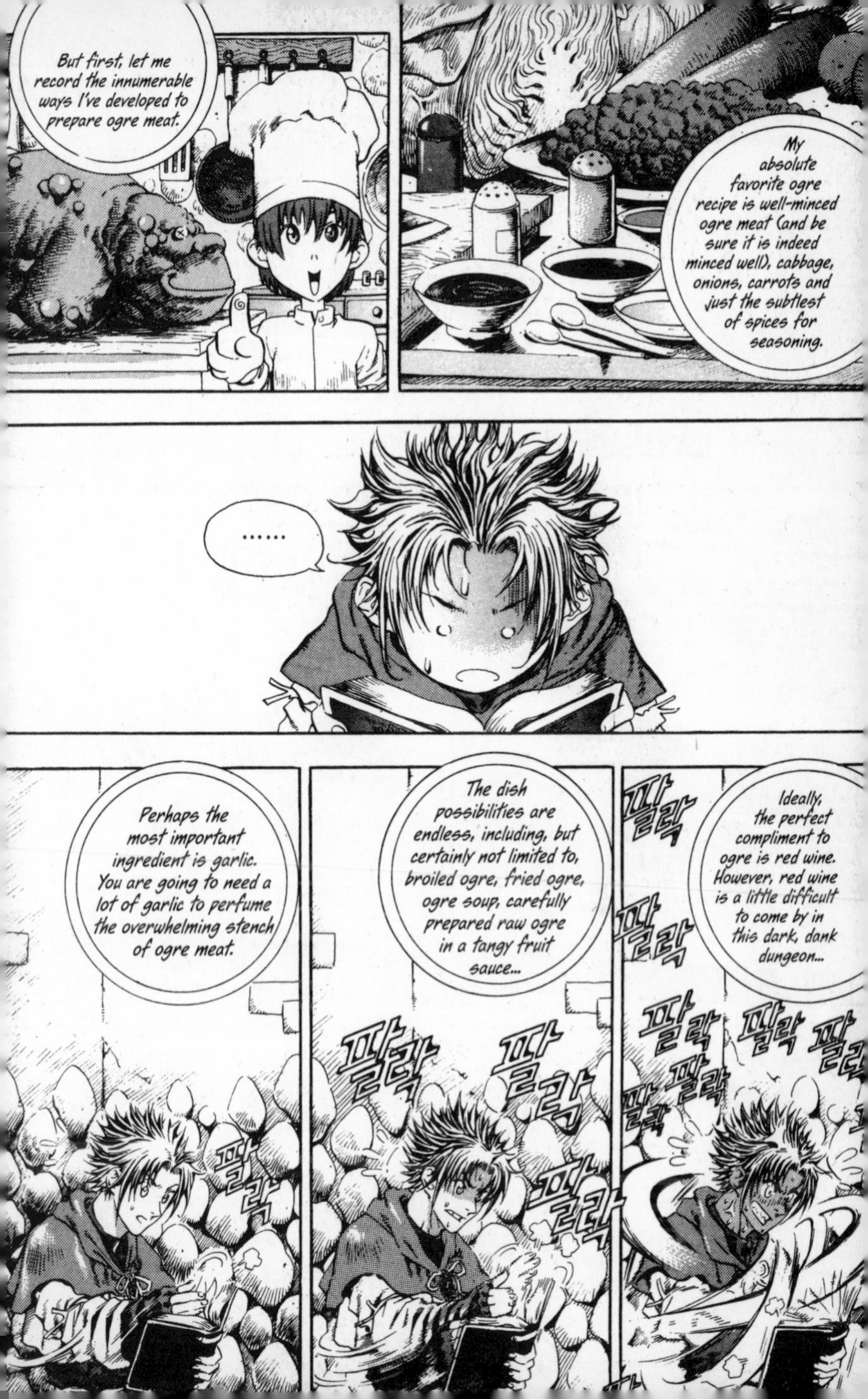
But first, let me record the innumerable ways I've developed to prepare ogre meat.
My absolute favorite ogre recipe is well-minced ogre meat (and be sure it is indeed minced well), cabbage, onions, carrots and just the subtlest of spices for seasoning.
......
Perhaps the most important ingredient is garlic. You are going to need a lot of garlic to perfume the overwhelming stench of ogre meat.
The dish possibilities are endless, including, but certainly not limited to, broiled ogre, fried ogre, ogre soup, carefully prepared raw ogre in a tangy fruit sauce...
Ideally, the perfect compliment to ogre is red wine. However, red wine is a little difficult to come by in this dark, dank dungeon...

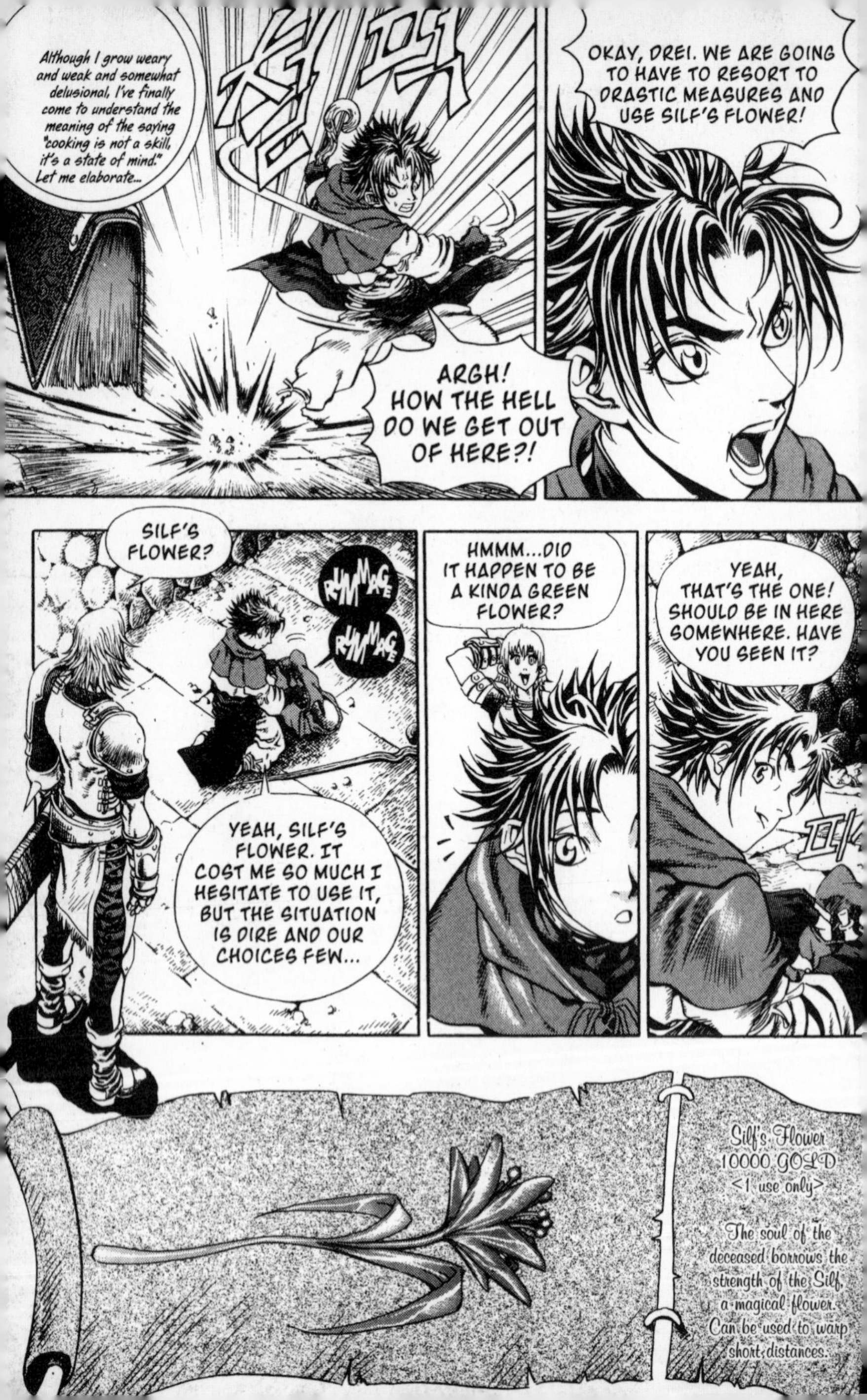
Although I grow weary and weak and somewhat delusional, I've finally come to understand the meaning of the saying "cooking is not a skill, it's a state of mind." Let me elaborate...
ARGH! HOW THE HELL DO WE GET OUT OF HERE?!
OKAY, DREI. WE ARE GOING TO HAVE TO RESORT TO DRASTIC MEASURES AND USE SILF'S FLOWER!
SILF'S FLOWER?
RUMMAGE
RUMMAGE
YEAH, SILF'S FLOWER. IT COST ME SO MUCH I HESITATE TO USE IT, BUT THE SITUATION IS DIRE AND OUR CHOICES FEW...
HMMM...DID IT HAPPEN TO BE A KINDA GREEN FLOWER?
YEAH, THAT'S THE ONE! SHOULD BE IN HERE SOMEWHERE. HAVE YOU SEEN IT?
Silf's Flower
10000 GOLD
<1 use only>
The soul of the deceased borrows the strength of the Silf, a magical flower. Can be used to warp short distances.

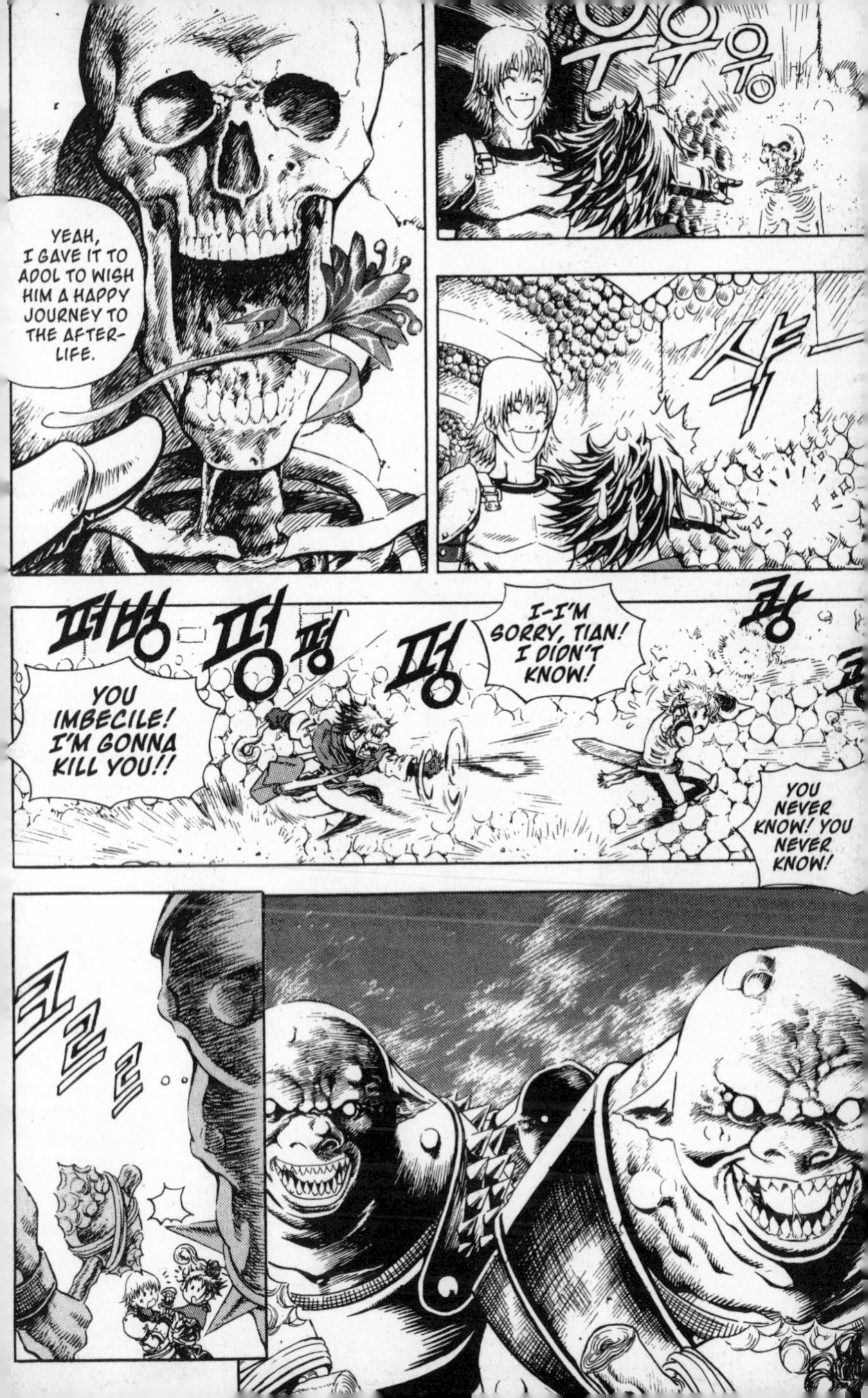
YEAH, I GAVE IT TO ADOL TO WISH HIM A HAPPY JOURNEY TO THE AFTER-LIFE.
YOU IMBECILE! I'M GONNA KILL YOU!!
I-I'M SORRY, TIAN! I DIDN'T KNOW!
YOU NEVER KNOW! YOU NEVER KNOW!

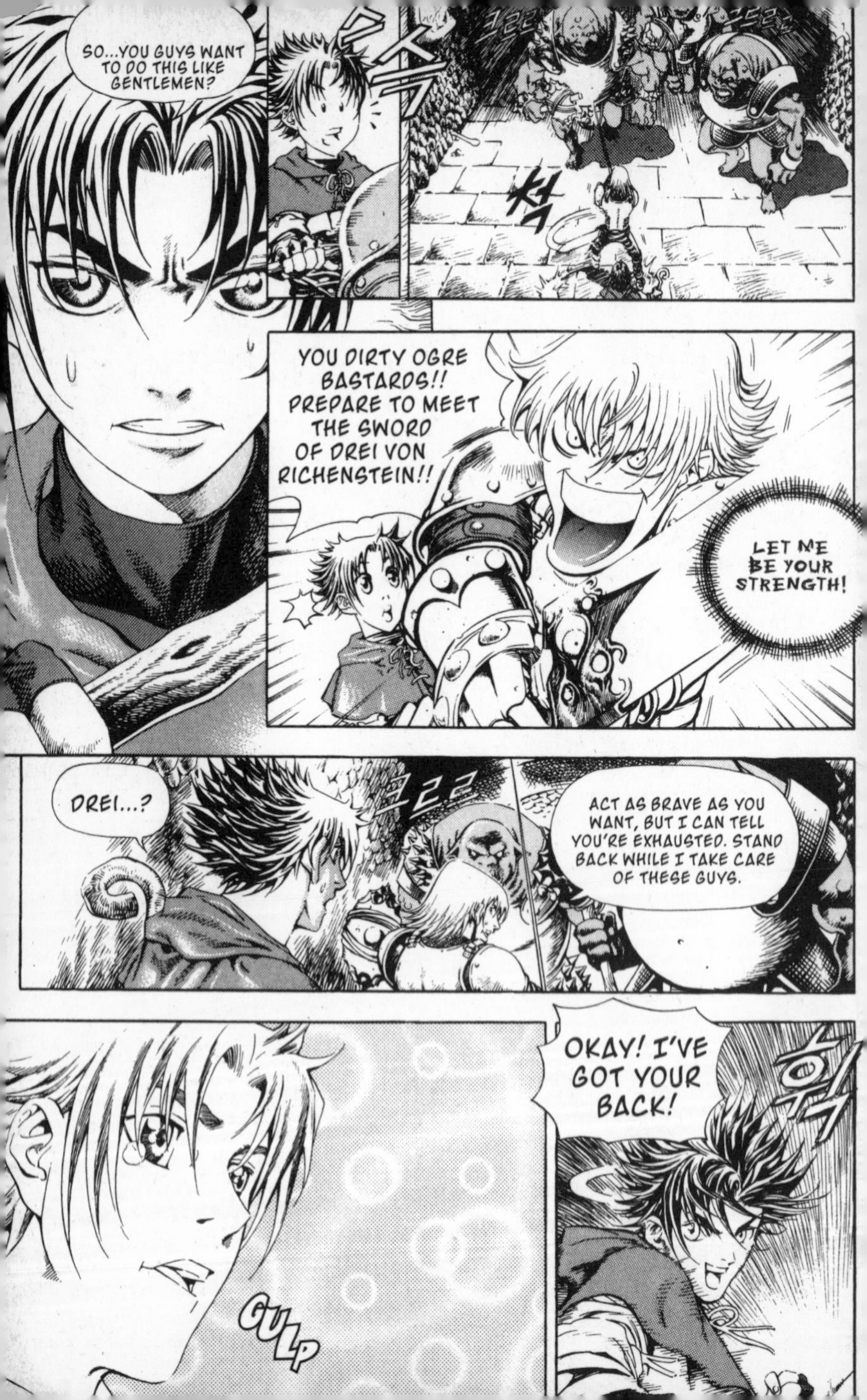
SO...YOU GUYS WANT TO DO THIS LIKE GENTLEMEN?
YOU DIRTY OGRE BASTARDS!! PREPARE TO MEET THE SWORD OF DREI VON RICHENSTEIN!!
LET ME BE YOUR STRENGTH!
DREI...?
ACT AS BRAVE AS YOU WANT, BUT I CAN TELL YOU'RE EXHAUSTED. STAND BACK WHILE I TAKE CARE OF THESE GUYS.
OKAY! I'VE GOT YOUR BACK!
GULP

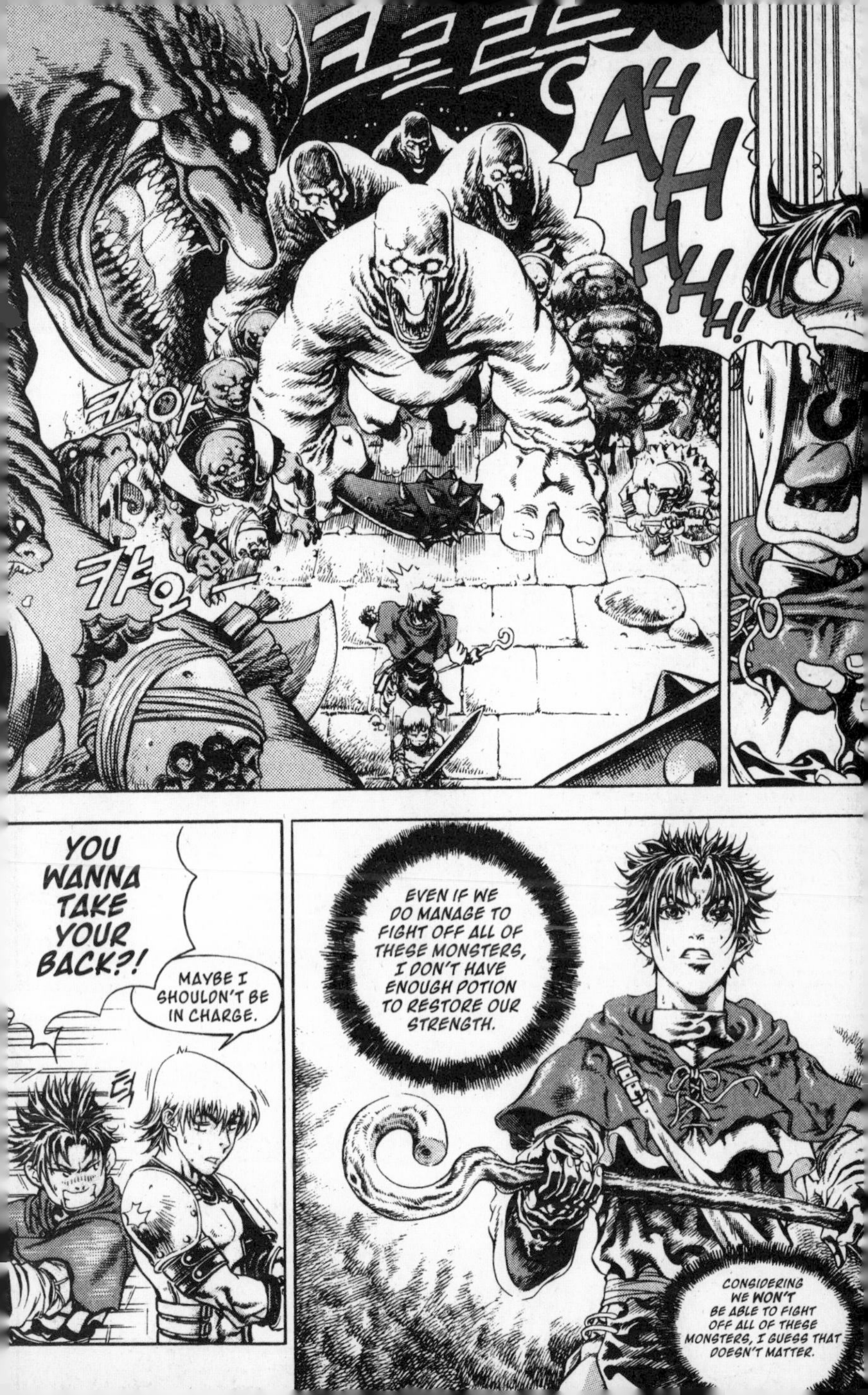
AHHHHHHH!
캬오
YOU WANNA TAKE YOUR BACK?!
MAYBE I SHOULDN'T BE IN CHARGE.
EVEN IF WE DO MANAGE TO FIGHT OFF ALL OF THESE MONSTERS, I DON'T HAVE ENOUGH POTION TO RESTORE OUR STRENGTH.
CONSIDERING WE WON'T BE ABLE TO FIGHT OFF ALL OF THESE MONSTERS, I GUESS THAT DOESN'T MATTER.

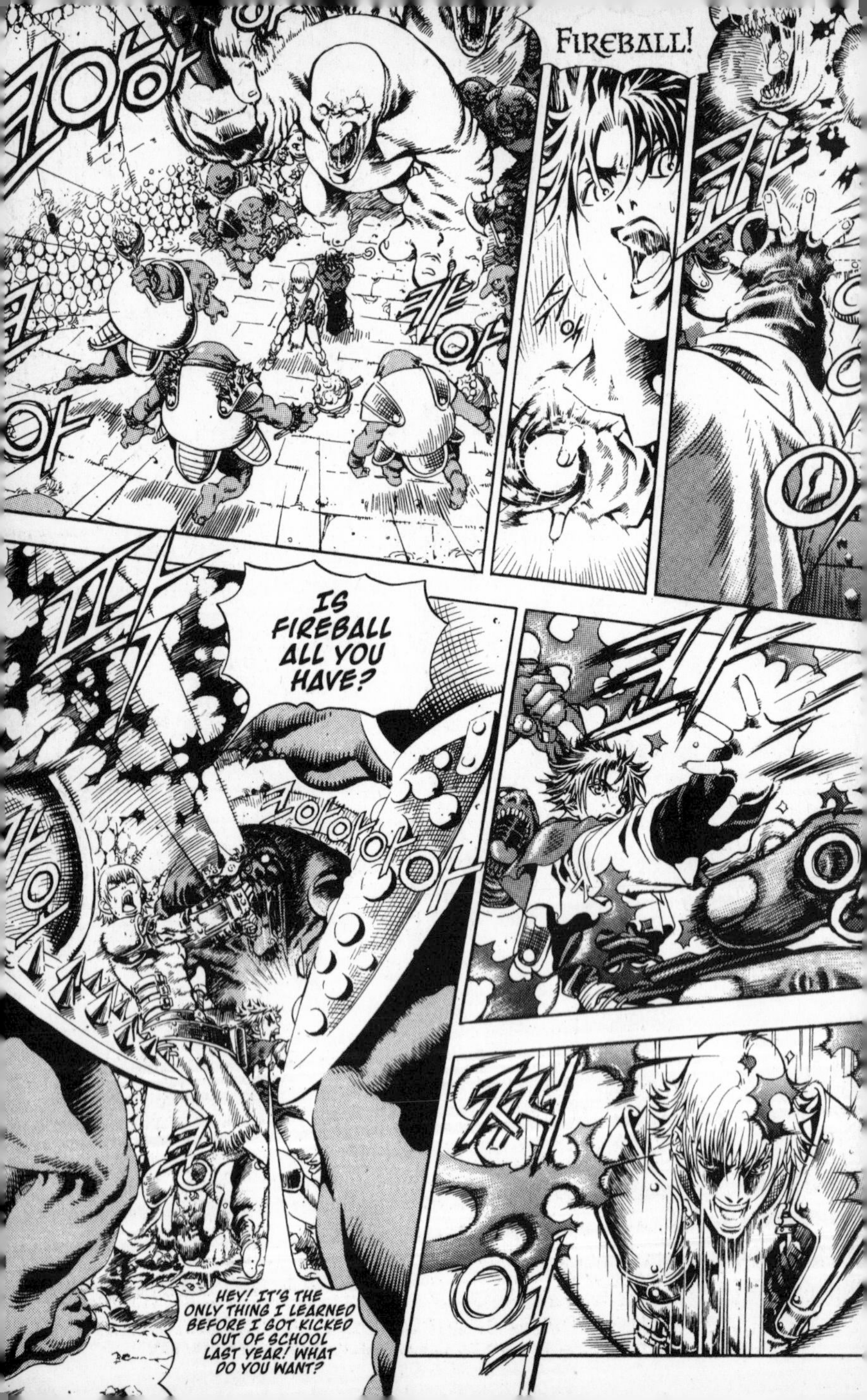
FIREBALL!
IS FIREBALL ALL YOU HAVE?
HEY! IT'S THE ONLY THING I LEARNED BEFORE I GOT KICKED OUT OF SCHOOL LAST YEAR! WHAT DO YOU WANT?

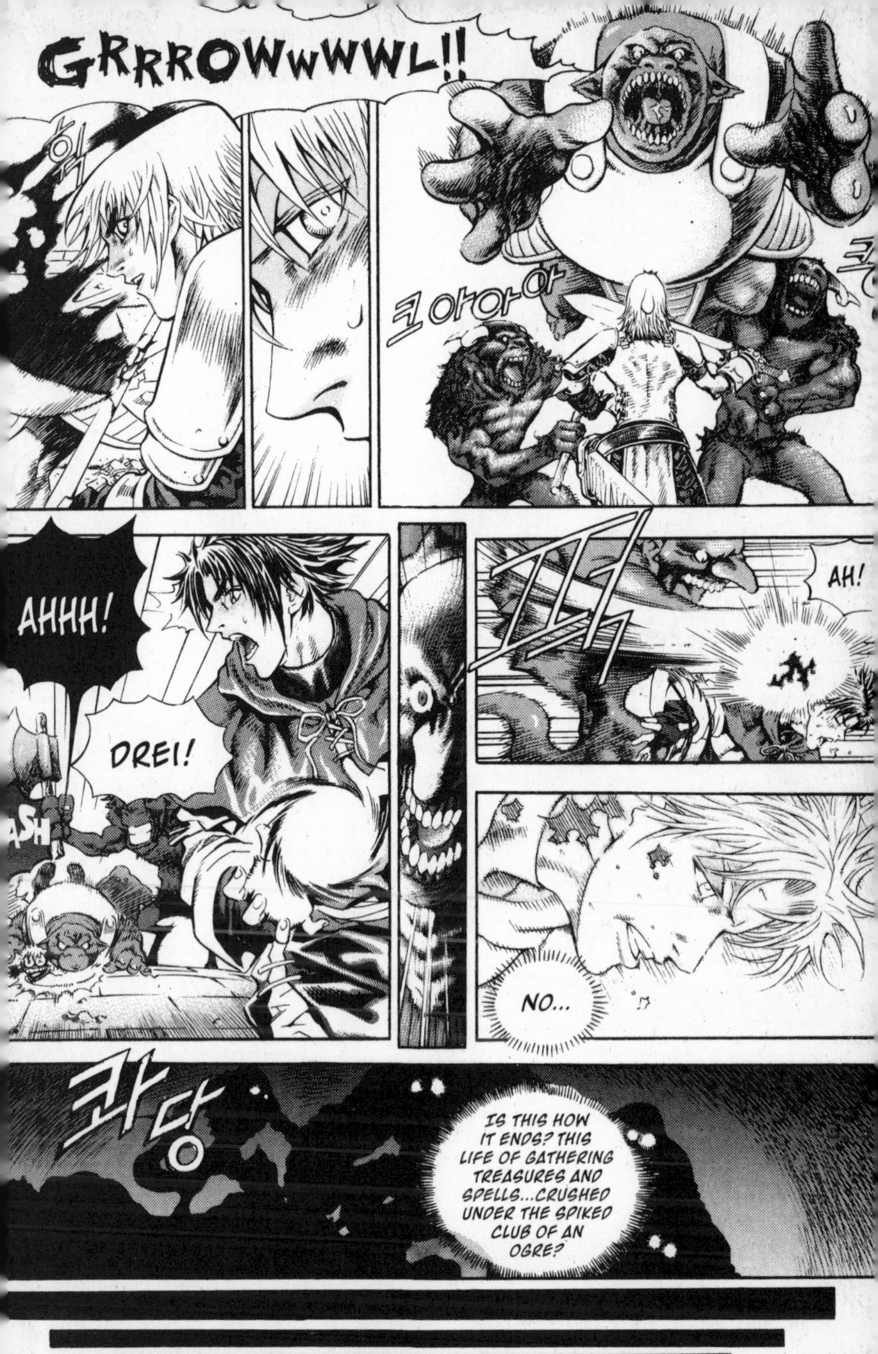
GRRROWWWWL!!
AHHH!
DREI!
AH!
NO...
콰당
IS THIS HOW IT ENDS? THIS LIFE OF GATHERING TREASURES AND SPELLS...CRUSHED UNDER THE SPIKED CLUB OF AN OGRE?

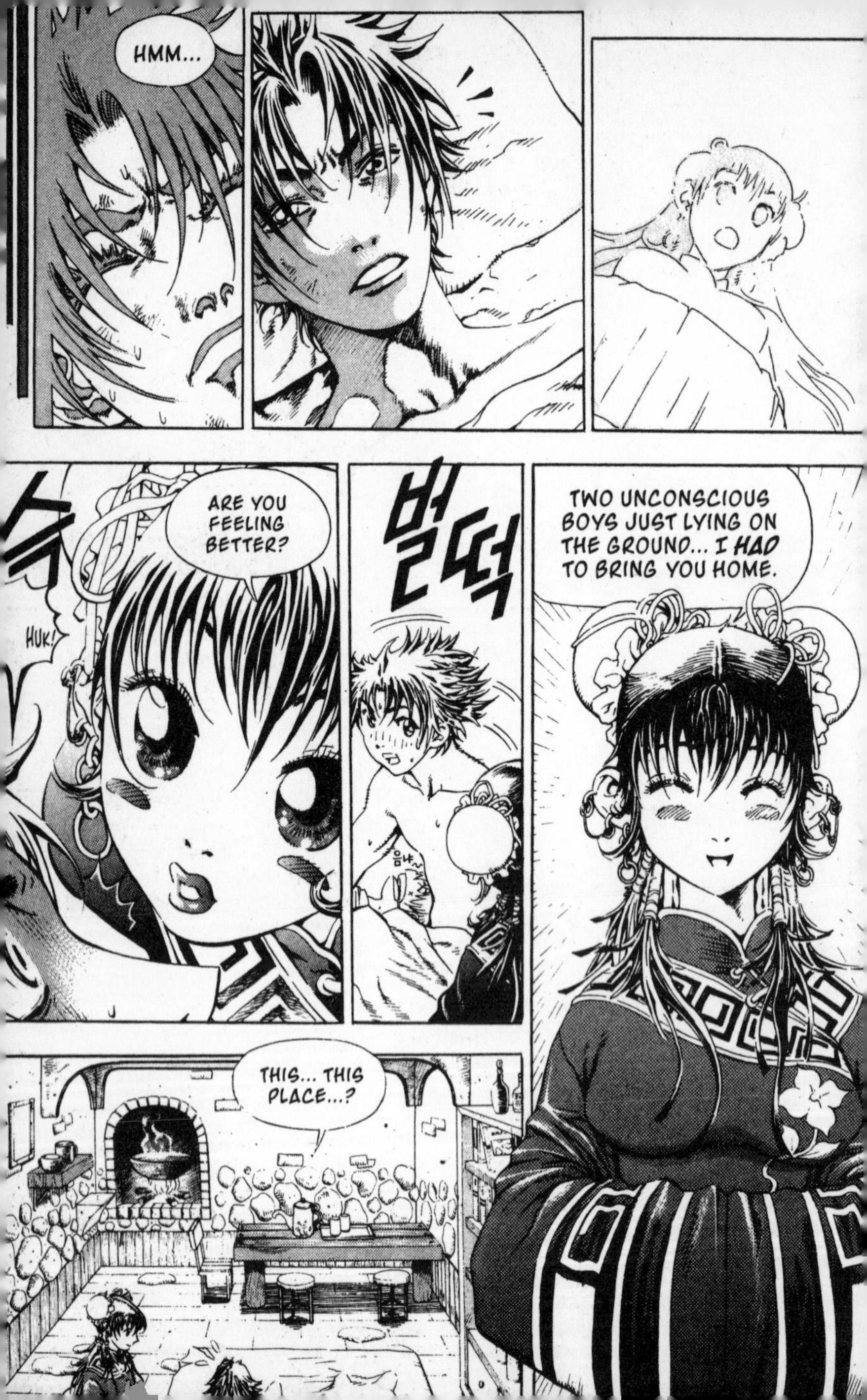
HMM...
ARE YOU FEELING BETTER?
HUK!
벌떡
TWO UNCONSCIOUS BOYS JUST LYING ON THE GROUND... I HAD TO BRING YOU HOME.
THIS... THIS PLACE...?

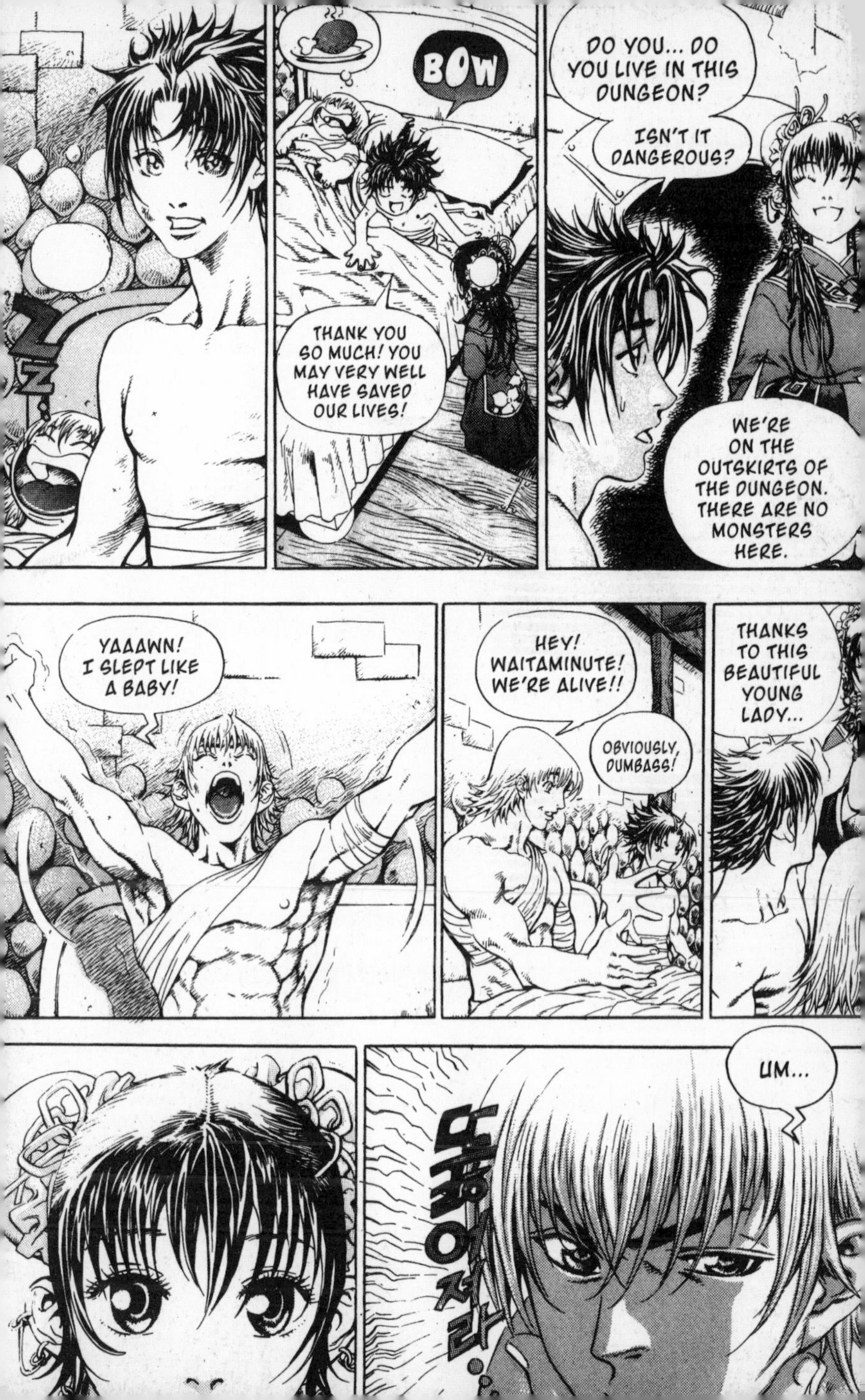
BOW
THANK YOU SO MUCH! YOU MAY VERY WELL HAVE SAVED OUR LIVES!
DO YOU... DO YOU LIVE IN THIS DUNGEON?
ISN'T IT DANGEROUS?
WE'RE ON THE OUTSKIRTS OF THE DUNGEON. THERE ARE NO MONSTERS HERE.
YAAAWN! I SLEPT LIKE A BABY!
HEY! WAITAMINUTE! WE'RE ALIVE!!
OBVIOUSLY, DUMBASS!
THANKS TO THIS BEAUTIFUL YOUNG LADY...
UM...

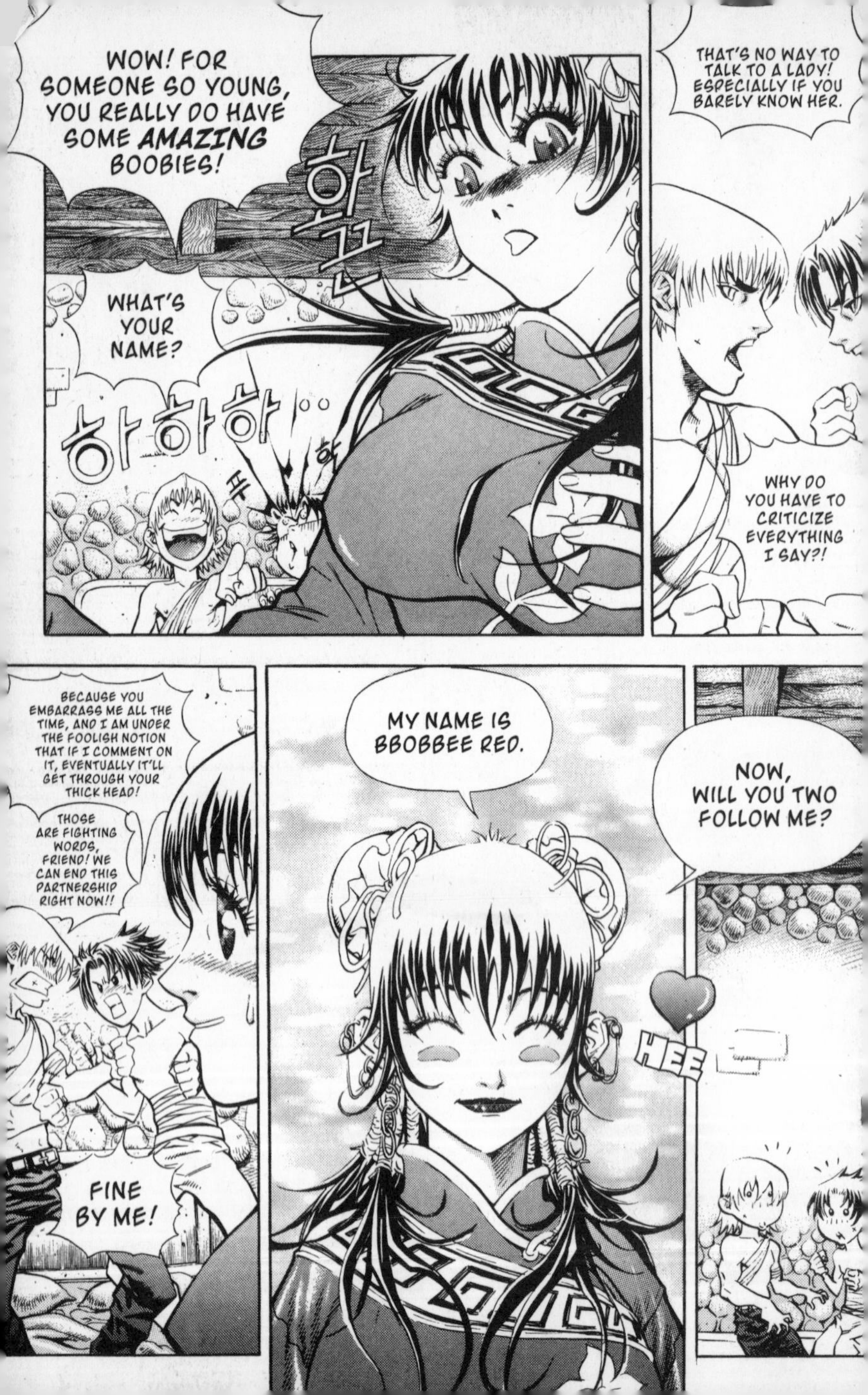
WOW! FOR SOMEONE SO YOUNG, YOU REALLY DO HAVE SOME **AMAZING** BOOBIES!
화끈
WHAT'S YOUR NAME?
하하하..
THAT'S NO WAY TO TALK TO A LADY! ESPECIALLY IF YOU BARELY KNOW HER.
WHY DO YOU HAVE TO CRITICIZE EVERYTHING I SAY?!
BECAUSE YOU EMBARRASS ME ALL THE TIME, AND I AM UNDER THE FOOLISH NOTION THAT IF I COMMENT ON IT, EVENTUALLY IT'LL GET THROUGH YOUR THICK HEAD!
THOSE ARE FIGHTING WORDS, FRIEND! WE CAN END THIS PARTNERSHIP RIGHT NOW!!
FINE BY ME!
MY NAME IS BBOBBEE RED.
NOW, WILL YOU TWO FOLLOW ME?
HEE

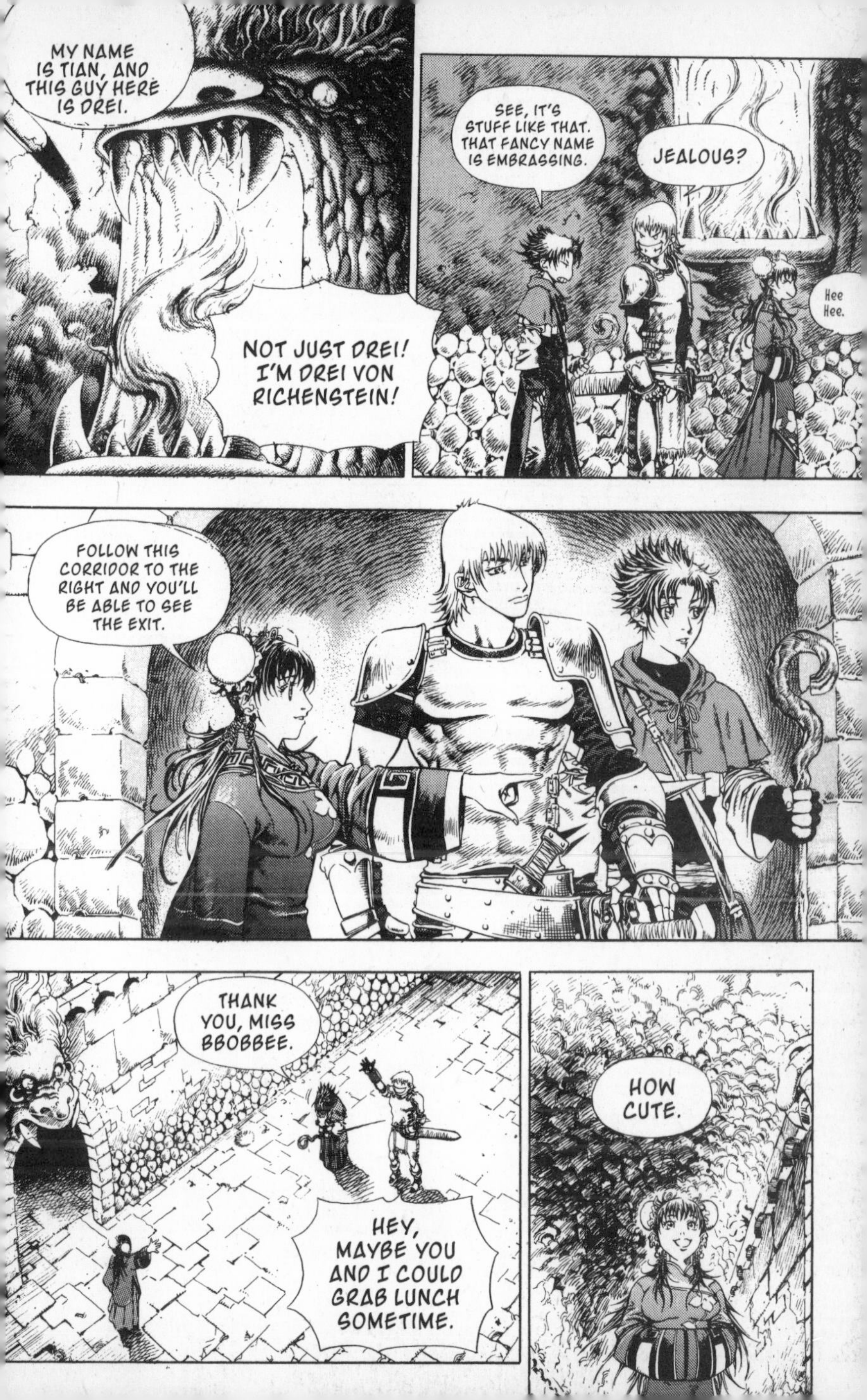
MY NAME IS TIAN, AND THIS GUY HERE IS DREI.
NOT JUST DREI! I'M DREI VON RICHENSTEIN!
SEE, IT'S STUFF LIKE THAT. THAT FANCY NAME IS EMBRASSING.
JEALOUS?
Hee Hee.
FOLLOW THIS CORRIDOR TO THE RIGHT AND YOU'LL BE ABLE TO SEE THE EXIT.
THANK YOU, MISS BBOBBEE.
HEY, MAYBE YOU AND I COULD GRAB LUNCH SOMETIME.
HOW CUTE.

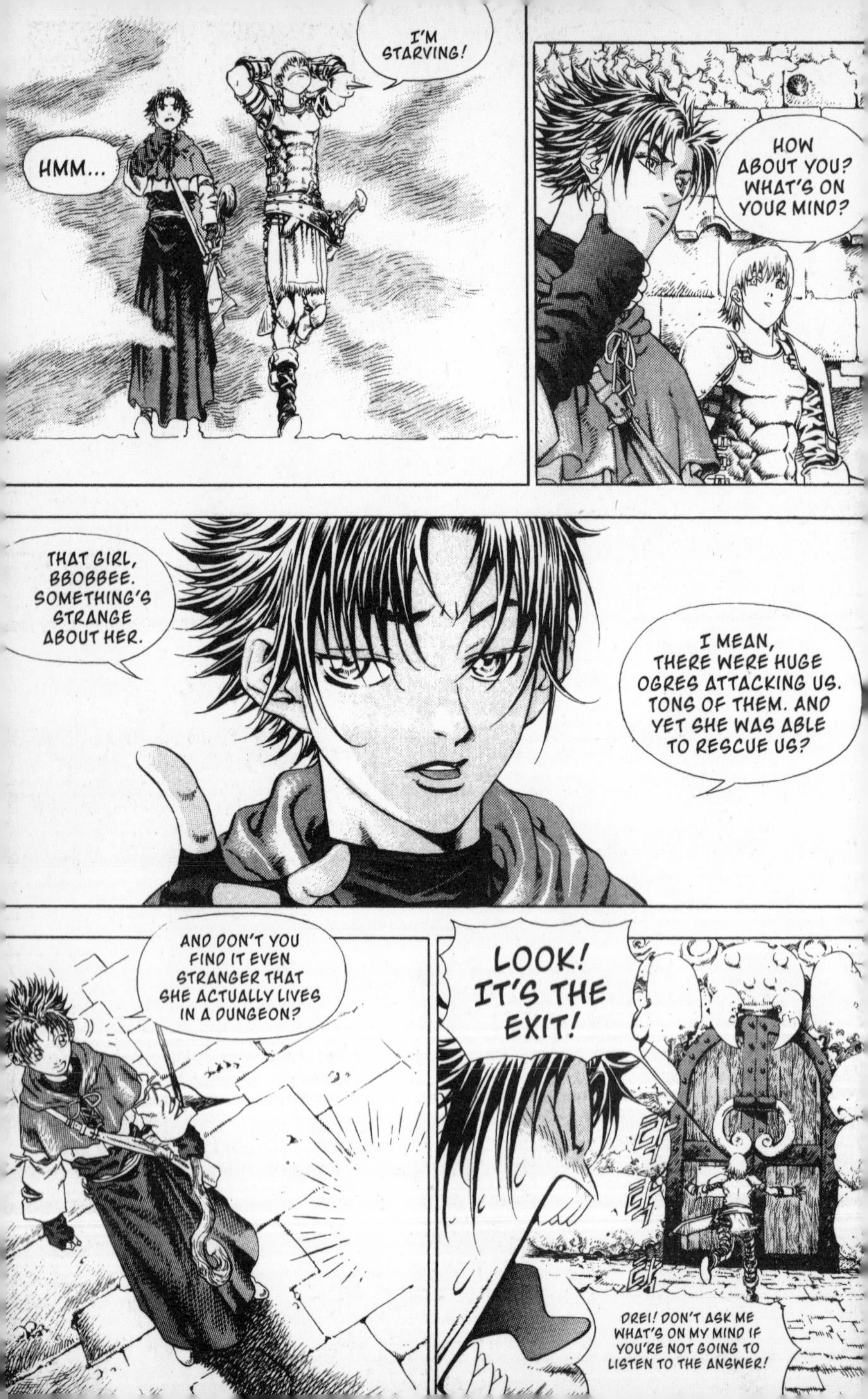
I'M STARVING!
HMM...
HOW ABOUT YOU? WHAT'S ON YOUR MIND?
THAT GIRL, BBOBBEE. SOMETHING'S STRANGE ABOUT HER.
I MEAN, THERE WERE HUGE OGRES ATTACKING US. TONS OF THEM. AND YET SHE WAS ABLE TO RESCUE US?
AND DON'T YOU FIND IT EVEN STRANGER THAT SHE ACTUALLY LIVES IN A DUNGEON?
LOOK! IT'S THE EXIT!
DREI! DON'T ASK ME WHAT'S ON MY MIND IF YOU'RE NOT GOING TO LISTEN TO THE ANSWER!

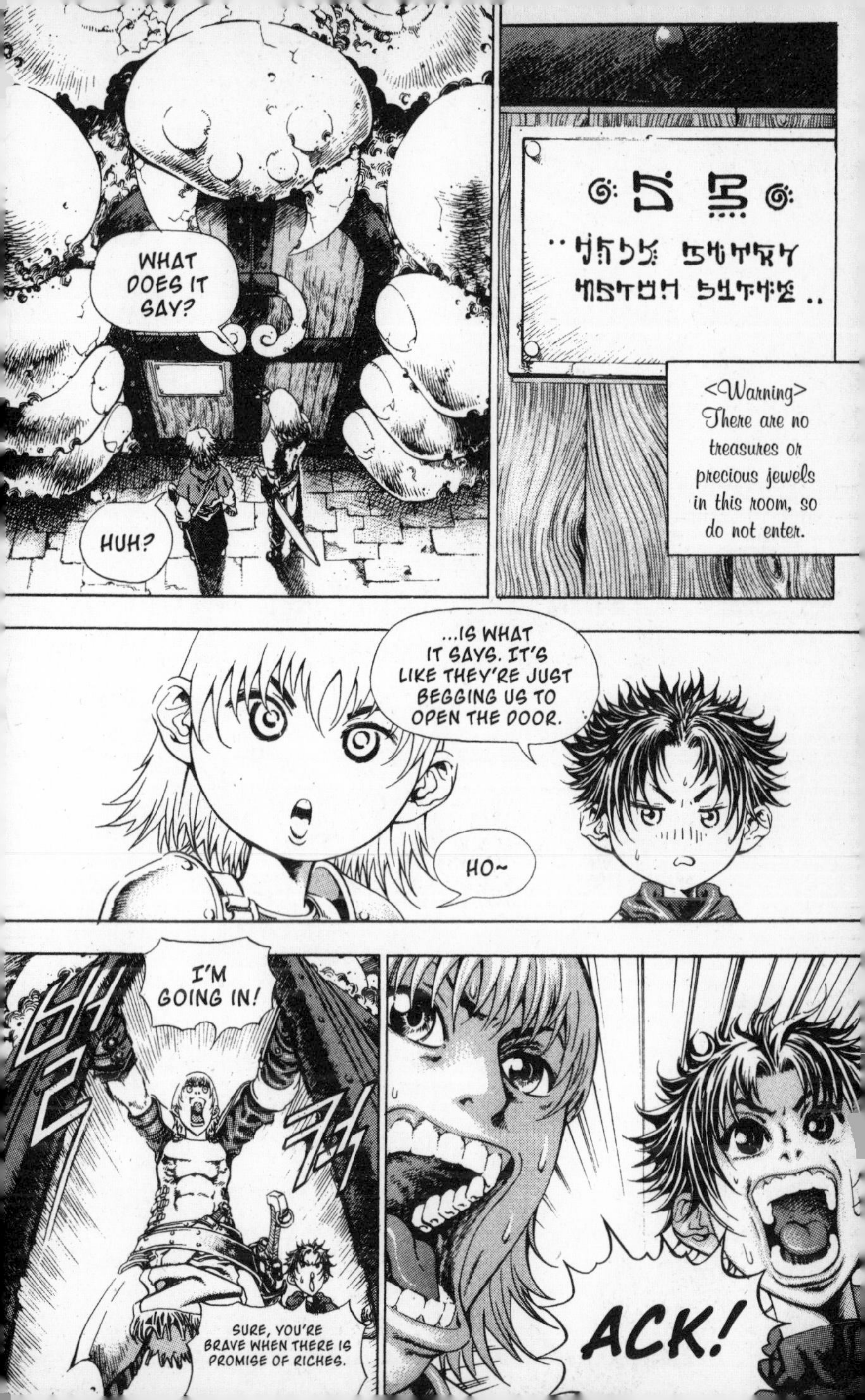

WHAT DOES IT SAY?
HUH?
<Warning>
There are no treasures or precious jewels in this room, so do not enter.
...IS WHAT IT SAYS. IT'S LIKE THEY'RE JUST BEGGING US TO OPEN THE DOOR.
HO~
I'M GOING IN!
SURE, YOU'RE BRAVE WHEN THERE IS PROMISE OF RICHES.
ACK!

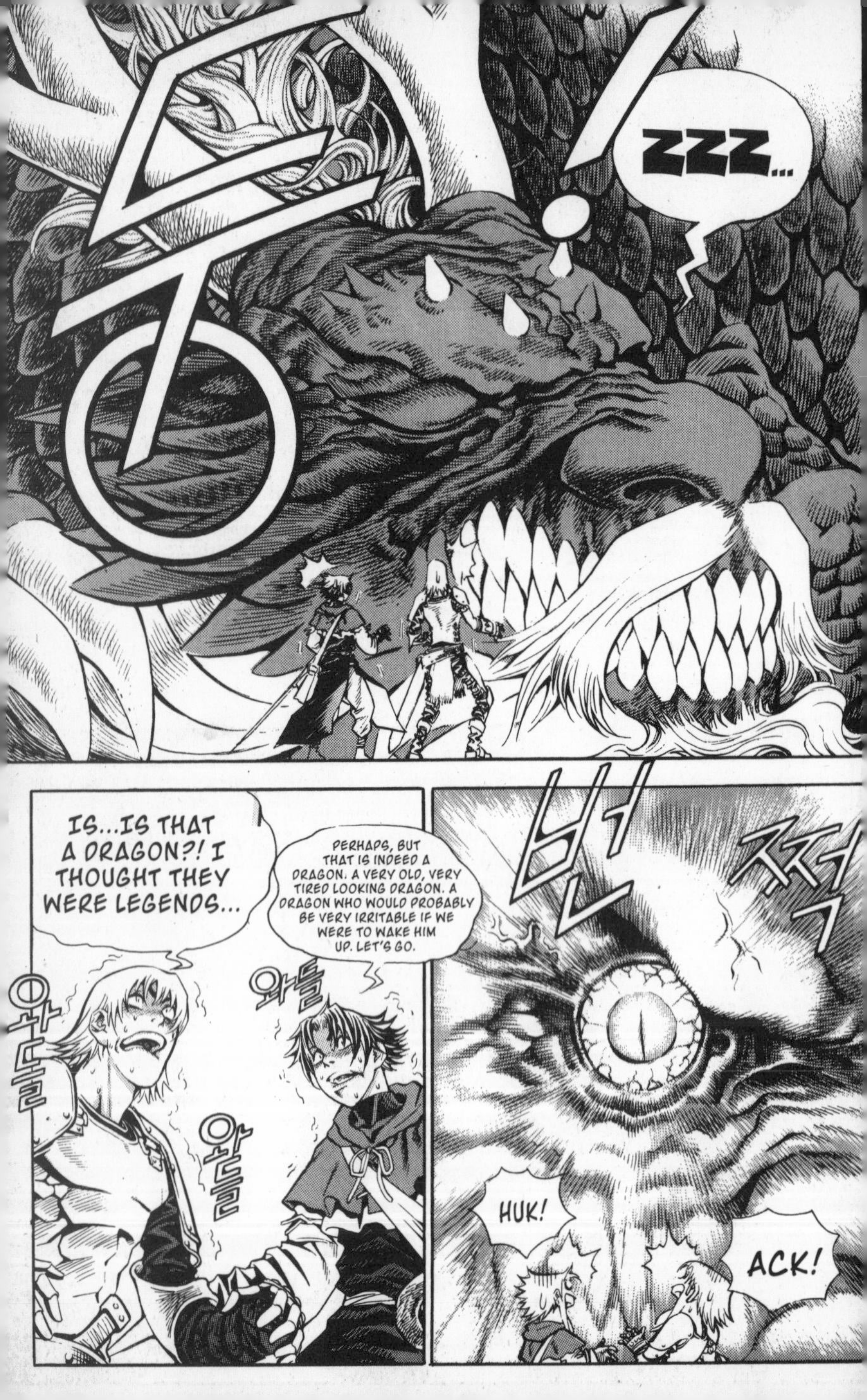
ZZZ...
IS...IS THAT A DRAGON?! I THOUGHT THEY WERE LEGENDS...
PERHAPS, BUT THAT IS INDEED A DRAGON. A VERY OLD, VERY TIRED LOOKING DRAGON. A DRAGON WHO WOULD PROBABLY BE VERY IRRITABLE IF WE WERE TO WAKE HIM UP. LET'S GO.
HUK!
ACK!

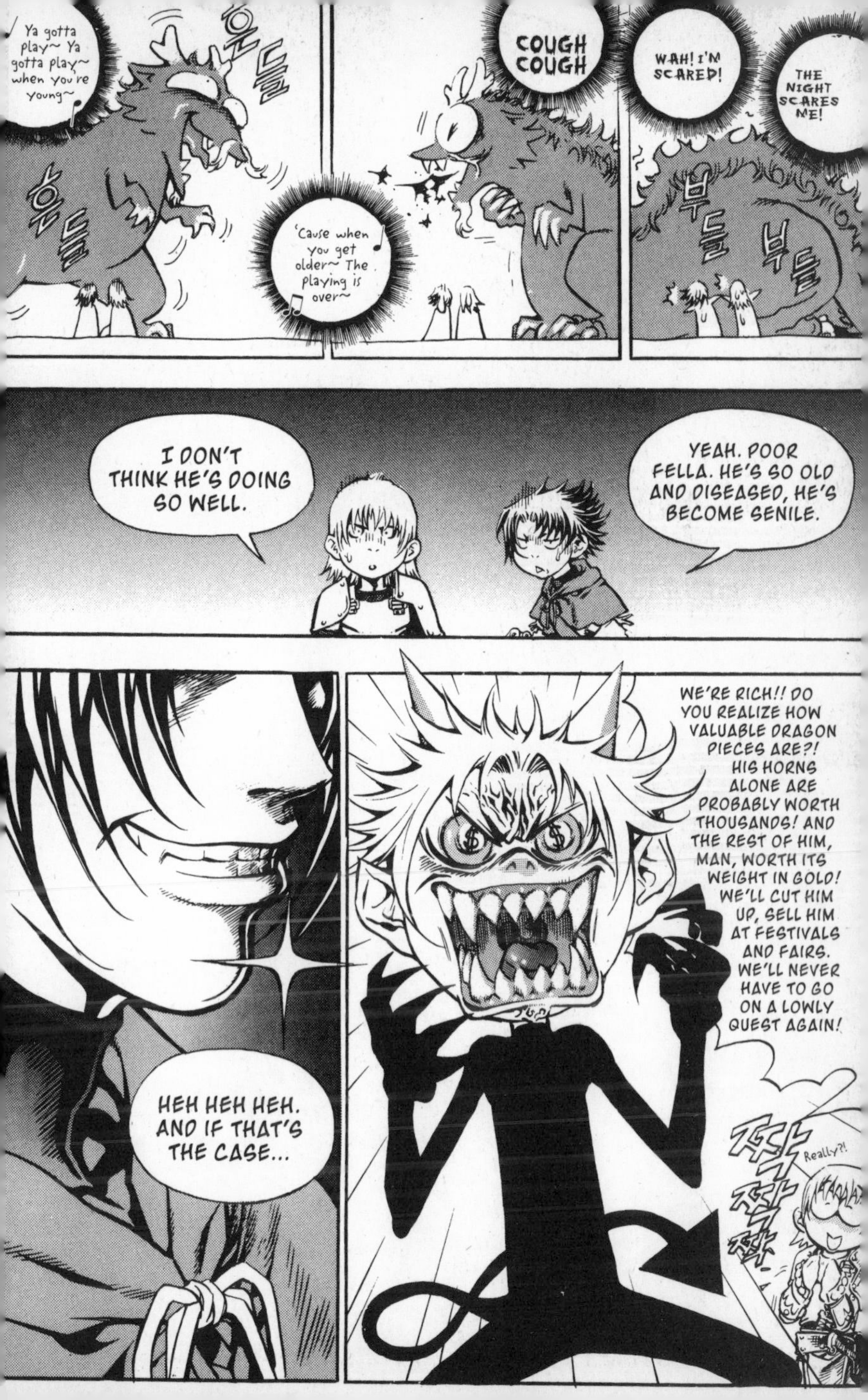

Ya gotta play~ Ya gotta play~ when you're young~
'Cause when you get older~ The playing is over~
COUGH COUGH
WAH! I'M SCARED!
THE NIGHT SCARES ME!
I DON'T THINK HE'S DOING SO WELL.
YEAH. POOR FELLA. HE'S SO OLD AND DISEASED, HE'S BECOME SENILE.
HEH HEH HEH. AND IF THAT'S THE CASE...
WE'RE RICH!! DO YOU REALIZE HOW VALUABLE DRAGON PIECES ARE?! HIS HORNS ALONE ARE PROBABLY WORTH THOUSANDS! AND THE REST OF HIM, MAN, WORTH ITS WEIGHT IN GOLD! WE'LL CUT HIM UP, SELL HIM AT FESTIVALS AND FAIRS. WE'LL NEVER HAVE TO GO ON A LOWLY QUEST AGAIN!
Really?!

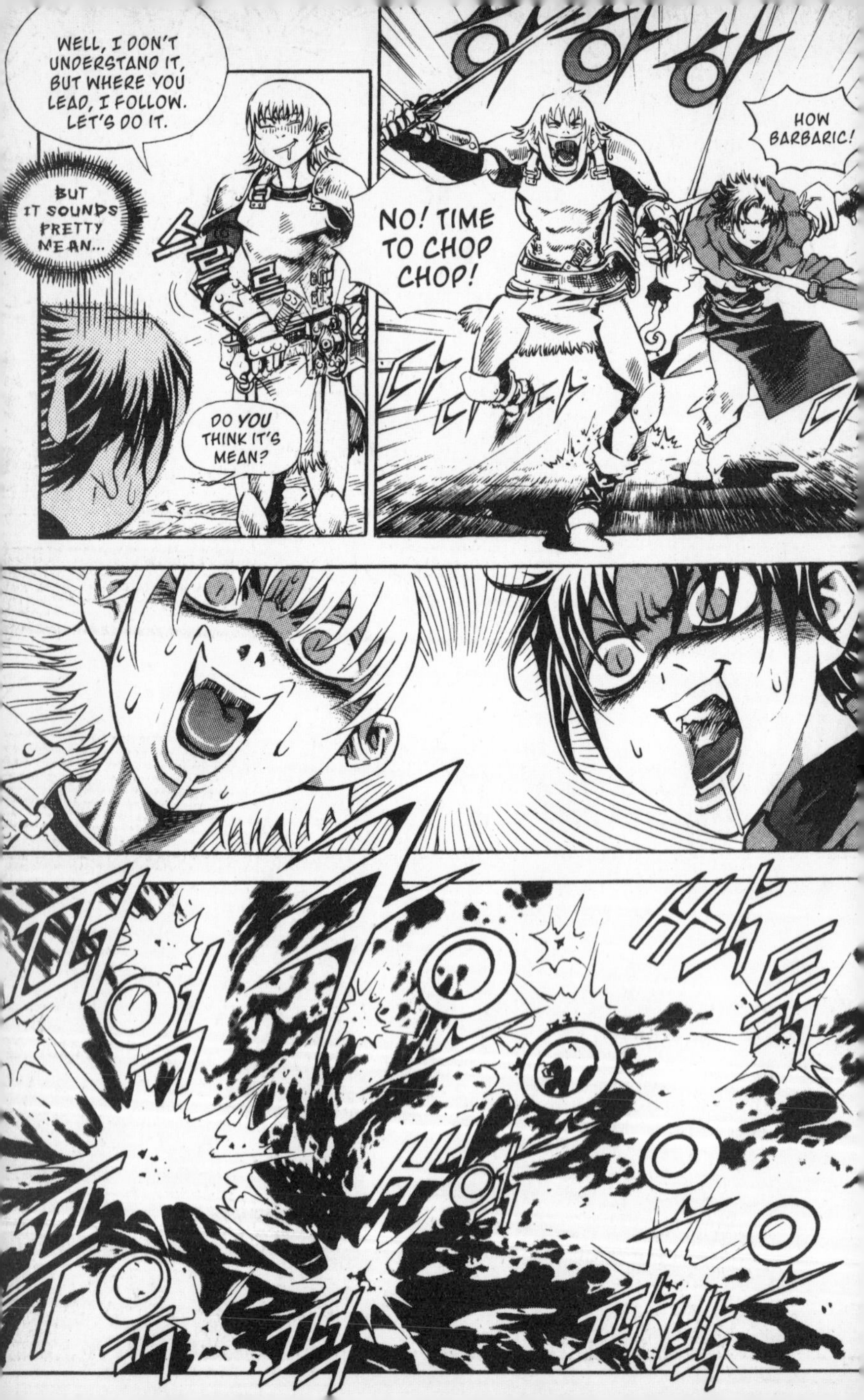
WELL, I DON'T UNDERSTAND IT, BUT WHERE YOU LEAD, I FOLLOW. LET'S DO IT.
BUT IT SOUNDS PRETTY MEAN...
DO YOU THINK IT'S MEAN?
NO! TIME TO CHOP CHOP!
HOW BARBARIC!

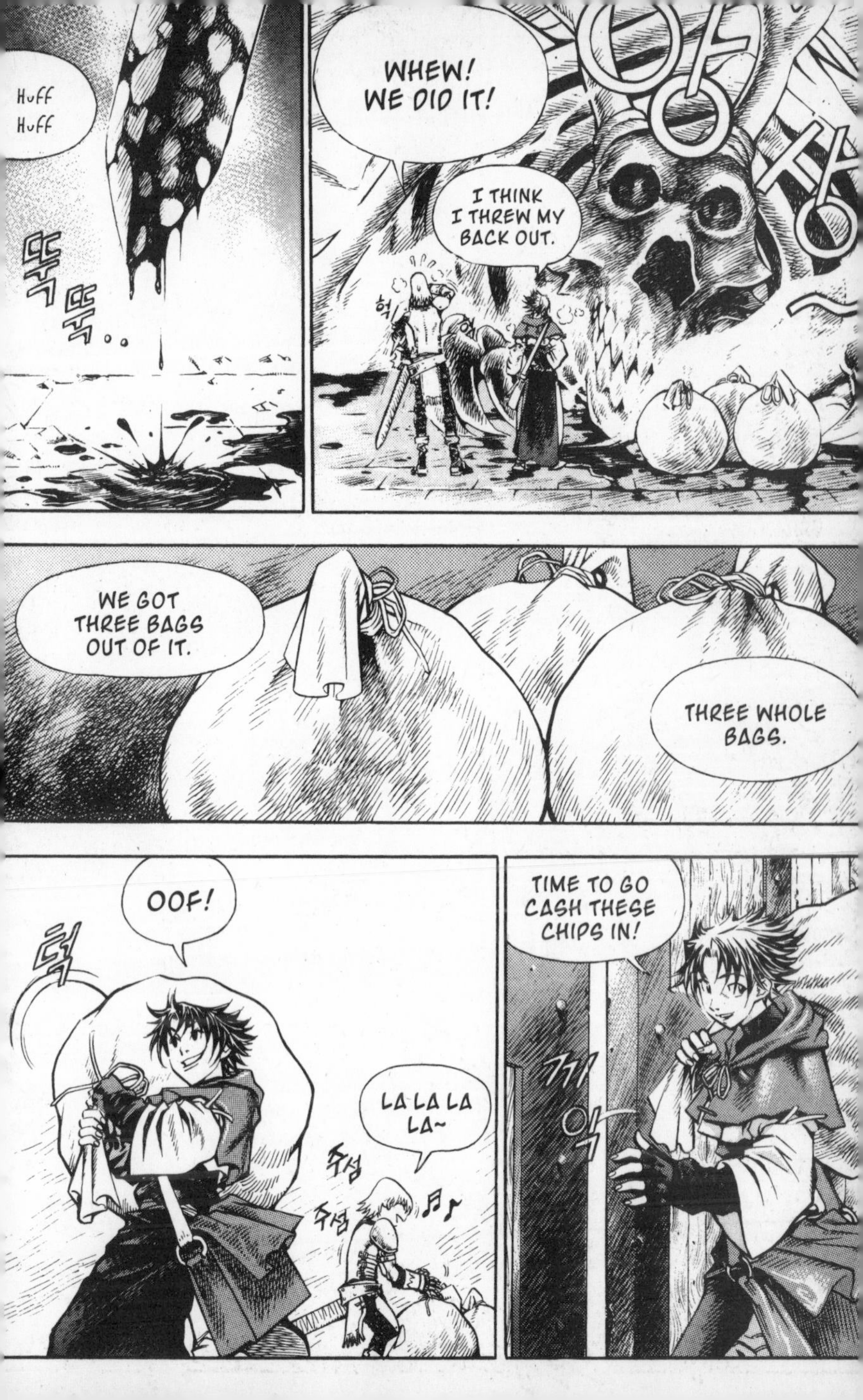
Huff
Huff
뚝 뚝..
WHEW! WE DID IT!
I THINK I THREW MY BACK OUT.
헉
WE GOT THREE BAGS OUT OF IT.
THREE WHOLE BAGS.
OOF!
LA LA LA LA~
주섬
주섬
TIME TO GO CASH THESE CHIPS IN!

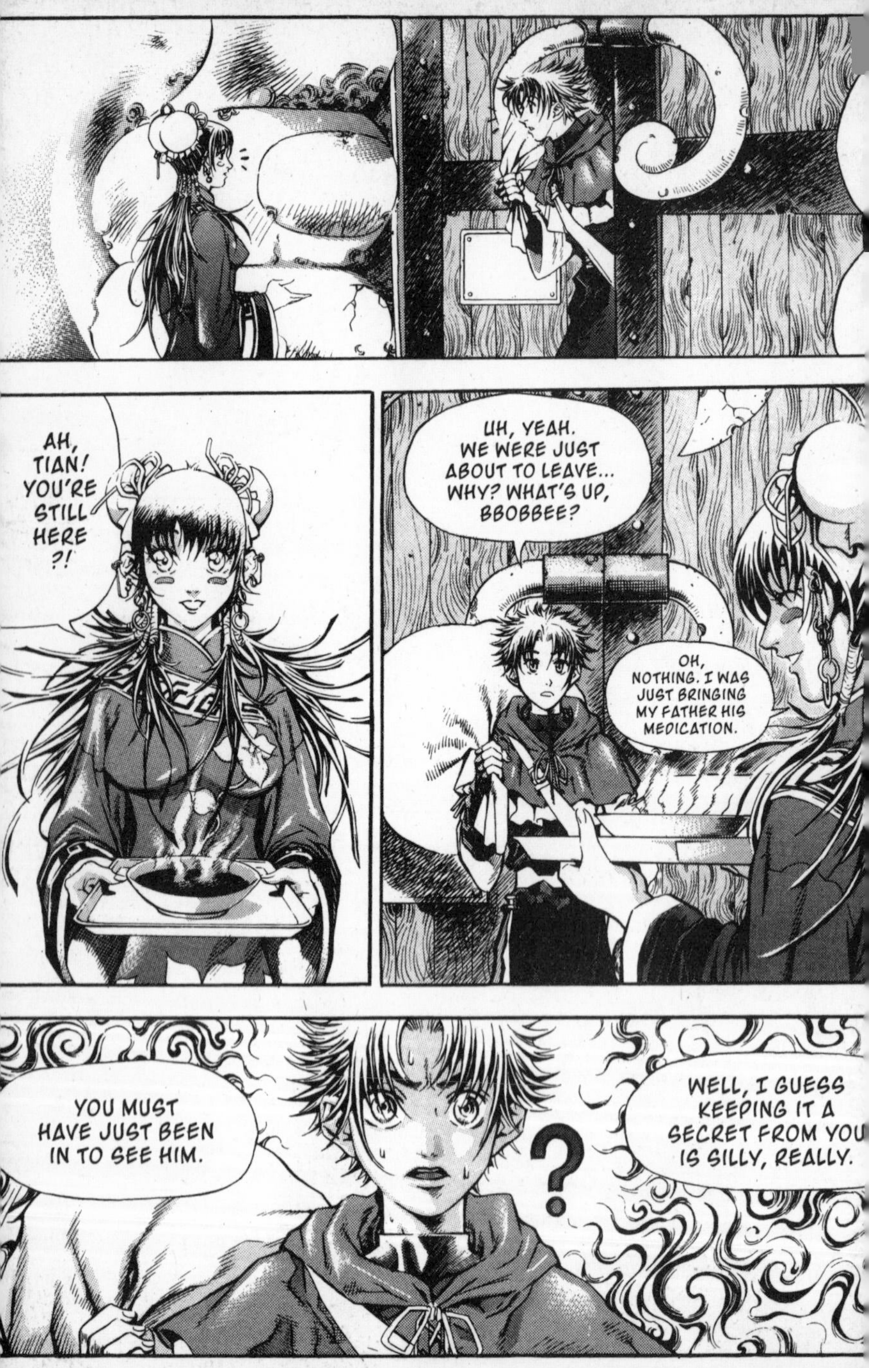
AH, TIAN! YOU'RE STILL HERE ?!
UH, YEAH. WE WERE JUST ABOUT TO LEAVE... WHY? WHAT'S UP, BBOBBEE?
OH, NOTHING. I WAS JUST BRINGING MY FATHER HIS MEDICATION.
YOU MUST HAVE JUST BEEN IN TO SEE HIM.
?
WELL, I GUESS KEEPING IT A SECRET FROM YOU IS SILLY, REALLY.

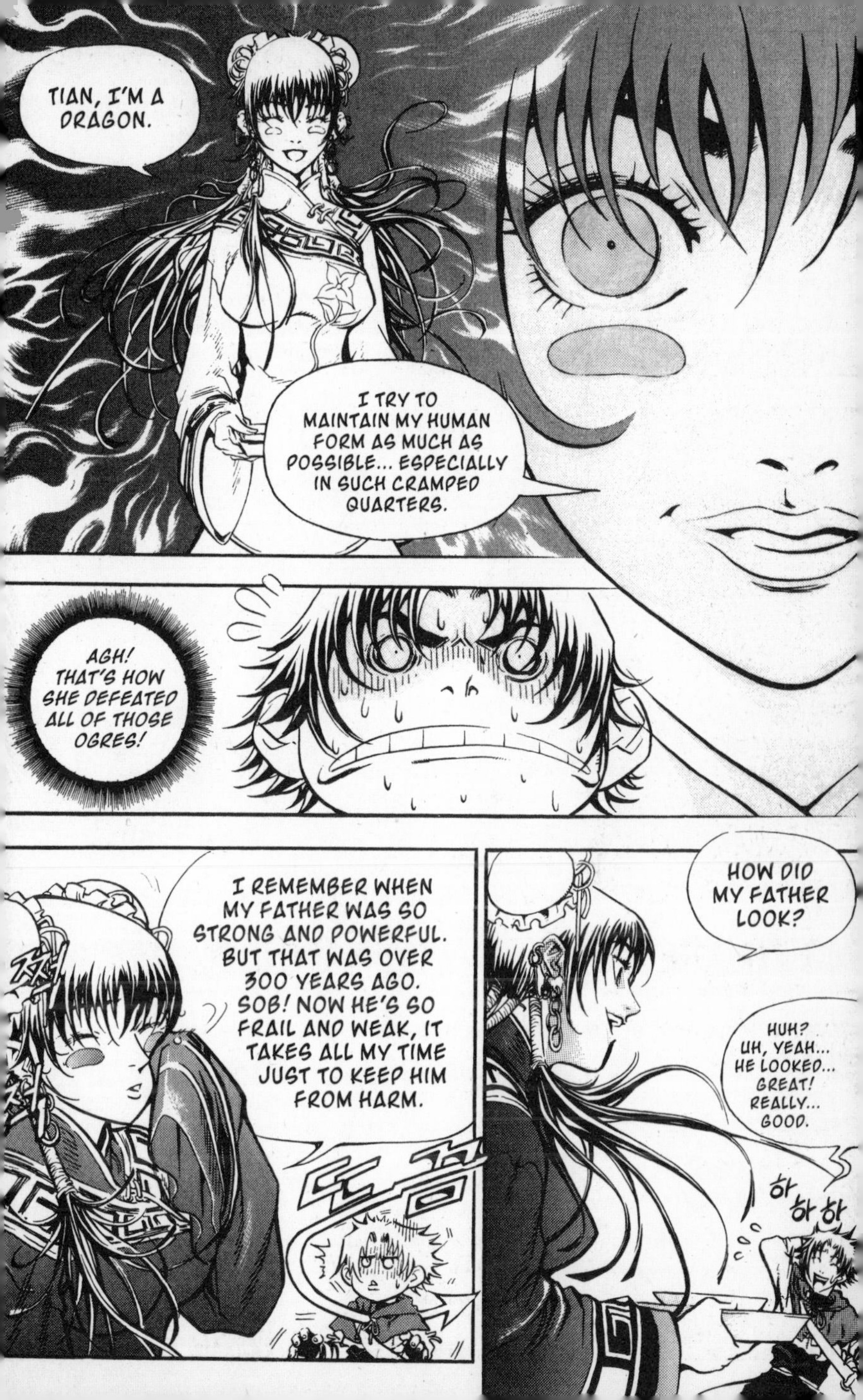
TIAN, I'M A DRAGON.
I TRY TO MAINTAIN MY HUMAN FORM AS MUCH AS POSSIBLE... ESPECIALLY IN SUCH CRAMPED QUARTERS.
AGH! THAT'S HOW SHE DEFEATED ALL OF THOSE OGRES!
I REMEMBER WHEN MY FATHER WAS SO STRONG AND POWERFUL. BUT THAT WAS OVER 300 YEARS AGO. SOB! NOW HE'S SO FRAIL AND WEAK, IT TAKES ALL MY TIME JUST TO KEEP HIM FROM HARM.
HOW DID MY FATHER LOOK?
HUH? UH, YEAH... HE LOOKED... GREAT! REALLY... GOOD.
하 하 하

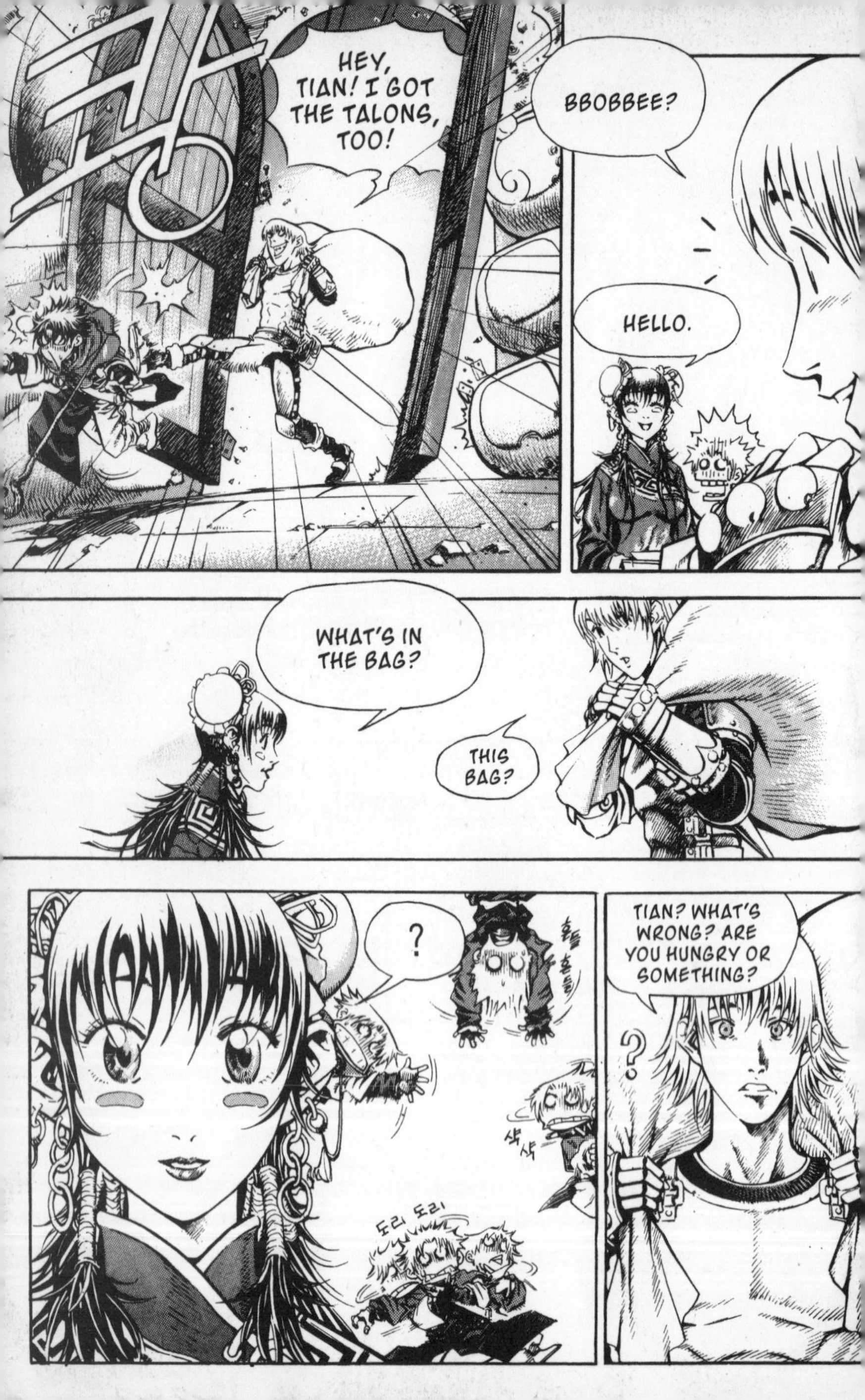
HEY, TIAN! I GOT THE TALONS, TOO!
BBOBBEE?
HELLO.
WHAT'S IN THE BAG?
THIS BAG?
?
흔들 흔들
삭 삭
도리 도리
TIAN? WHAT'S WRONG? ARE YOU HUNGRY OR SOMETHING?
?

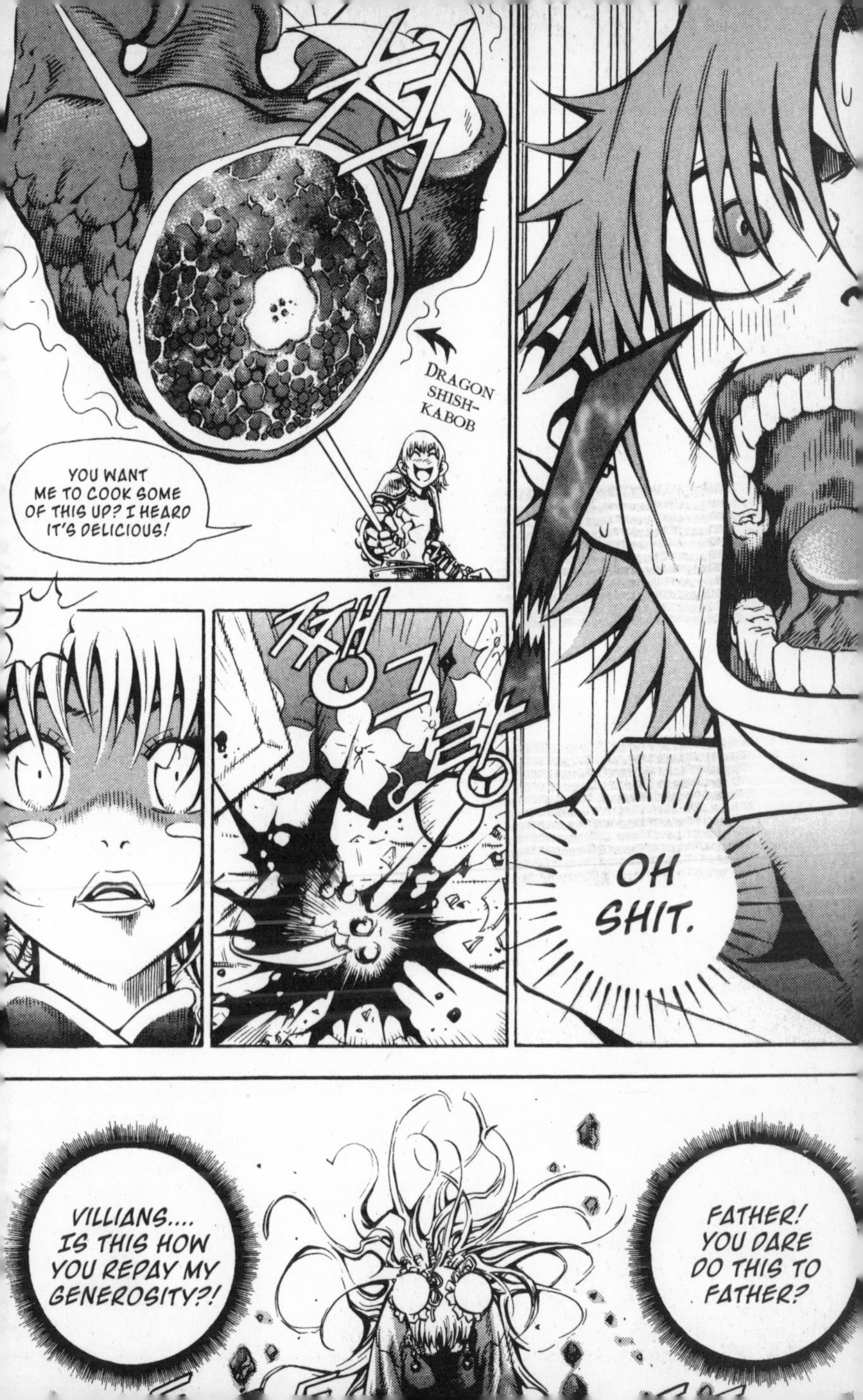
DRAGON SHISH-KABOB
YOU WANT ME TO COOK SOME OF THIS UP? I HEARD IT'S DELICIOUS!
OH SHIT.
VILLIANS.... IS THIS HOW YOU REPAY MY GENEROSITY?!
FATHER! YOU DARE DO THIS TO FATHER?

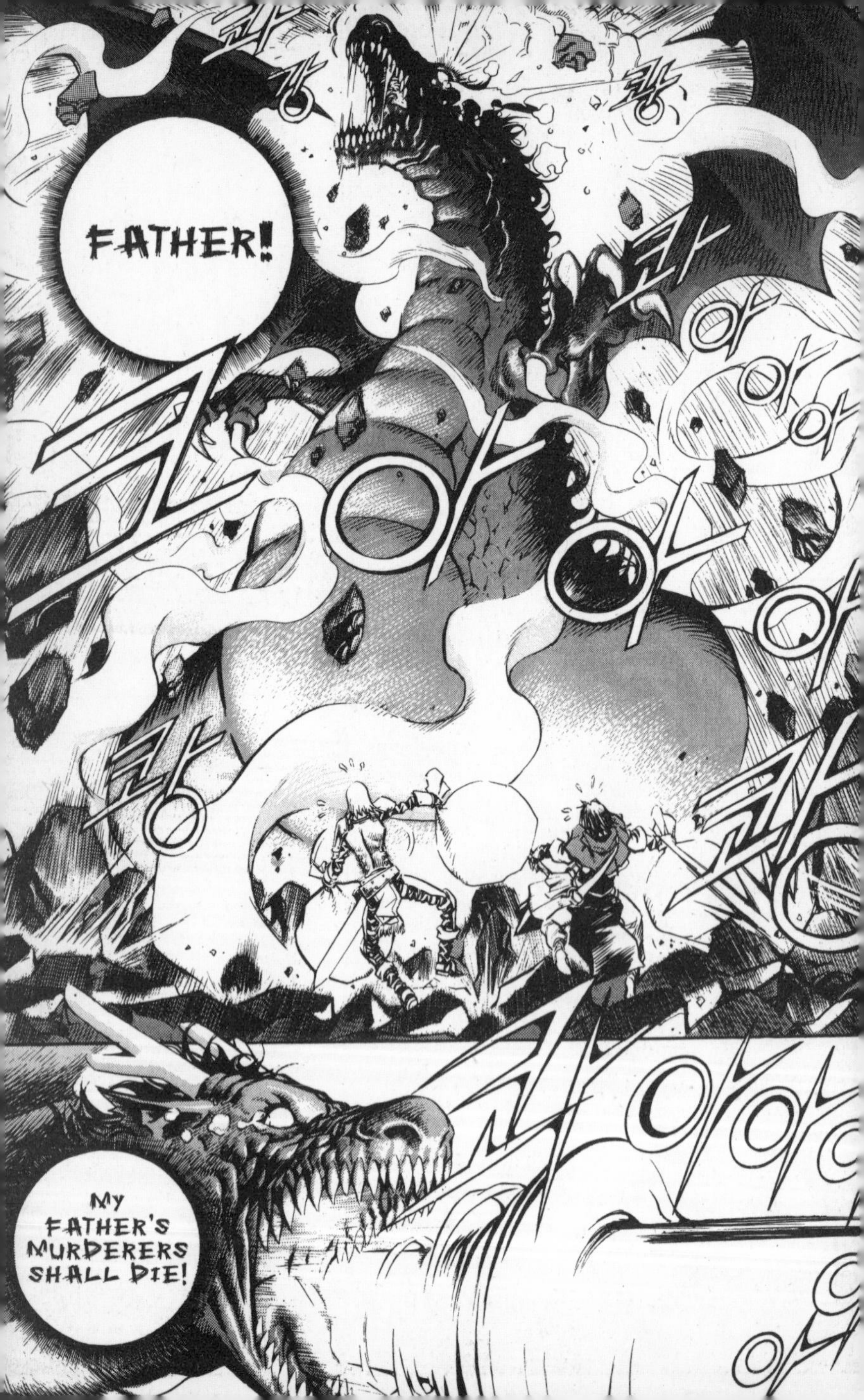
FATHER!
MY FATHER'S MURDERERS SHALL DIE!

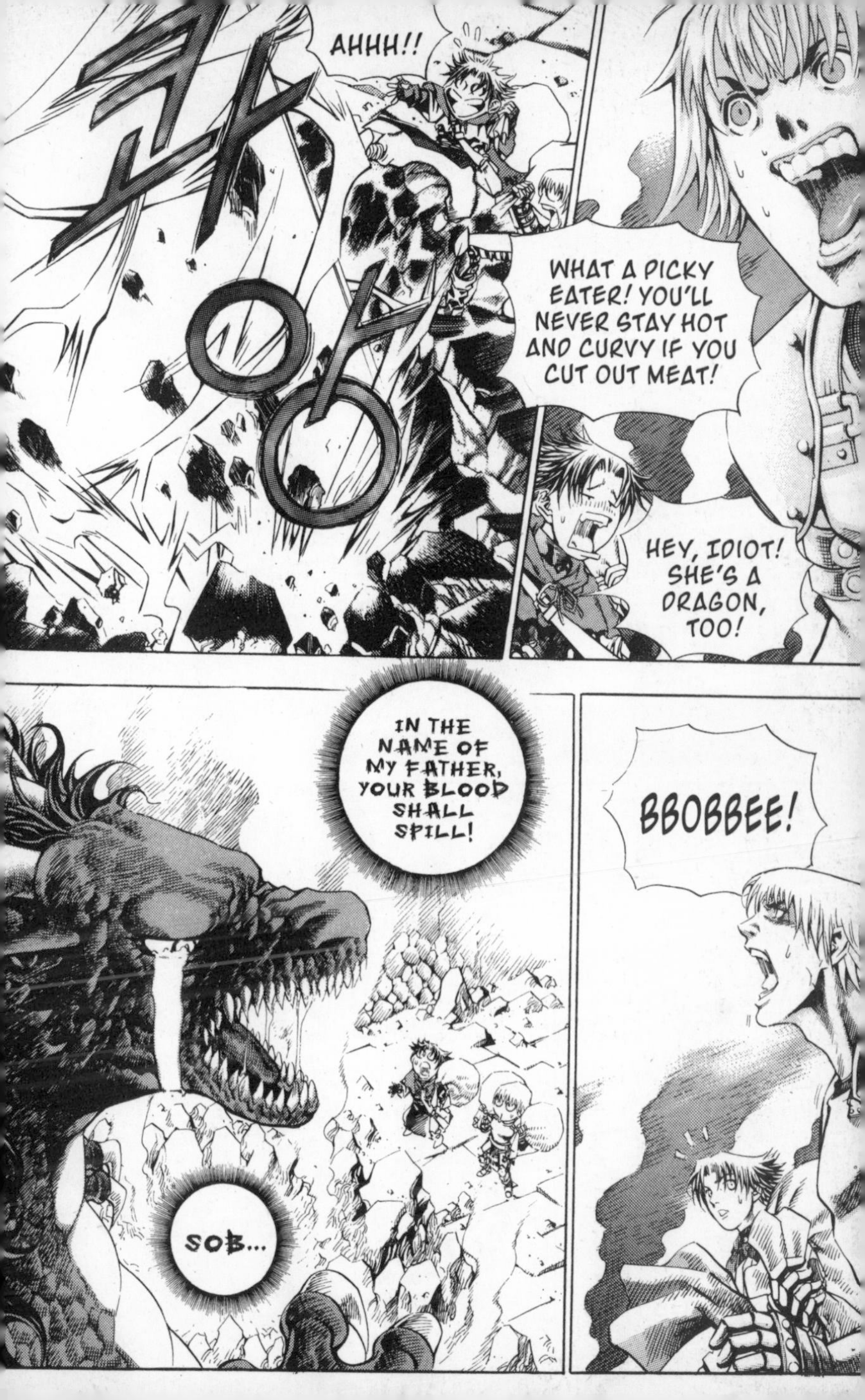
AHHH!!
WHAT A PICKY EATER! YOU'LL NEVER STAY HOT AND CURVY IF YOU CUT OUT MEAT!
HEY, IDIOT! SHE'S A DRAGON, TOO!
IN THE NAME OF MY FATHER, YOUR BLOOD SHALL SPILL!
SOB...
BBOBBEE!

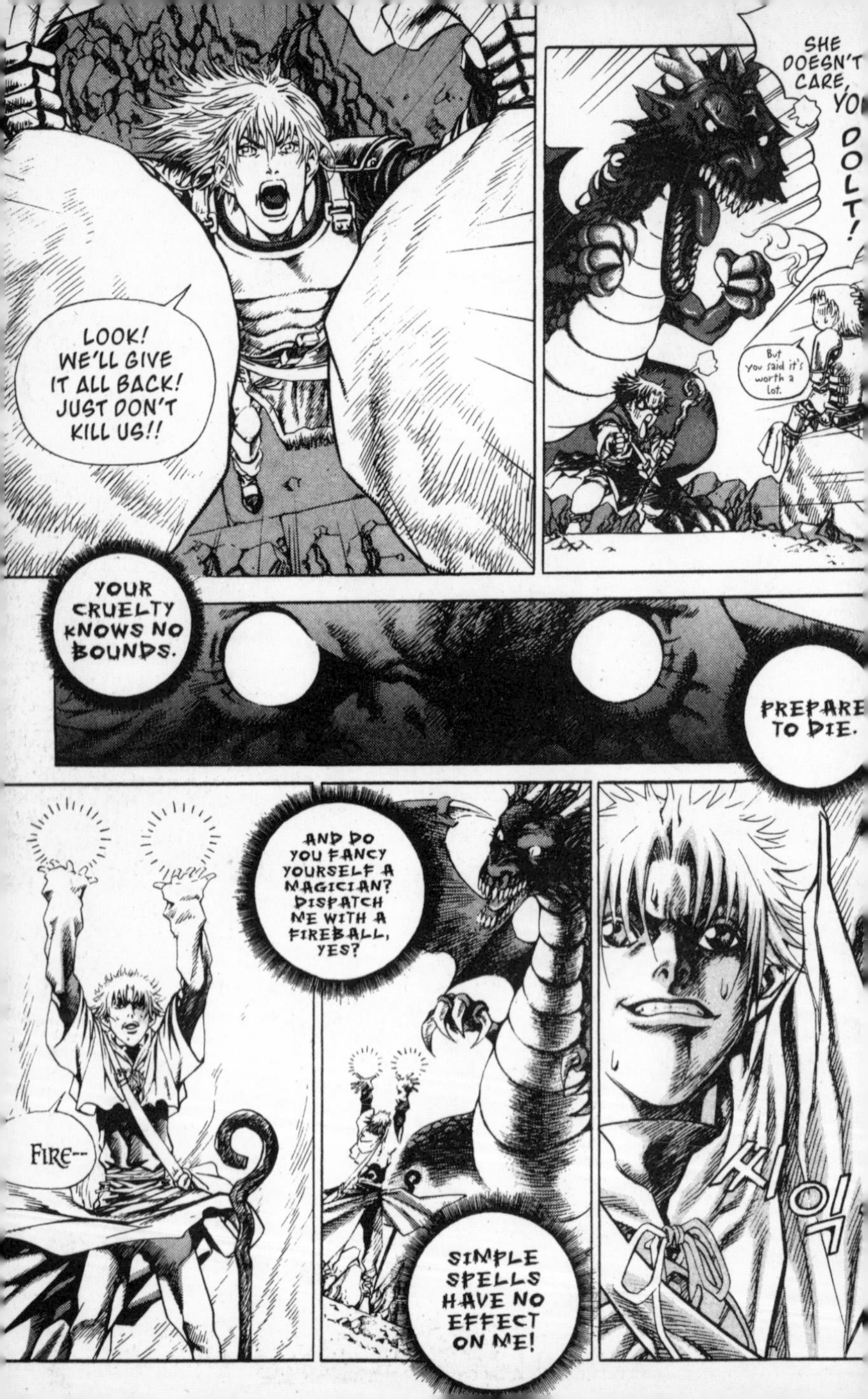
LOOK! WE'LL GIVE IT ALL BACK! JUST DON'T KILL US!!
SHE DOESN'T CARE, YO DOLT!
But you said it's worth a lot.
YOUR CRUELTY KNOWS NO BOUNDS.
PREPARE TO DIE.
FIRE--
AND DO YOU FANCY YOURSELF A MAGICIAN? DISPATCH ME WITH A FIREBALL, YES?
SIMPLE SPELLS HAVE NO EFFECT ON ME!

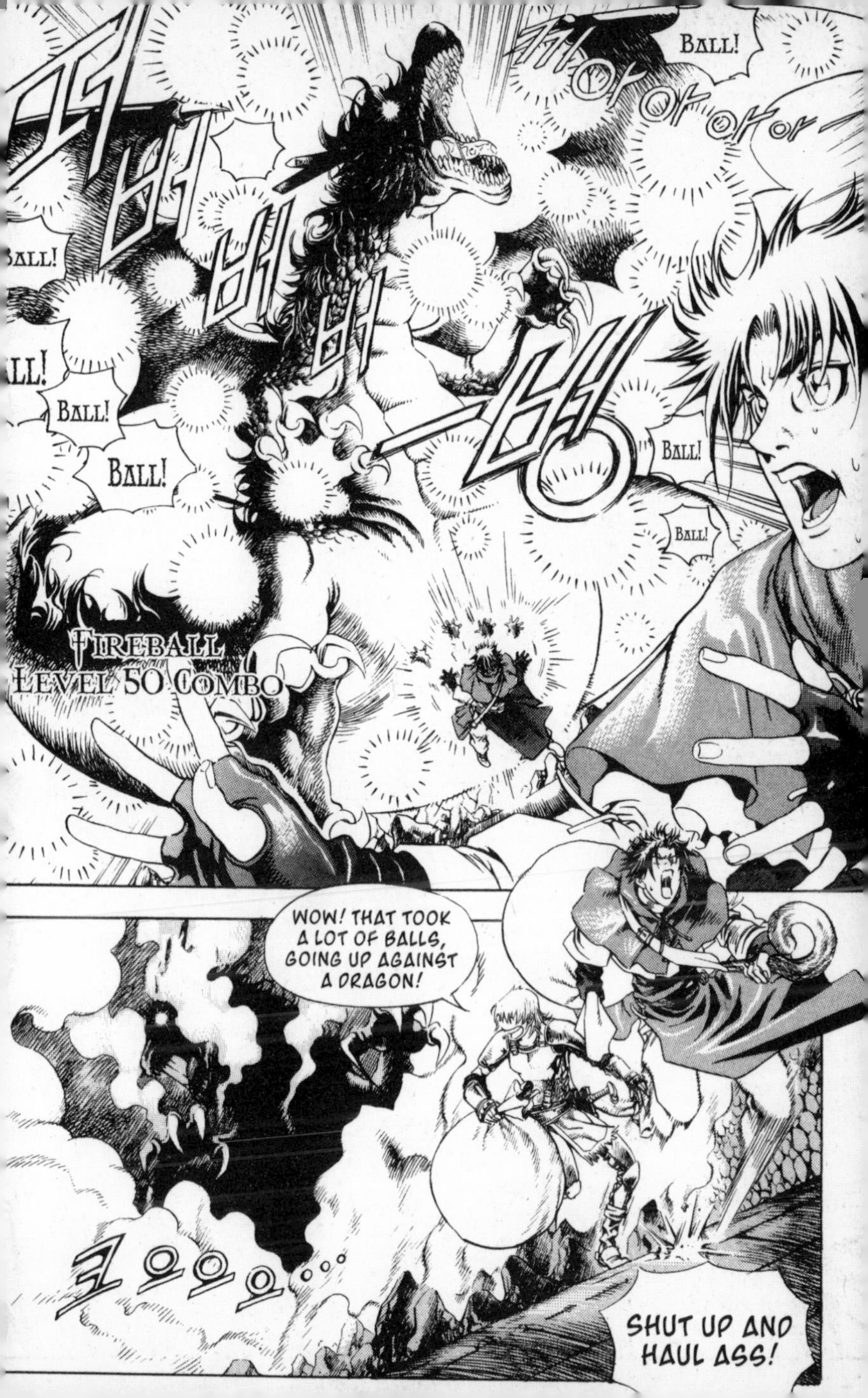
BALL!
BALL!
BALL!
BALL!
BALL!
FIREBALL
LEVEL 50 COMBO
WOW! THAT TOOK A LOT OF BALLS, GOING UP AGAINST A DRAGON!
SHUT UP AND HAUL ASS!

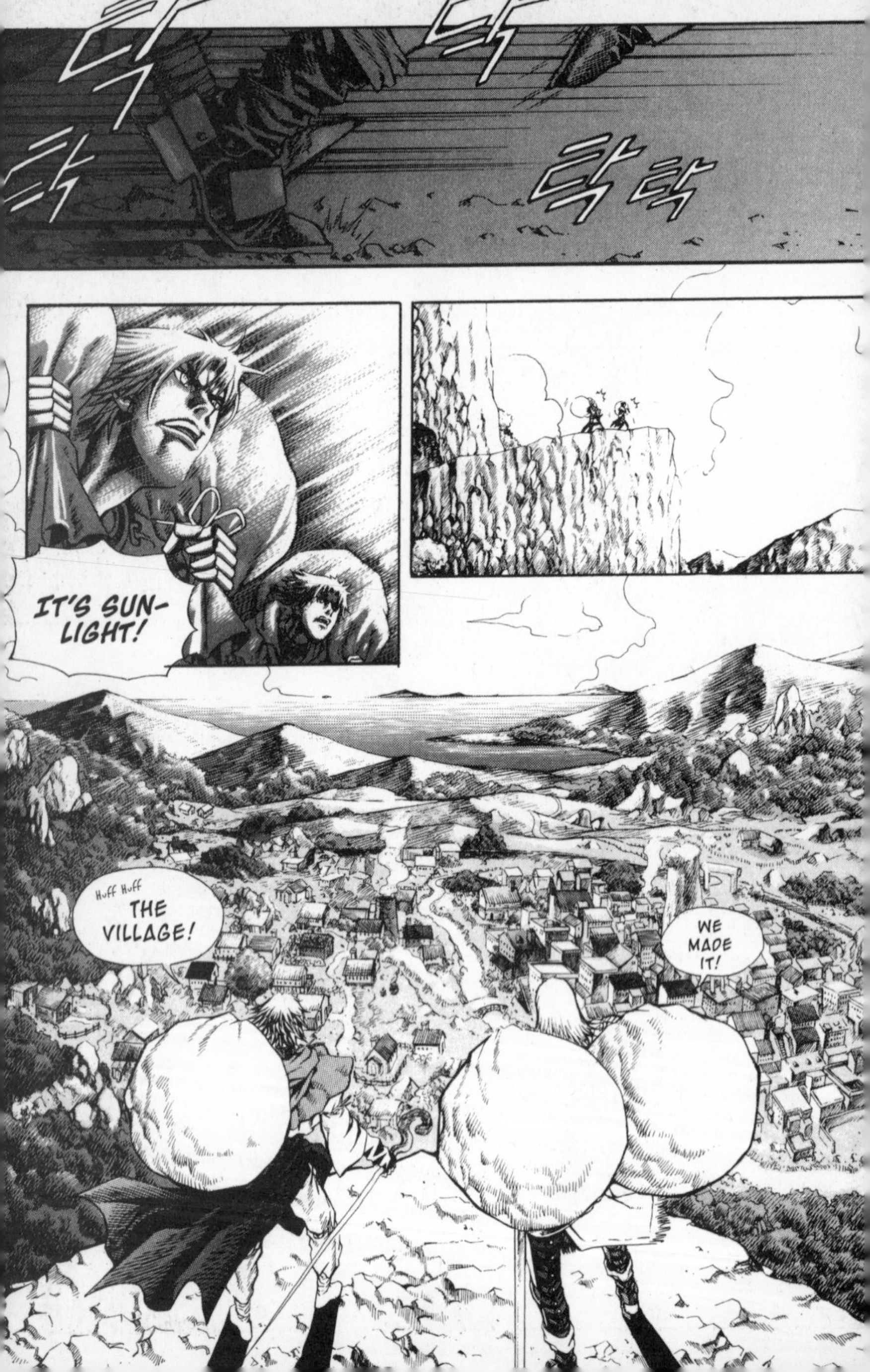
닥
닥
닥
닥닥
IT'S SUN-LIGHT!
Huff Huff
THE VILLAGE!
WE MADE IT!

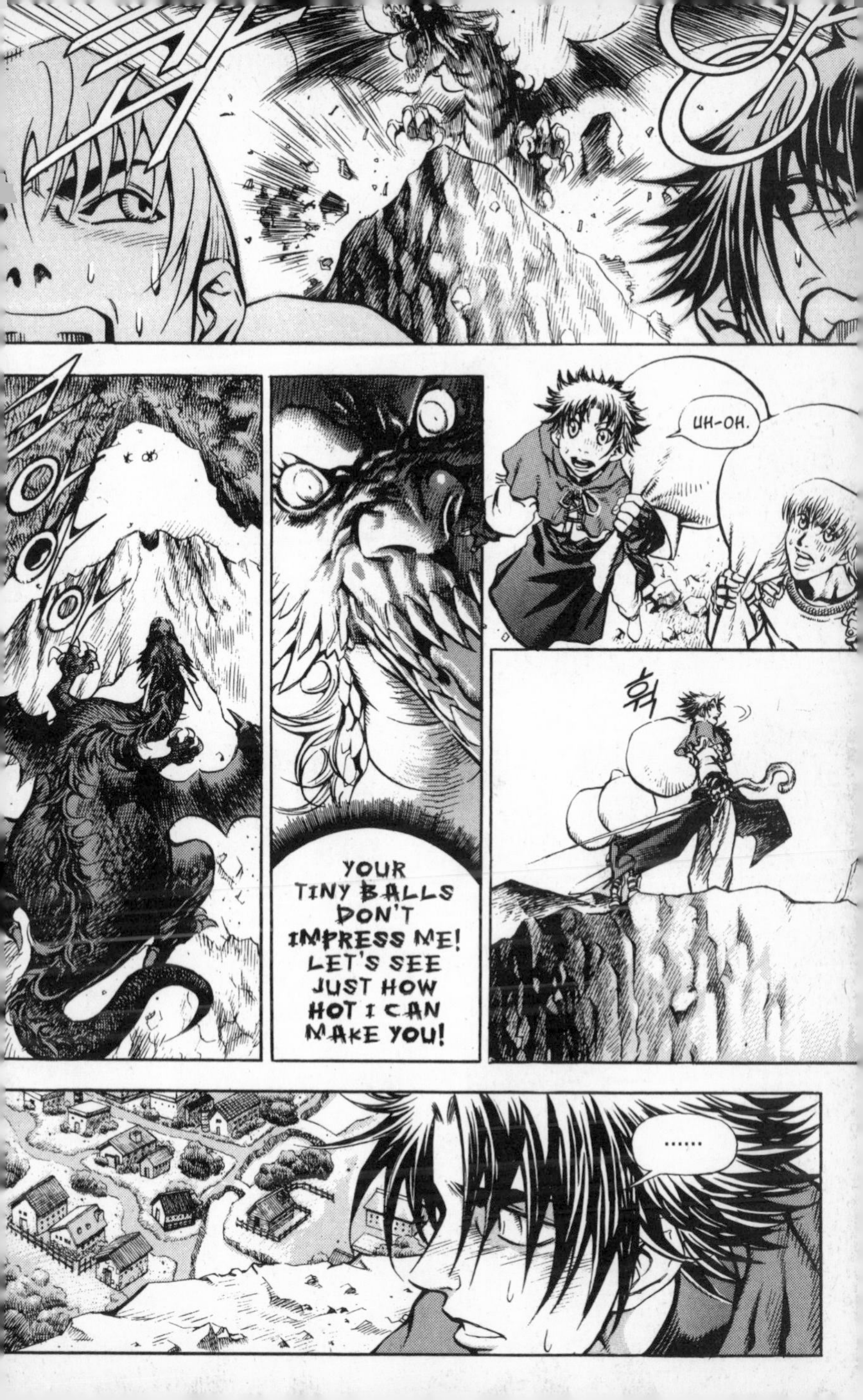
UH-OH.
YOUR TINY BALLS DON'T IMPRESS ME! LET'S SEE JUST HOW HOT I CAN MAKE YOU!
......

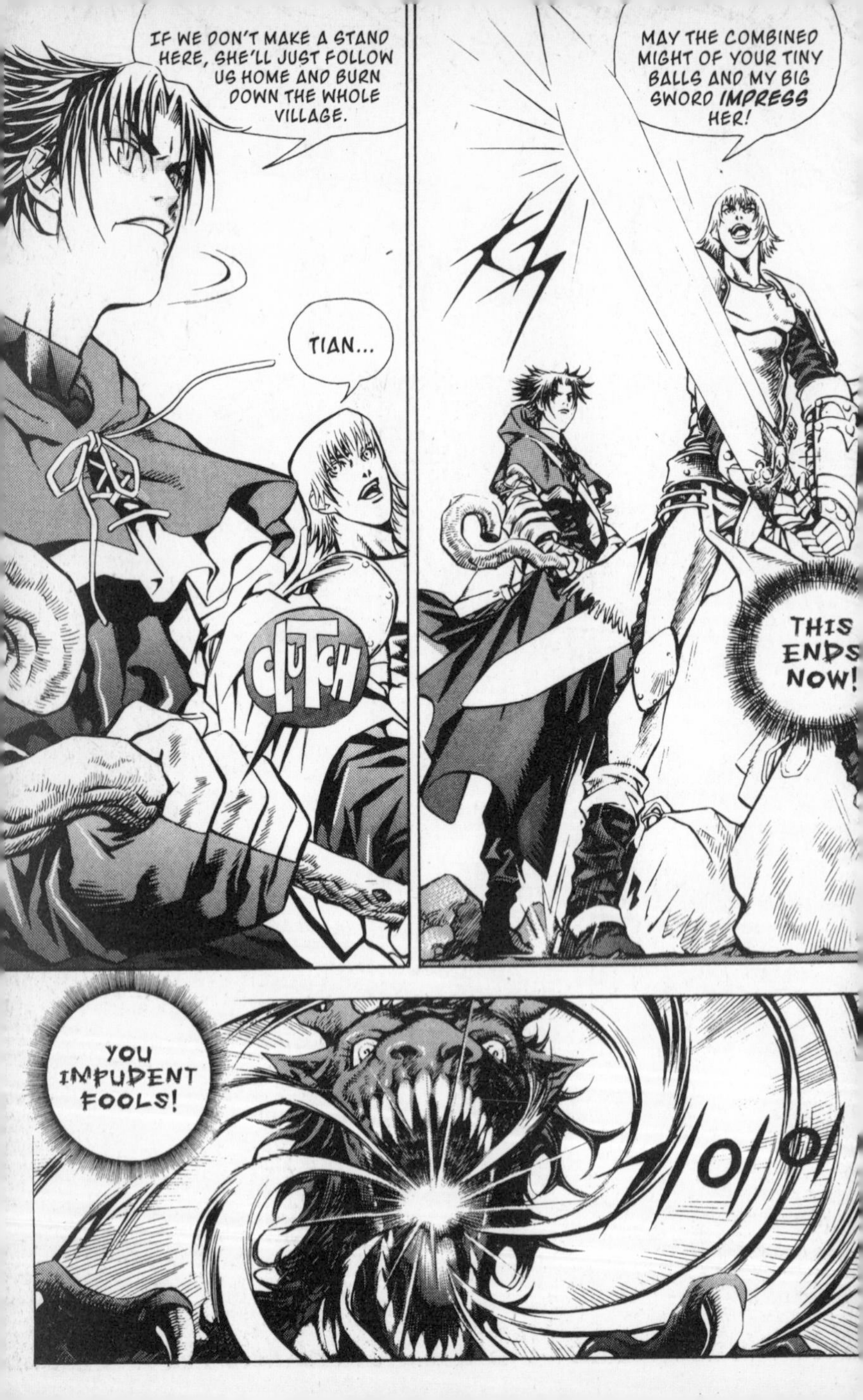
IF WE DON'T MAKE A STAND HERE, SHE'LL JUST FOLLOW US HOME AND BURN DOWN THE WHOLE VILLAGE.
TIAN...
CLUTCH
MAY THE COMBINED MIGHT OF YOUR TINY BALLS AND MY BIG SWORD IMPRESS HER!
THIS ENDS NOW!
YOU IMPUDENT FOOLS!

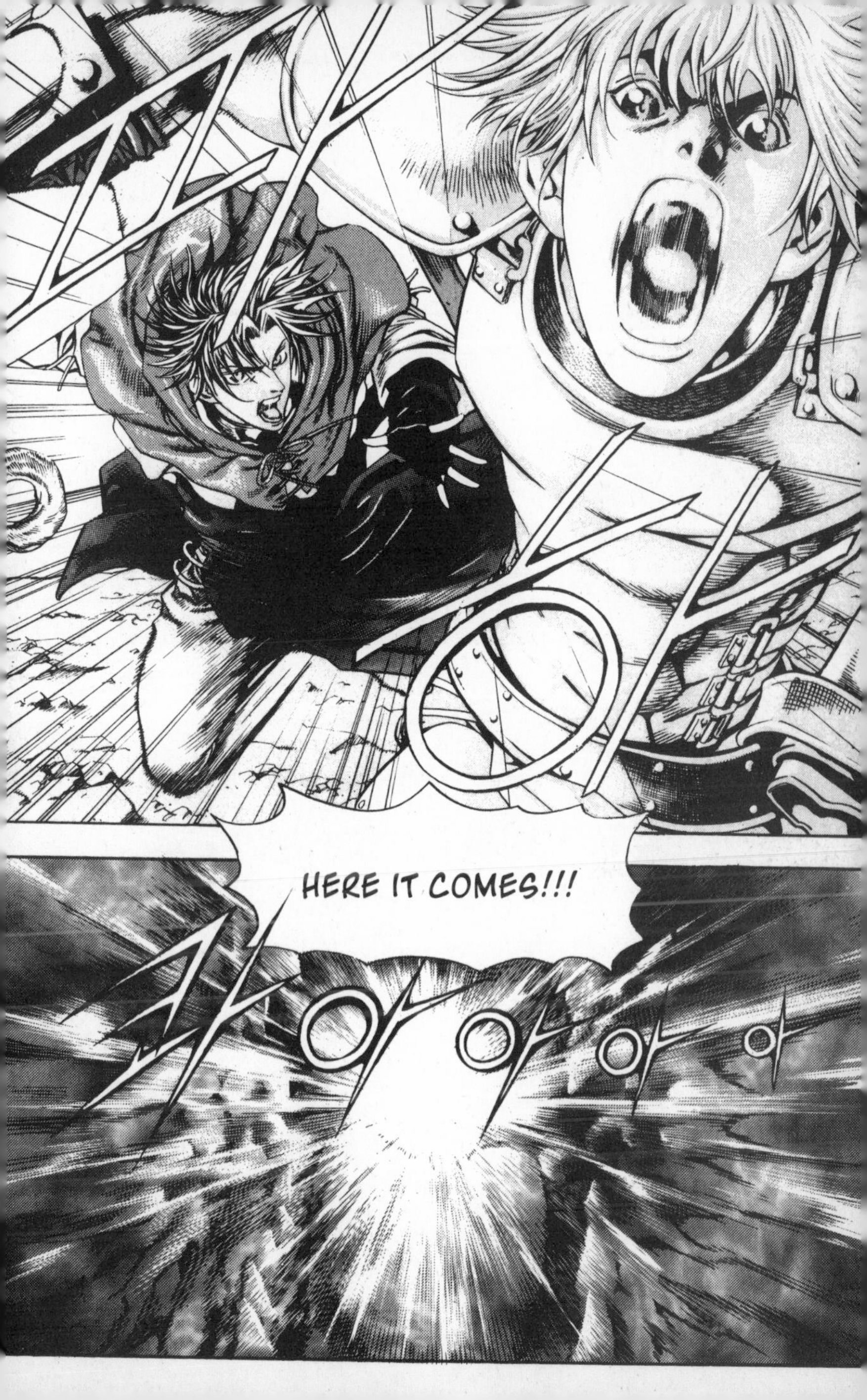
HERE IT COMES!!!

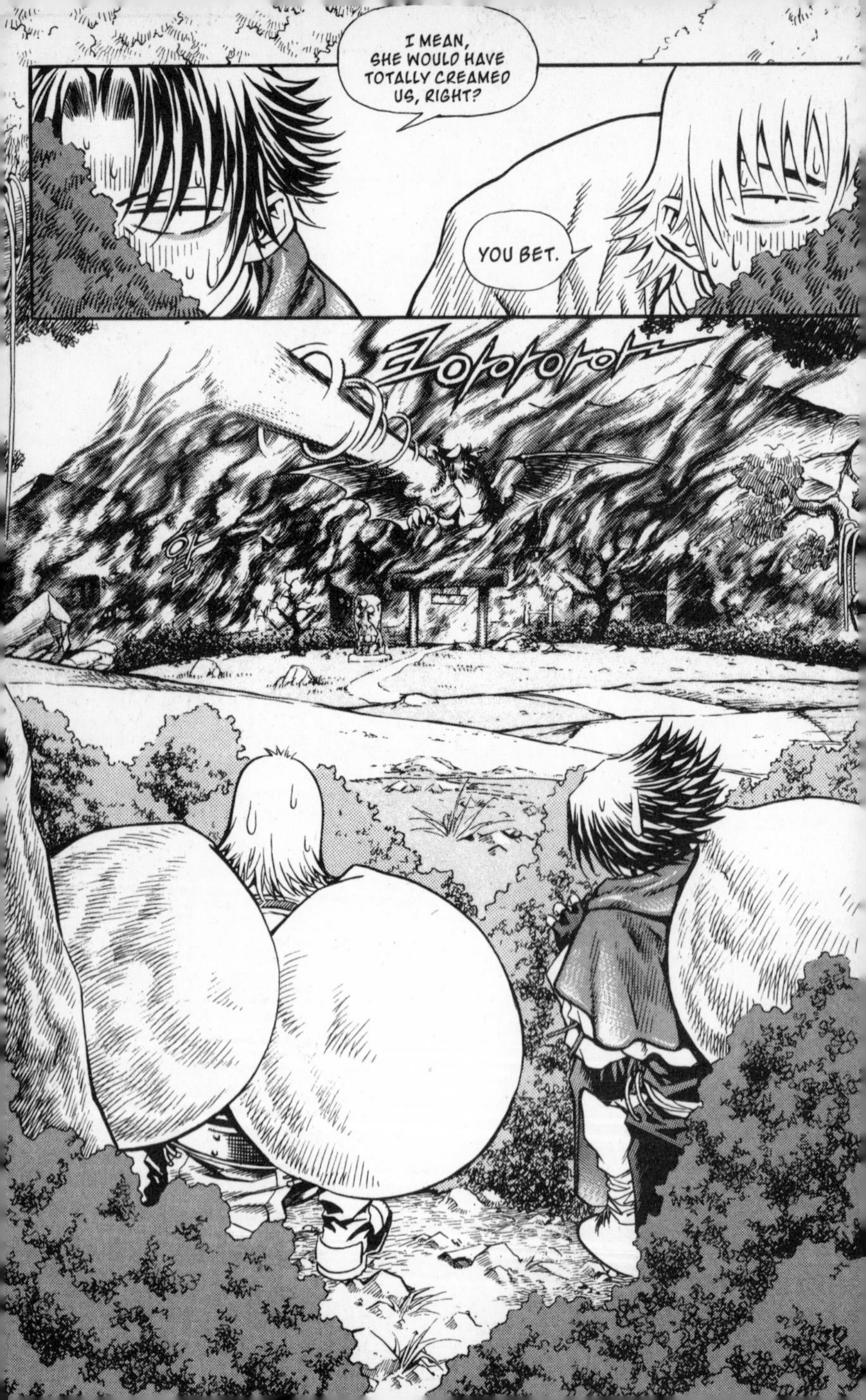
I MEAN, SHE WOULD HAVE TOTALLY CREAMED US, RIGHT?
YOU BET.

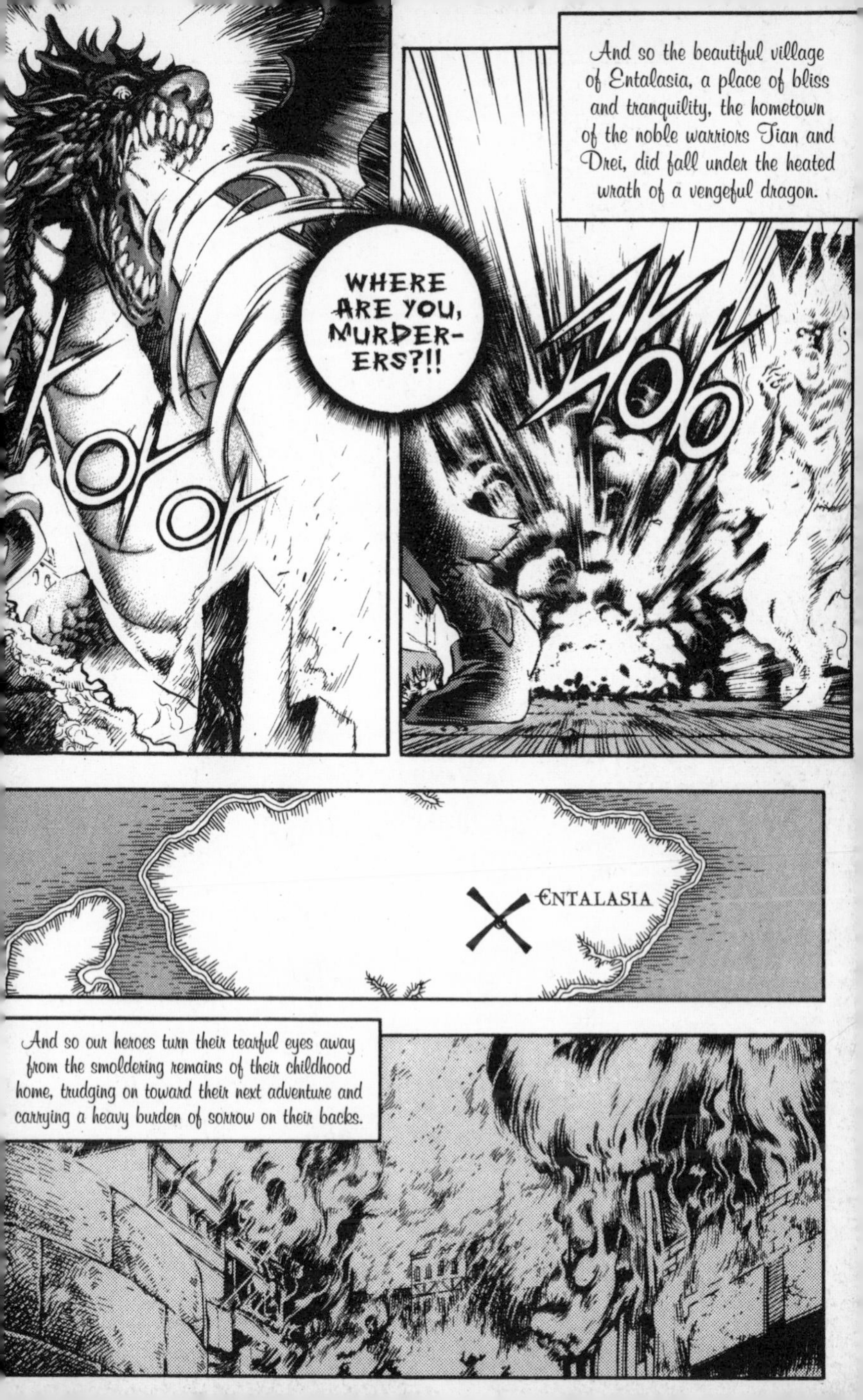
And so the beautiful village of Entalasia, a place of bliss and tranquility, the hometown of the noble warriors Tian and Drei, did fall under the heated wrath of a vengeful dragon.
WHERE ARE YOU, MURDER-ERS?!!
ENTALASIA
And so our heroes turn their tearful eyes away from the smoldering remains of their childhood home, trudging on toward their next adventure and carrying a heavy burden of sorrow on their backs.

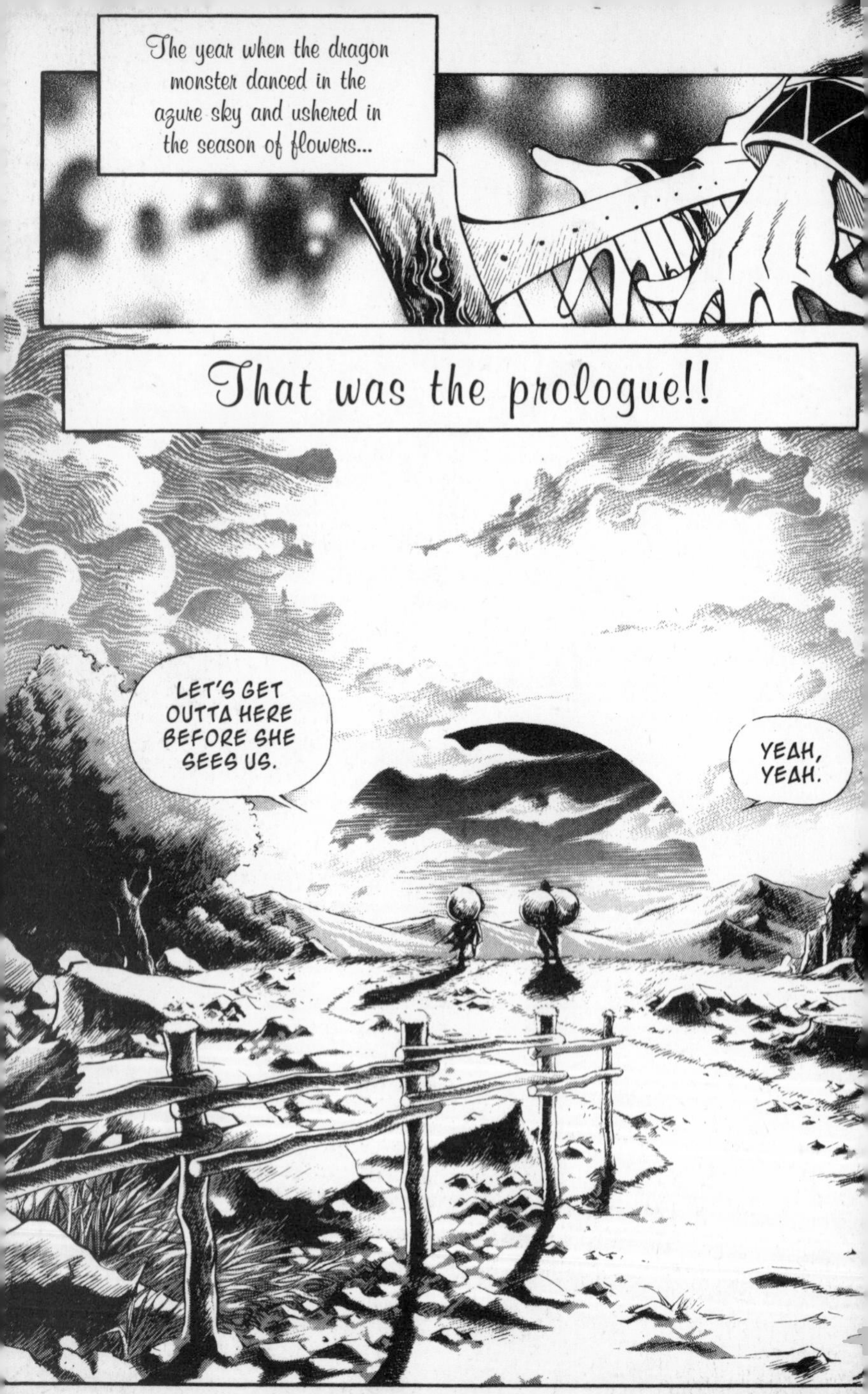
The year when the dragon monster danced in the azure sky and ushered in the season of flowers...
That was the prologue!!
LET'S GET OUTTA HERE BEFORE SHE SEES US.
YEAH, YEAH.

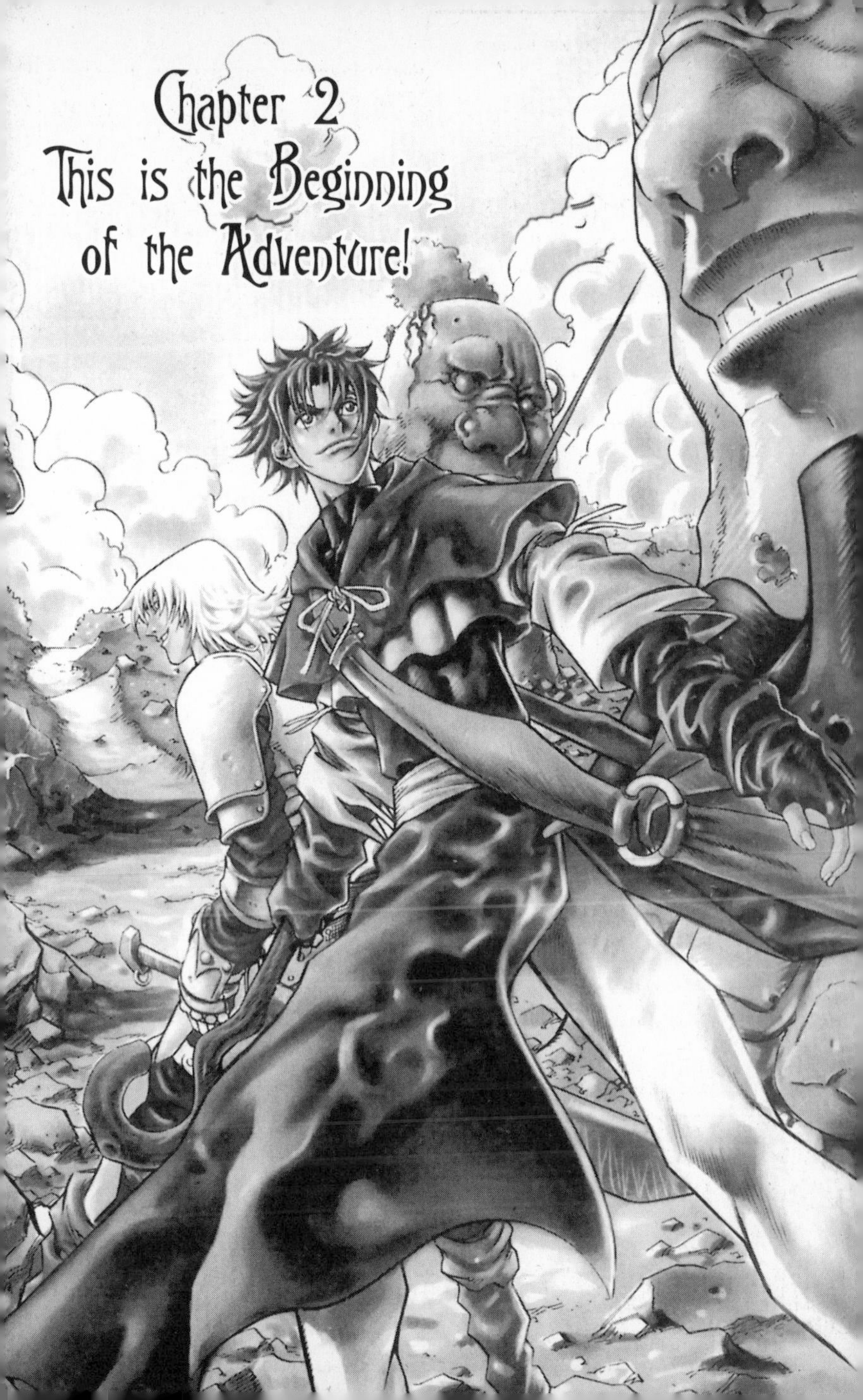
Chapter 2
This is the Beginning
of the Adventure!

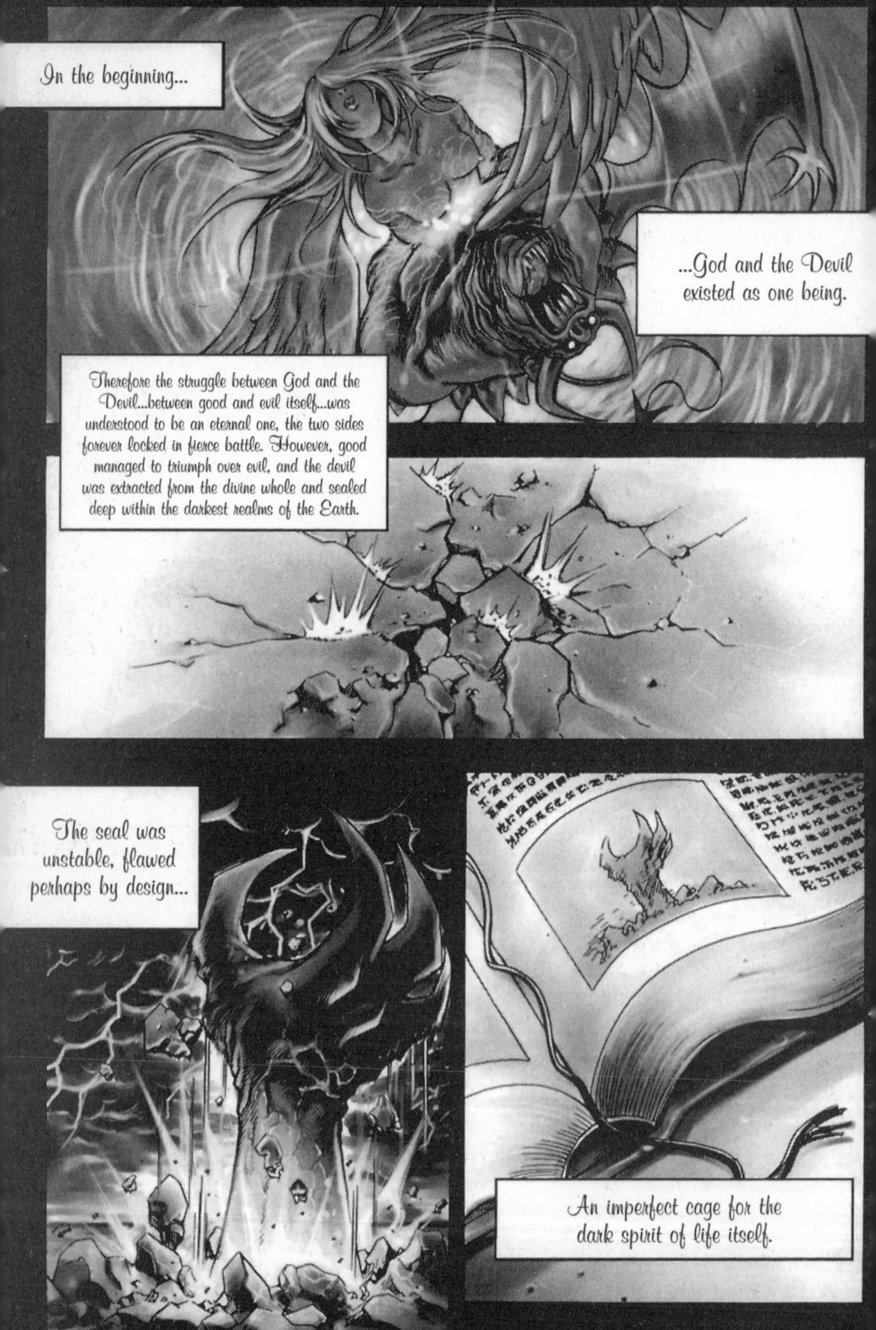
In the beginning...
...God and the Devil existed as one being.
Therefore the struggle between God and the Devil...between good and evil itself...was understood to be an eternal one, the two sides forever locked in fierce battle. However, good managed to triumph over evil, and the devil was extracted from the divine whole and sealed deep within the darkest realms of the Earth.
The seal was unstable, flawed perhaps by design...
An imperfect cage for the dark spirit of life itself.

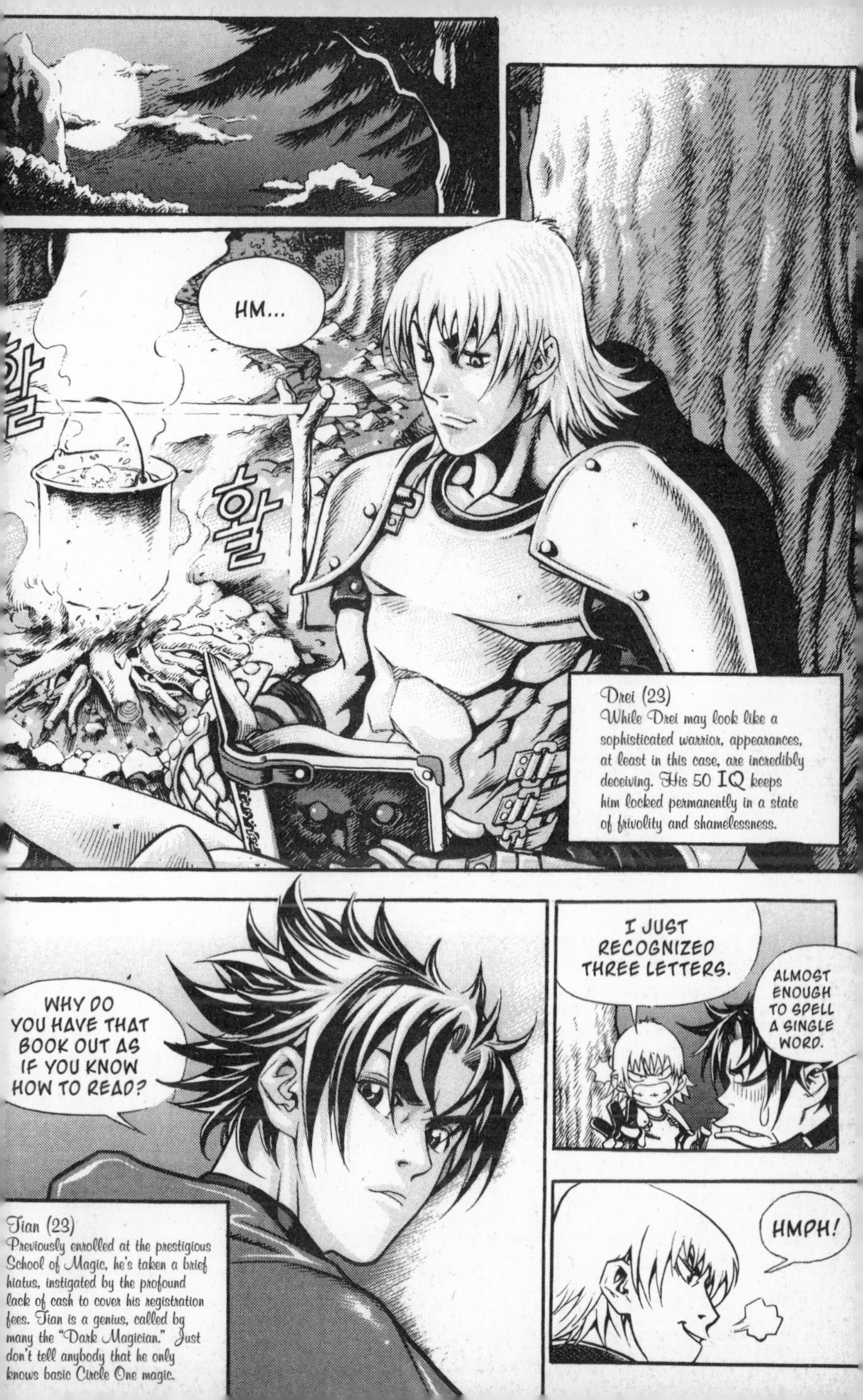
HM...
활활
Drei (23)
While Drei may look like a sophisticated warrior, appearances, at least in this case, are incredibly deceiving. His 50 IQ keeps him locked permanently in a state of frivolity and shamelessness.
WHY DO YOU HAVE THAT BOOK OUT AS IF YOU KNOW HOW TO READ?
Tian (23)
Previously enrolled at the prestigious School of Magic, he's taken a brief hiatus, instigated by the profound lack of cash to cover his registration fees. Tian is a genius, called by many the "Dark Magician." Just don't tell anybody that he only knows basic Circle One magic.
I JUST RECOGNIZED THREE LETTERS.
ALMOST ENOUGH TO SPELL A SINGLE WORD.
HMPH!

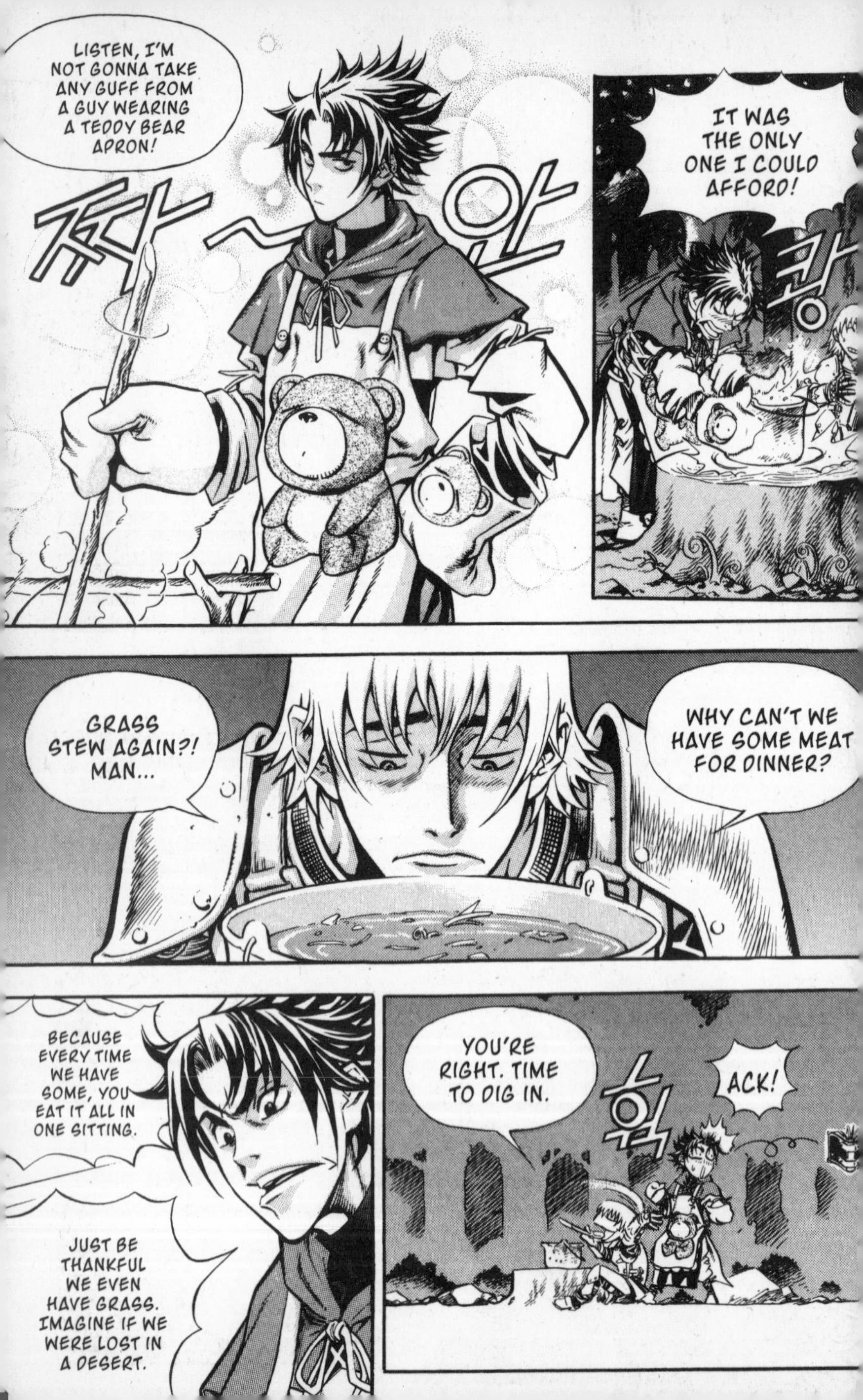

LISTEN, I'M NOT GONNA TAKE ANY GUFF FROM A GUY WEARING A TEDDY BEAR APRON!
IT WAS THE ONLY ONE I COULD AFFORD!
GRASS STEW AGAIN?! MAN...
WHY CAN'T WE HAVE SOME MEAT FOR DINNER?
BECAUSE EVERY TIME WE HAVE SOME, YOU EAT IT ALL IN ONE SITTING.
JUST BE THANKFUL WE EVEN HAVE GRASS. IMAGINE IF WE WERE LOST IN A DESERT.
YOU'RE RIGHT. TIME TO DIG IN.
ACK!

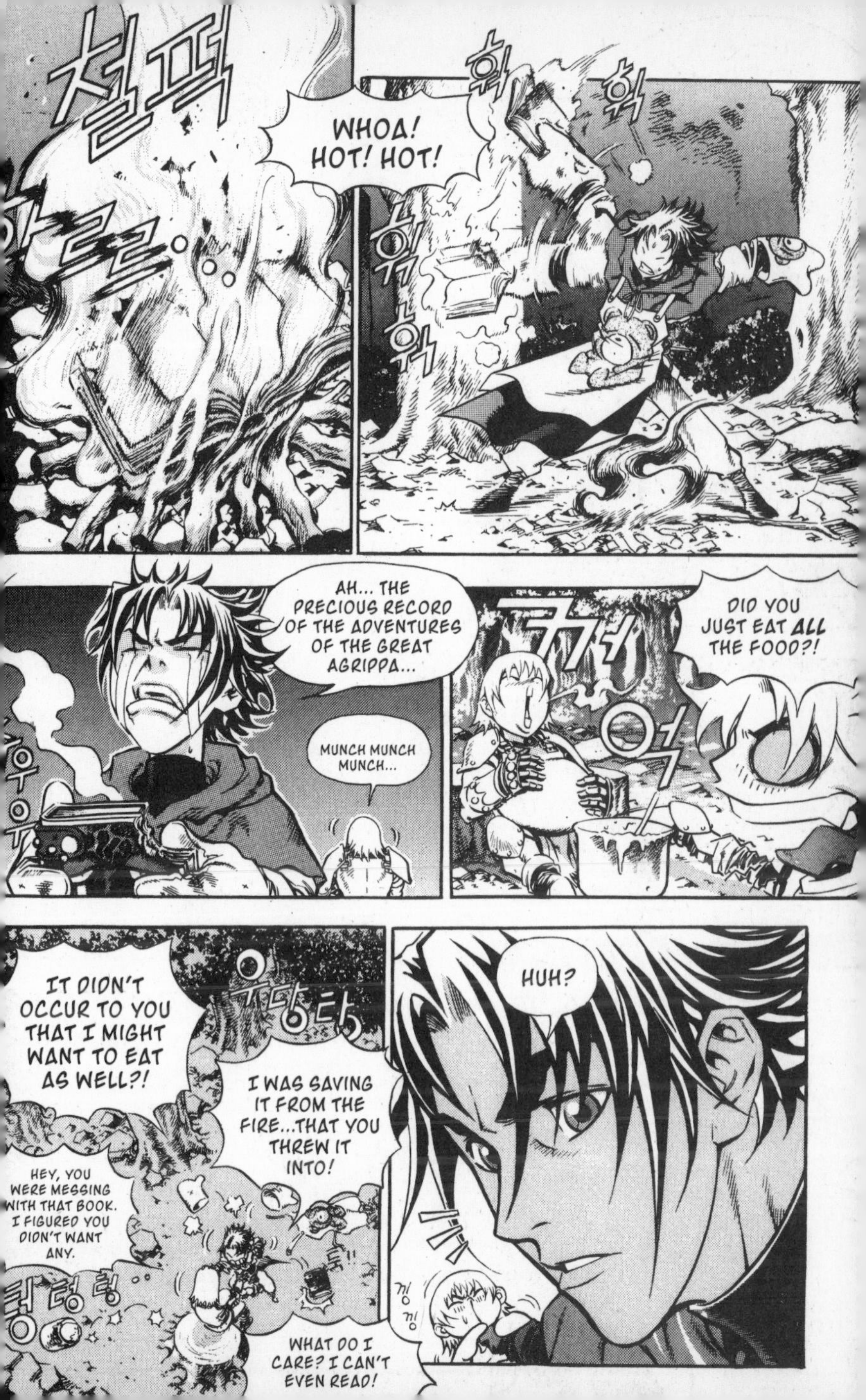
WHOA! HOT! HOT!
AH... THE PRECIOUS RECORD OF THE ADVENTURES OF THE GREAT AGRIPPA...
MUNCH MUNCH MUNCH...
DID YOU JUST EAT ALL THE FOOD?!
IT DIDN'T OCCUR TO YOU THAT I MIGHT WANT TO EAT AS WELL?!
I WAS SAVING IT FROM THE FIRE...THAT YOU THREW IT INTO!
HEY, YOU WERE MESSING WITH THAT BOOK. I FIGURED YOU DIDN'T WANT ANY.
HUH?
WHAT DO I CARE? I CAN'T EVEN READ!

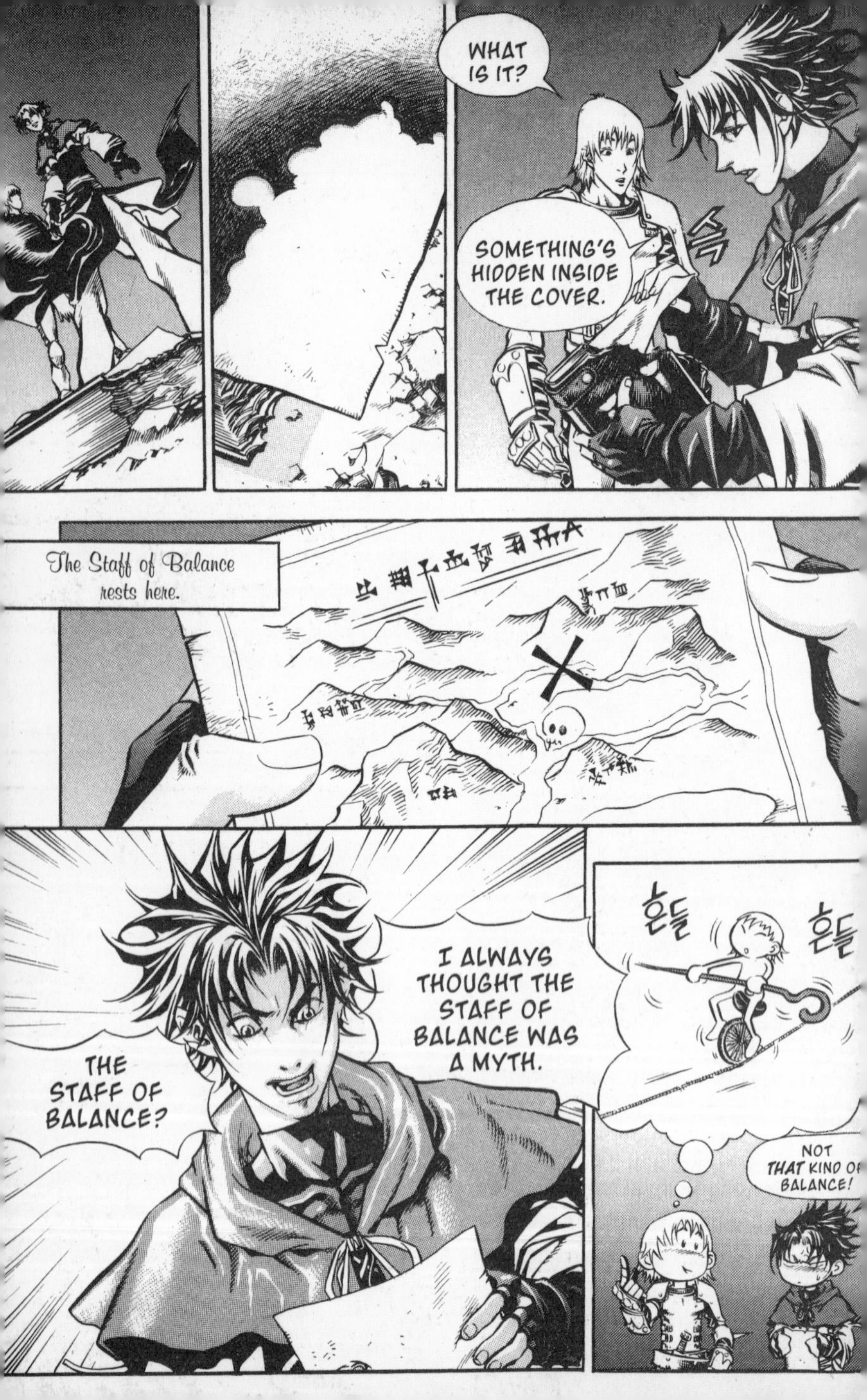
WHAT IS IT?
SOMETHING'S HIDDEN INSIDE THE COVER.
The Staff of Balance rests here.
THE STAFF OF BALANCE?
I ALWAYS THOUGHT THE STAFF OF BALANCE WAS A MYTH.
흔들
흔들
NOT THAT KIND OF BALANCE!

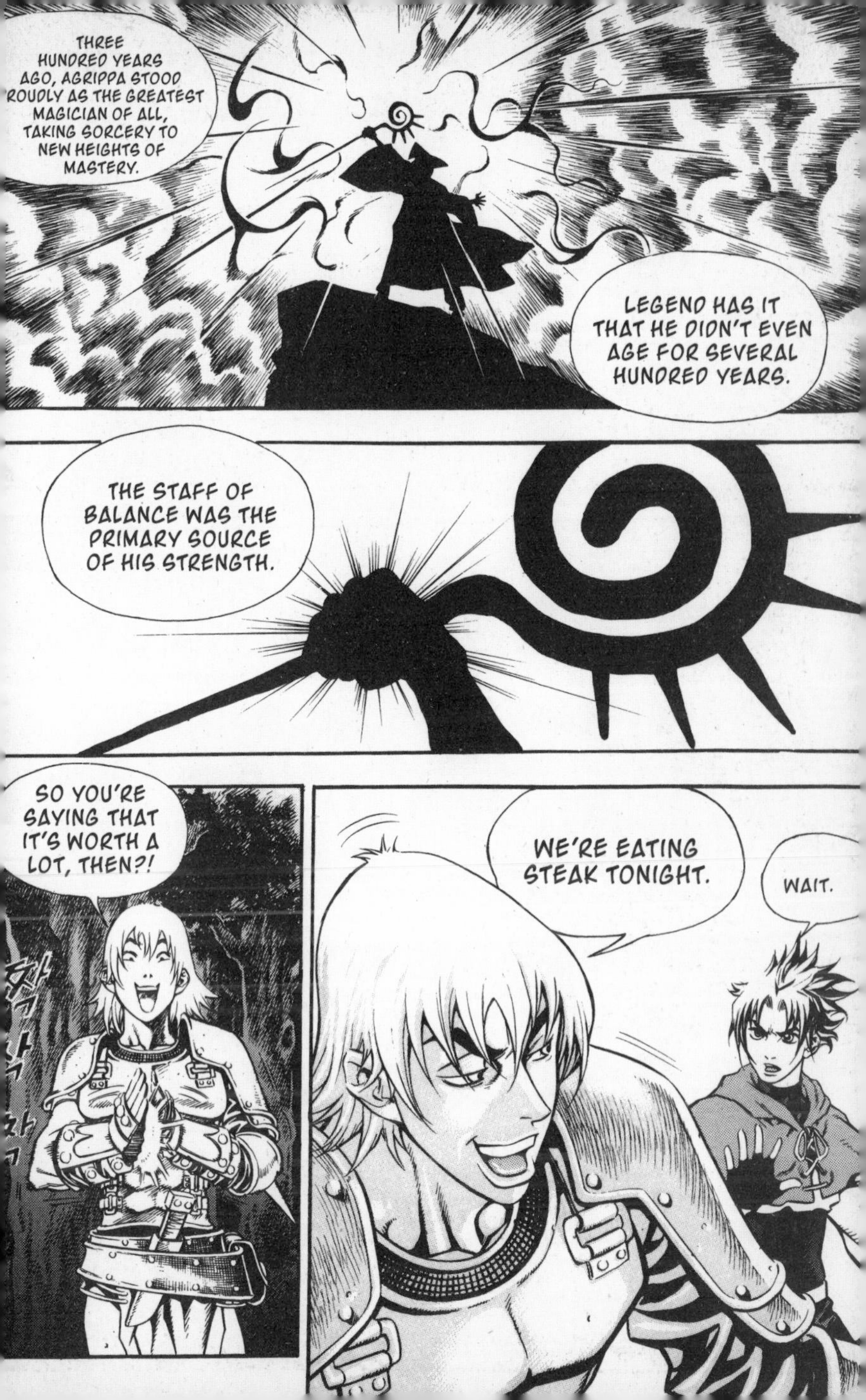
THREE HUNDRED YEARS AGO, AGRIPPA STOOD ROUDLY AS THE GREATEST MAGICIAN OF ALL, TAKING SORCERY TO NEW HEIGHTS OF MASTERY.
LEGEND HAS IT THAT HE DIDN'T EVEN AGE FOR SEVERAL HUNDRED YEARS.
THE STAFF OF BALANCE WAS THE PRIMARY SOURCE OF HIS STRENGTH.
SO YOU'RE SAYING THAT IT'S WORTH A LOT, THEN?!
WE'RE EATING STEAK TONIGHT.
WAIT.

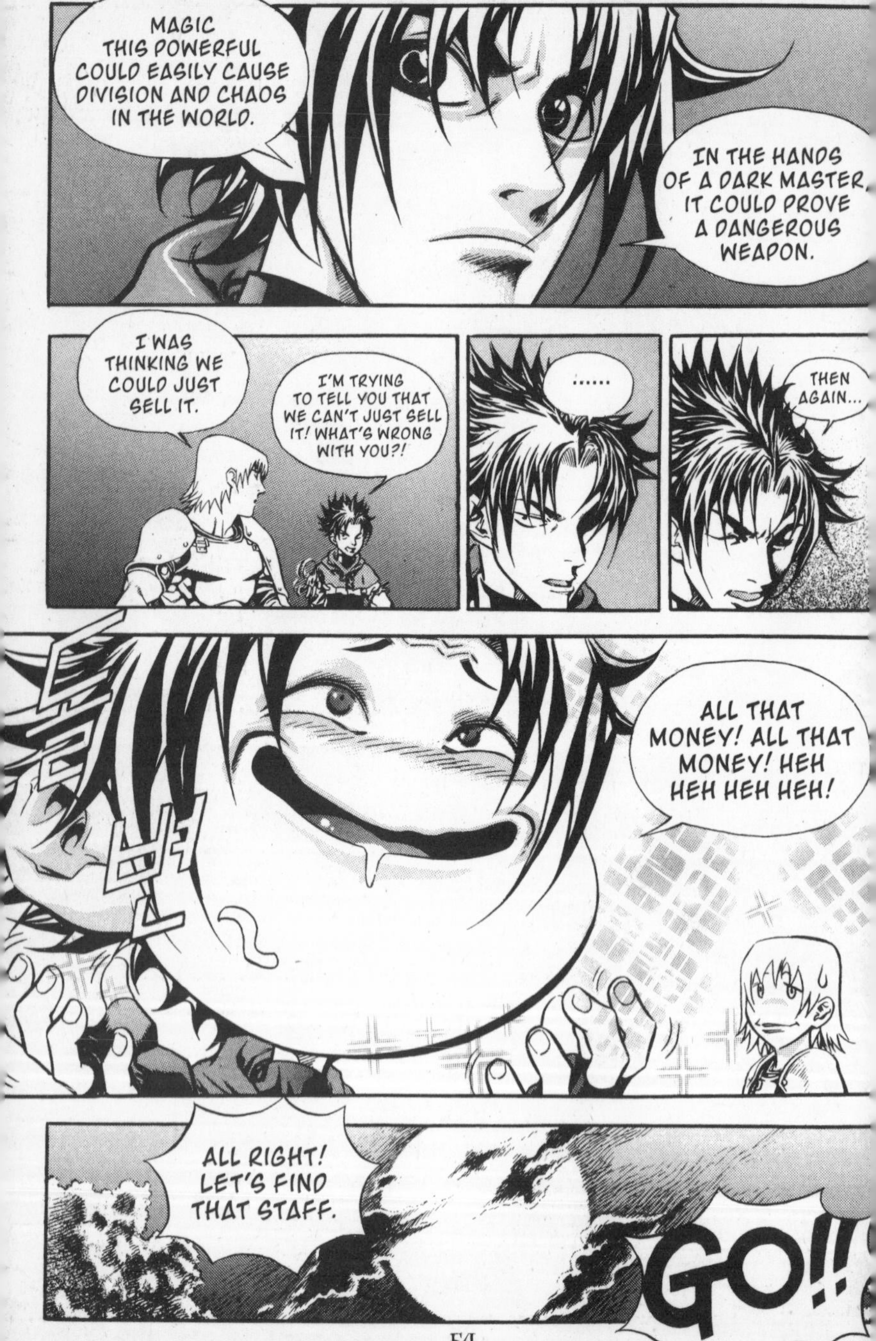
MAGIC THIS POWERFUL COULD EASILY CAUSE DIVISION AND CHAOS IN THE WORLD.
IN THE HANDS OF A DARK MASTER, IT COULD PROVE A DANGEROUS WEAPON.
I WAS THINKING WE COULD JUST SELL IT.
I'M TRYING TO TELL YOU THAT WE CAN'T JUST SELL IT! WHAT'S WRONG WITH YOU?!
......
THEN AGAIN...
ALL THAT MONEY! ALL THAT MONEY! HEH HEH HEH HEH!
ALL RIGHT! LET'S FIND THAT STAFF.
GO!!

I'M STARVING.

MAN, MAYBE I REALLY SHOULD HAVE LEFT SOME FOOD FOR YOU...

YA THINK?!

YOU WOLFED DOWN TWO DAYS WORTH IN TWO SECONDS!

SORRY, SORRY. CALM DOWN.

HMM... I THINK I'M EXPERIENCING MY GROWTH SPURT...

......

I'M ALREADY HUNGRY AGAIN.

UGH!

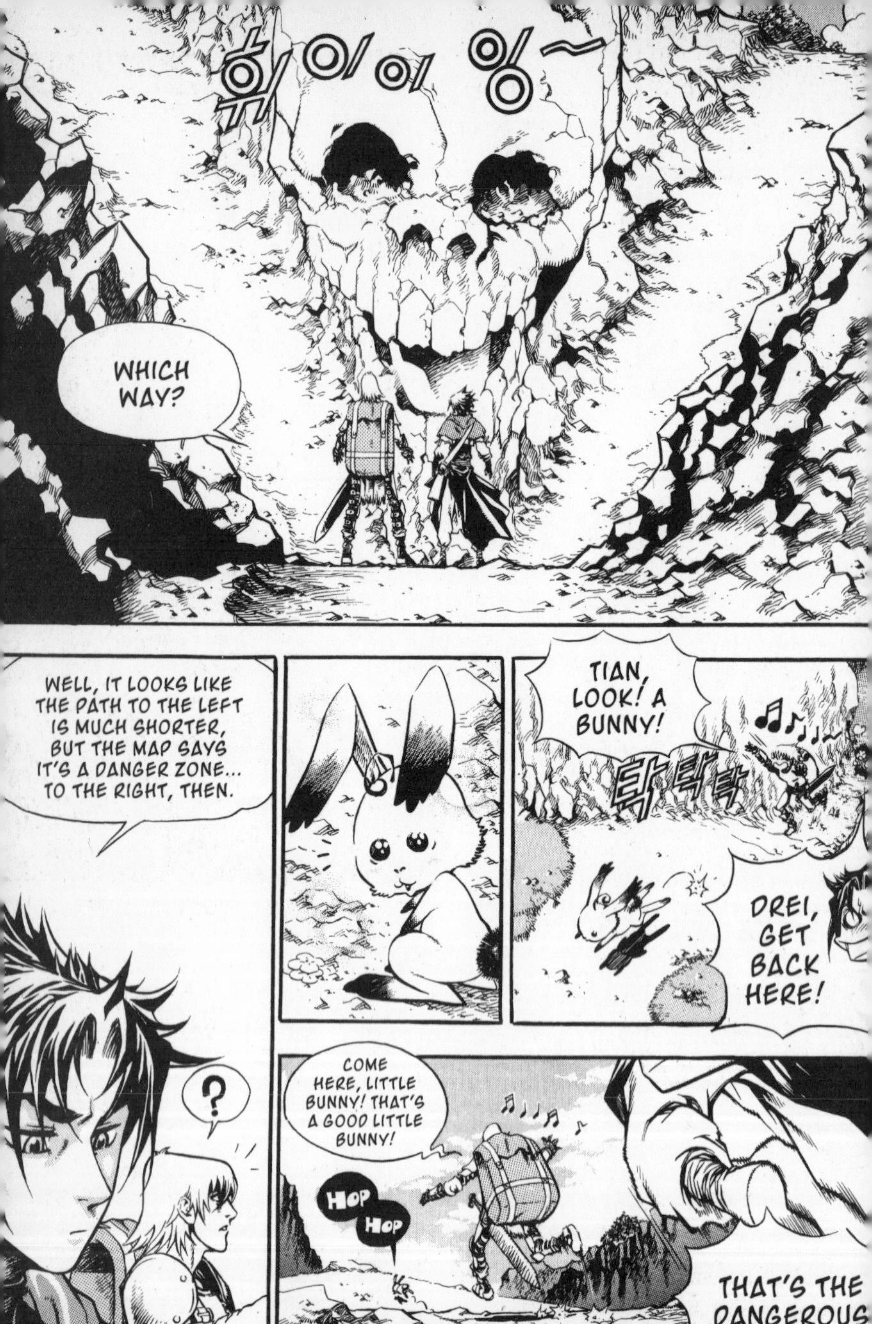

휘이이잉~
WHICH WAY?
WELL, IT LOOKS LIKE THE PATH TO THE LEFT IS MUCH SHORTER, BUT THE MAP SAYS IT'S A DANGER ZONE... TO THE RIGHT, THEN.
TIAN, LOOK! A BUNNY!
DREI, GET BACK HERE!
?
COME HERE, LITTLE BUNNY! THAT'S A GOOD LITTLE BUNNY!
HOP
HOP
THAT'S THE DANGEROUS PATH!

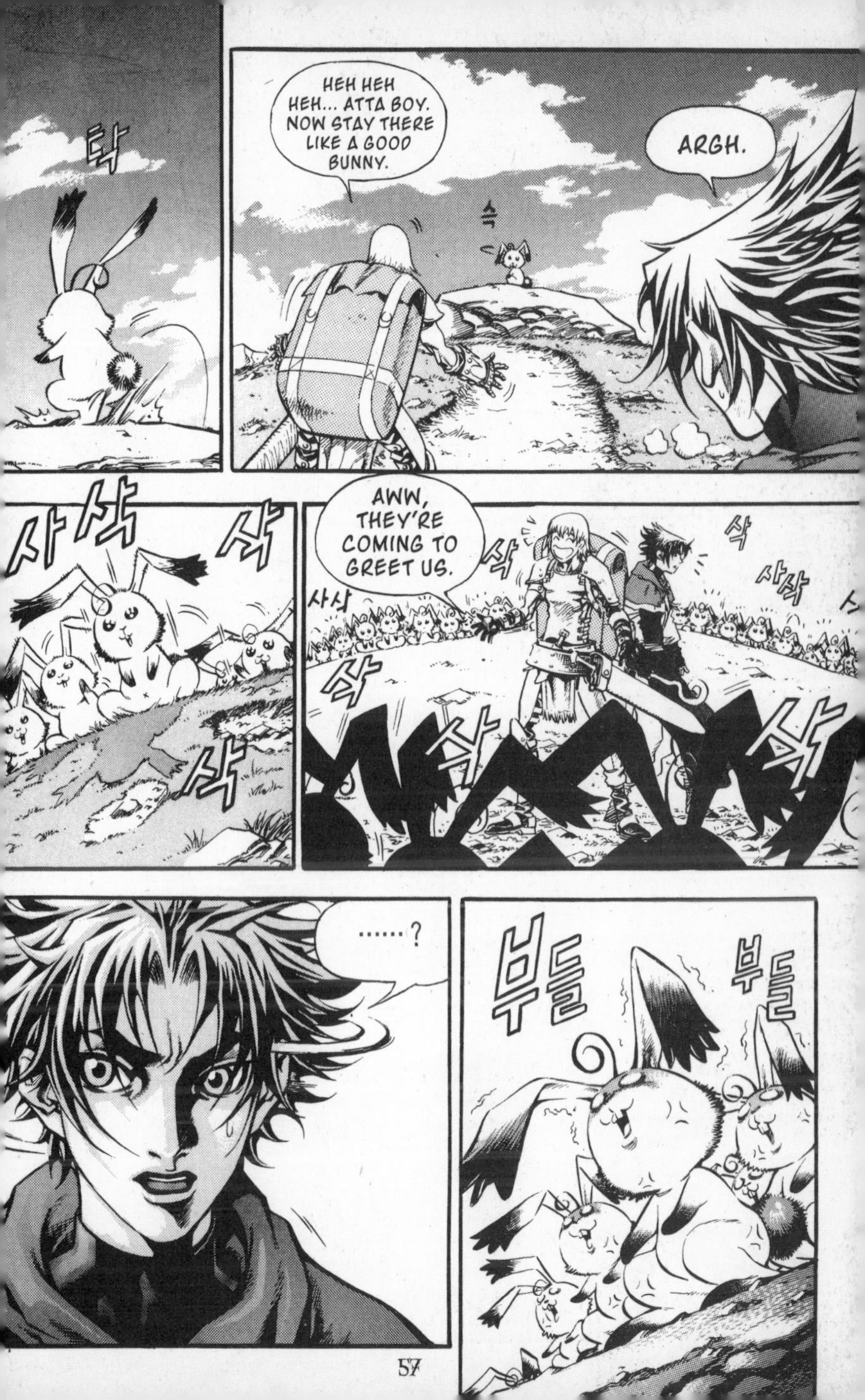

탁
HEH HEH HEH... ATTA BOY. NOW STAY THERE LIKE A GOOD BUNNY.
슥
ARGH.
사삭
삭
삭
AWW, THEY'RE COMING TO GREET US.
사삭
삭
사삭
삭
삭
삭
......?
부들
부들

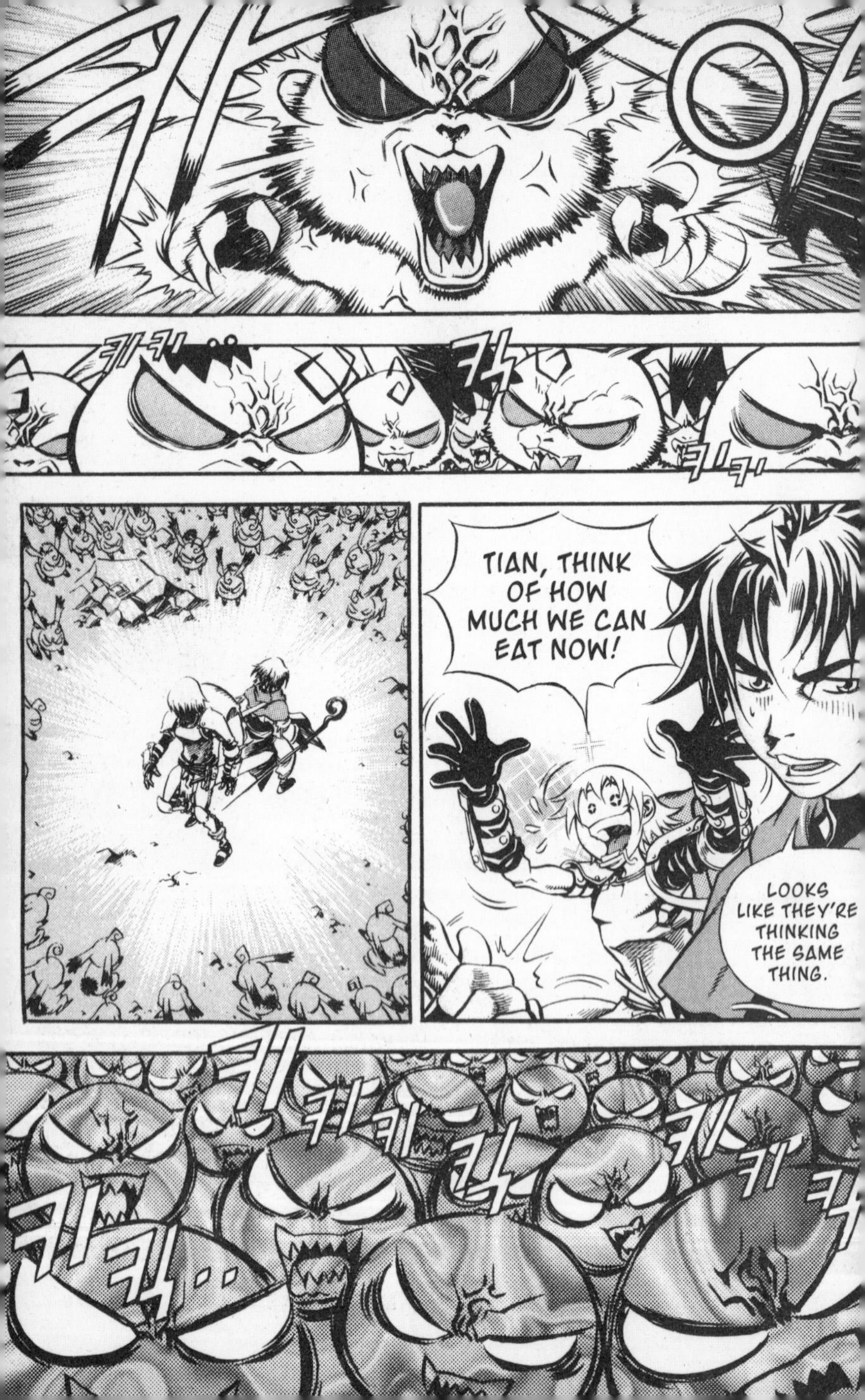
TIAN, THINK OF HOW MUCH WE CAN EAT NOW!
LOOKS LIKE THEY'RE THINKING THE SAME THING.

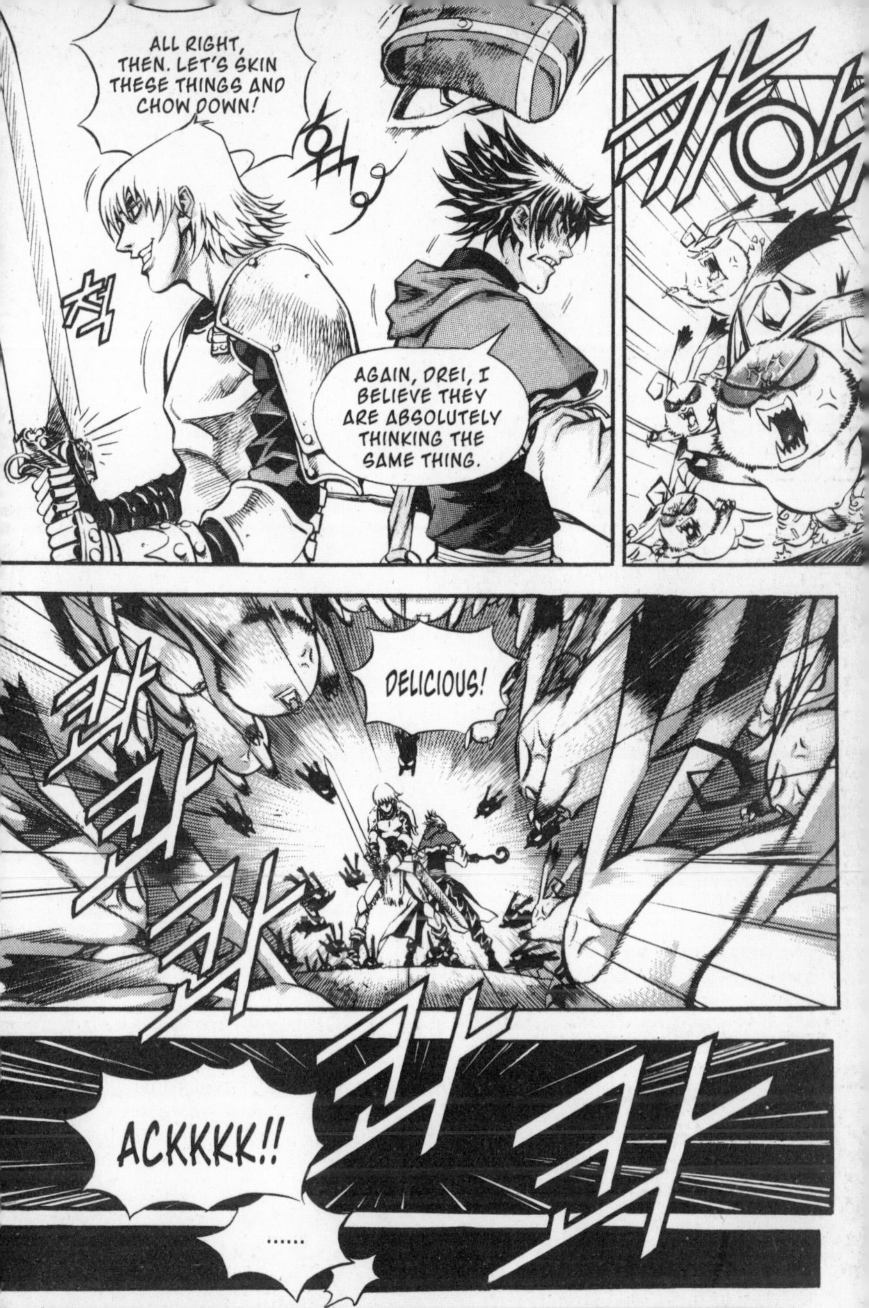
ALL RIGHT, THEN. LET'S SKIN THESE THINGS AND CHOW DOWN!
AGAIN, DREI, I BELIEVE THEY ARE ABSOLUTELY THINKING THE SAME THING.
DELICIOUS!
ACKKKK!!
......

D... DREI...

I'M SORRY... I...I TRIED TO KEEP UP...

But...but... I can't...

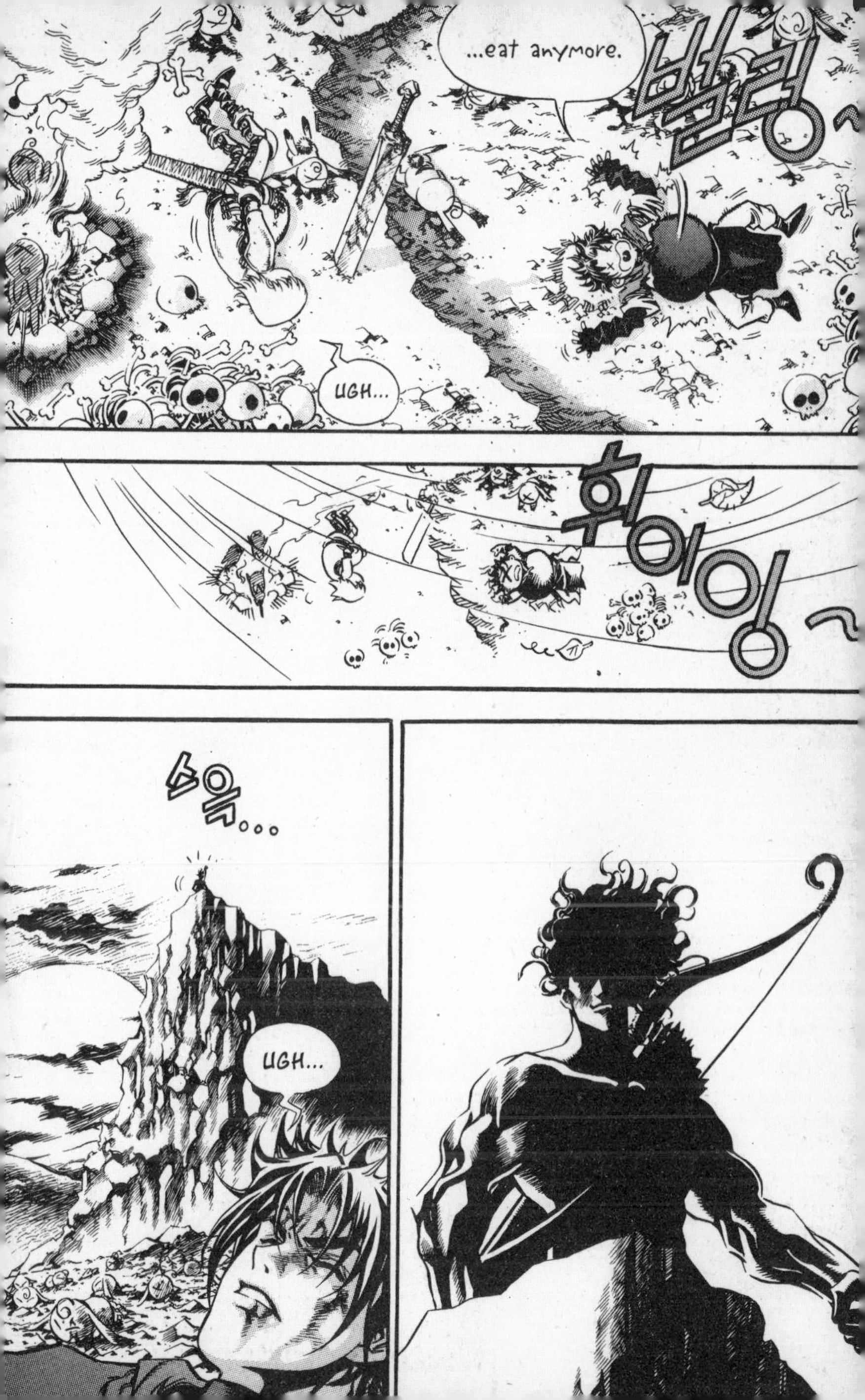

...eat anymore.
벌렁~
UGH...
휘이이잉~
UGH...

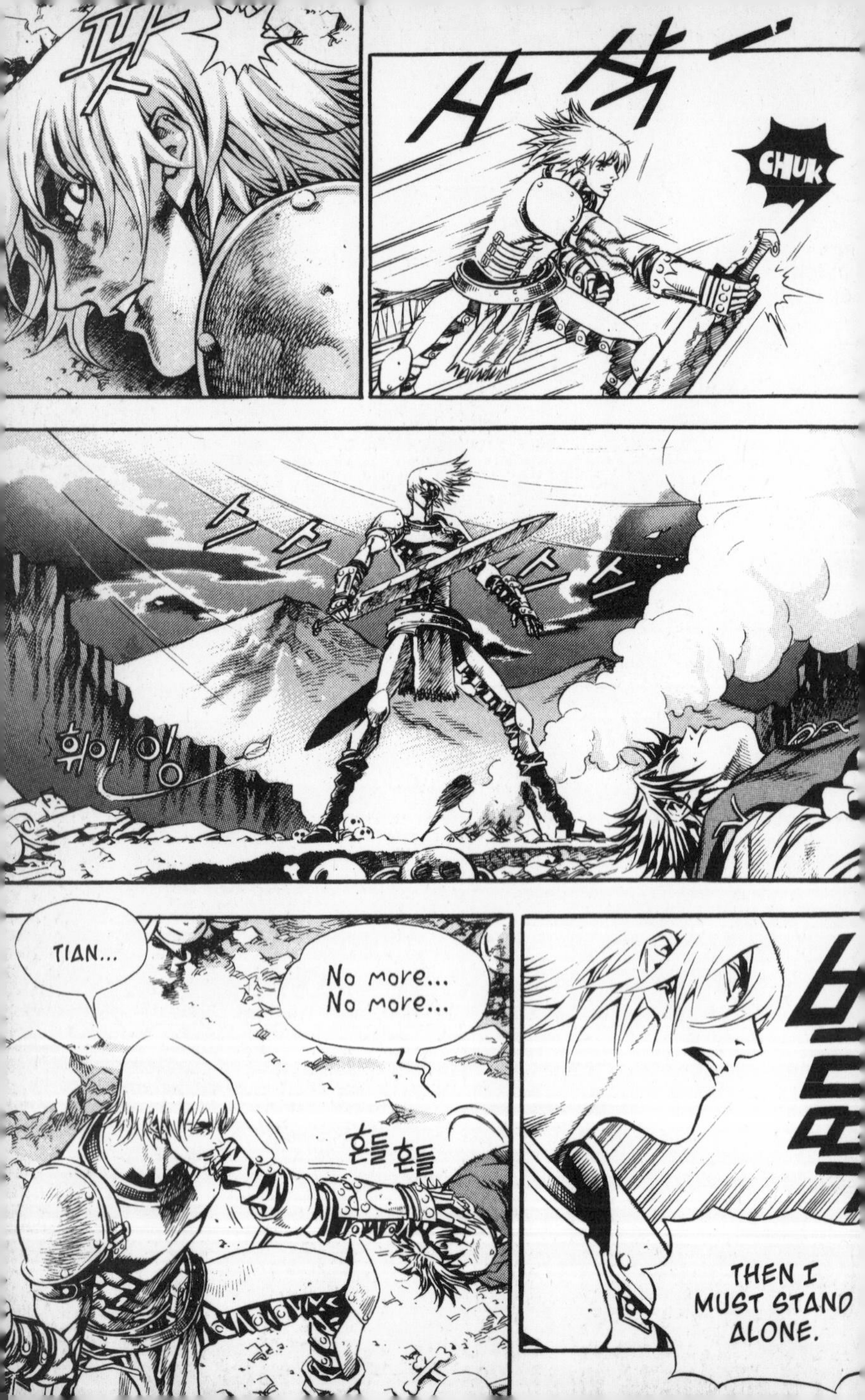
CHUK
TIAN...
No more...
No more...
흔들흔들
THEN I MUST STAND ALONE.

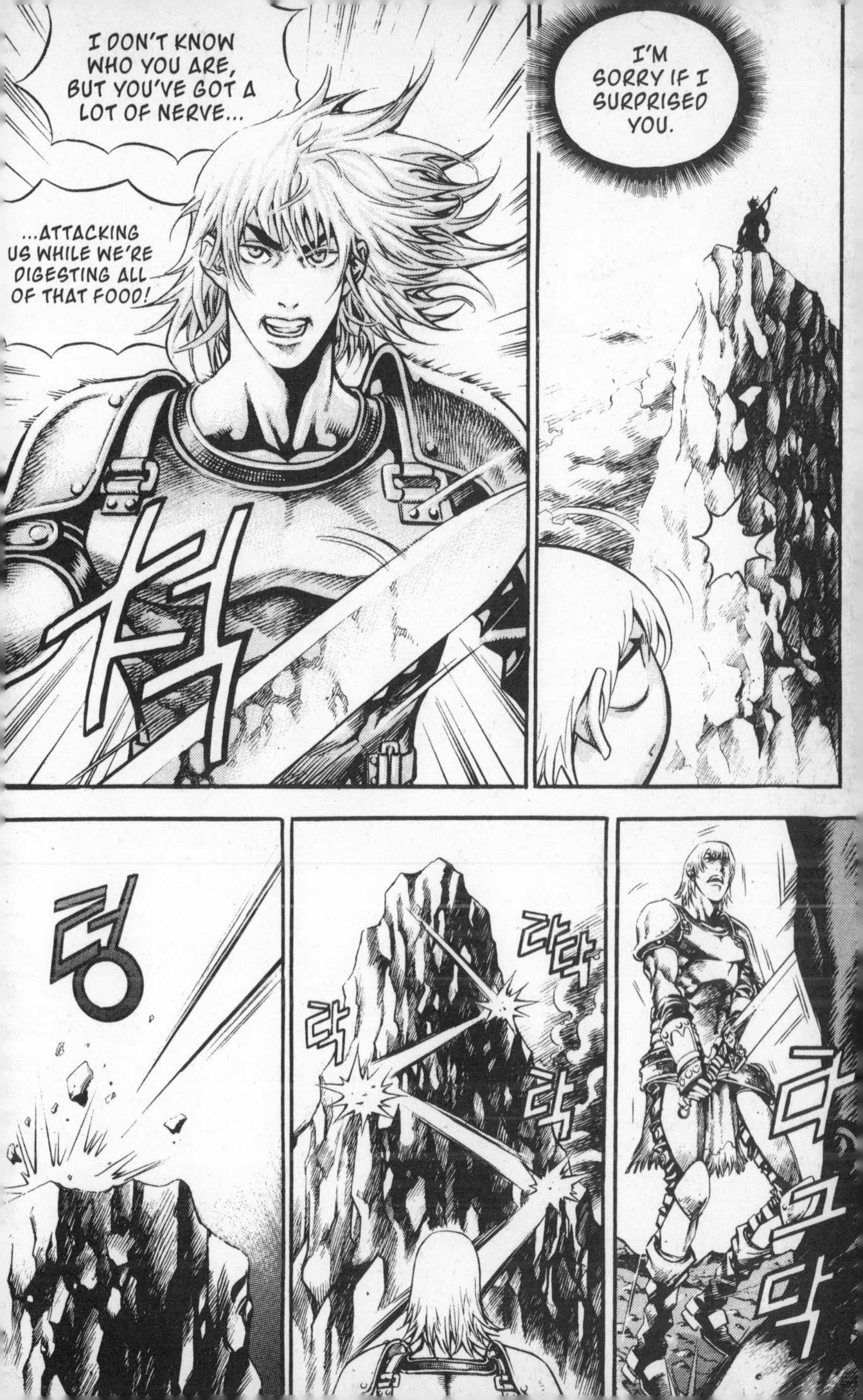
I DON'T KNOW WHO YOU ARE, BUT YOU'VE GOT A LOT OF NERVE...
...ATTACKING US WHILE WE'RE DIGESTING ALL OF THAT FOOD!
I'M SORRY IF I SURPRISED YOU.

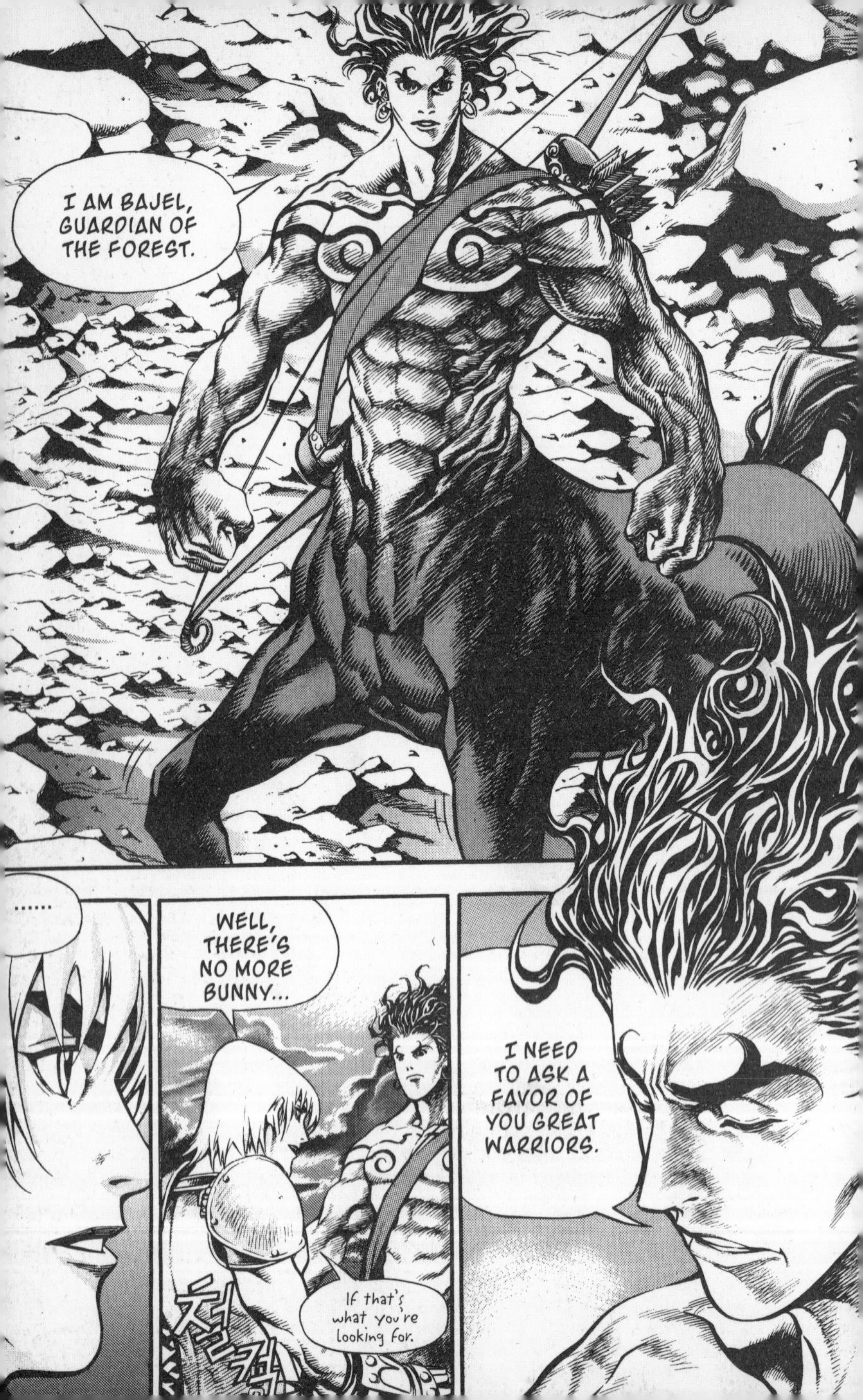
I AM BAJEL, GUARDIAN OF THE FOREST.
......
WELL, THERE'S NO MORE BUNNY...
If that's what you're looking for.
I NEED TO ASK A FAVOR OF YOU GREAT WARRIORS.

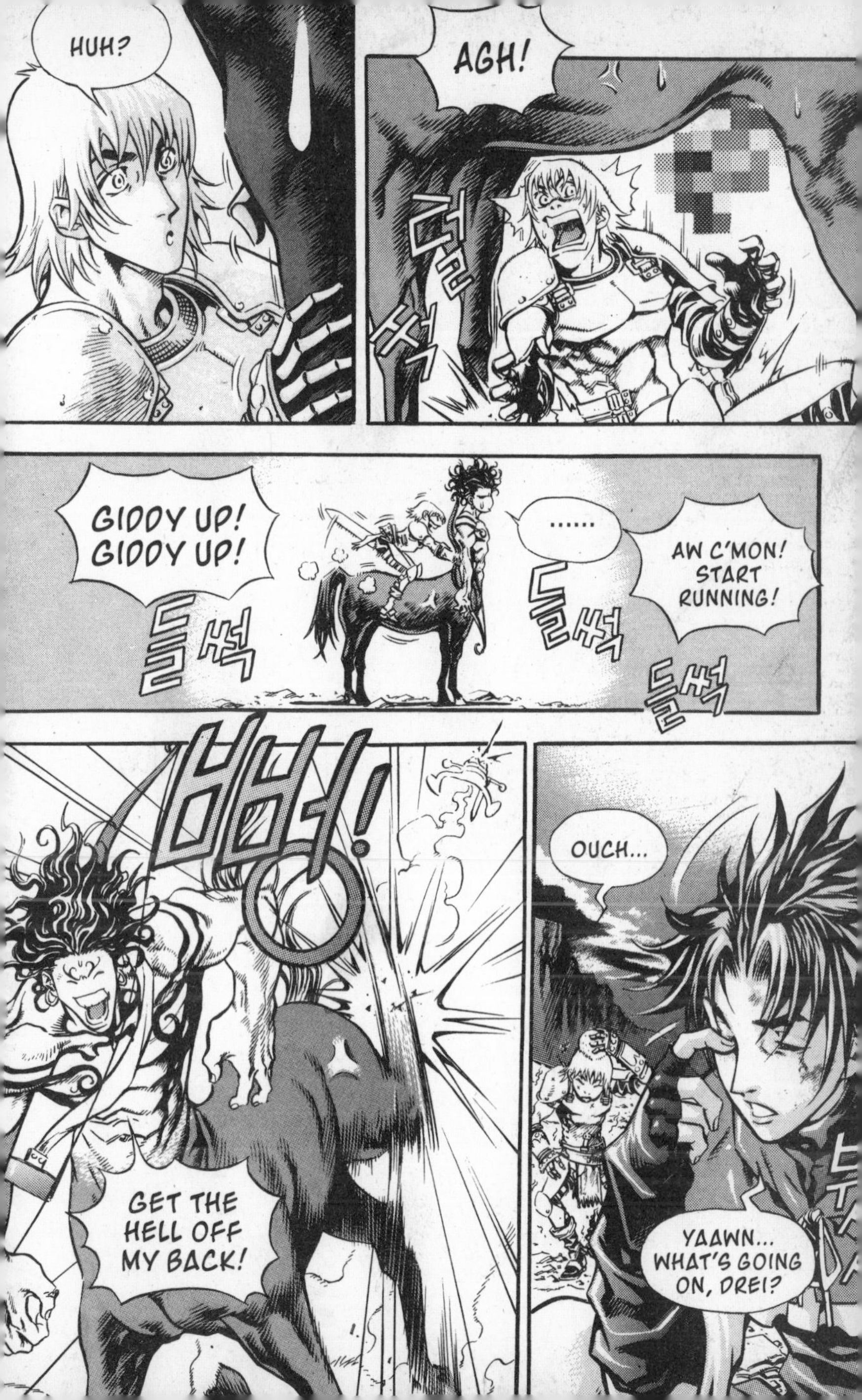
HUH?
AGH!
GIDDY UP! GIDDY UP!
......
AW C'MON! START RUNNING!
GET THE HELL OFF MY BACK!
OUCH...
YAAWN... WHAT'S GOING ON, DREI?

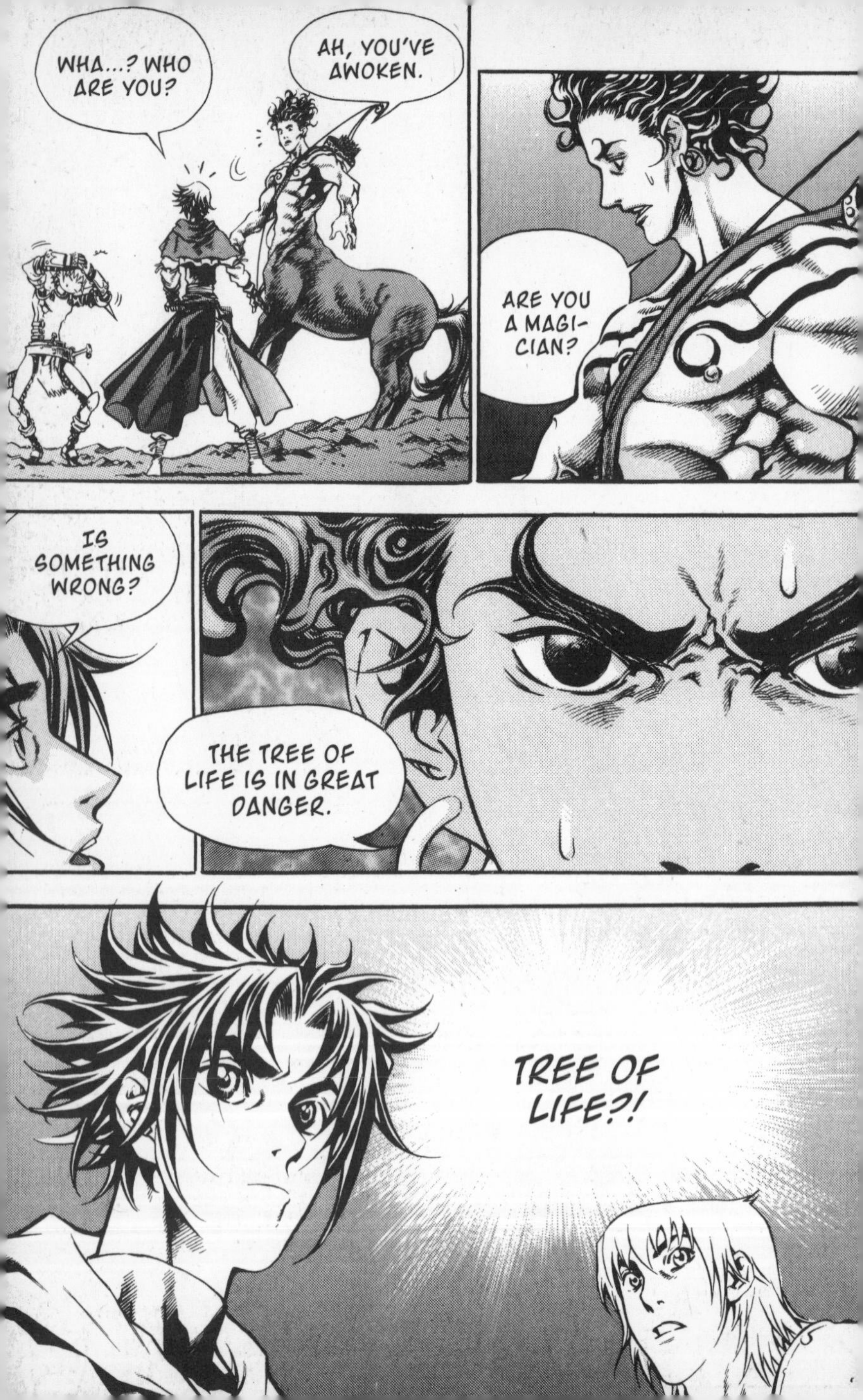
WHA...? WHO ARE YOU?
AH, YOU'VE AWOKEN.
ARE YOU A MAGI-CIAN?
IS SOMETHING WRONG?
THE TREE OF LIFE IS IN GREAT DANGER.
TREE OF LIFE?!

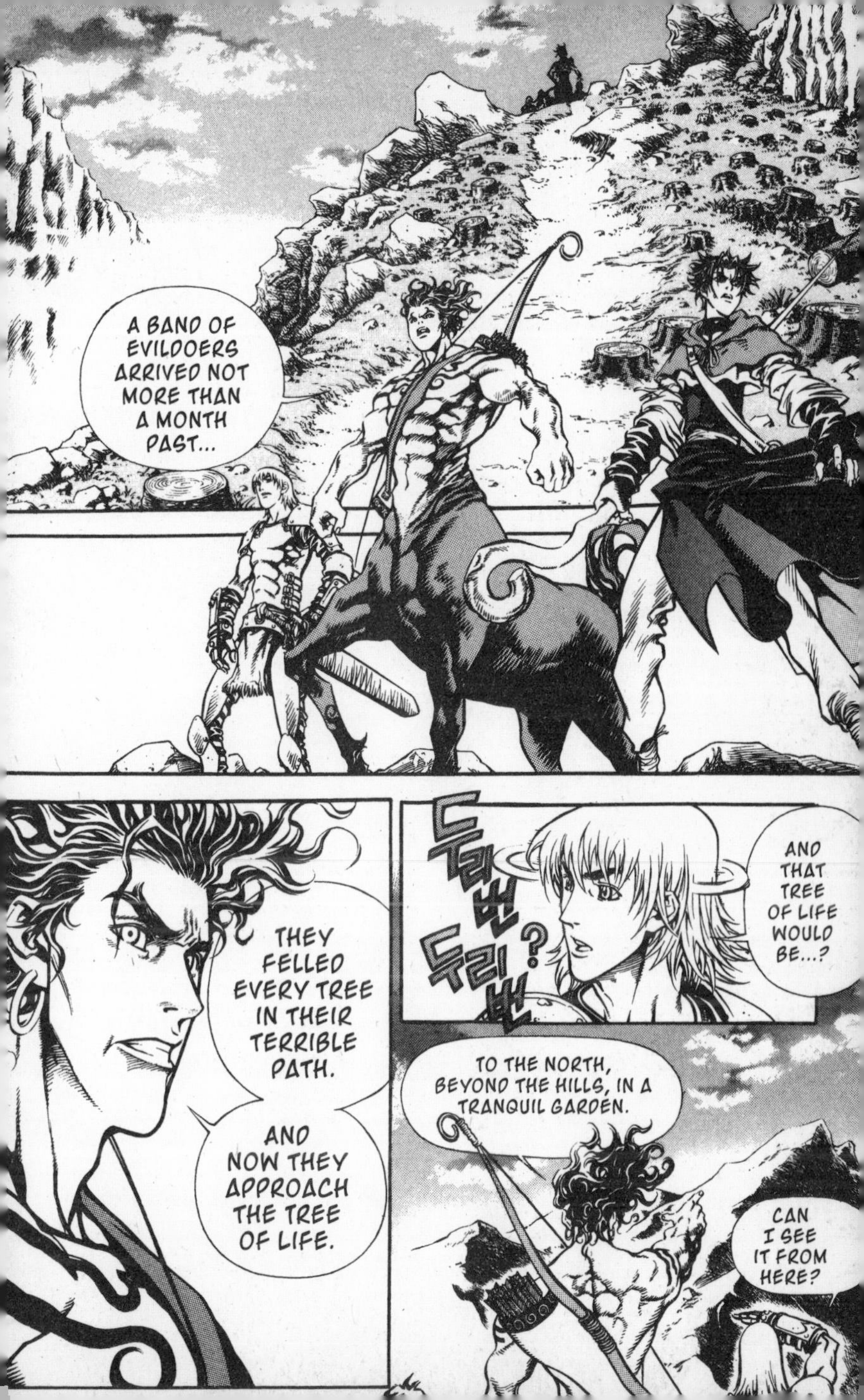
A BAND OF EVILDOERS ARRIVED NOT MORE THAN A MONTH PAST...
THEY FELLED EVERY TREE IN THEIR TERRIBLE PATH.
AND NOW THEY APPROACH THE TREE OF LIFE.
두리번 두리번
?
AND THAT TREE OF LIFE WOULD BE...?
TO THE NORTH, BEYOND THE HILLS, IN A TRANQUIL GARDEN.
CAN I SEE IT FROM HERE?

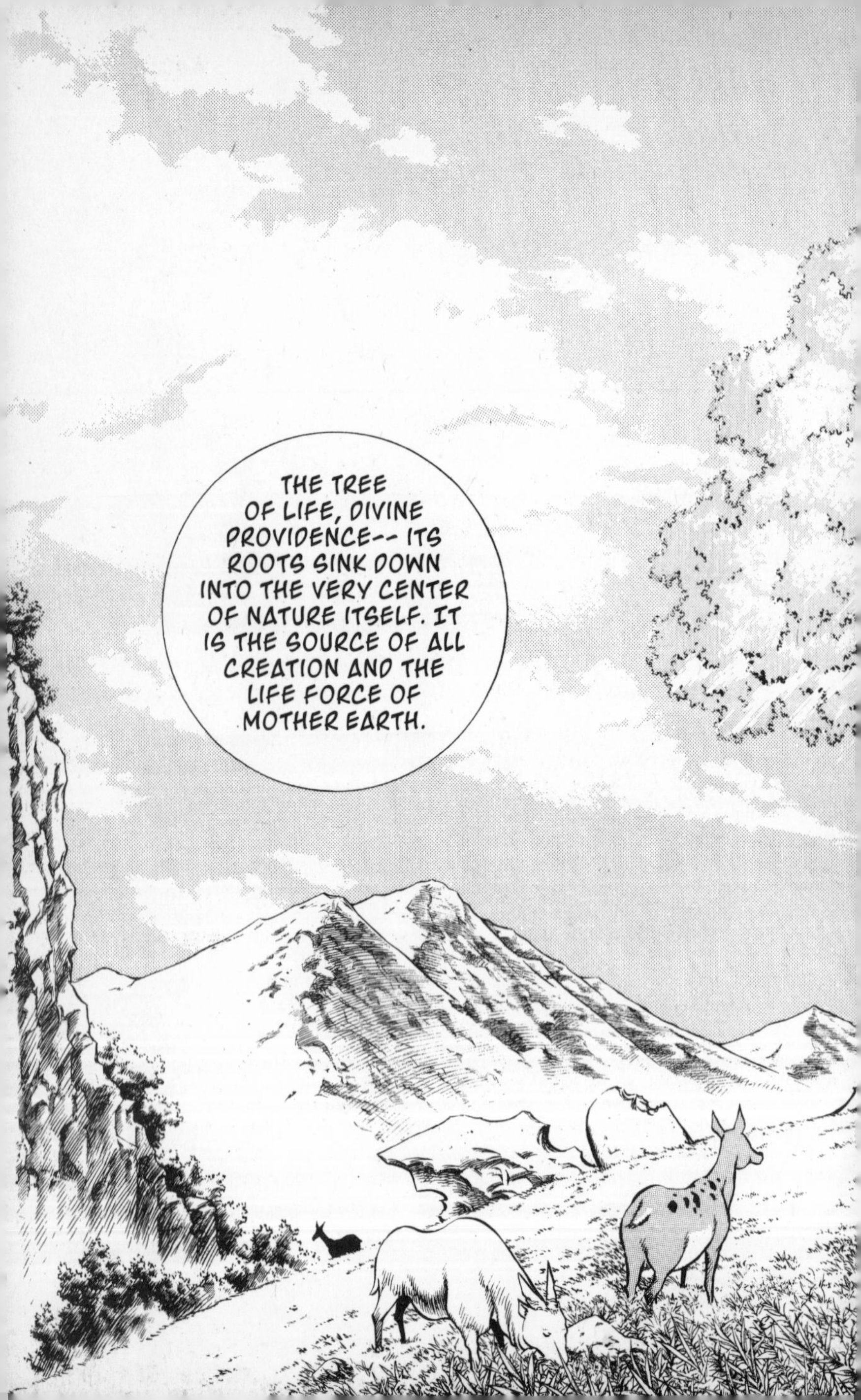
THE TREE OF LIFE, DIVINE PROVIDENCE-- ITS ROOTS SINK DOWN INTO THE VERY CENTER OF NATURE ITSELF. IT IS THE SOURCE OF ALL CREATION AND THE LIFE FORCE OF MOTHER EARTH.

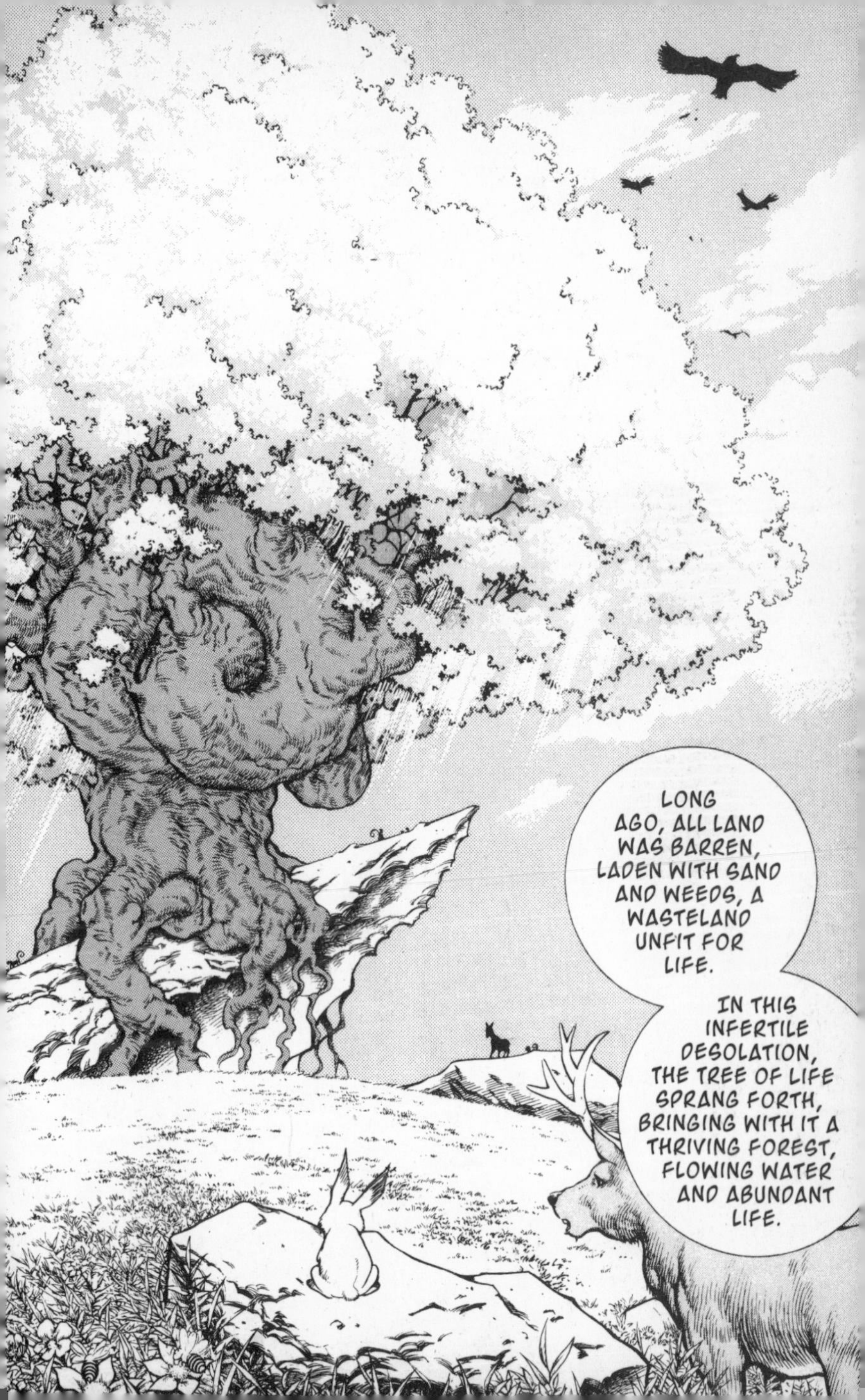
LONG AGO, ALL LAND WAS BARREN, LADEN WITH SAND AND WEEDS, A WASTELAND UNFIT FOR LIFE.
IN THIS INFERTILE DESOLATION, THE TREE OF LIFE SPRANG FORTH, BRINGING WITH IT A THRIVING FOREST, FLOWING WATER AND ABUNDANT LIFE.

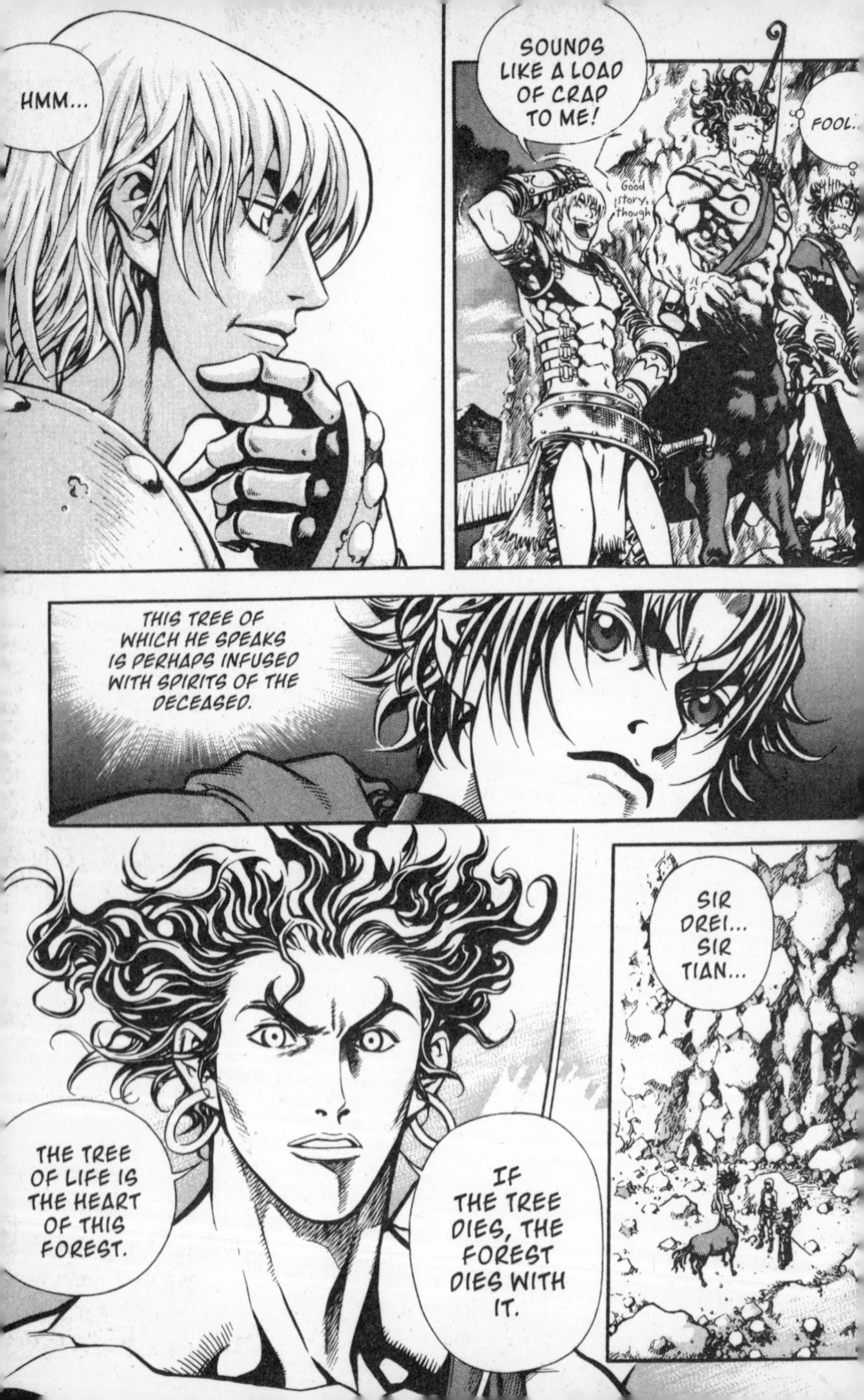
HMM...
SOUNDS LIKE A LOAD OF CRAP TO ME!
Good story, though
FOOL...
THIS TREE OF WHICH HE SPEAKS IS PERHAPS INFUSED WITH SPIRITS OF THE DECEASED.
THE TREE OF LIFE IS THE HEART OF THIS FOREST.
IF THE TREE DIES, THE FOREST DIES WITH IT.
SIR DREI... SIR TIAN...

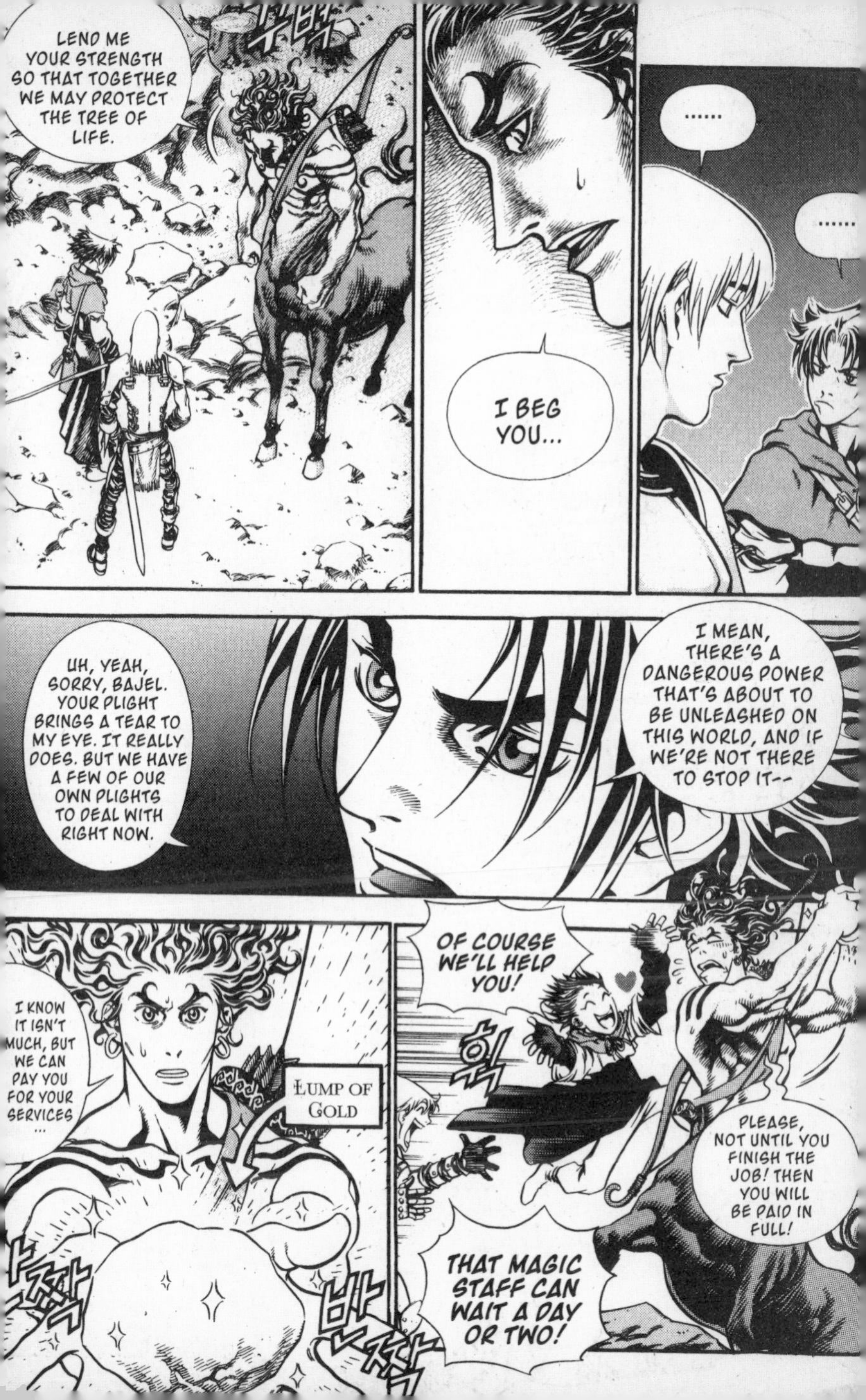
LEND ME YOUR STRENGTH SO THAT TOGETHER WE MAY PROTECT THE TREE OF LIFE.
I BEG YOU...
......
......
UH, YEAH, SORRY, BAJEL. YOUR PLIGHT BRINGS A TEAR TO MY EYE. IT REALLY DOES. BUT WE HAVE A FEW OF OUR OWN PLIGHTS TO DEAL WITH RIGHT NOW.
I MEAN, THERE'S A DANGEROUS POWER THAT'S ABOUT TO BE UNLEASHED ON THIS WORLD, AND IF WE'RE NOT THERE TO STOP IT--
I KNOW IT ISN'T MUCH, BUT WE CAN PAY YOU FOR YOUR SERVICES...
LUMP OF GOLD
OF COURSE WE'LL HELP YOU!
THAT MAGIC STAFF CAN WAIT A DAY OR TWO!
PLEASE, NOT UNTIL YOU FINISH THE JOB! THEN YOU WILL BE PAID IN FULL!

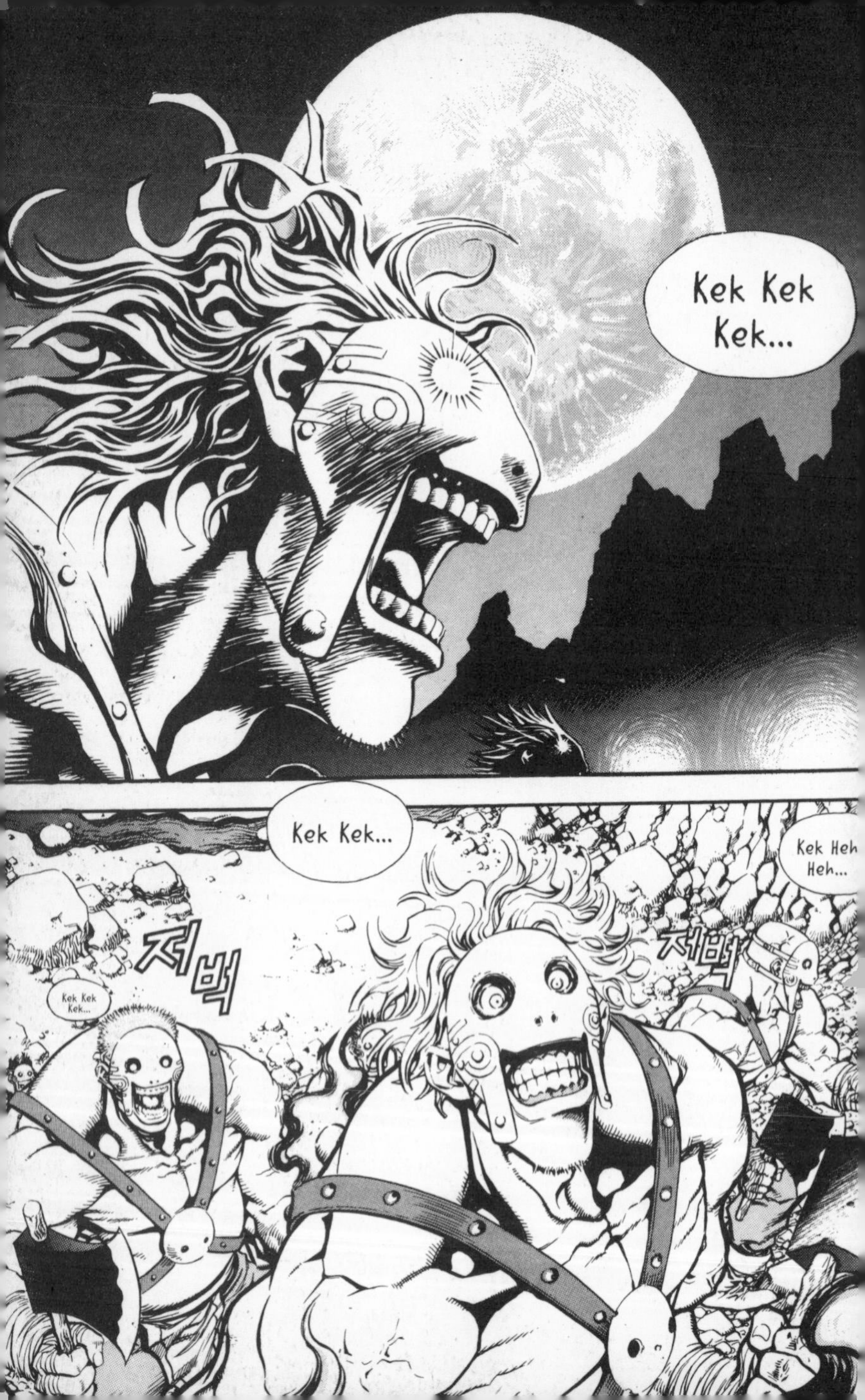
Kek Kek Kek...
Kek Kek...
Kek Heh Heh...
저벅
저벅
Kek Kek Kek...

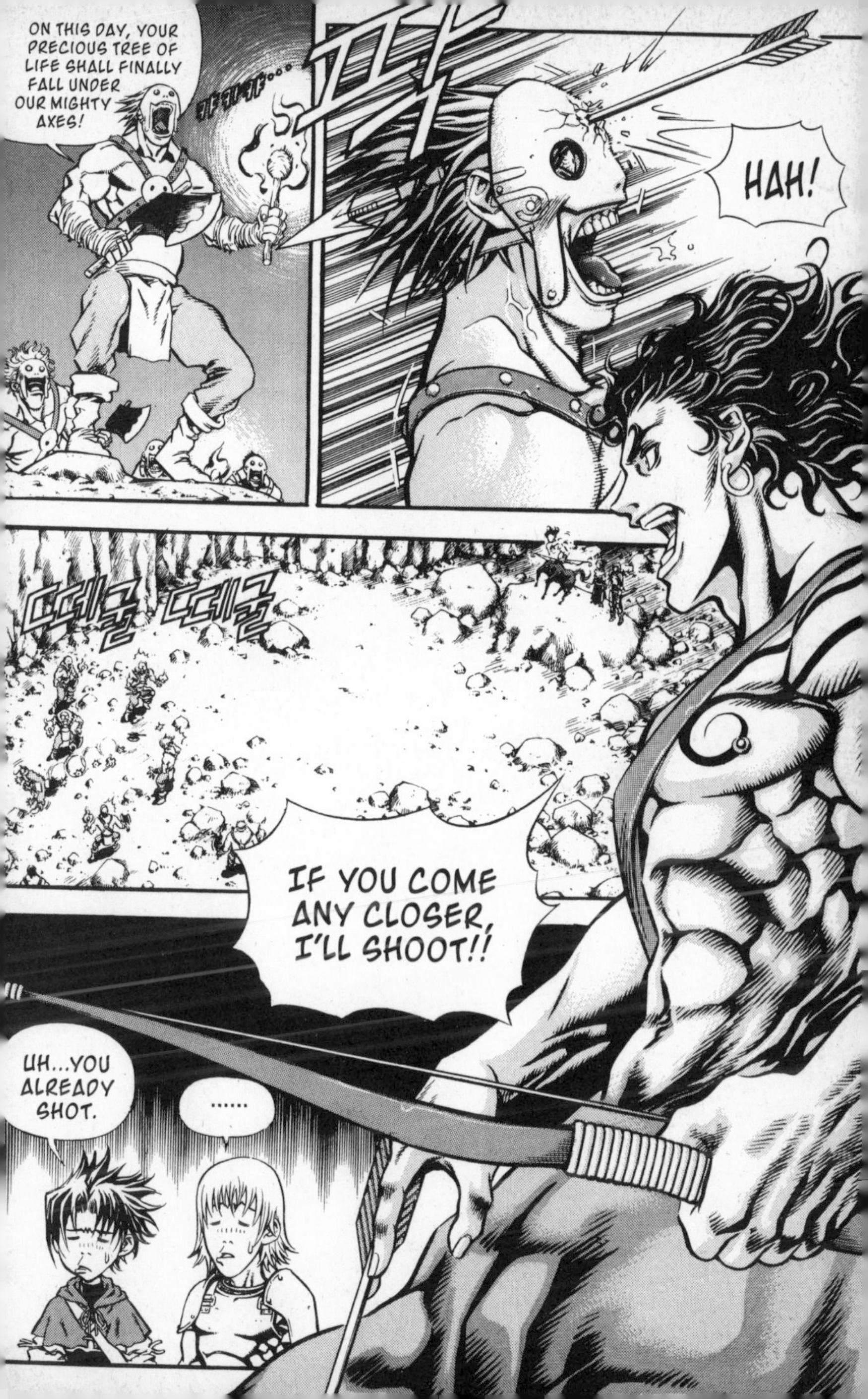
ON THIS DAY, YOUR PRECIOUS TREE OF LIFE SHALL FINALLY FALL UNDER OUR MIGHTY AXES!
HAH!
데굴 데굴
IF YOU COME ANY CLOSER, I'LL SHOOT!!
UH...YOU ALREADY SHOT.
......

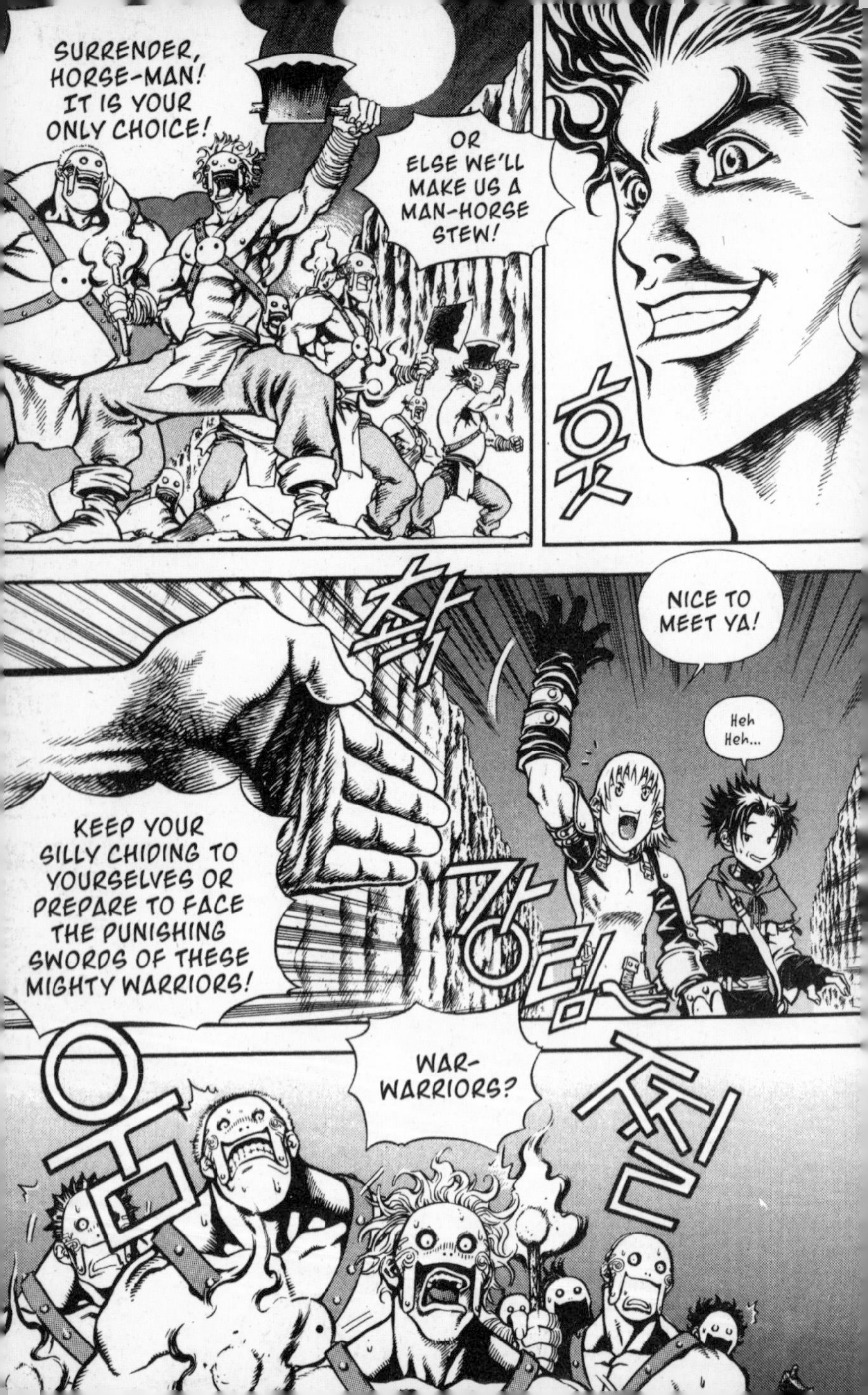
SURRENDER, HORSE-MAN! IT IS YOUR ONLY CHOICE!
OR ELSE WE'LL MAKE US A MAN-HORSE STEW!
NICE TO MEET YA!
Heh Heh...
KEEP YOUR SILLY CHIDING TO YOURSELVES OR PREPARE TO FACE THE PUNISHING SWORDS OF THESE MIGHTY WARRIORS!
WAR-WARRIORS?

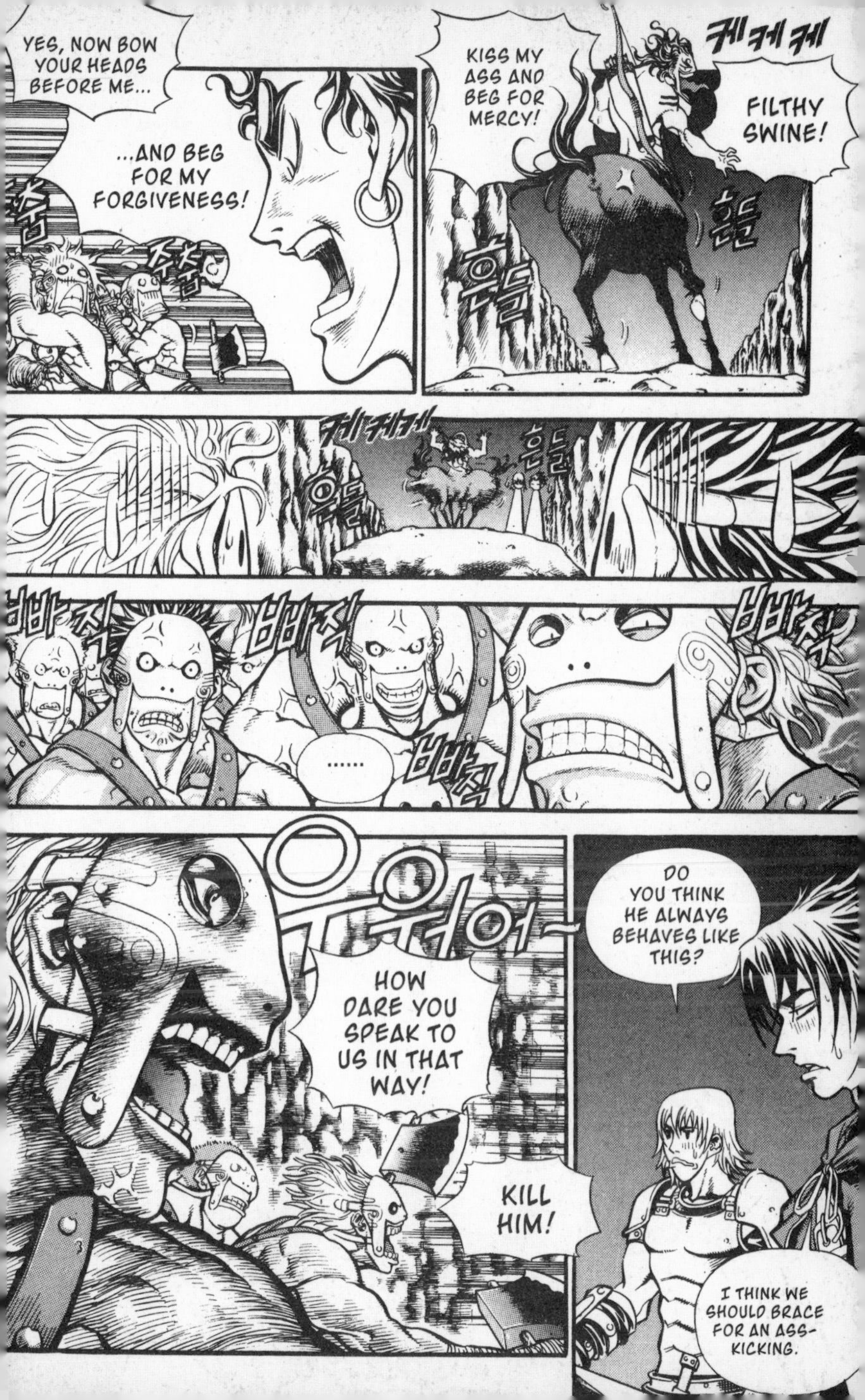
YES, NOW BOW YOUR HEADS BEFORE ME...
...AND BEG FOR MY FORGIVENESS!
KISS MY ASS AND BEG FOR MERCY!
케케케
FILTHY SWINE!
......
DO YOU THINK HE ALWAYS BEHAVES LIKE THIS?
HOW DARE YOU SPEAK TO US IN THAT WAY!
KILL HIM!
I THINK WE SHOULD BRACE FOR AN ASS-KICKING.

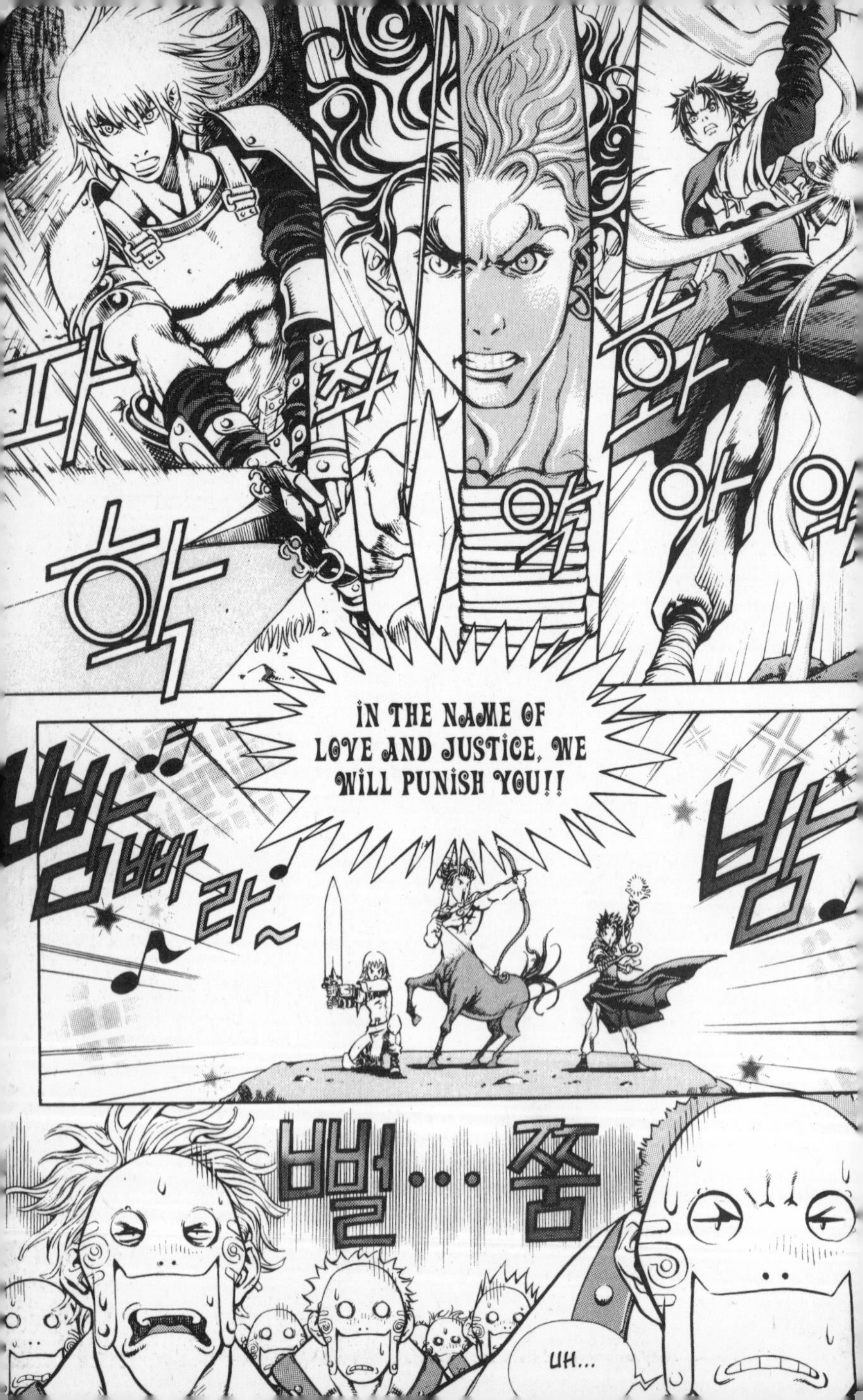

IN THE NAME OF LOVE AND JUSTICE, WE WILL PUNISH YOU!!
UH...

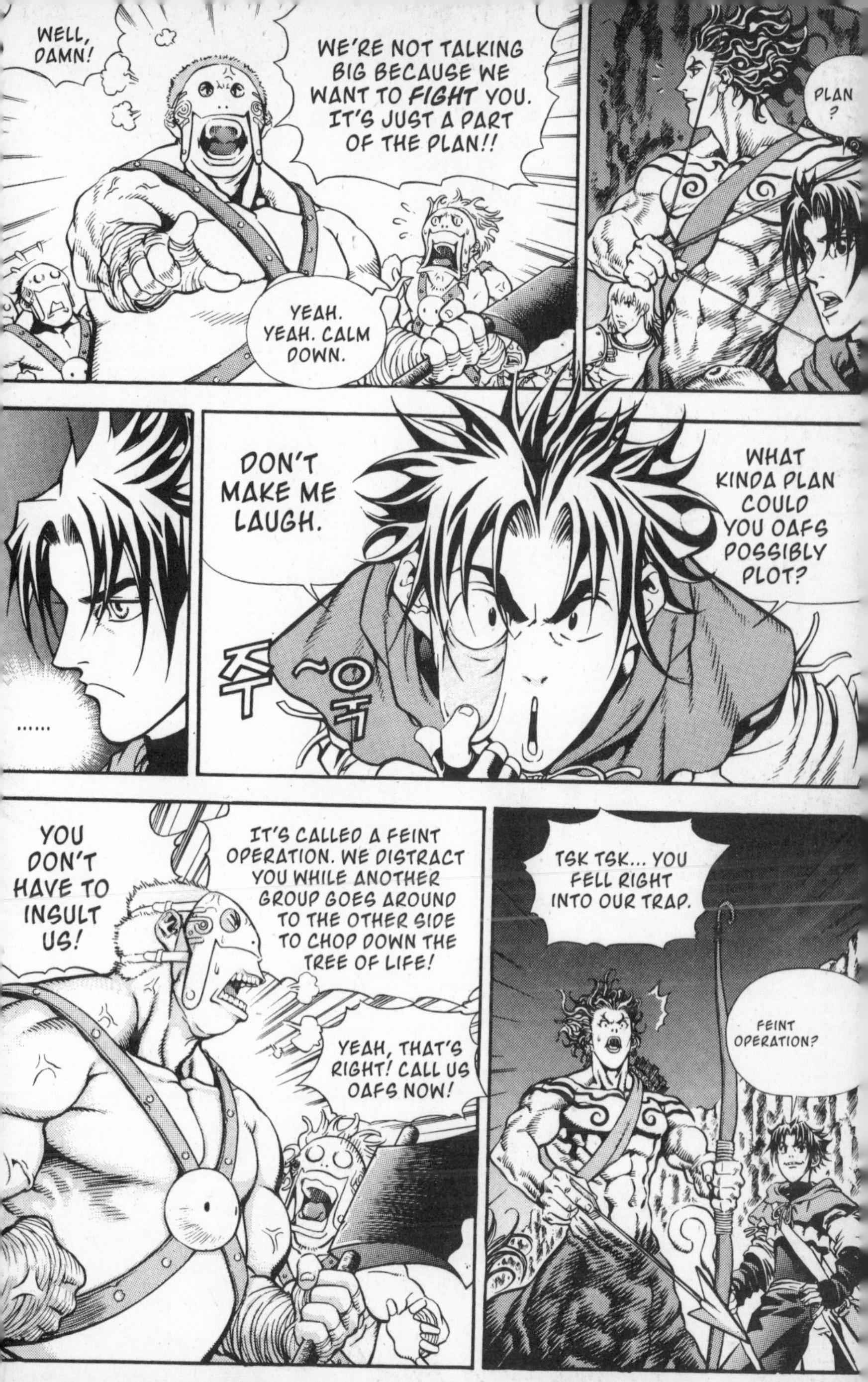

WELL, DAMN!
WE'RE NOT TALKING BIG BECAUSE WE WANT TO FIGHT YOU. IT'S JUST A PART OF THE PLAN!!
YEAH. YEAH. CALM DOWN.
PLAN?
......
DON'T MAKE ME LAUGH.
WHAT KINDA PLAN COULD YOU OAFS POSSIBLY PLOT?
YOU DON'T HAVE TO INSULT US!
IT'S CALLED A FEINT OPERATION. WE DISTRACT YOU WHILE ANOTHER GROUP GOES AROUND TO THE OTHER SIDE TO CHOP DOWN THE TREE OF LIFE!
YEAH, THAT'S RIGHT! CALL US OAFS NOW!
TSK TSK... YOU FELL RIGHT INTO OUR TRAP.
FEINT OPERATION?

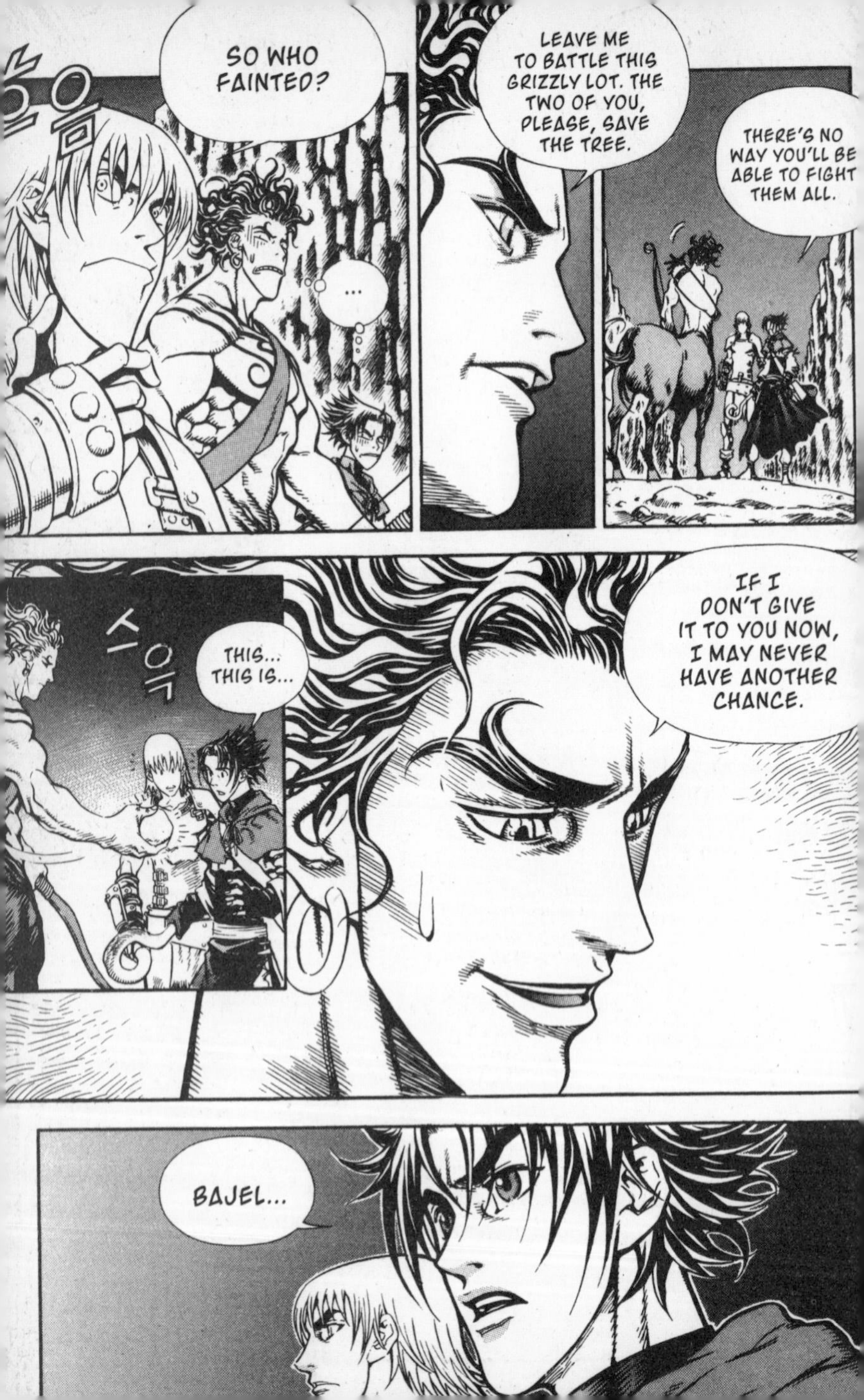

SO WHO FAINTED?
...
LEAVE ME TO BATTLE THIS GRIZZLY LOT. THE TWO OF YOU, PLEASE, SAVE THE TREE.
THERE'S NO WAY YOU'LL BE ABLE TO FIGHT THEM ALL.
THIS... THIS IS...
IF I DON'T GIVE IT TO YOU NOW, I MAY NEVER HAVE ANOTHER CHANCE.
BAJEL...

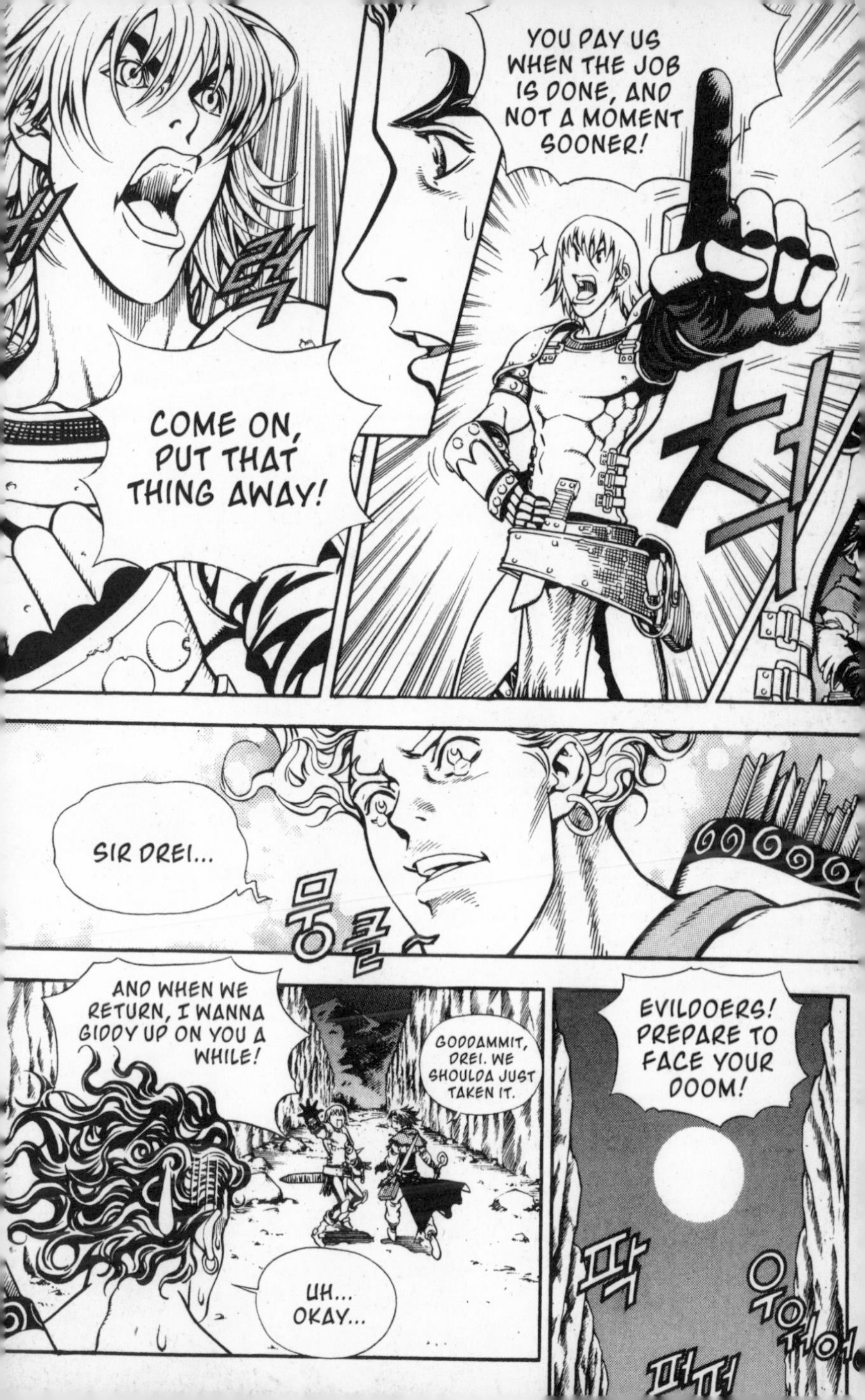
COME ON, PUT THAT THING AWAY!
YOU PAY US WHEN THE JOB IS DONE, AND NOT A MOMENT SOONER!
SIR DREI...
AND WHEN WE RETURN, I WANNA GIDDY UP ON YOU A WHILE!
GODDAMMIT, DREI. WE SHOULDA JUST TAKEN IT.
UH... OKAY...
EVILDOERS! PREPARE TO FACE YOUR DOOM!

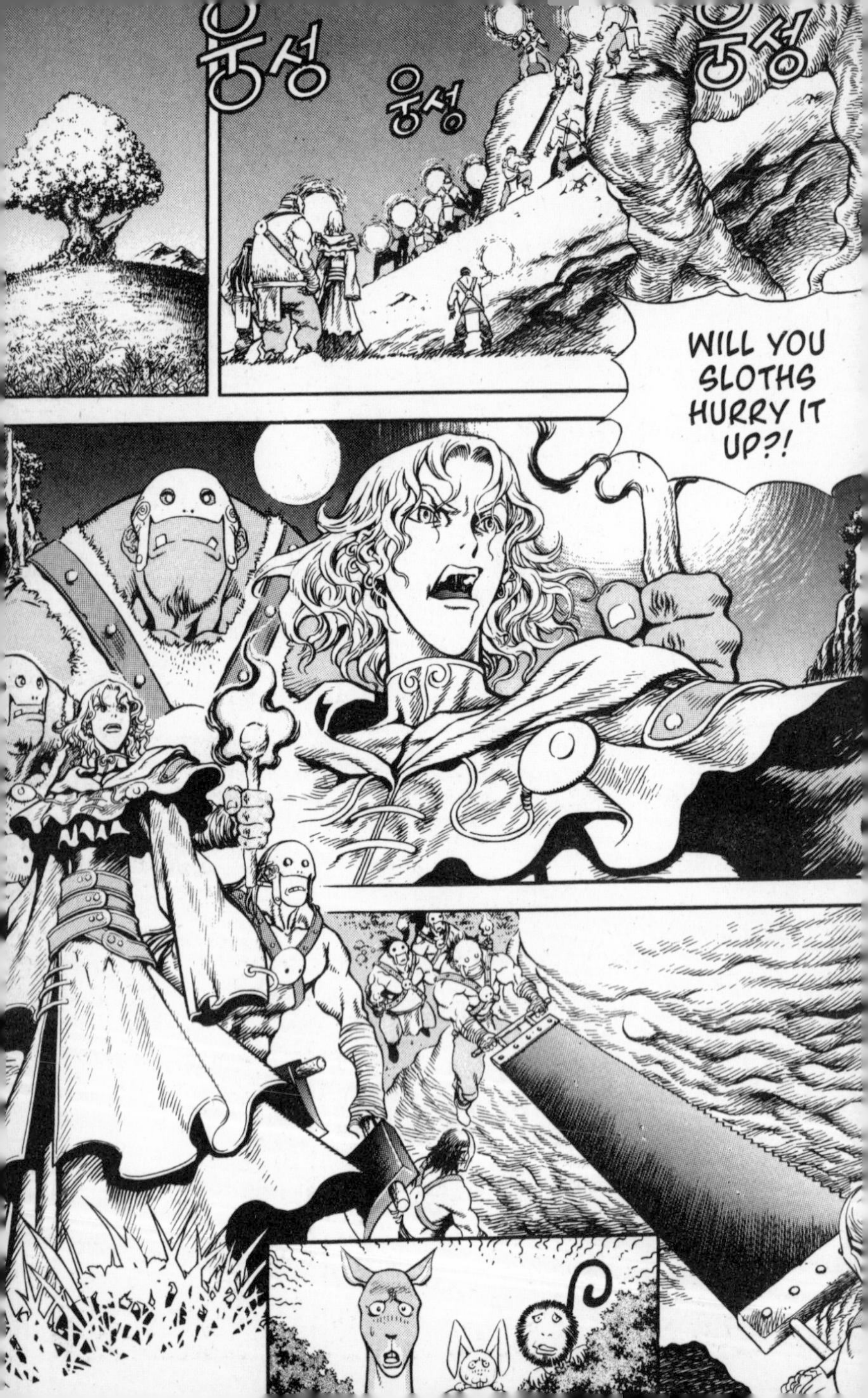
웅성
웅성
웅성
WILL YOU SLOTHS HURRY IT UP?!

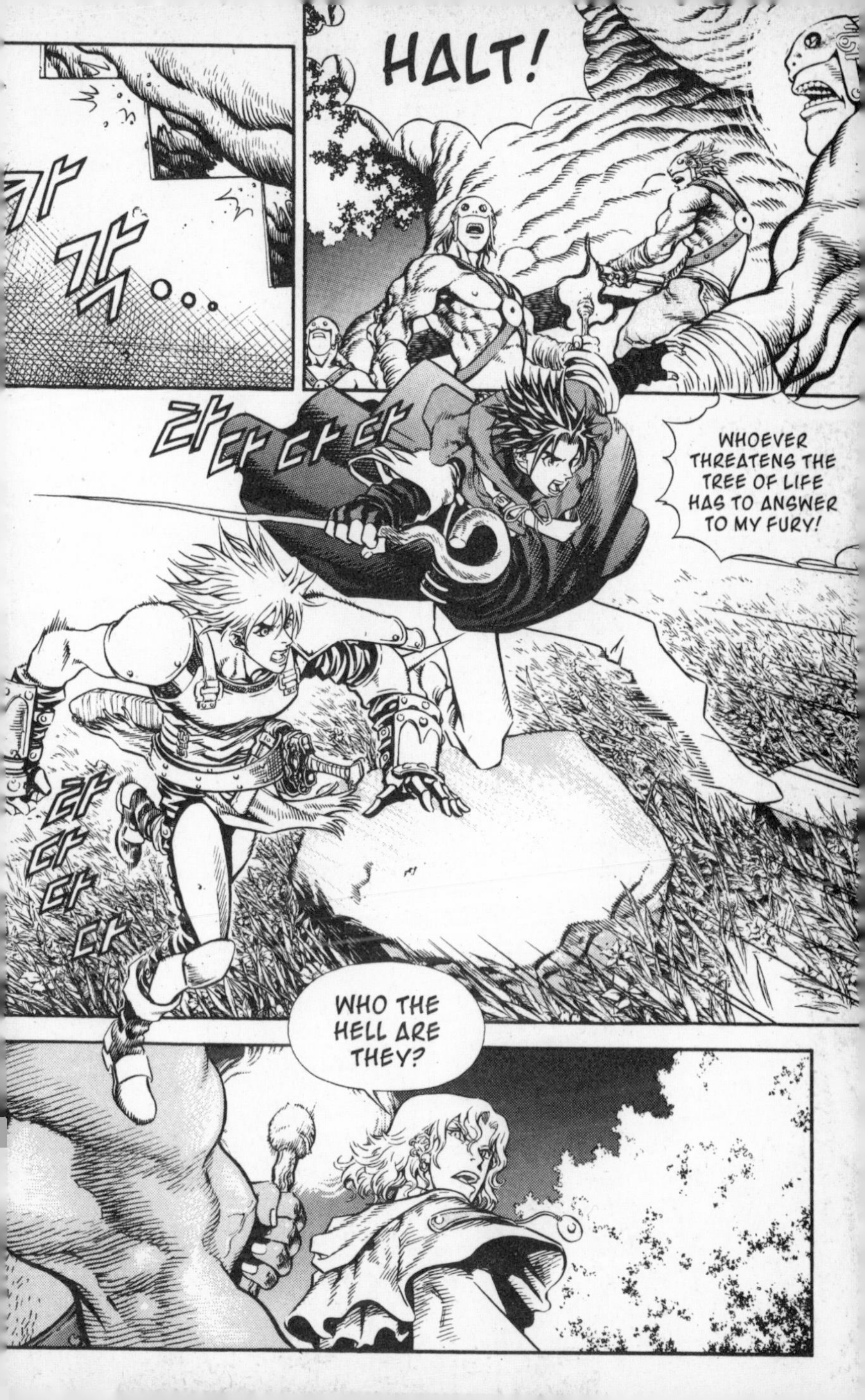
HALT!
WHOEVER THREATENS THE TREE OF LIFE HAS TO ANSWER TO MY FURY!
WHO THE HELL ARE THEY?

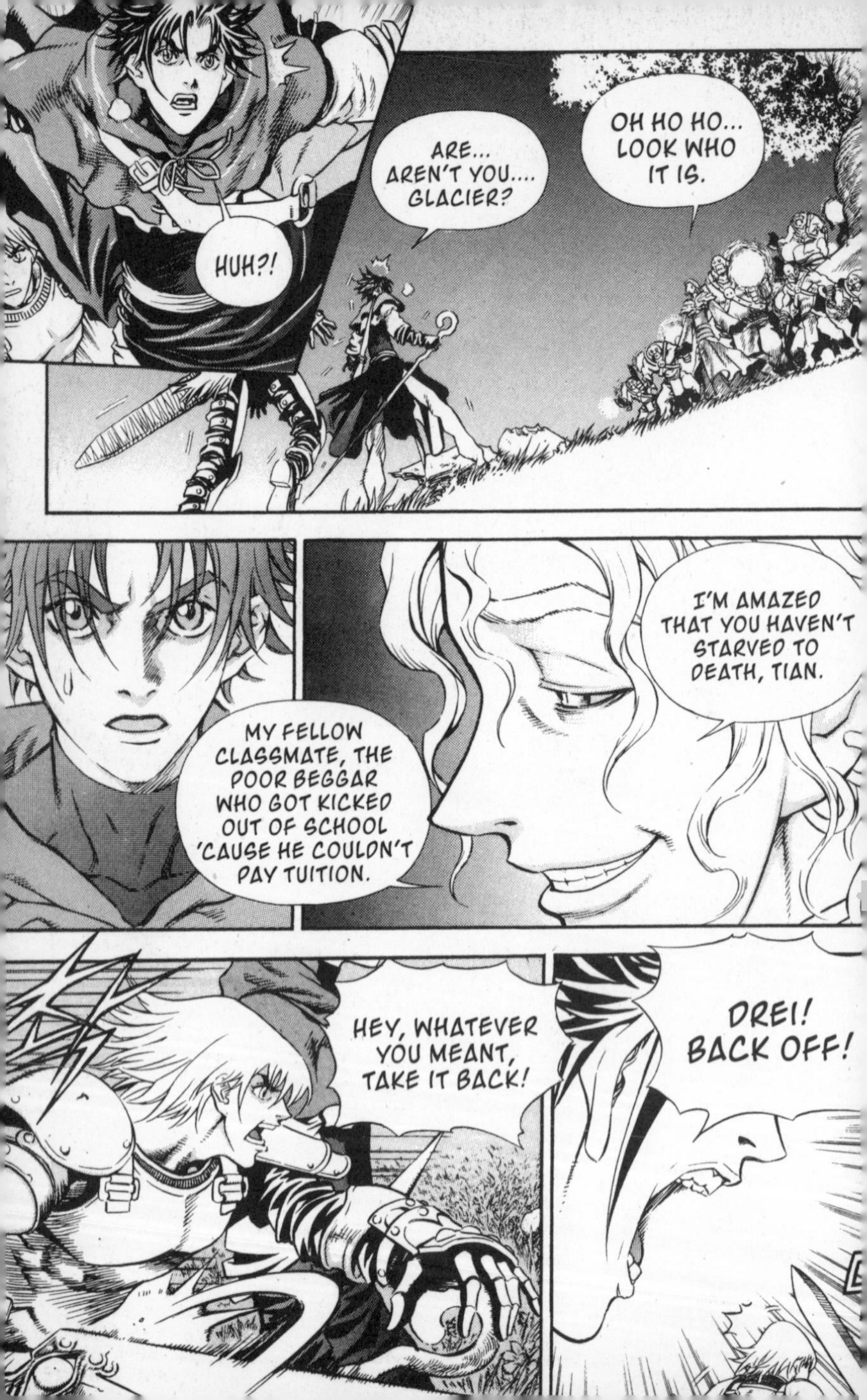
HUH?!
ARE... AREN'T YOU.... GLACIER?
OH HO HO... LOOK WHO IT IS.
I'M AMAZED THAT YOU HAVEN'T STARVED TO DEATH, TIAN.
MY FELLOW CLASSMATE, THE POOR BEGGAR WHO GOT KICKED OUT OF SCHOOL 'CAUSE HE COULDN'T PAY TUITION.
HEY, WHATEVER YOU MEANT, TAKE IT BACK!
DREI! BACK OFF!

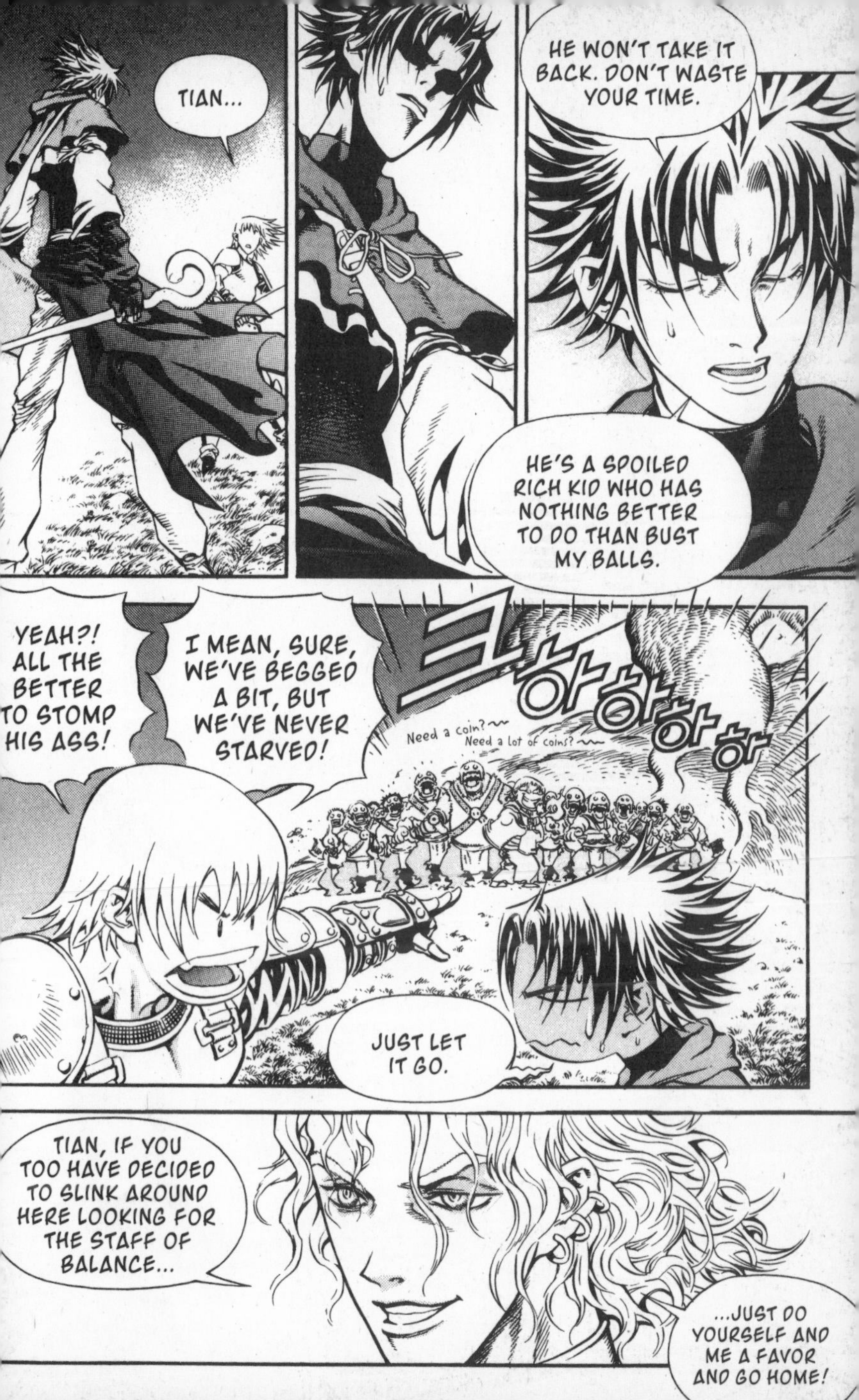
TIAN...
HE WON'T TAKE IT BACK. DON'T WASTE YOUR TIME.
HE'S A SPOILED RICH KID WHO HAS NOTHING BETTER TO DO THAN BUST MY BALLS.
YEAH?! ALL THE BETTER TO STOMP HIS ASS!
I MEAN, SURE, WE'VE BEGGED A BIT, BUT WE'VE NEVER STARVED!
크하하하하하
Need a coin?~
Need a lot of coins?~
JUST LET IT GO.
TIAN, IF YOU TOO HAVE DECIDED TO SLINK AROUND HERE LOOKING FOR THE STAFF OF BALANCE...
...JUST DO YOURSELF AND ME A FAVOR AND GO HOME!

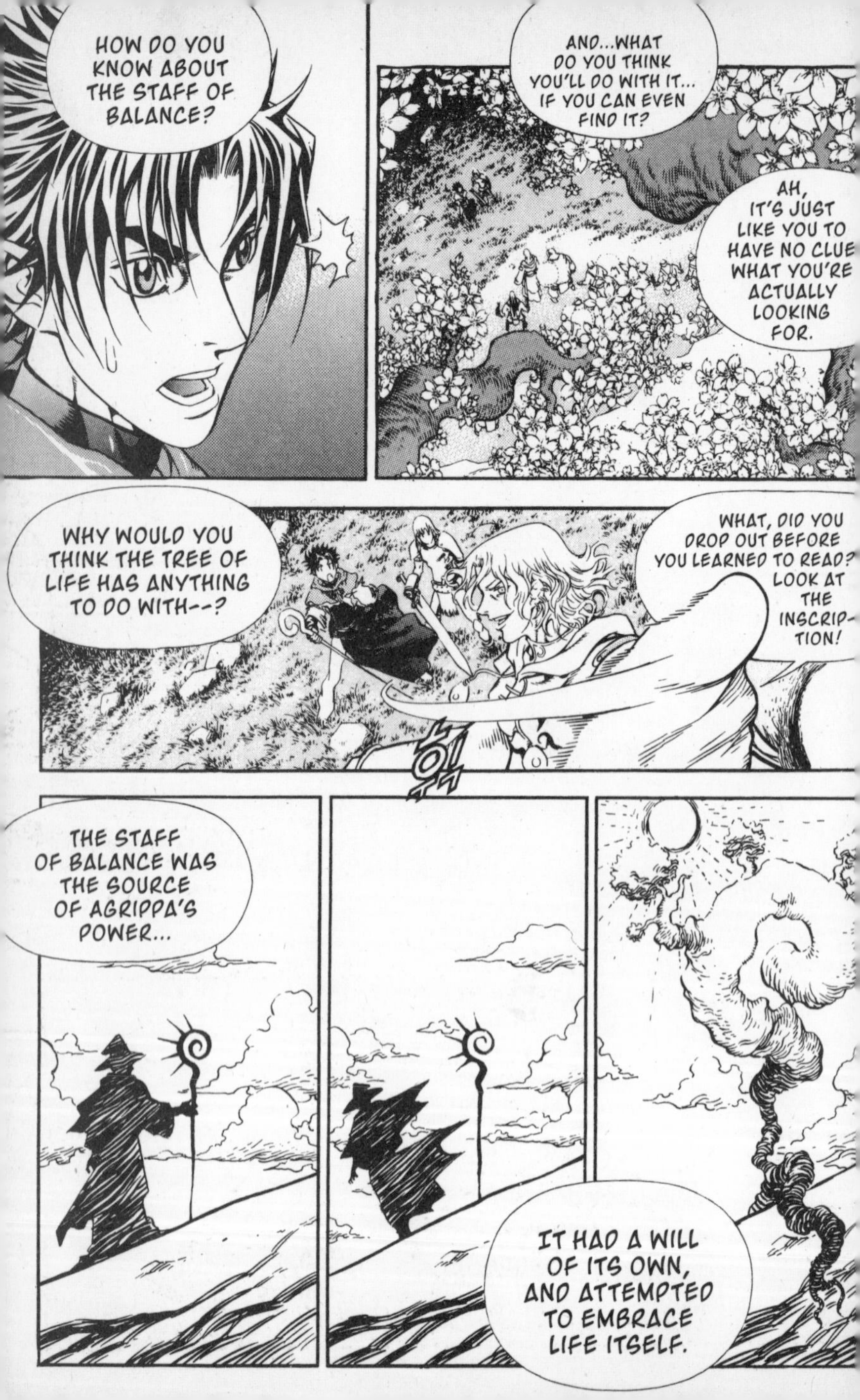
HOW DO YOU KNOW ABOUT THE STAFF OF BALANCE?
AND...WHAT DO YOU THINK YOU'LL DO WITH IT... IF YOU CAN EVEN FIND IT?
AH, IT'S JUST LIKE YOU TO HAVE NO CLUE WHAT YOU'RE ACTUALLY LOOKING FOR.
WHY WOULD YOU THINK THE TREE OF LIFE HAS ANYTHING TO DO WITH--?
WHAT, DID YOU DROP OUT BEFORE YOU LEARNED TO READ? LOOK AT THE INSCRIPTION!
THE STAFF OF BALANCE WAS THE SOURCE OF AGRIPPA'S POWER...
IT HAD A WILL OF ITS OWN, AND ATTEMPTED TO EMBRACE LIFE ITSELF.

HERE LIES THE
STAFF OF BALANCE.

I CAN'T BELIEVE IT...

WHAT, TIAN? WHAT DOES IT SAY?

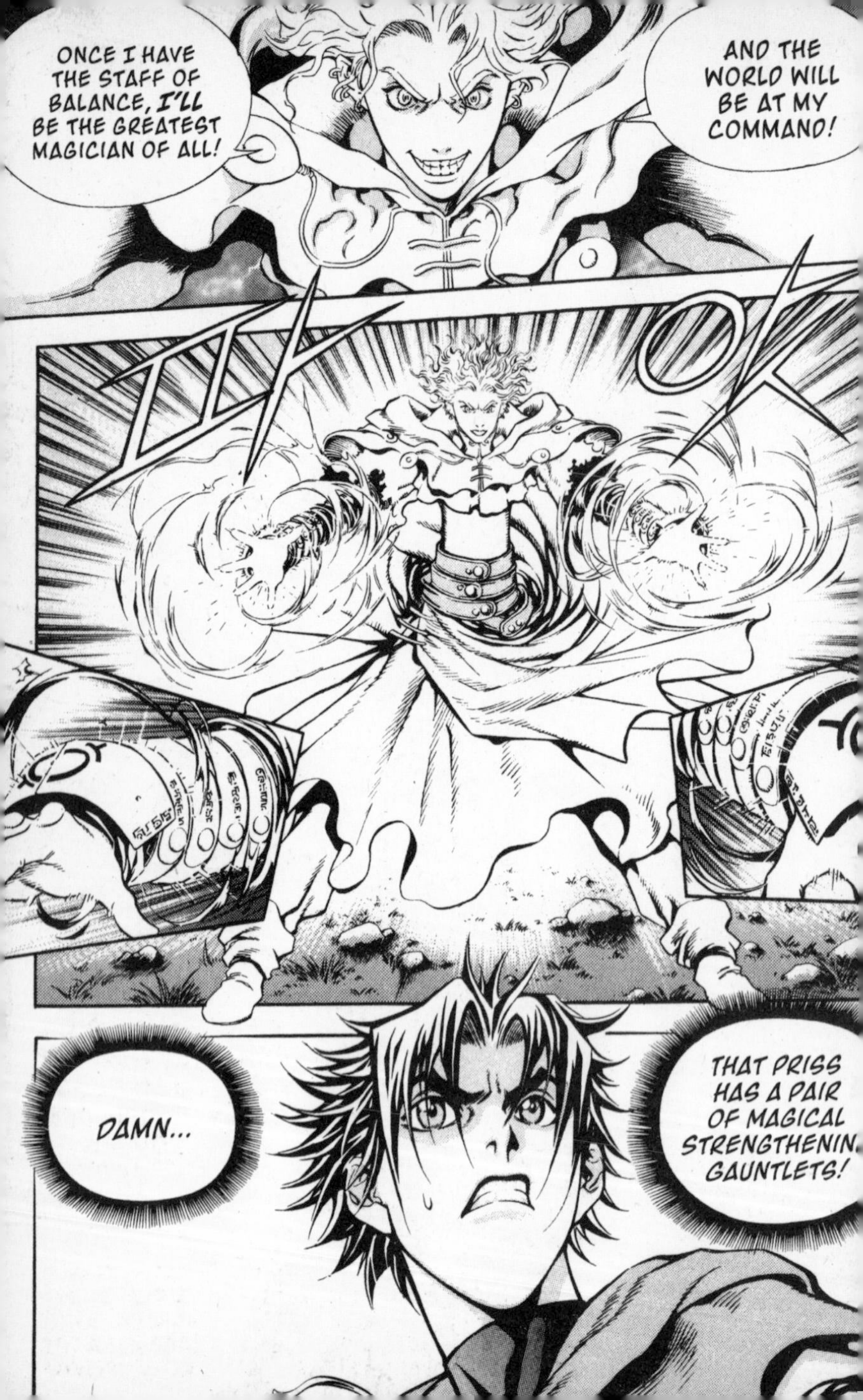
ONCE I HAVE THE STAFF OF BALANCE, I'LL BE THE GREATEST MAGICIAN OF ALL!
AND THE WORLD WILL BE AT MY COMMAND!
TTTOK
DAMN...
THAT PRISS HAS A PAIR OF MAGICAL STRENGTHENIN GAUNTLETS!

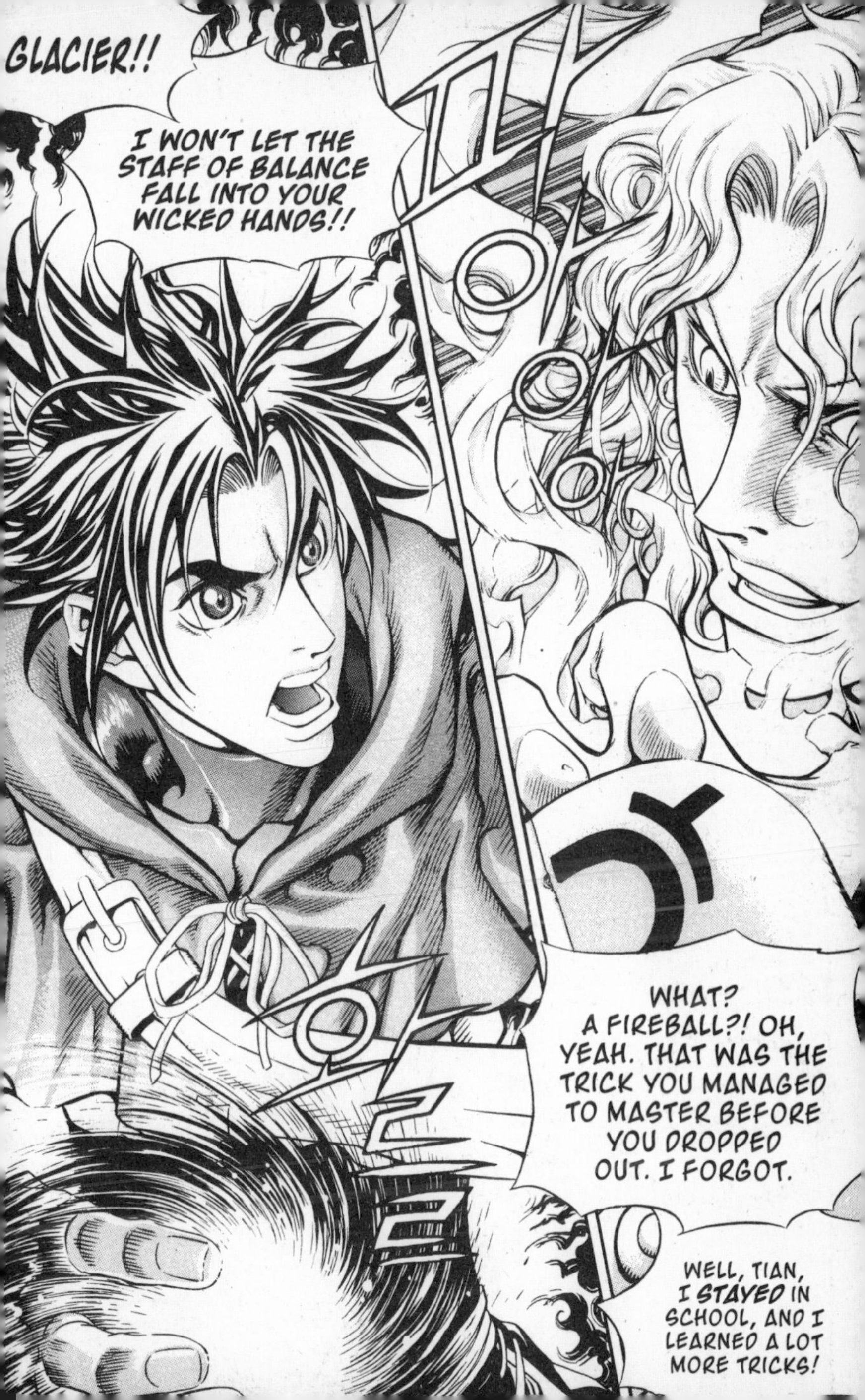
GLACIER!!
I WON'T LET THE STAFF OF BALANCE FALL INTO YOUR WICKED HANDS!!
WHAT? A FIREBALL?! OH, YEAH. THAT WAS THE TRICK YOU MANAGED TO MASTER BEFORE YOU DROPPED OUT. I FORGOT.
WELL, TIAN, I STAYED IN SCHOOL, AND I LEARNED A LOT MORE TRICKS!

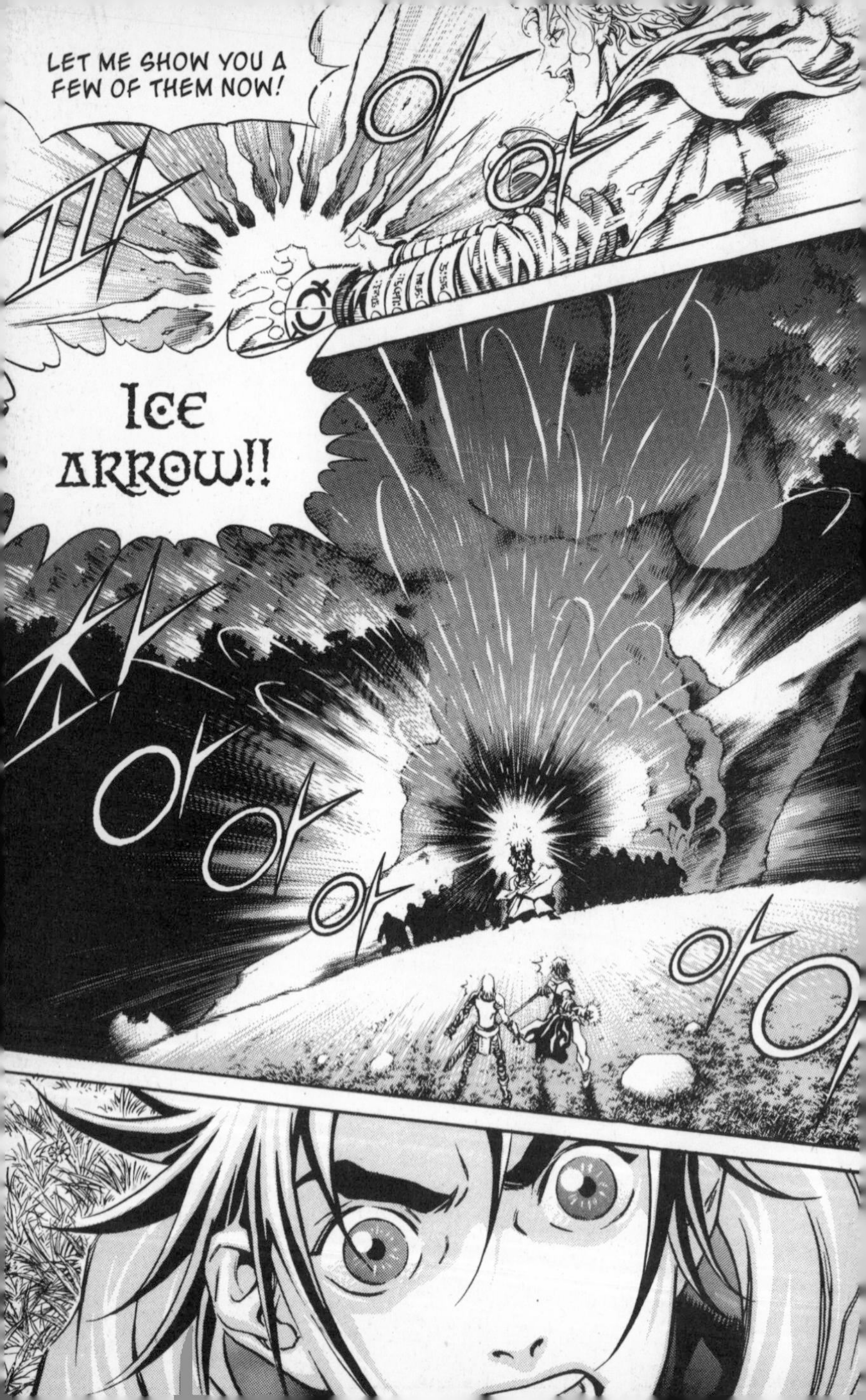
LET ME SHOW YOU A FEW OF THEM NOW!
ICE ARROW!!

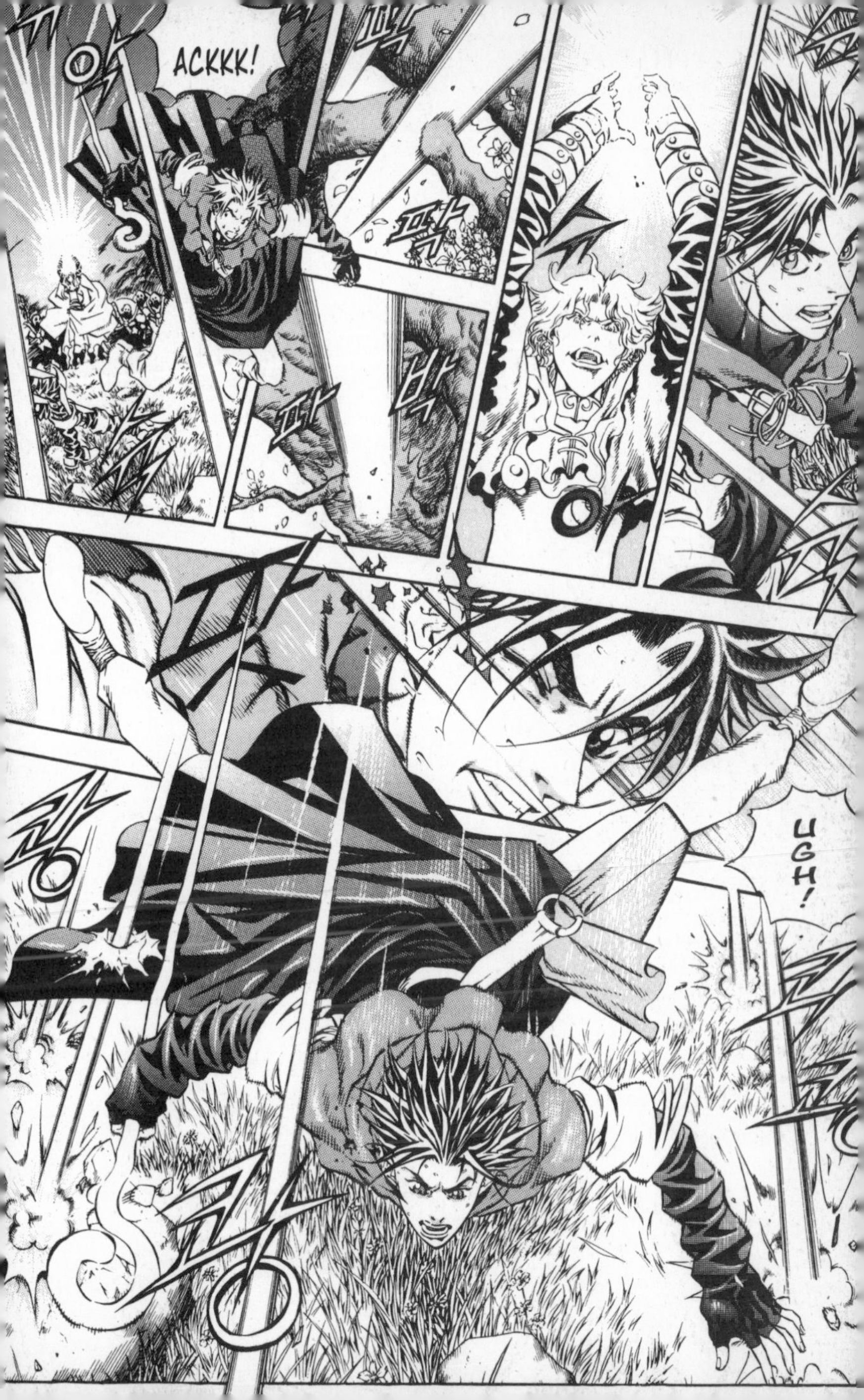
ACKKK!
UGH!

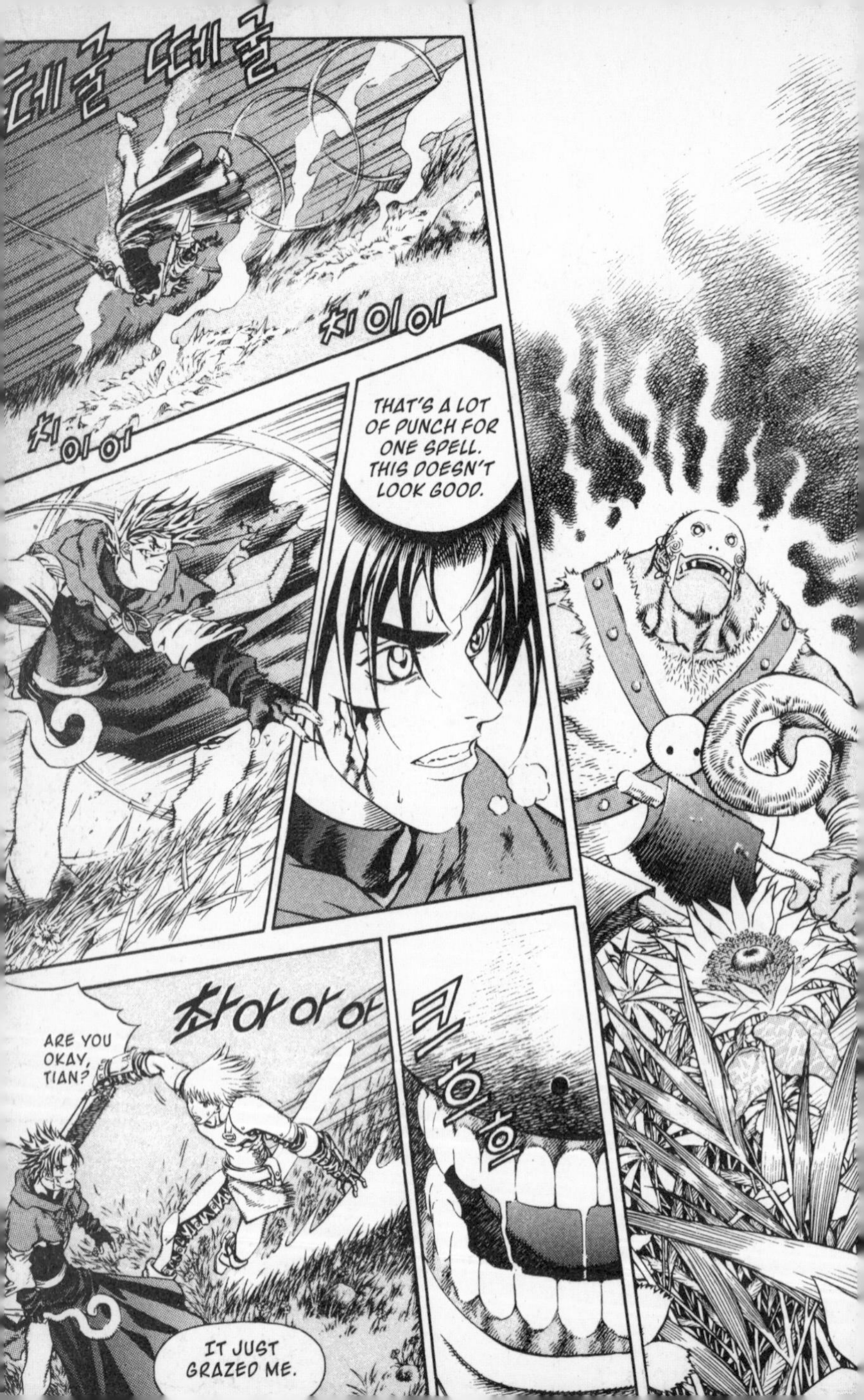
데굴 데굴
치이이
치이이
THAT'S A LOT OF PUNCH FOR ONE SPELL. THIS DOESN'T LOOK GOOD.
좌아아아
ARE YOU OKAY, TIAN?
IT JUST GRAZED ME.
크히히

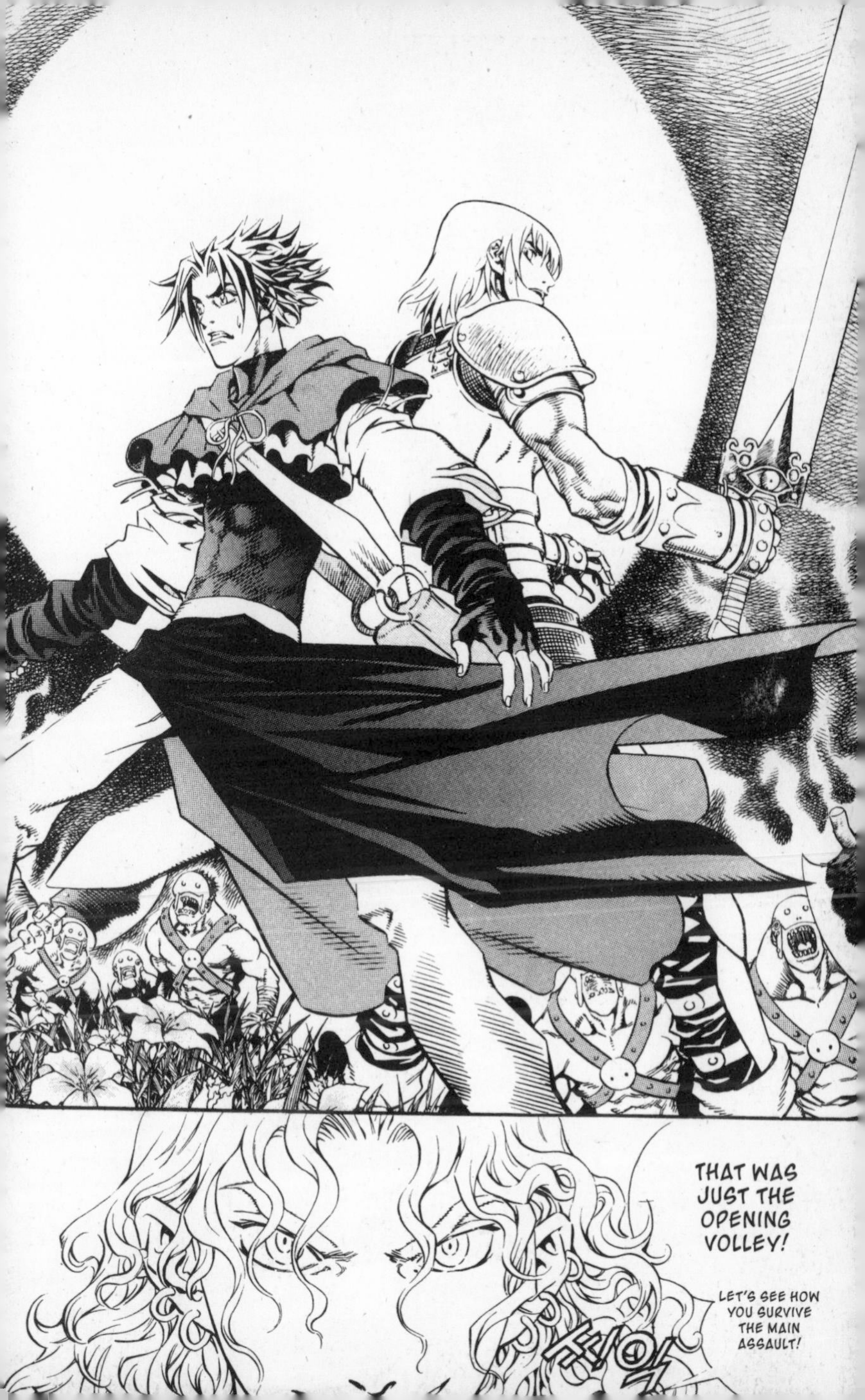
THAT WAS JUST THE OPENING VOLLEY!
LET'S SEE HOW YOU SURVIVE THE MAIN ASSAULT!

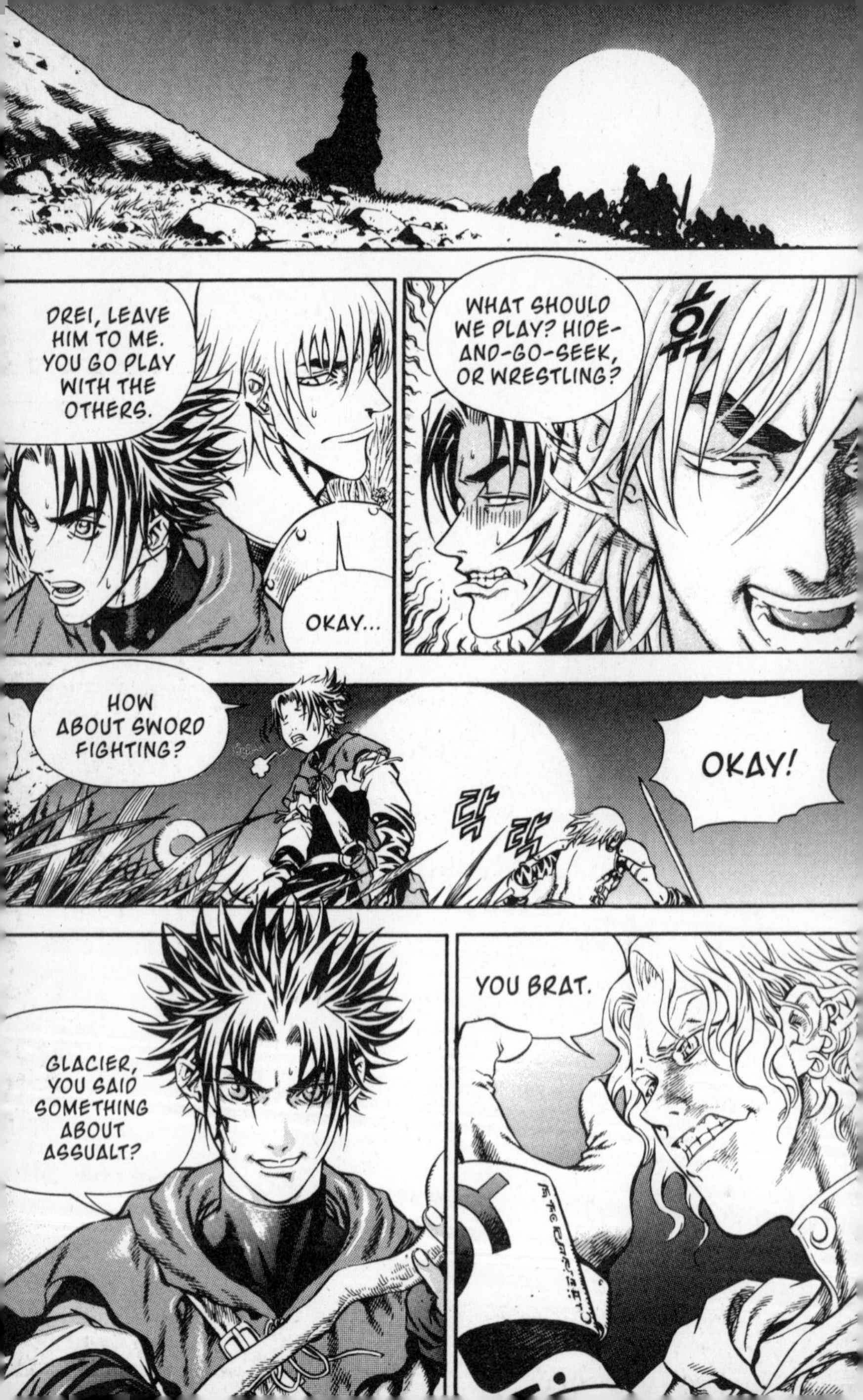
DREI, LEAVE HIM TO ME. YOU GO PLAY WITH THE OTHERS.
OKAY...
WHAT SHOULD WE PLAY? HIDE-AND-GO-SEEK, OR WRESTLING?
휙
HOW ABOUT SWORD FIGHTING?
OKAY!
GLACIER, YOU SAID SOMETHING ABOUT ASSUALT?
YOU BRAT.

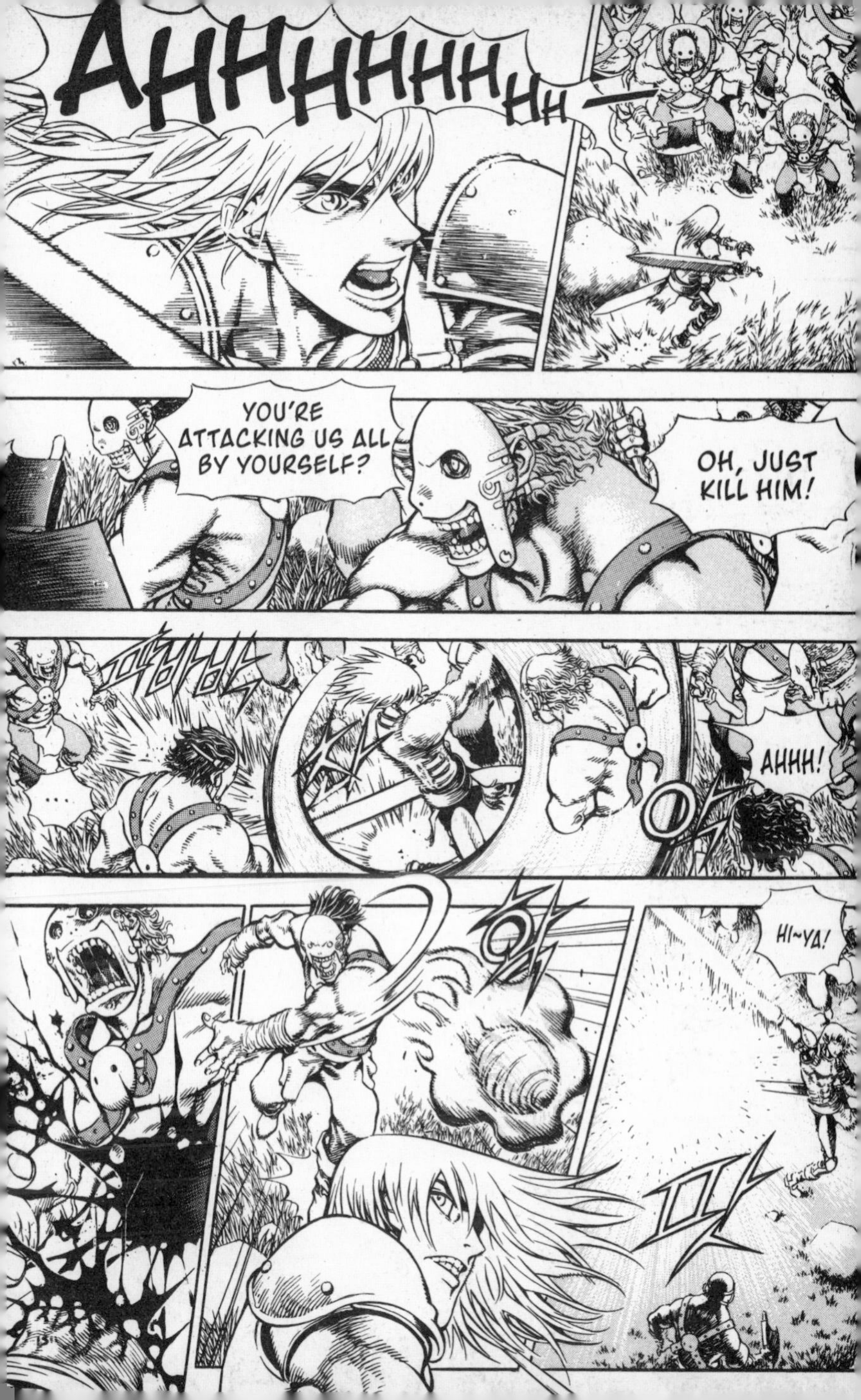
AHHHHHHHH—
YOU'RE ATTACKING US ALL BY YOURSELF?
OH, JUST KILL HIM!
...
AHHH!
HI~YA!

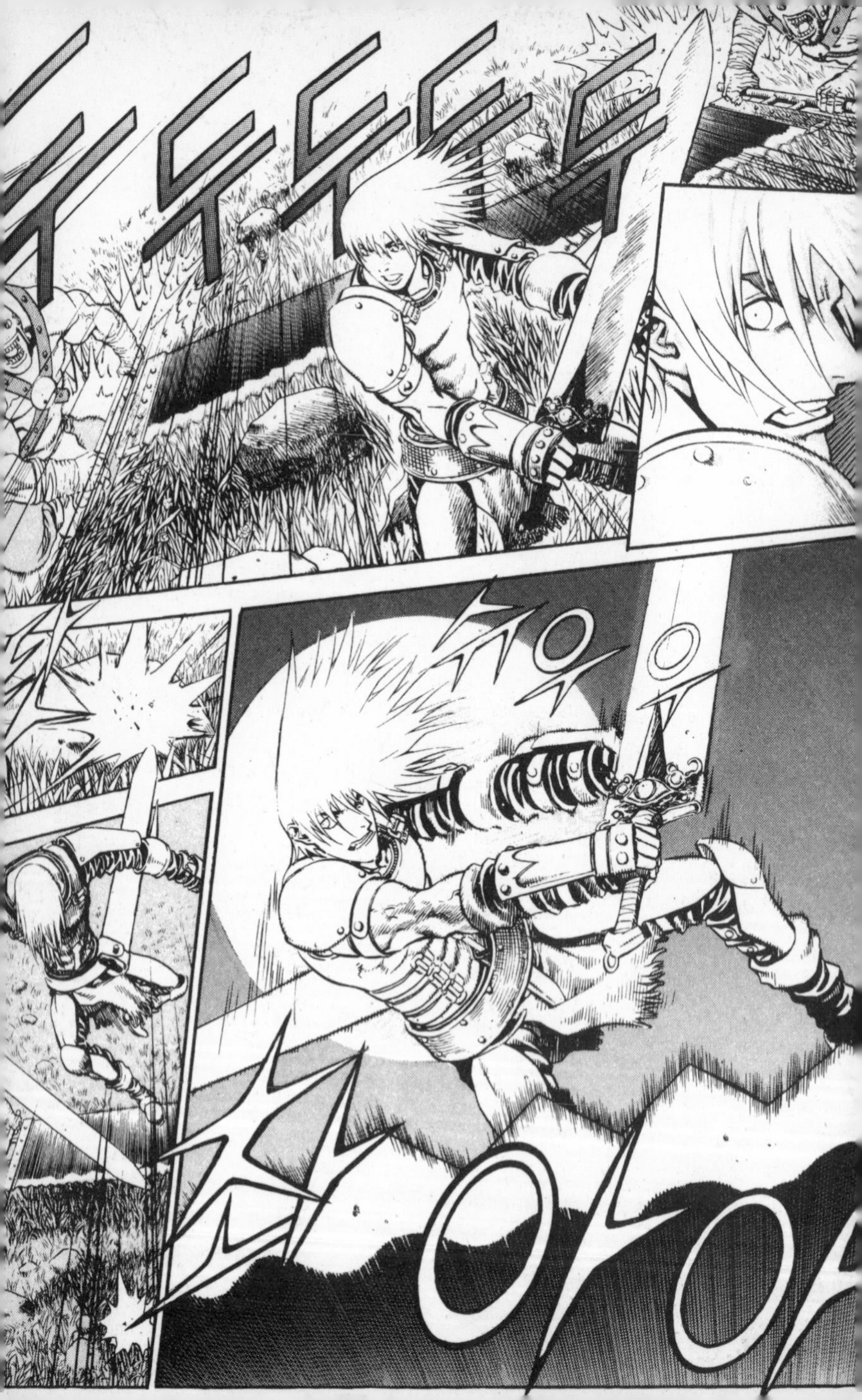

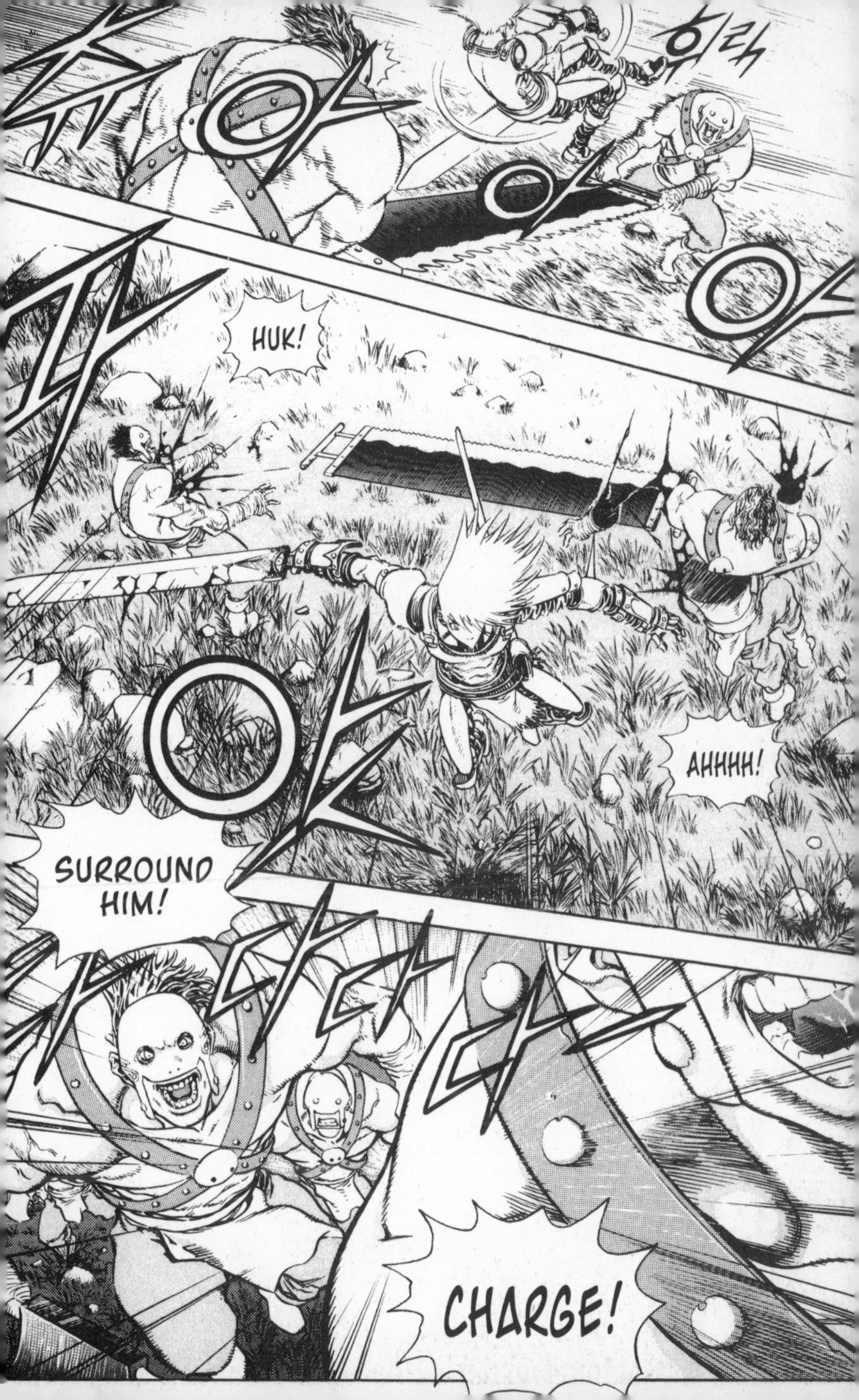
HUK!
AHHHH!
SURROUND HIM!
CHARGE!

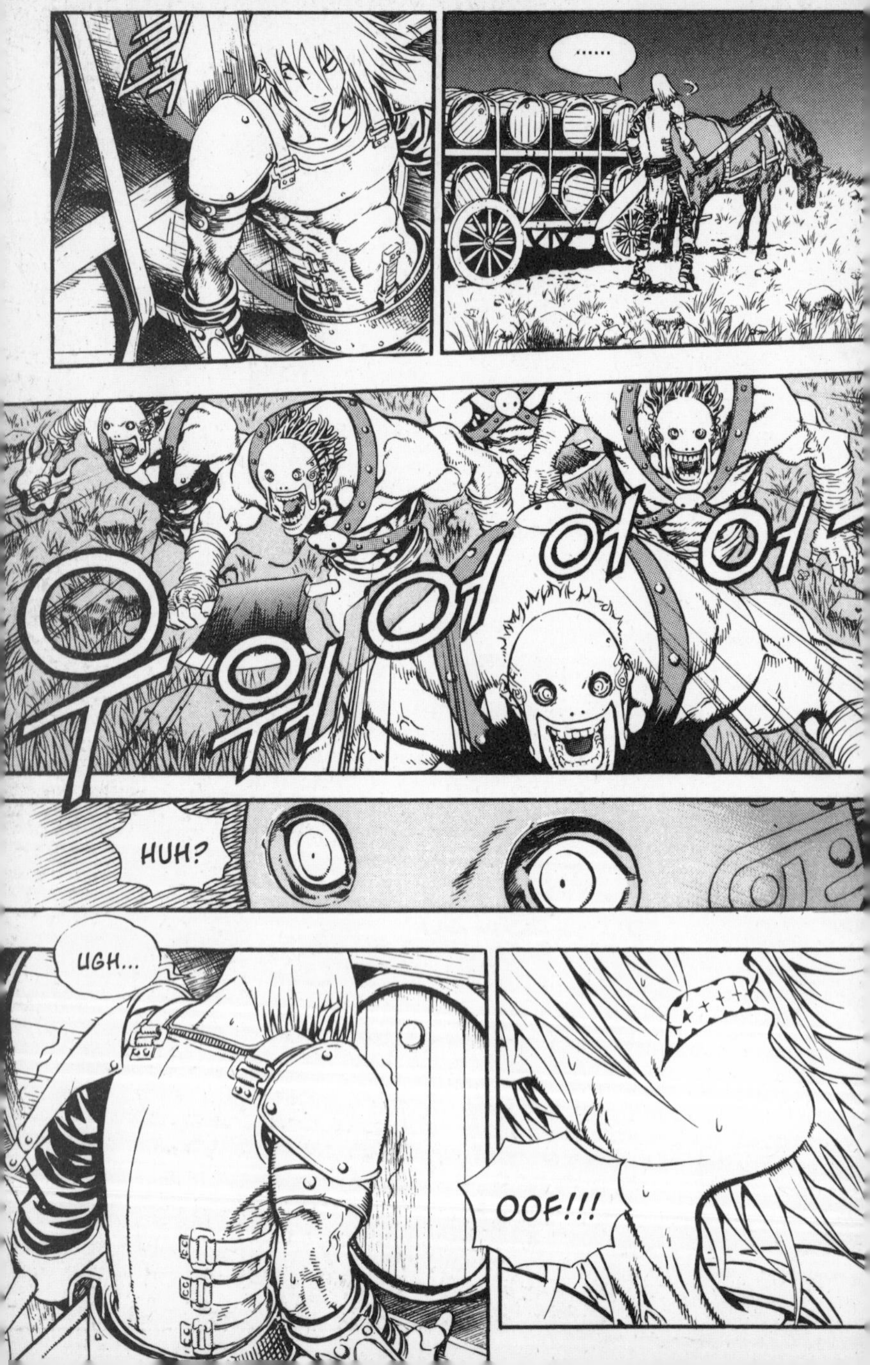
......
HUH?
UGH...
OOF!!!

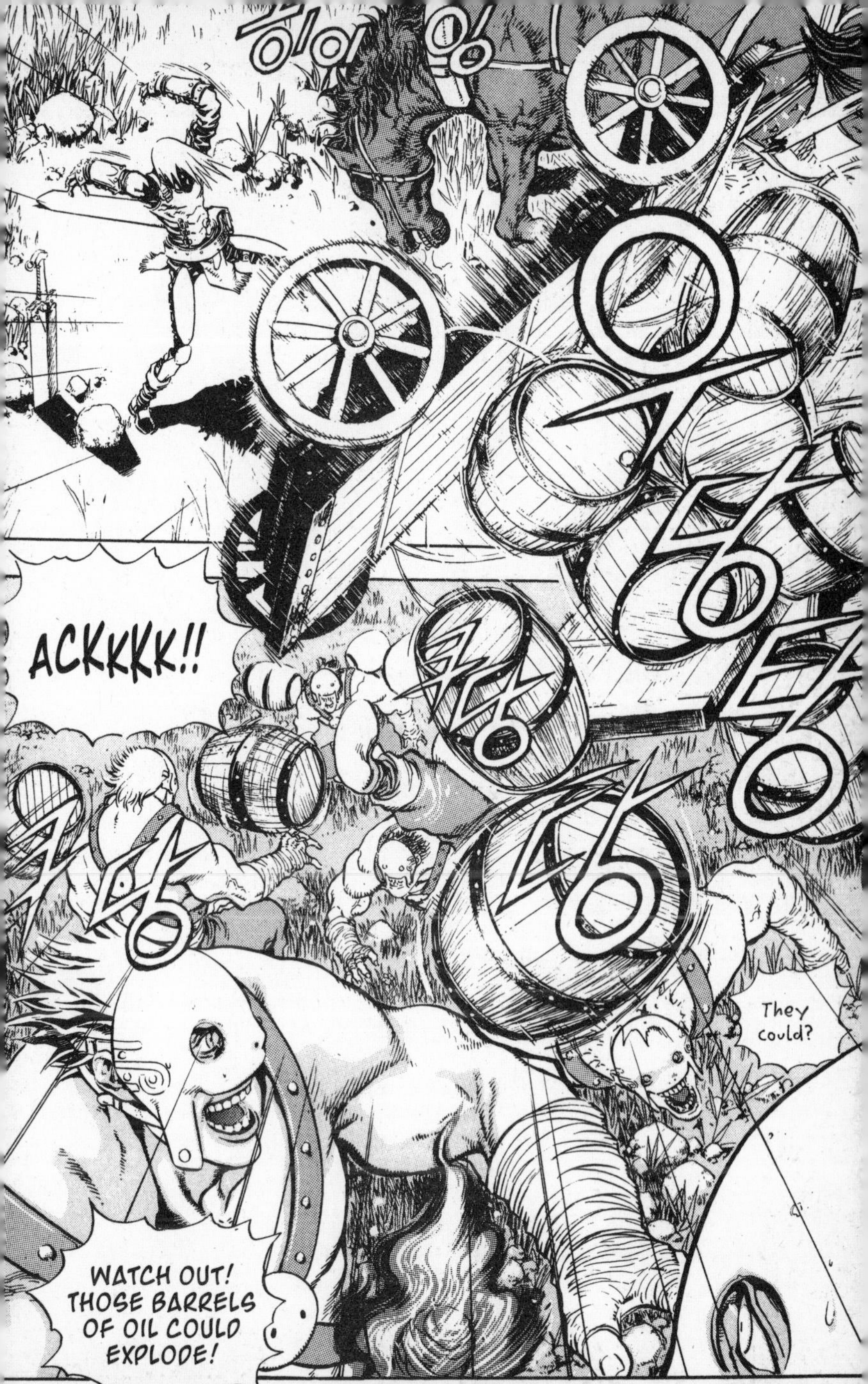
ACKKKK!!
WATCH OUT! THOSE BARRELS OF OIL COULD EXPLODE!
They could?

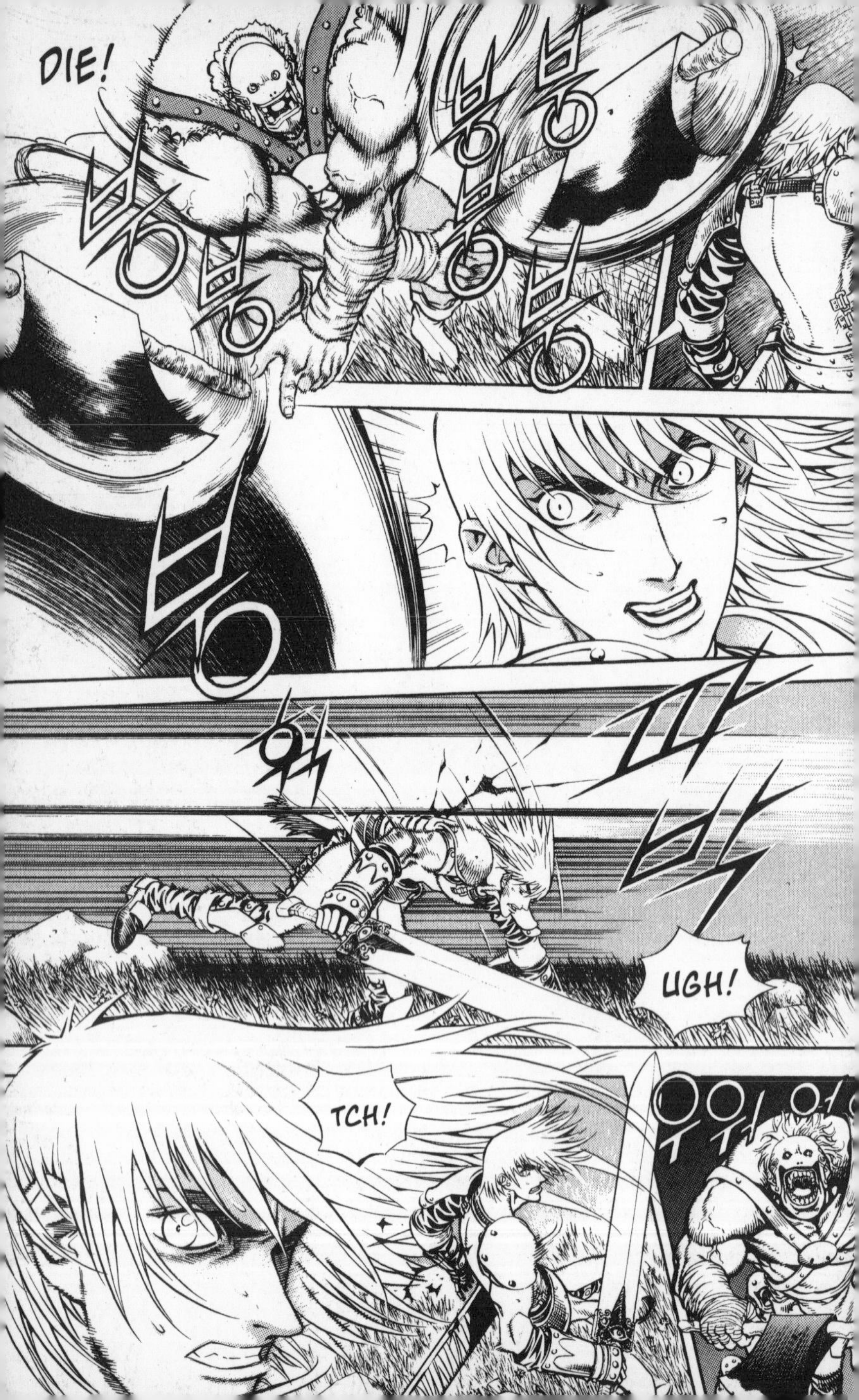
DIE!
UGH!
TCH!

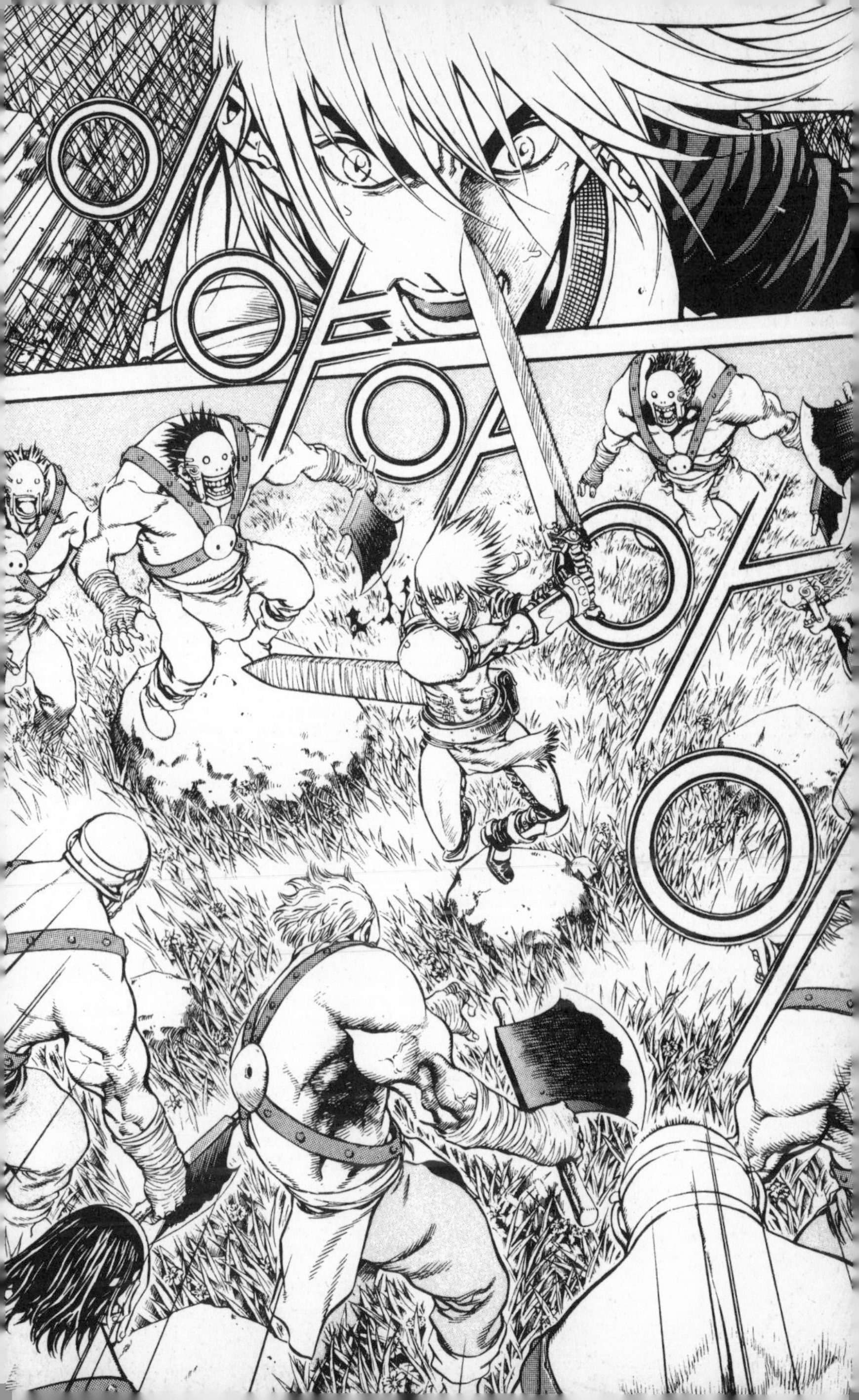

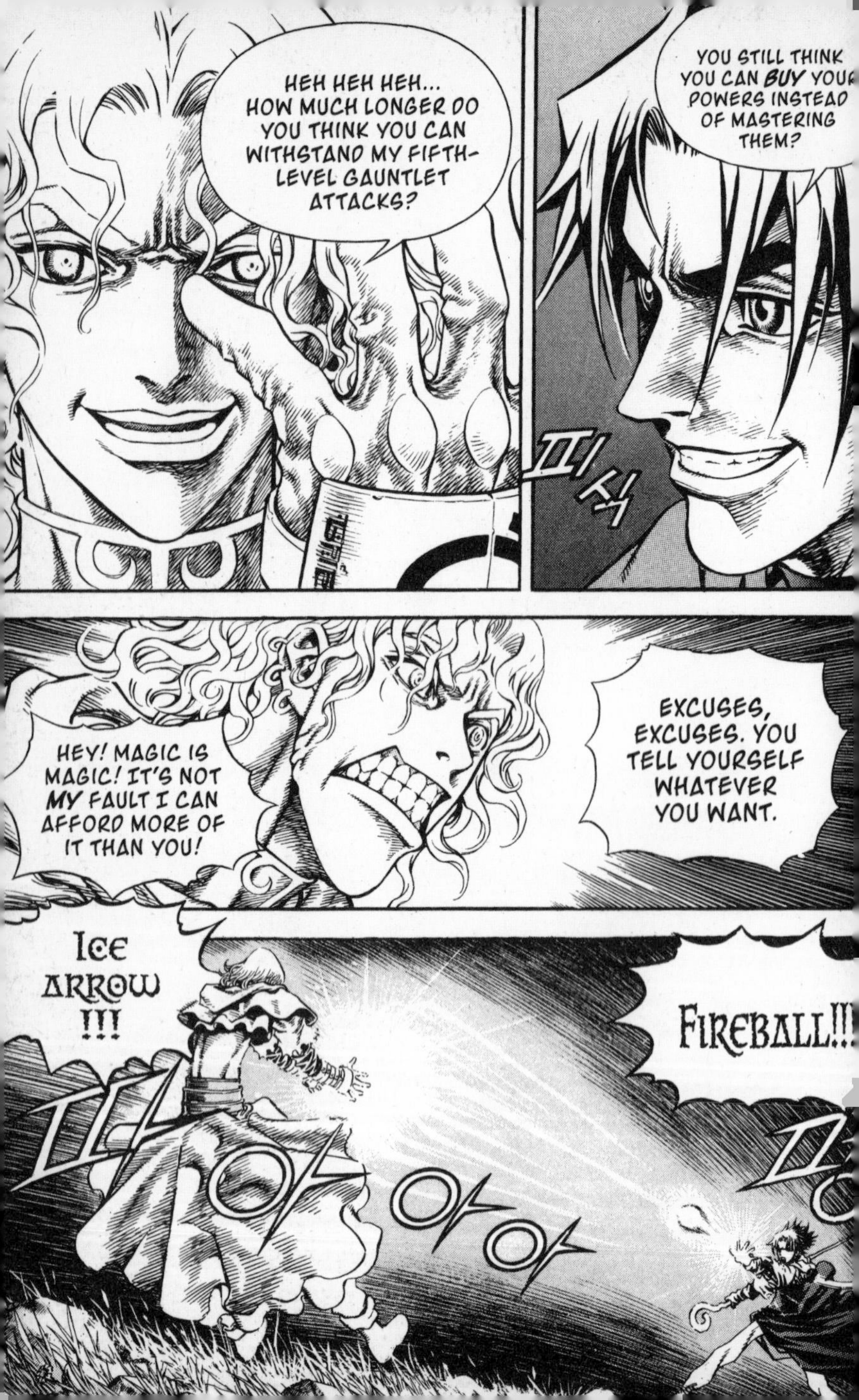
HEH HEH HEH... HOW MUCH LONGER DO YOU THINK YOU CAN WITHSTAND MY FIFTH-LEVEL GAUNTLET ATTACKS?
YOU STILL THINK YOU CAN BUY YOUR POWERS INSTEAD OF MASTERING THEM?
HEY! MAGIC IS MAGIC! IT'S NOT MY FAULT I CAN AFFORD MORE OF IT THAN YOU!
EXCUSES, EXCUSES. YOU TELL YOURSELF WHATEVER YOU WANT.
ICE ARROW !!!
FIREBALL!!!

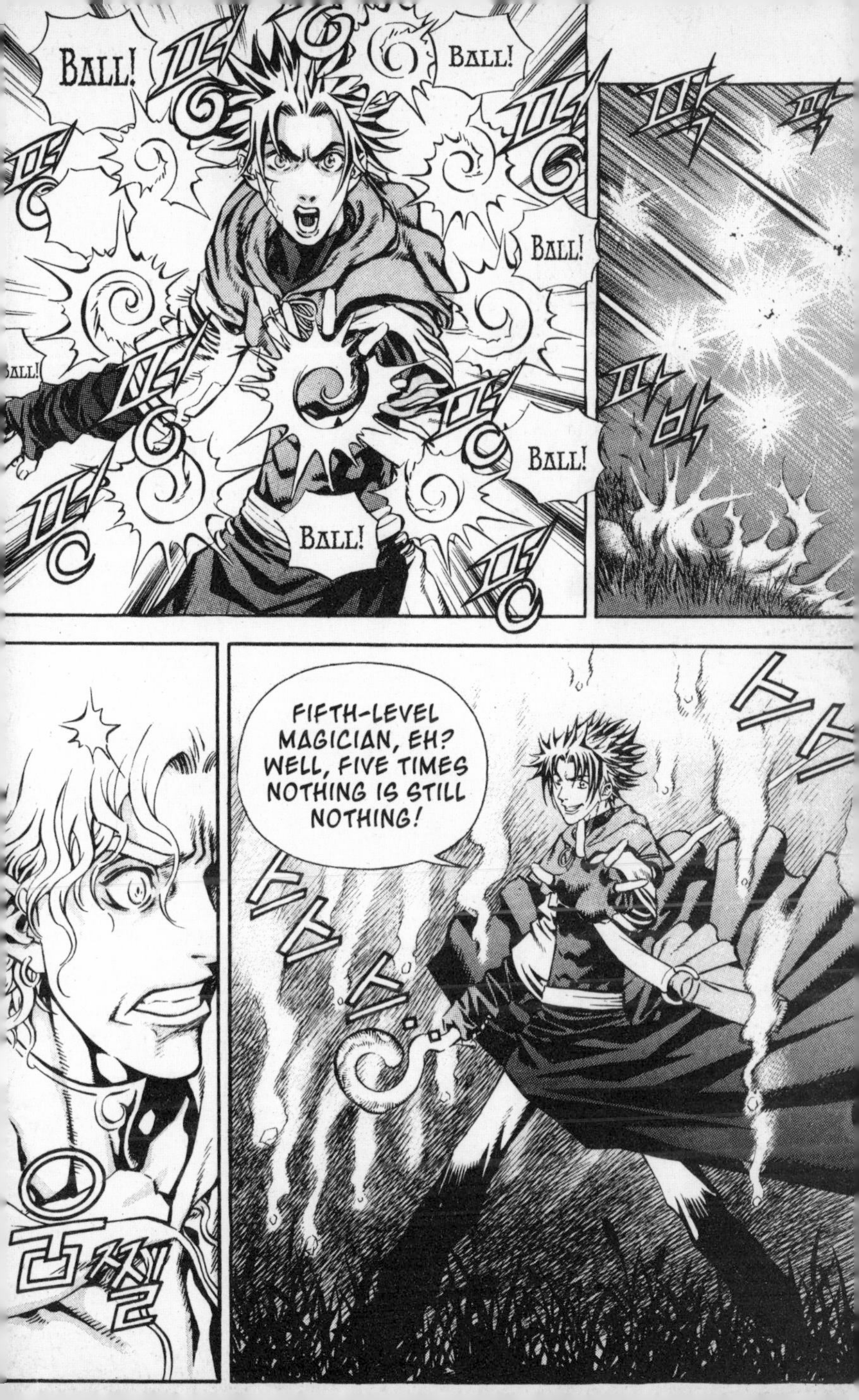
BALL!
BALL!
BALL!
BALL!
BALL!
FIFTH-LEVEL MAGICIAN, EH? WELL, FIVE TIMES NOTHING IS STILL NOTHING!

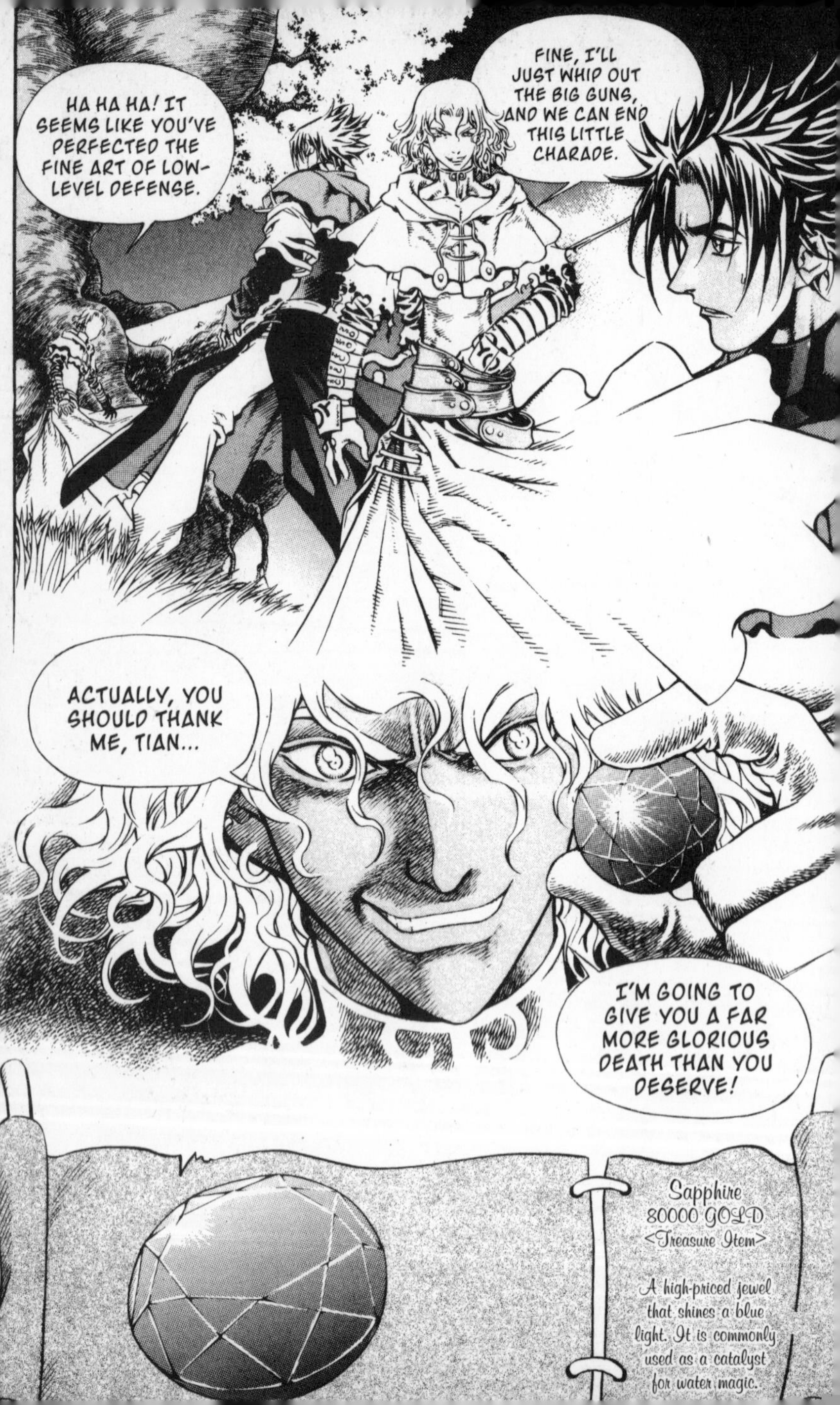
FINE, I'LL JUST WHIP OUT THE BIG GUNS, AND WE CAN END THIS LITTLE CHARADE.
HA HA HA! IT SEEMS LIKE YOU'VE PERFECTED THE FINE ART OF LOW-LEVEL DEFENSE.
ACTUALLY, YOU SHOULD THANK ME, TIAN...
I'M GOING TO GIVE YOU A FAR MORE GLORIOUS DEATH THAN YOU DESERVE!
Sapphire
80000 GOLD
<Treasure Item>
A high-priced jewel that shines a blue light. It is commonly used as a catalyst for water magic.

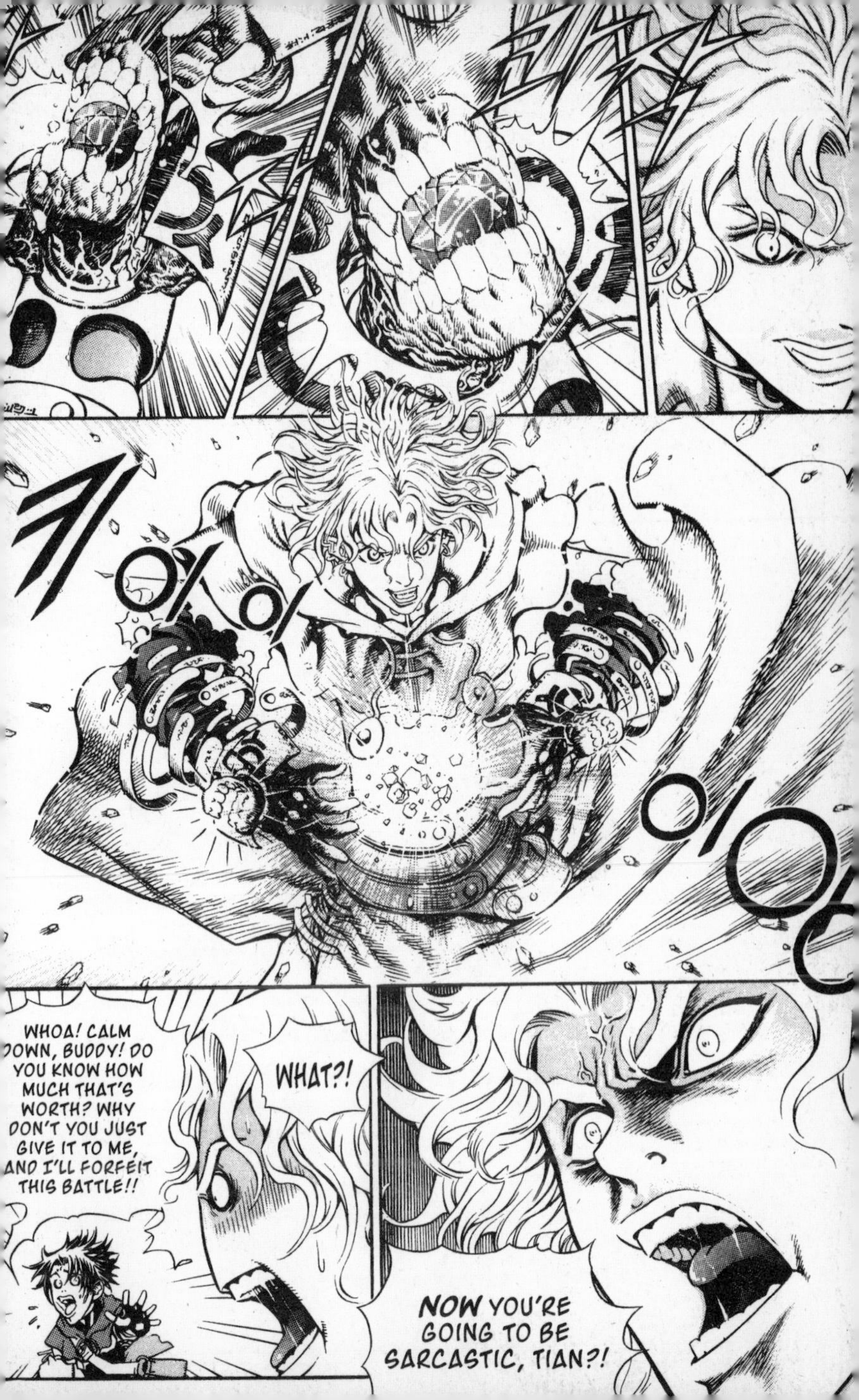
WHOA! CALM DOWN, BUDDY! DO YOU KNOW HOW MUCH THAT'S WORTH? WHY DON'T YOU JUST GIVE IT TO ME, AND I'LL FORFEIT THIS BATTLE!!
WHAT?!
NOW YOU'RE GOING TO BE SARCASTIC, TIAN?!

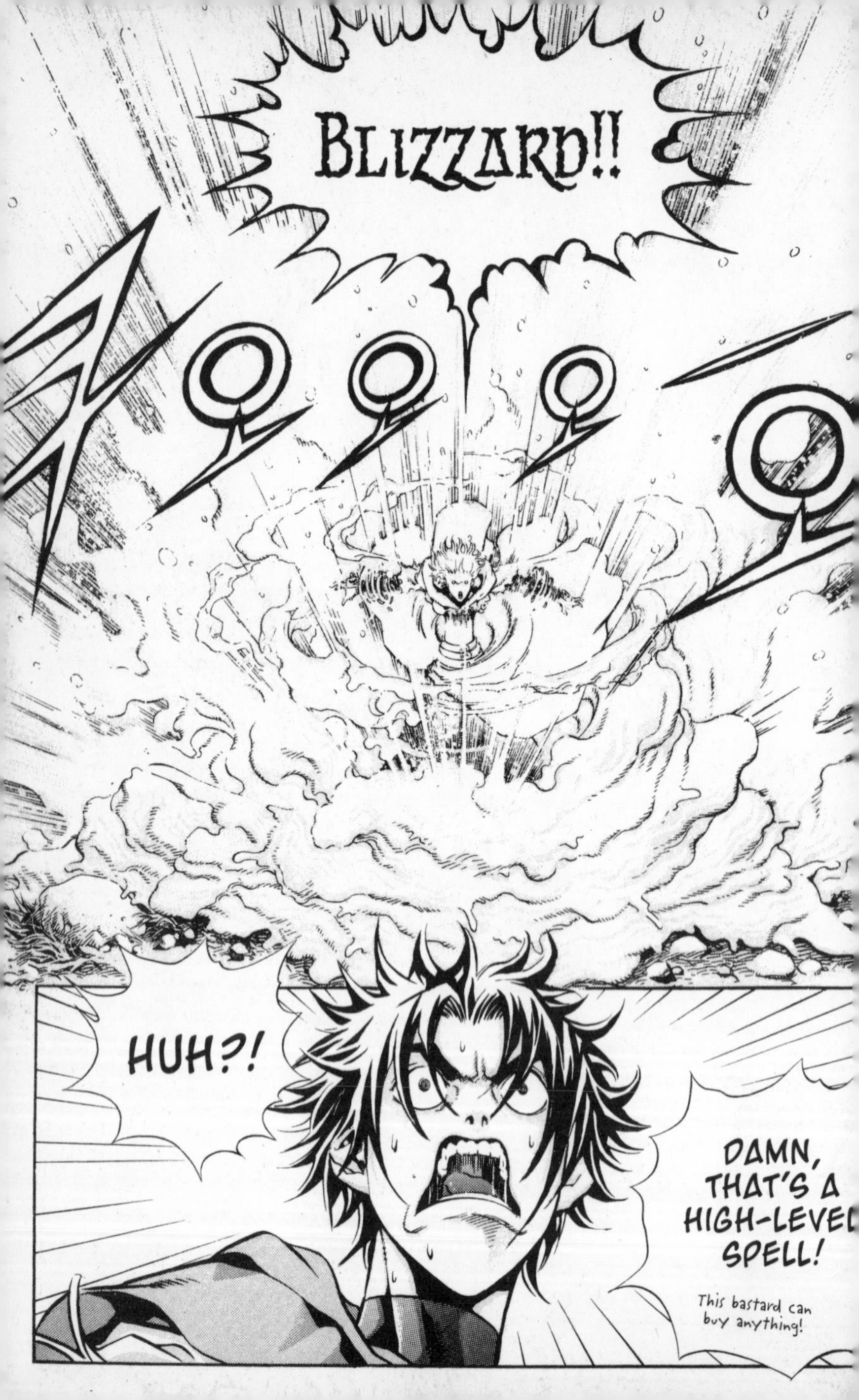
BLIZZARD!!
HUH?!
DAMN, THAT'S A HIGH-LEVEL SPELL!
This bastard can buy anything!

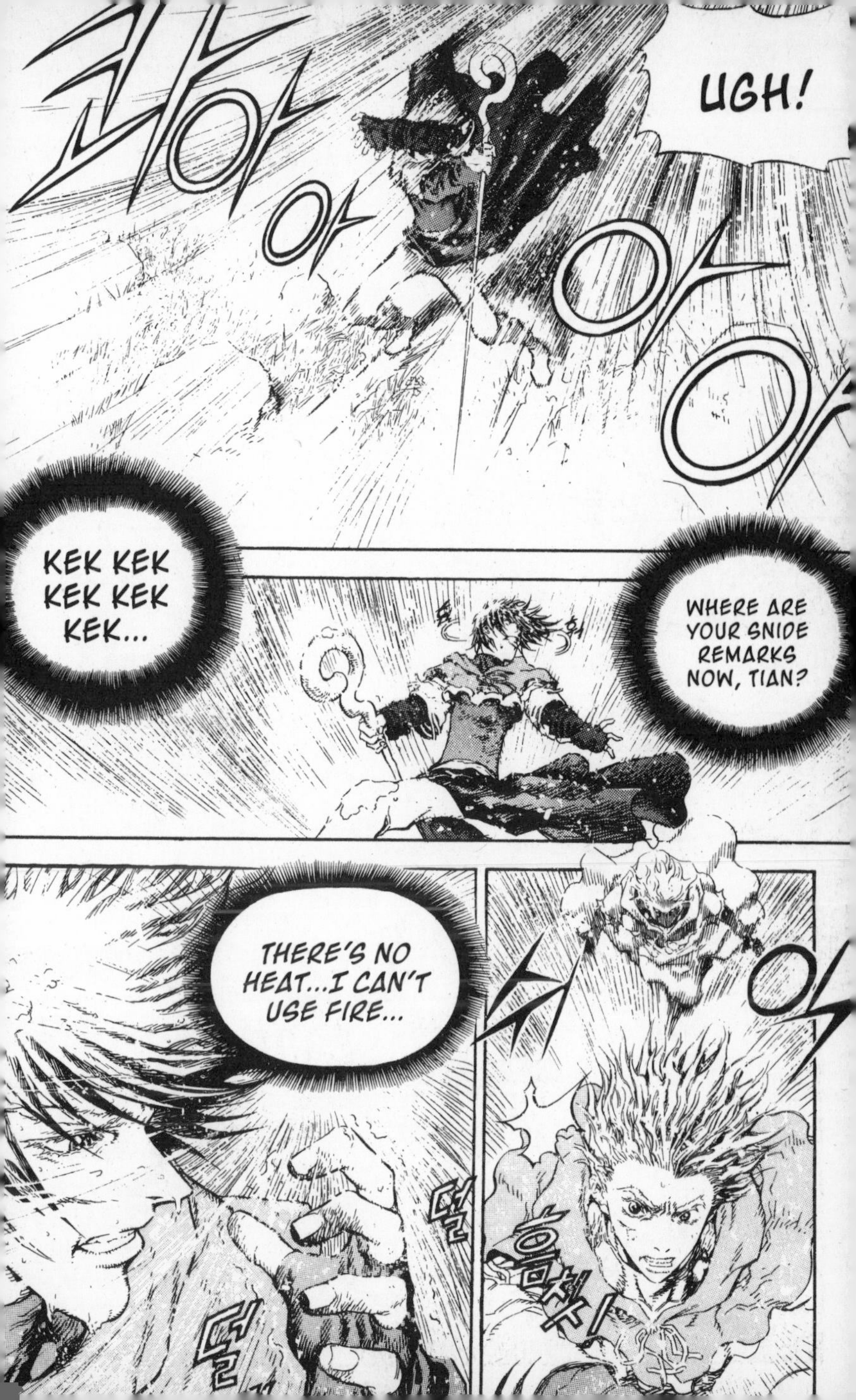
UGH!
KEK KEK KEK KEK KEK...
WHERE ARE YOUR SNIDE REMARKS NOW, TIAN?
THERE'S NO HEAT...I CAN'T USE FIRE...

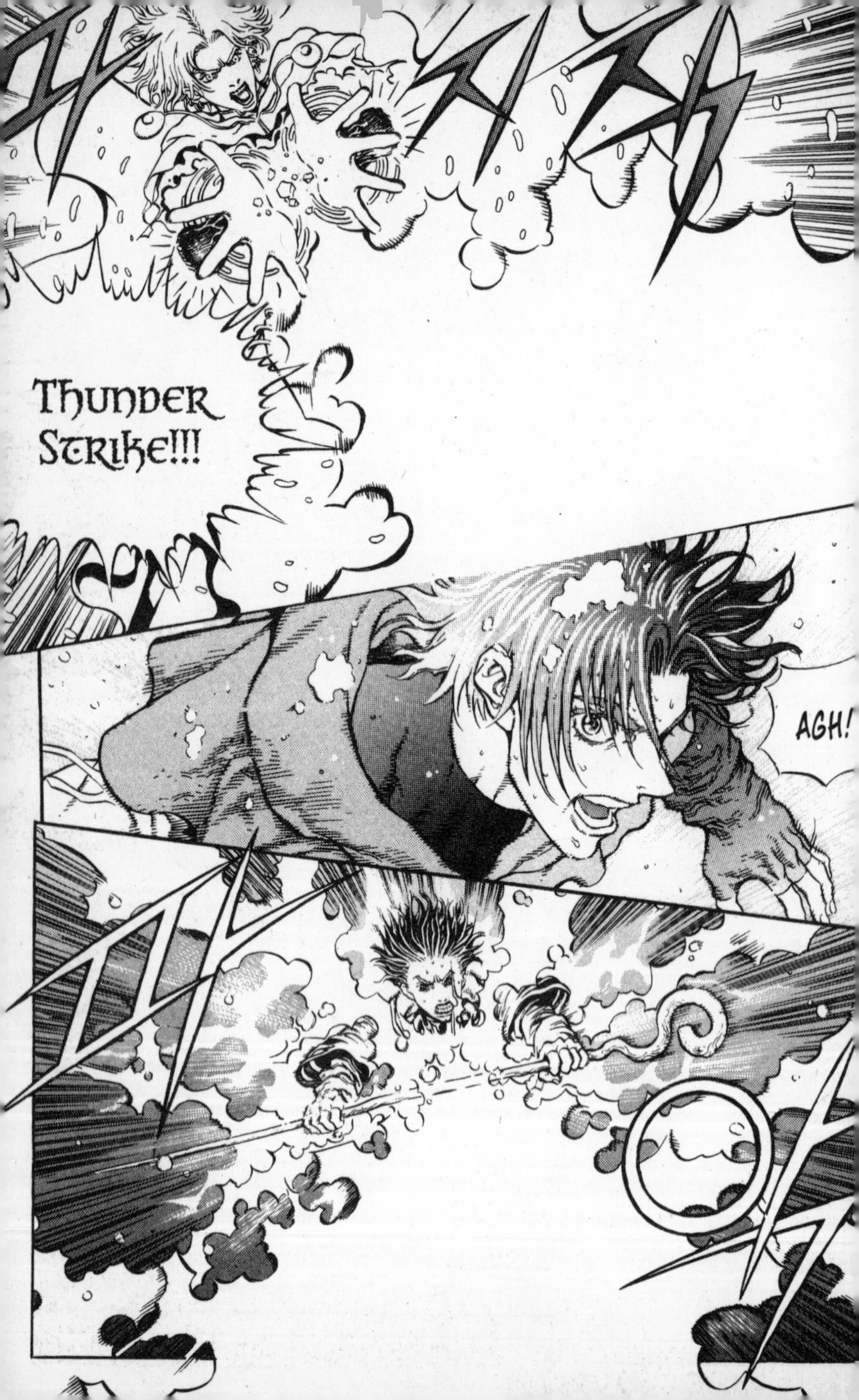
THUNDER STRIKE!!!
AGH!

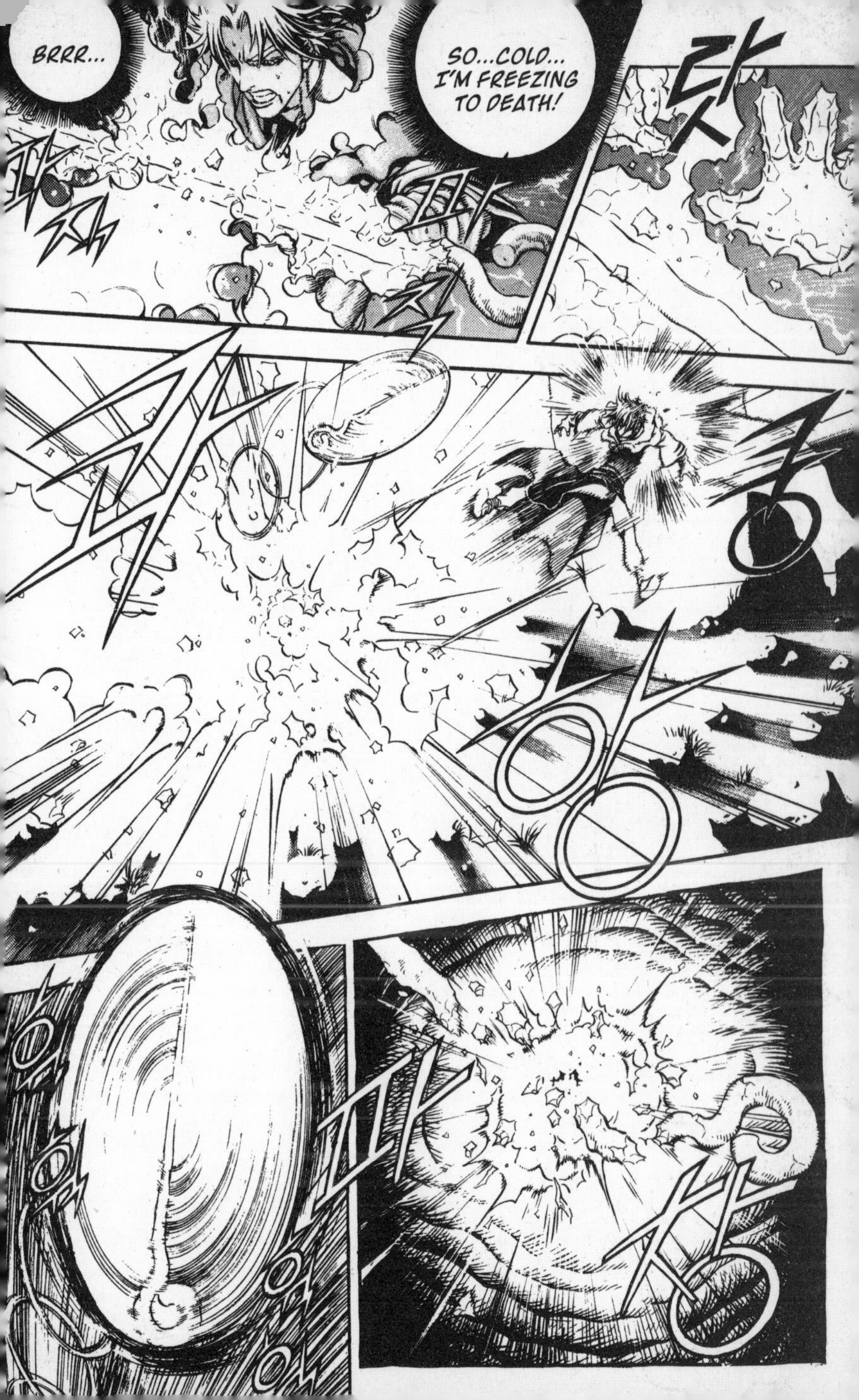
BRRR...
SO...COLD... I'M FREEZING TO DEATH!

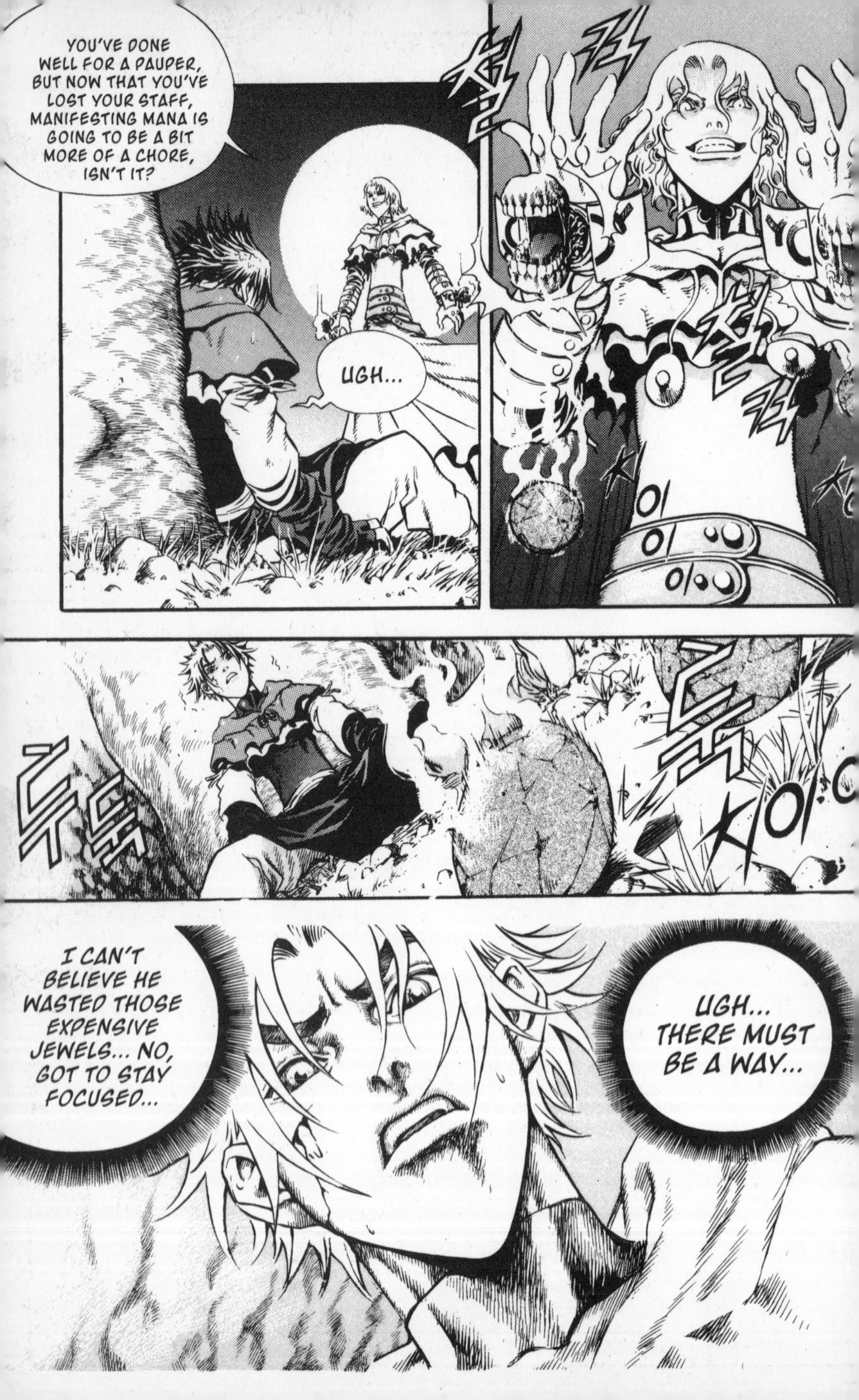
YOU'VE DONE WELL FOR A PAUPER, BUT NOW THAT YOU'VE LOST YOUR STAFF, MANIFESTING MANA IS GOING TO BE A BIT MORE OF A CHORE, ISN'T IT?
UGH...
I CAN'T BELIEVE HE WASTED THOSE EXPENSIVE JEWELS... NO, GOT TO STAY FOCUSED...
UGH... THERE MUST BE A WAY...

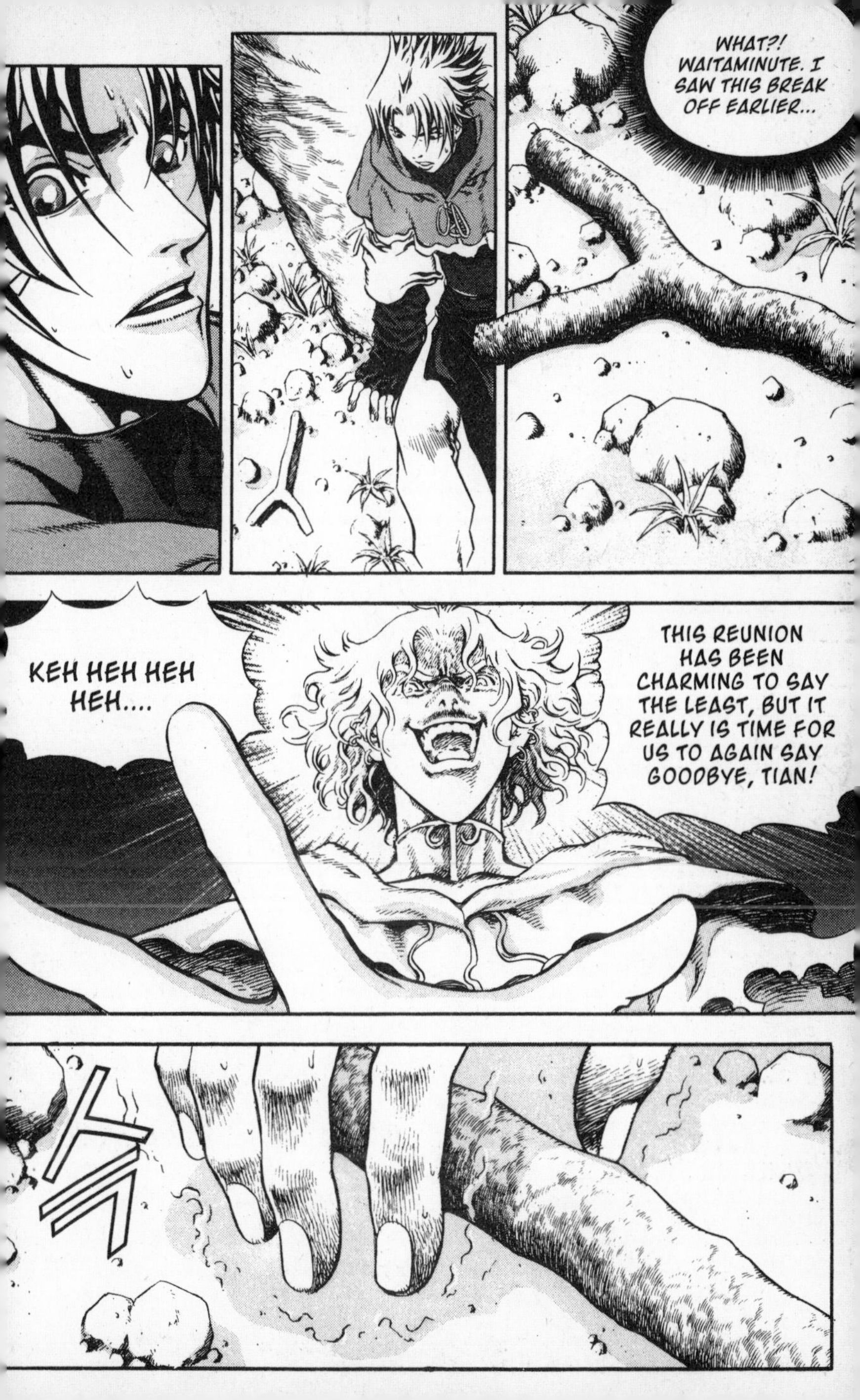
WHAT?! WAITAMINUTE. I SAW THIS BREAK OFF EARLIER...
KEH HEH HEH HEH....
THIS REUNION HAS BEEN CHARMING TO SAY THE LEAST, BUT IT REALLY IS TIME FOR US TO AGAIN SAY GOODBYE, TIAN!

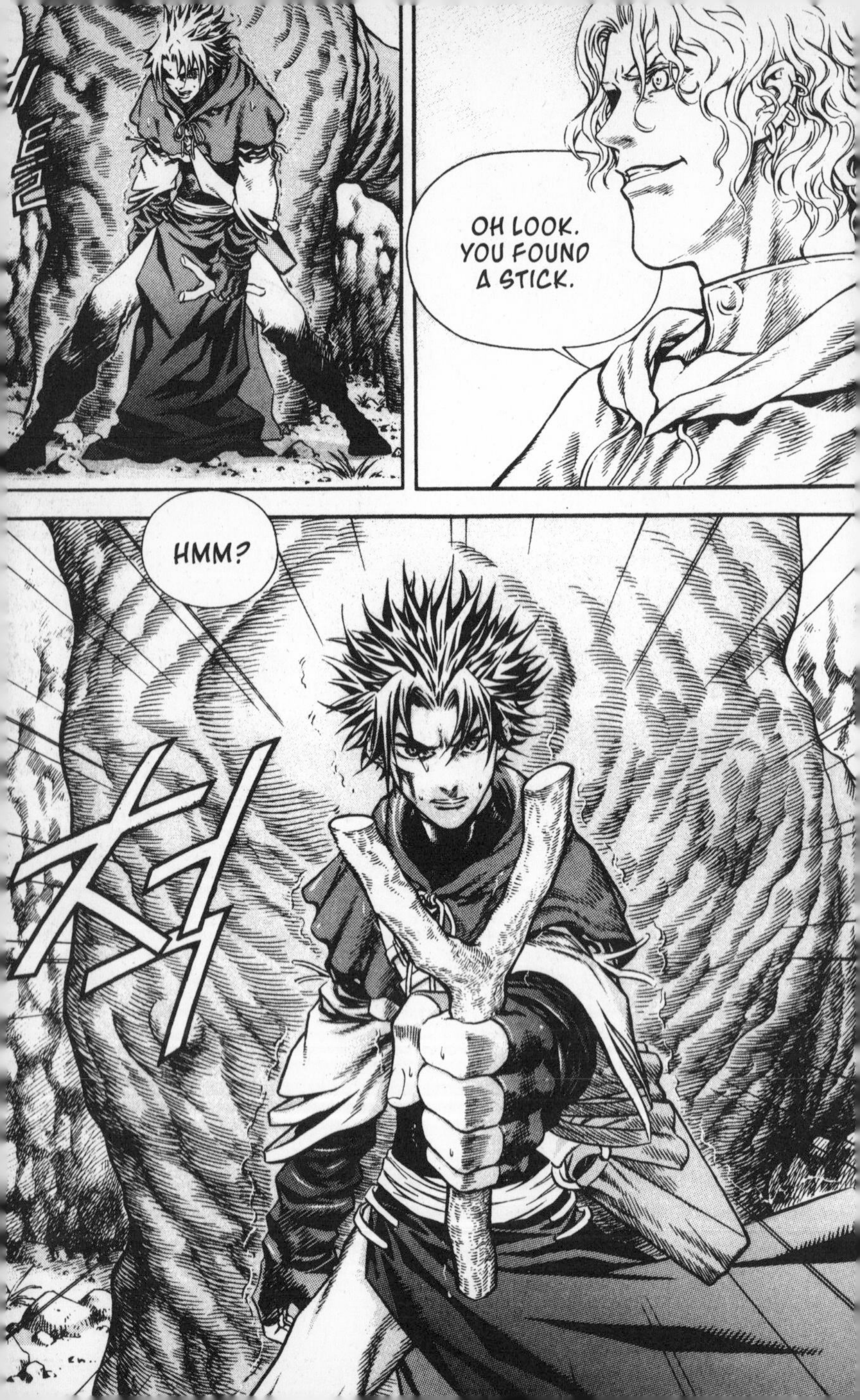
OH LOOK.
YOU FOUND
A STICK.
HMM?

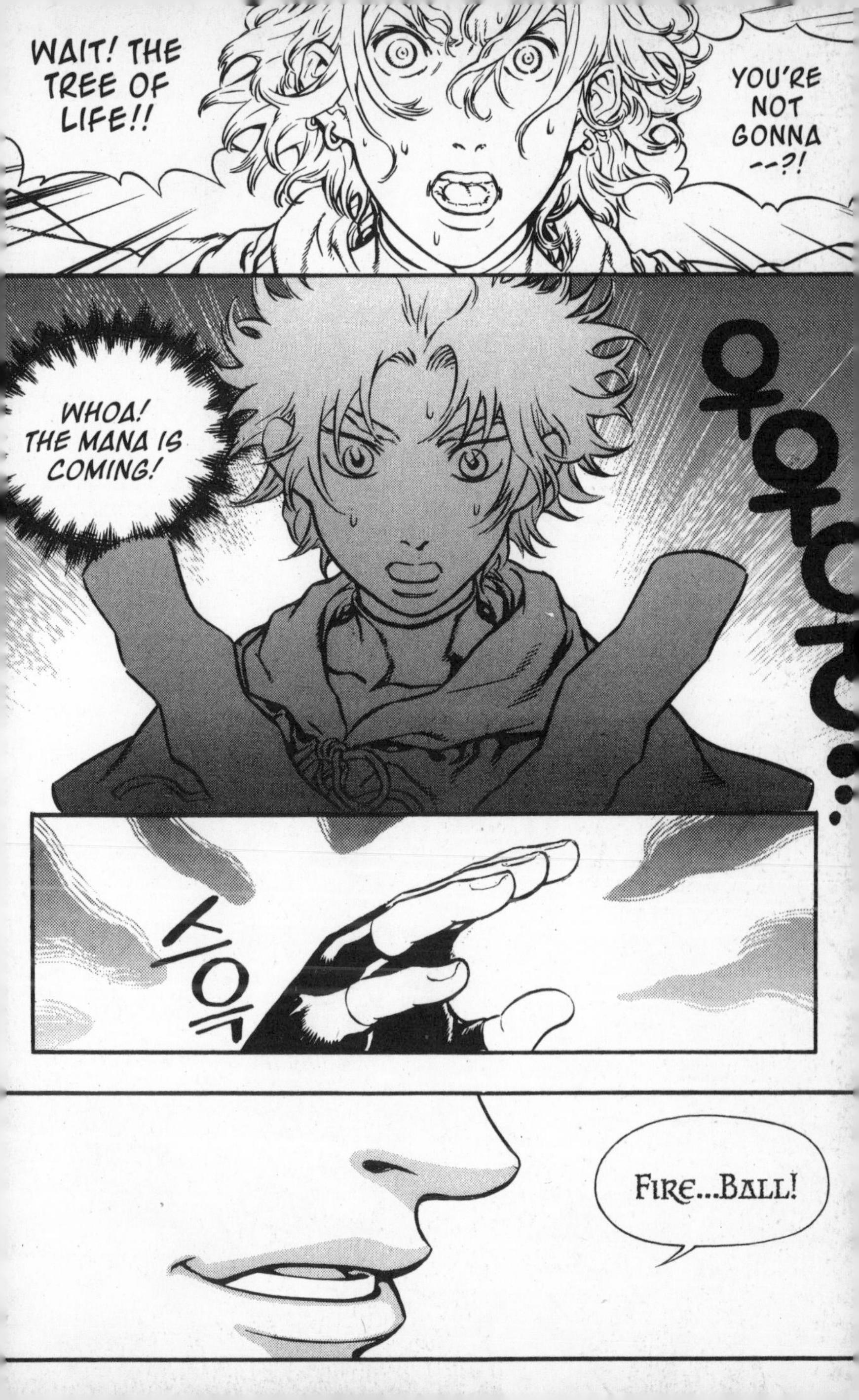
WAIT! THE TREE OF LIFE!!
YOU'RE NOT GONNA --?!
WHOA! THE MANA IS COMING!
FIRE...BALL!

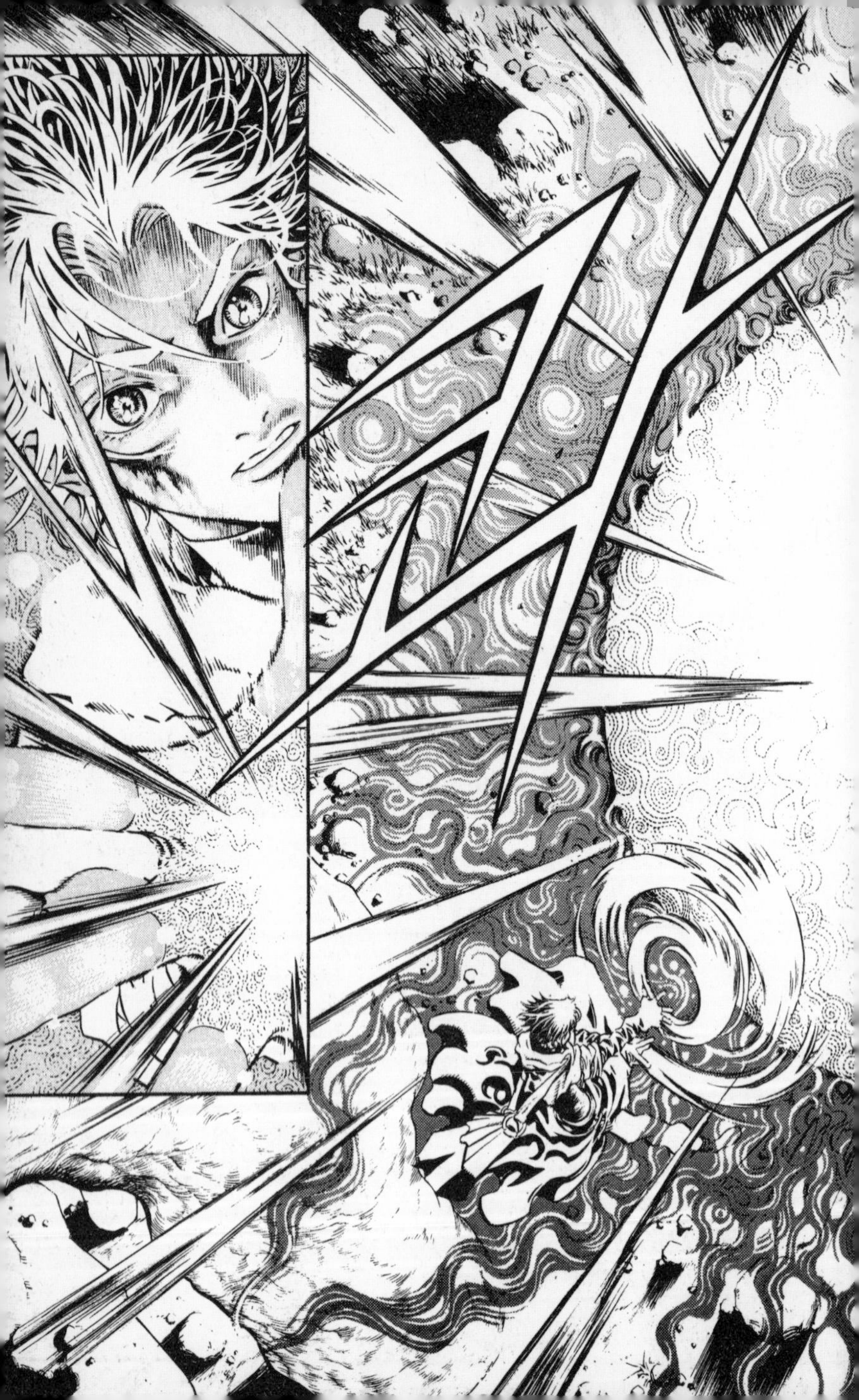

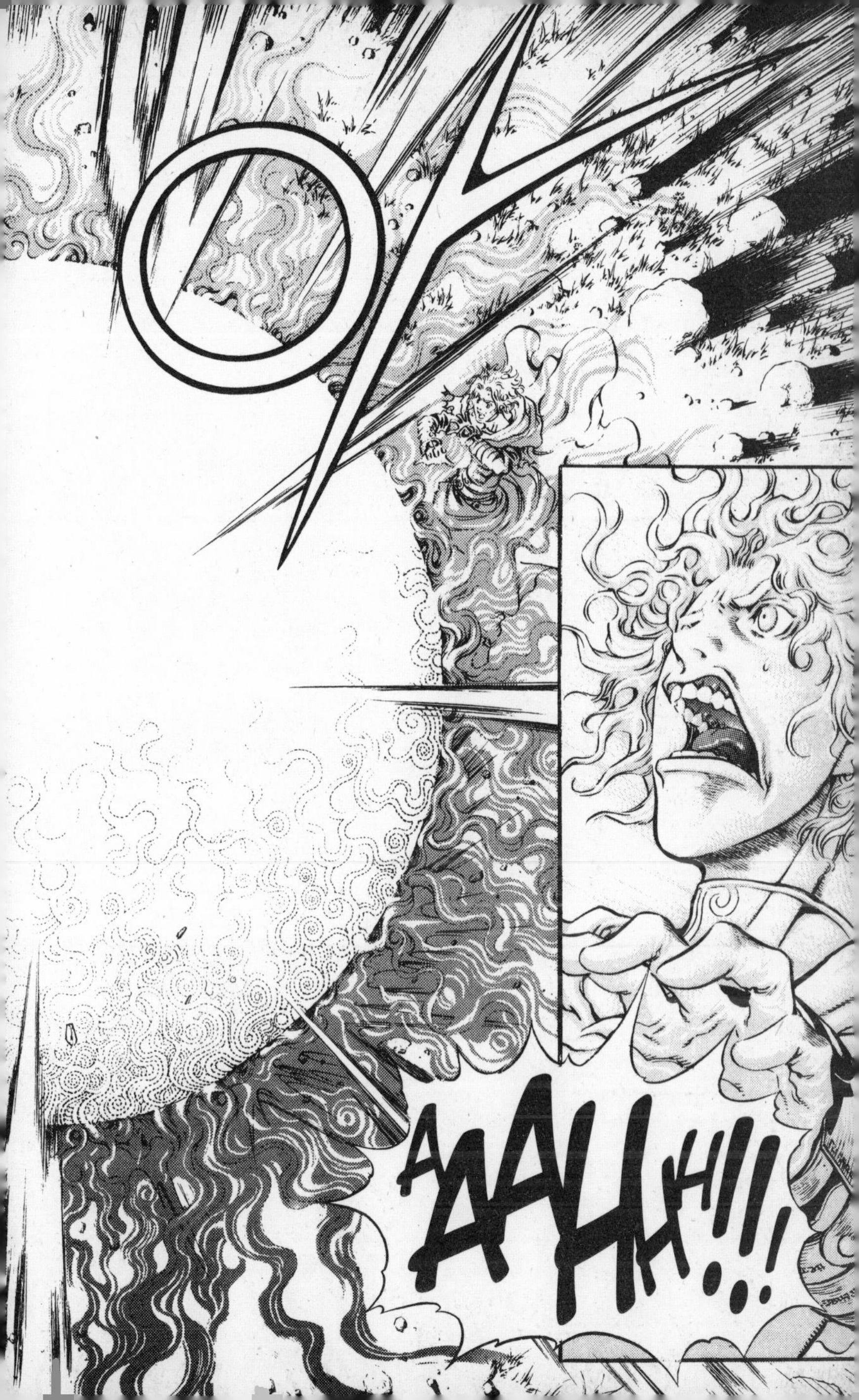
AAHHH!!!

SO MUCH POWER... FROM ONE TINY BRANCH...I CAN'T IMAGINE...

UGH...

I...LIKE IT...

IT'S OVER. JUST QUIT NOW WHILE YOU'RE AHEAD.

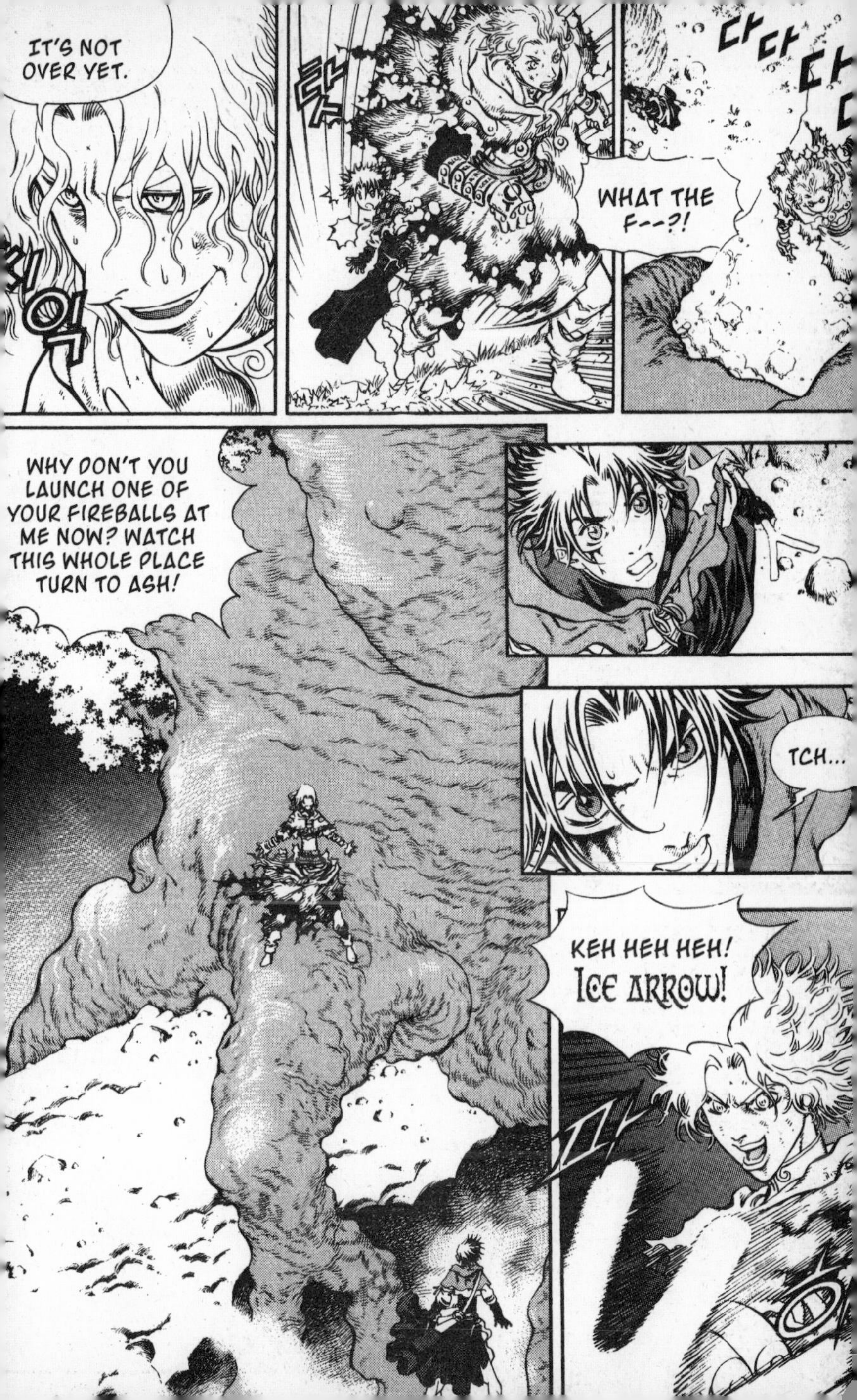
IT'S NOT OVER YET.
WHAT THE F--?!
WHY DON'T YOU LAUNCH ONE OF YOUR FIREBALLS AT ME NOW? WATCH THIS WHOLE PLACE TURN TO ASH!
TCH...
KEH HEH HEH! ICE ARROW!

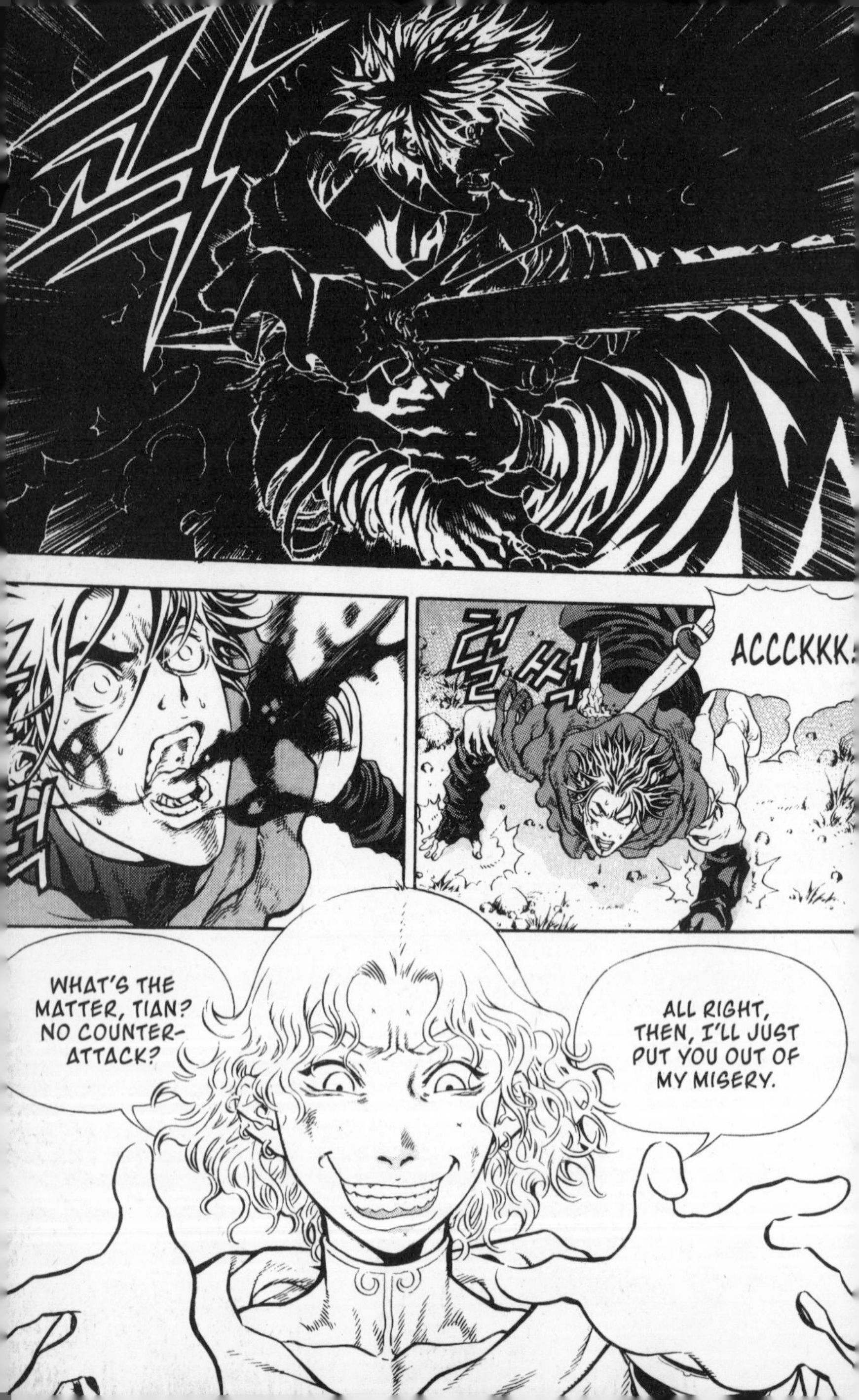
ACCCKKK...
WHAT'S THE MATTER, TIAN? NO COUNTER-ATTACK?
ALL RIGHT, THEN, I'LL JUST PUT YOU OUT OF MY MISERY.

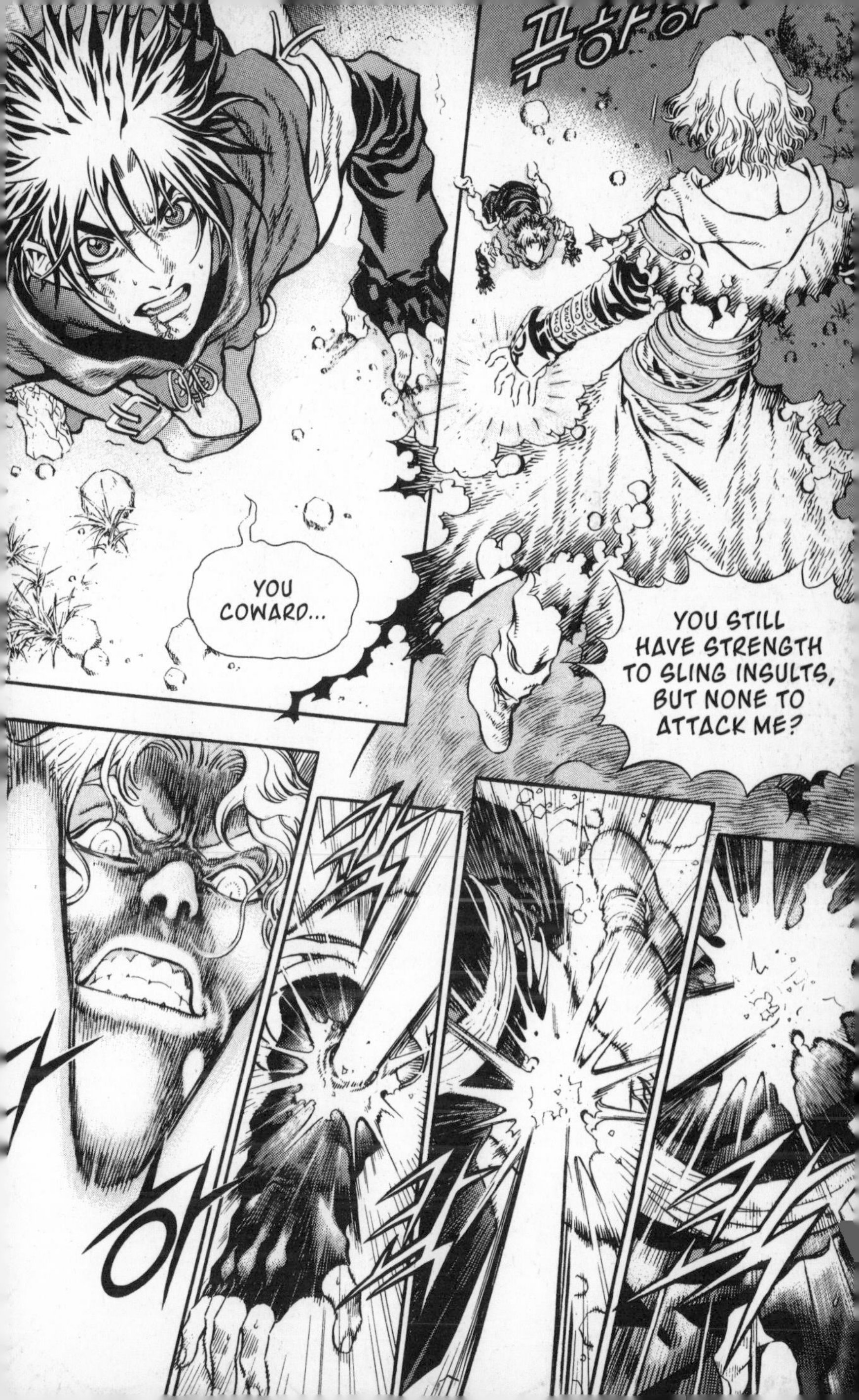
푸하아
YOU COWARD...
YOU STILL HAVE STRENGTH TO SLING INSULTS, BUT NONE TO ATTACK ME?

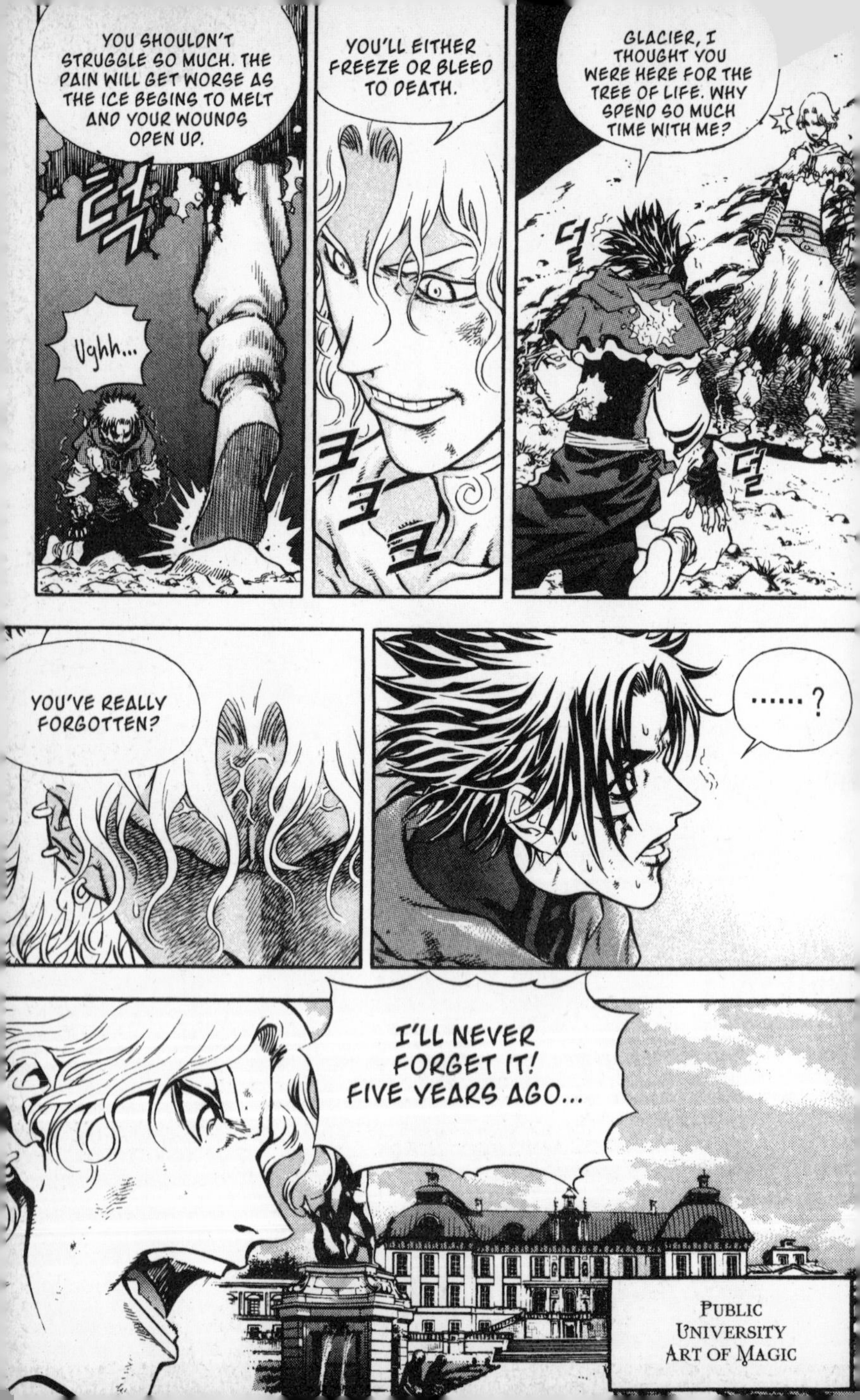
YOU SHOULDN'T STRUGGLE SO MUCH. THE PAIN WILL GET WORSE AS THE ICE BEGINS TO MELT AND YOUR WOUNDS OPEN UP.
Ughh...
YOU'LL EITHER FREEZE OR BLEED TO DEATH.
GLACIER, I THOUGHT YOU WERE HERE FOR THE TREE OF LIFE. WHY SPEND SO MUCH TIME WITH ME?
YOU'VE REALLY FORGOTTEN?
......?
I'LL NEVER FORGET IT! FIVE YEARS AGO...
PUBLIC UNIVERSITY ART OF MAGIC

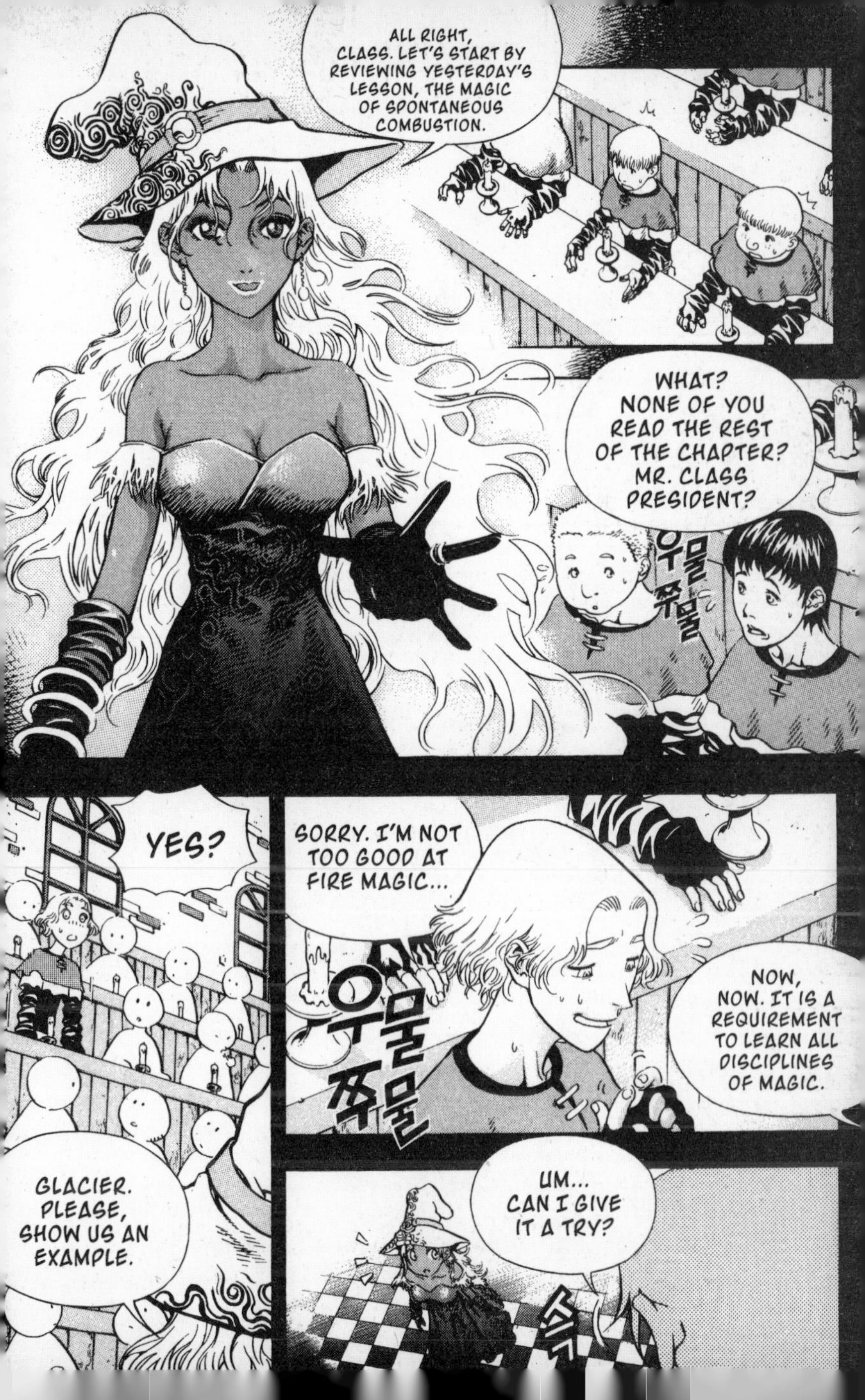
ALL RIGHT, CLASS. LET'S START BY REVIEWING YESTERDAY'S LESSON, THE MAGIC OF SPONTANEOUS COMBUSTION.
WHAT? NONE OF YOU READ THE REST OF THE CHAPTER? MR. CLASS PRESIDENT?
우물 쭈물
YES?
SORRY. I'M NOT TOO GOOD AT FIRE MAGIC...
우물 쭈물
NOW, NOW. IT IS A REQUIREMENT TO LEARN ALL DISCIPLINES OF MAGIC.
GLACIER. PLEASE, SHOW US AN EXAMPLE.
UM... CAN I GIVE IT A TRY?

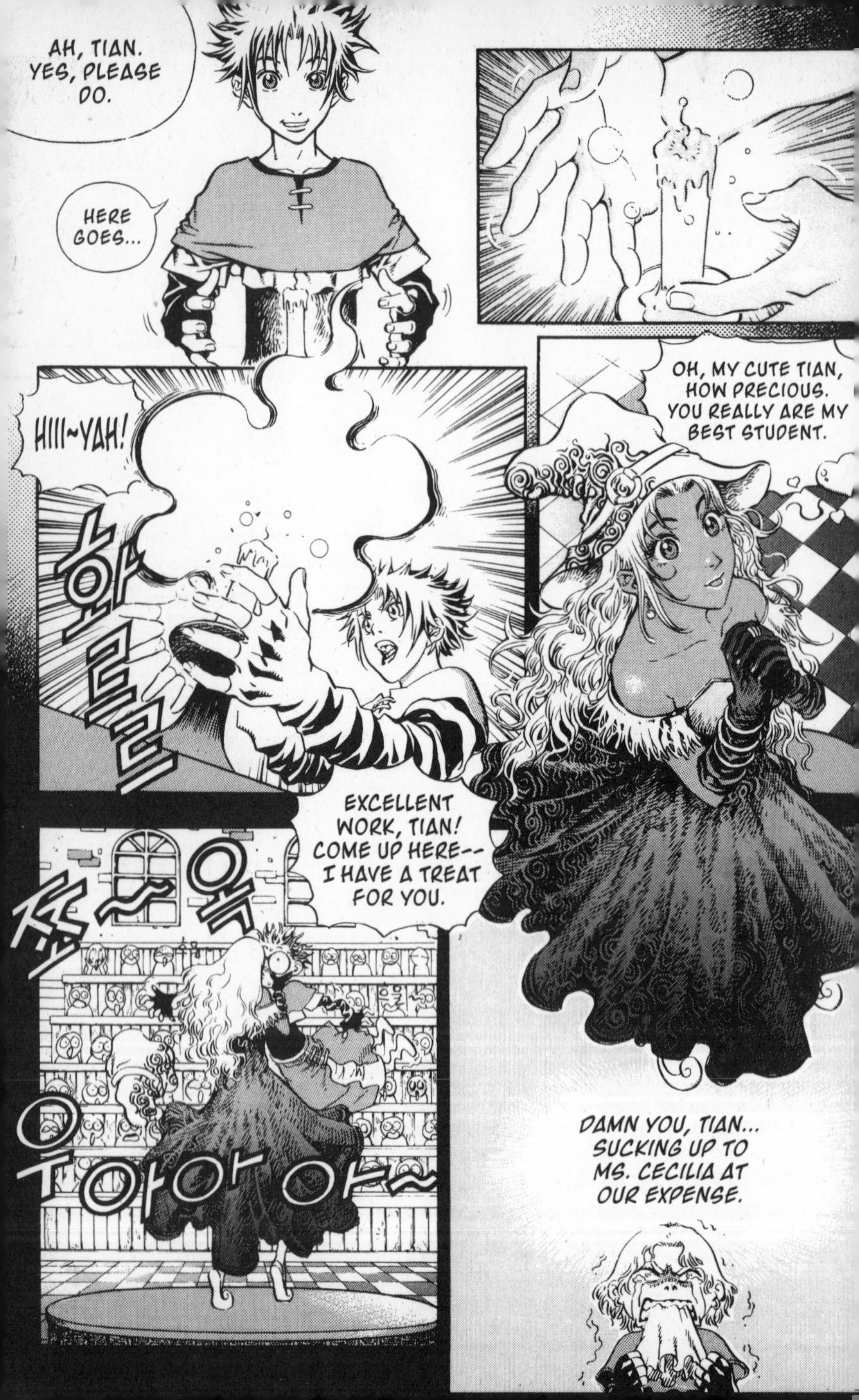
AH, TIAN. YES, PLEASE DO.
HERE GOES...
HIII~YAH!
화르르
OH, MY CUTE TIAN, HOW PRECIOUS. YOU REALLY ARE MY BEST STUDENT.
EXCELLENT WORK, TIAN! COME UP HERE-- I HAVE A TREAT FOR YOU.
쭈~욱
우아아 아~
DAMN YOU, TIAN... SUCKING UP TO MS. CECILIA AT OUR EXPENSE.

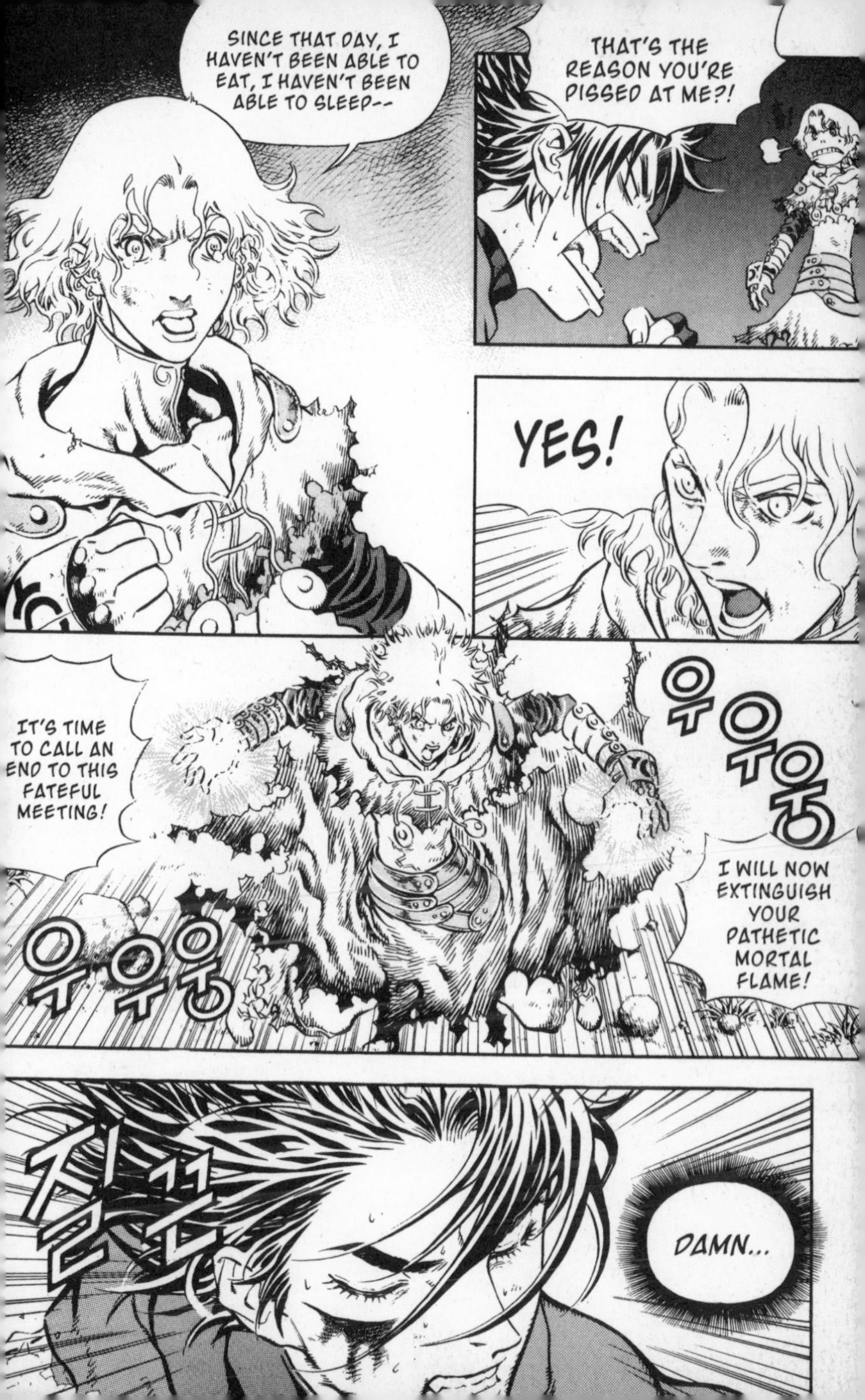

SINCE THAT DAY, I HAVEN'T BEEN ABLE TO EAT, I HAVEN'T BEEN ABLE TO SLEEP--
THAT'S THE REASON YOU'RE PISSED AT ME?!
YES!
IT'S TIME TO CALL AN END TO THIS FATEFUL MEETING!
오오오옹
I WILL NOW EXTINGUISH YOUR PATHETIC MORTAL FLAME!
우우웅
DAMN...

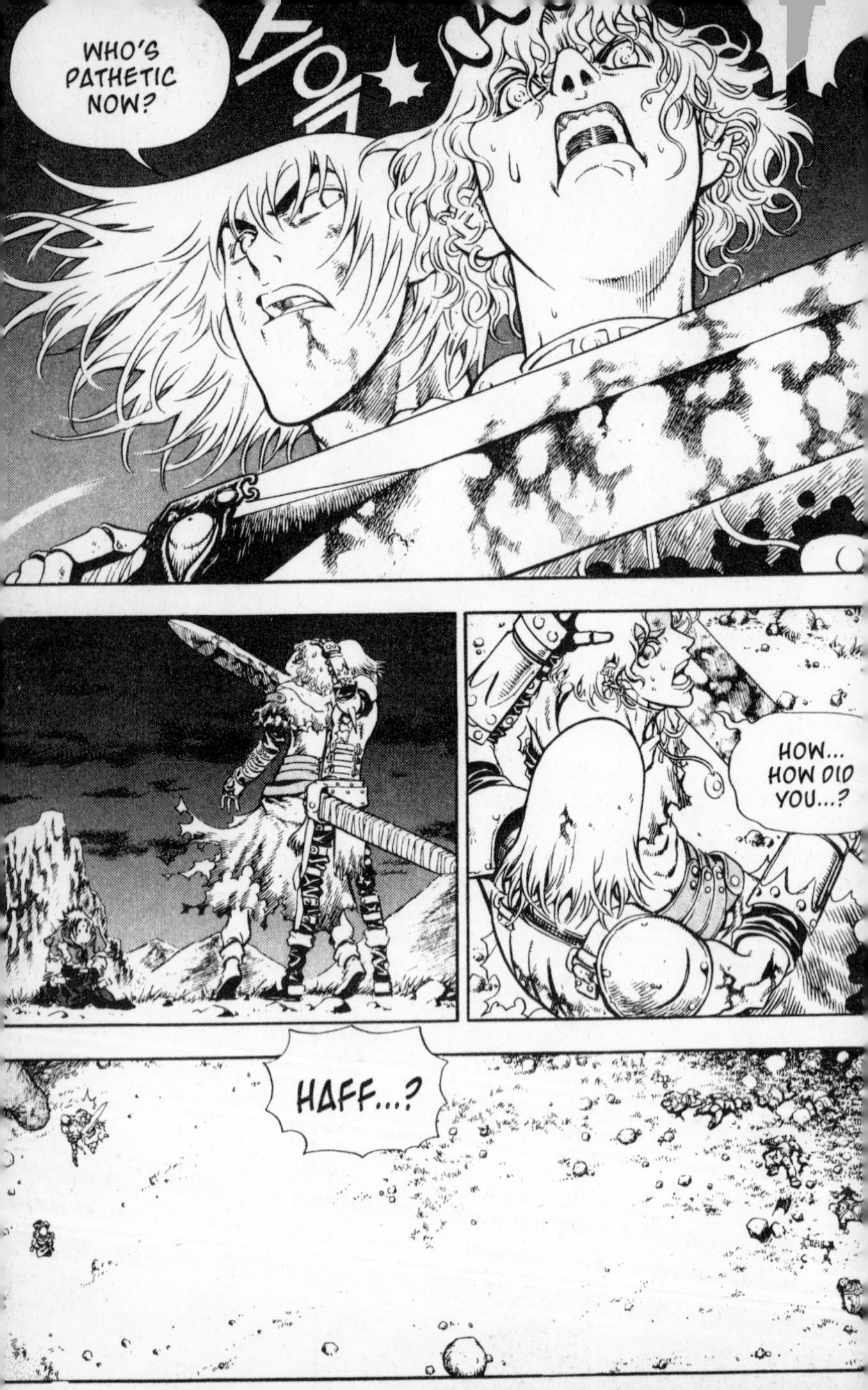
WHO'S PATHETIC NOW?
HOW... HOW DID YOU...?
HAFF...?

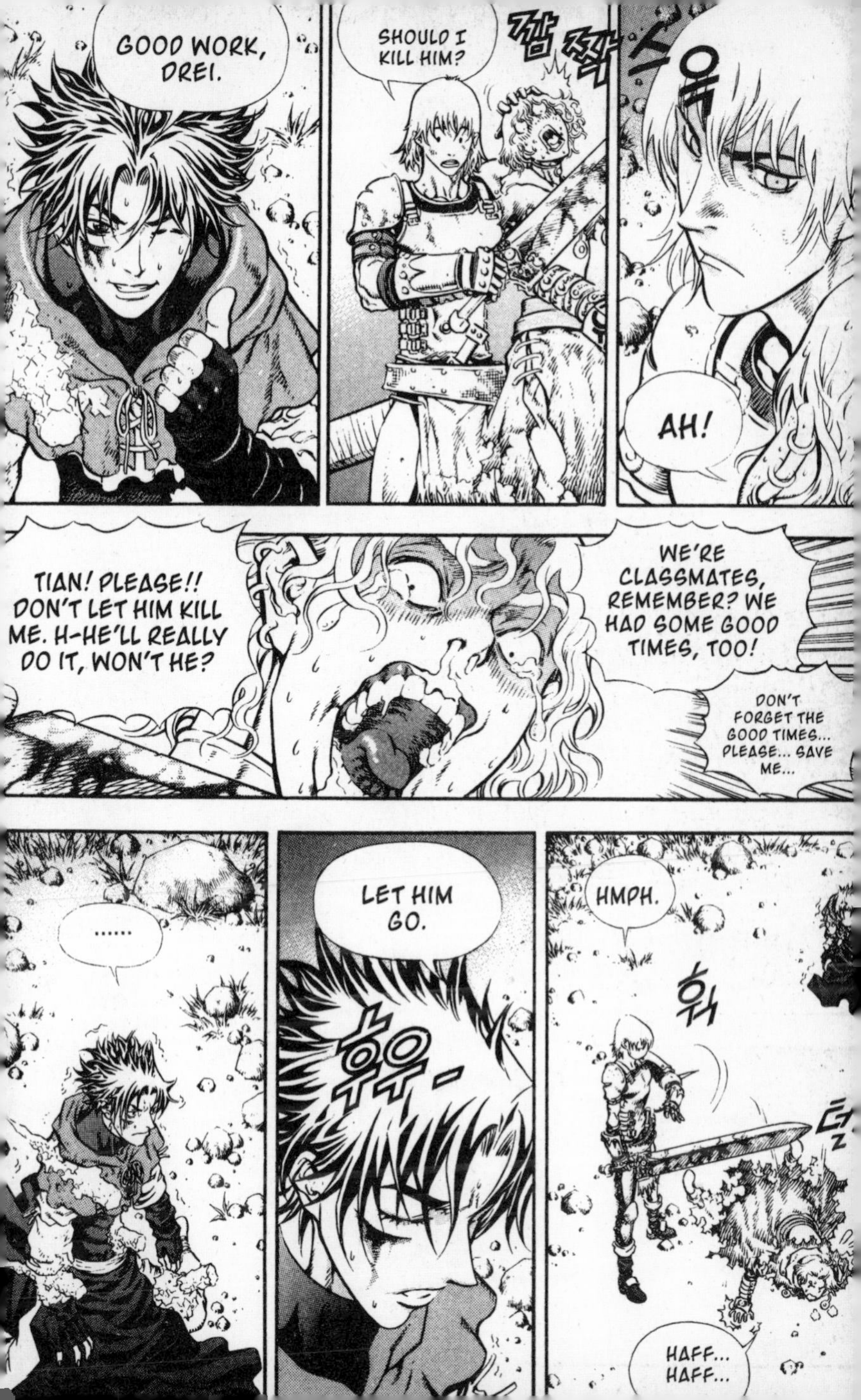
GOOD WORK, DREI.
SHOULD I KILL HIM?
AH!
TIAN! PLEASE!! DON'T LET HIM KILL ME. H-HE'LL REALLY DO IT, WON'T HE?
WE'RE CLASSMATES, REMEMBER? WE HAD SOME GOOD TIMES, TOO!
DON'T FORGET THE GOOD TIMES... PLEASE... SAVE ME...
......
LET HIM GO.
HMPH.
HAFF... HAFF...

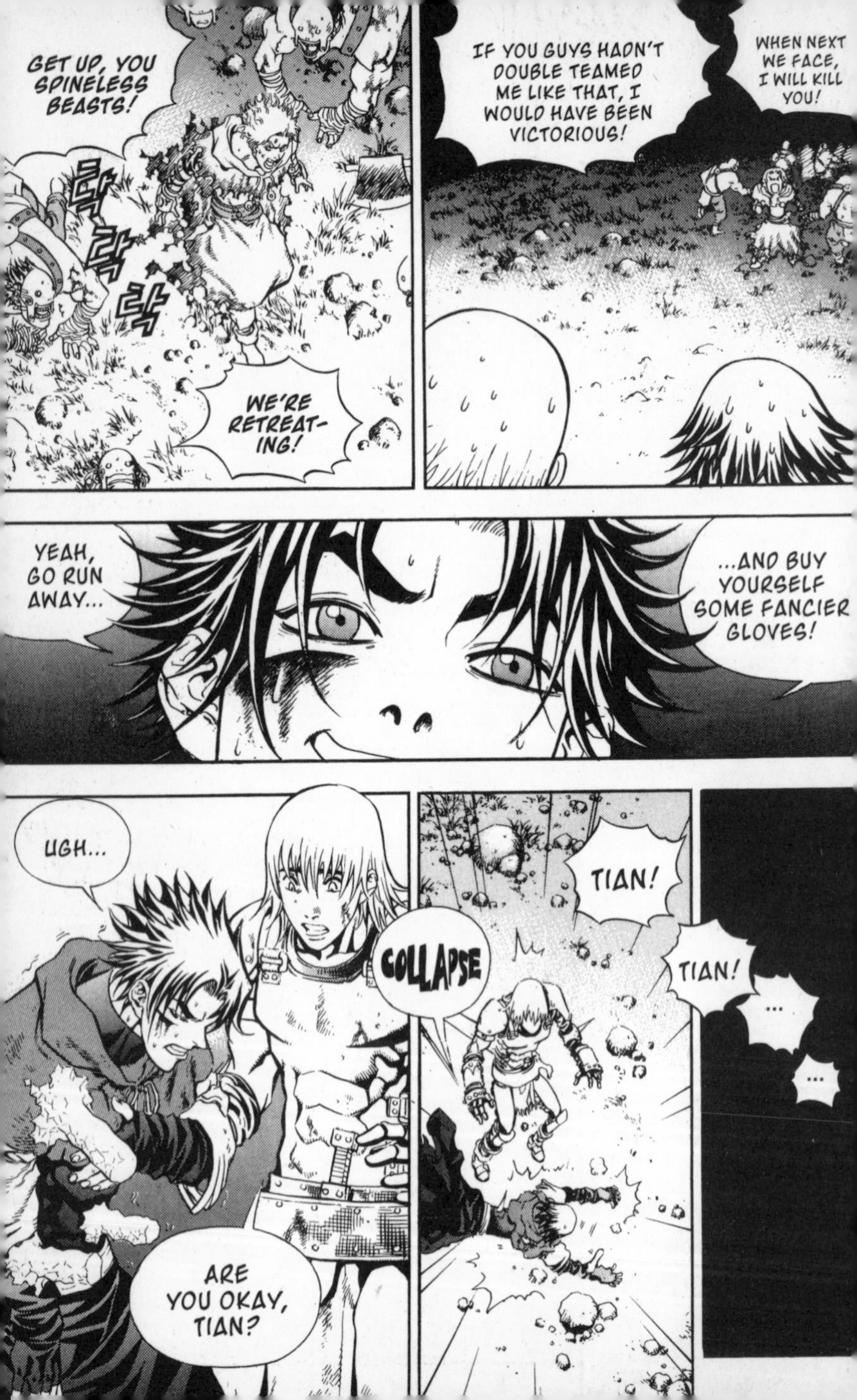
GET UP, YOU SPINELESS BEASTS!
WE'RE RETREATING!
IF YOU GUYS HADN'T DOUBLE TEAMED ME LIKE THAT, I WOULD HAVE BEEN VICTORIOUS!
WHEN NEXT WE FACE, I WILL KILL YOU!
YEAH, GO RUN AWAY...
...AND BUY YOURSELF SOME FANCIER GLOVES!
UGH...
COLLAPSE
ARE YOU OKAY, TIAN?
TIAN!
TIAN!
...
...

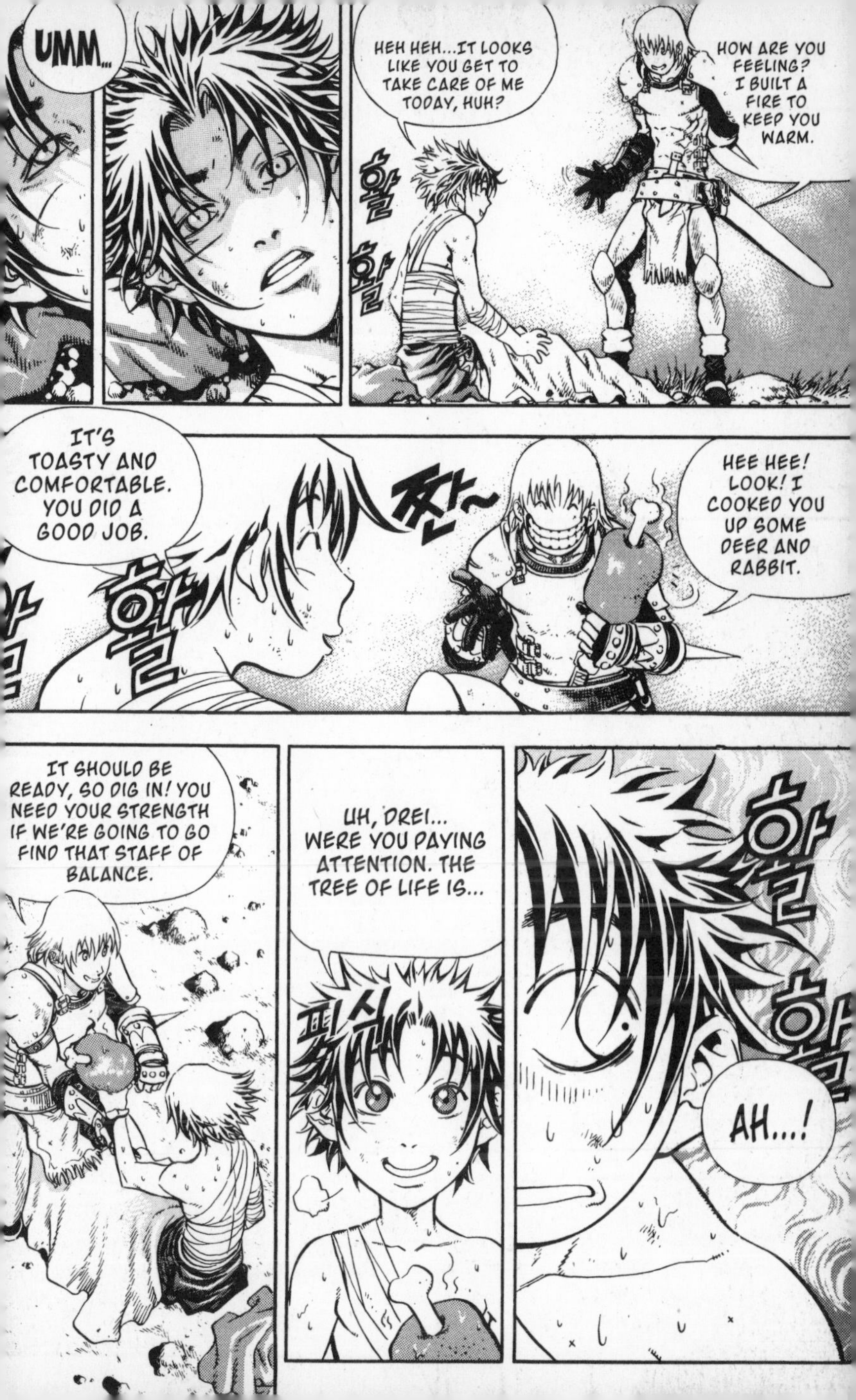
UMM...
HEH HEH...IT LOOKS LIKE YOU GET TO TAKE CARE OF ME TODAY, HUH?
HOW ARE YOU FEELING? I BUILT A FIRE TO KEEP YOU WARM.
IT'S TOASTY AND COMFORTABLE. YOU DID A GOOD JOB.
HEE HEE! LOOK! I COOKED YOU UP SOME DEER AND RABBIT.
IT SHOULD BE READY, SO DIG IN! YOU NEED YOUR STRENGTH IF WE'RE GOING TO GO FIND THAT STAFF OF BALANCE.
UH, DREI... WERE YOU PAYING ATTENTION. THE TREE OF LIFE IS...
피식
AH...!

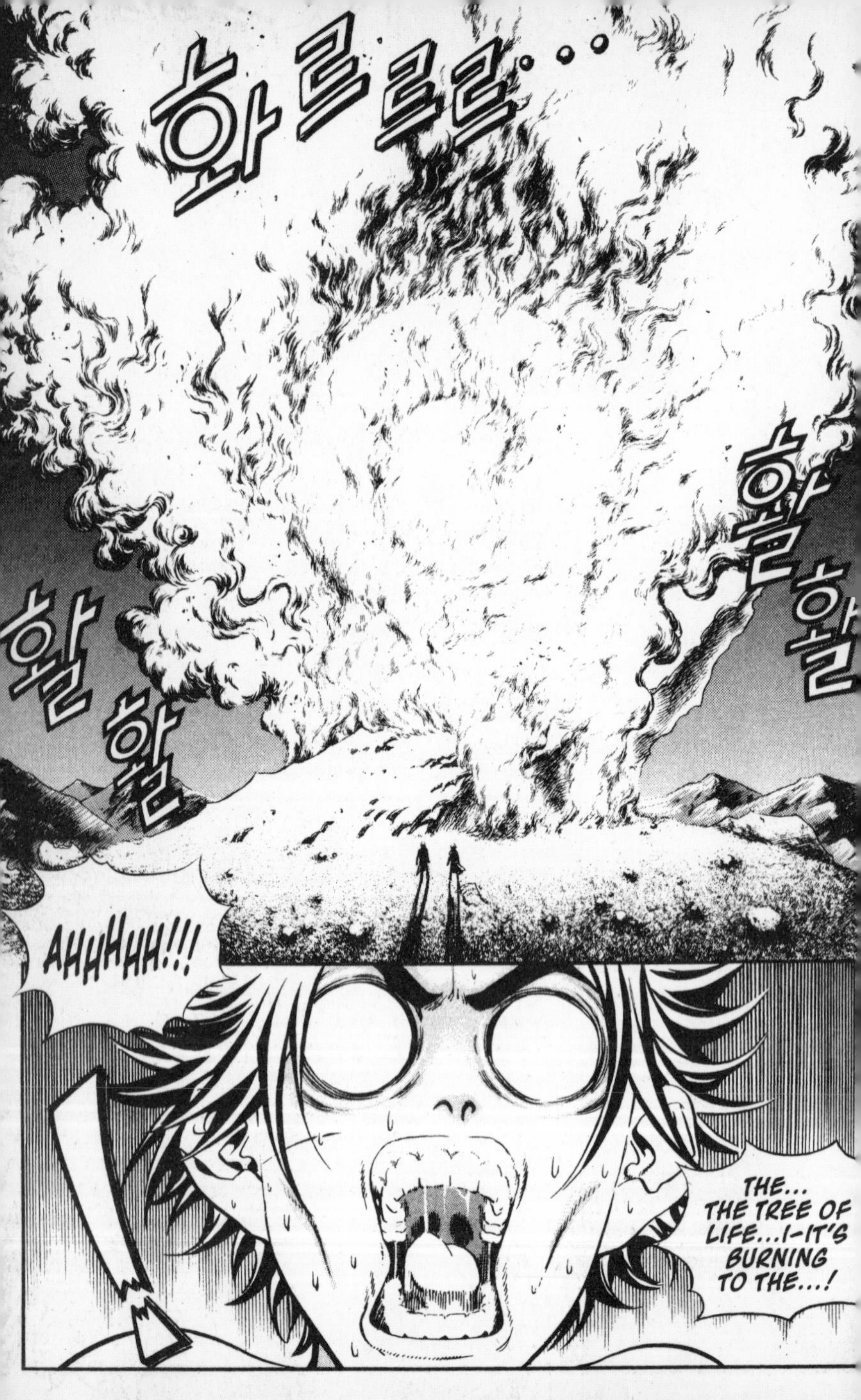
화르르...
활활
활활
AHHHHH!!!
THE... THE TREE OF LIFE...I-IT'S BURNING TO THE...!

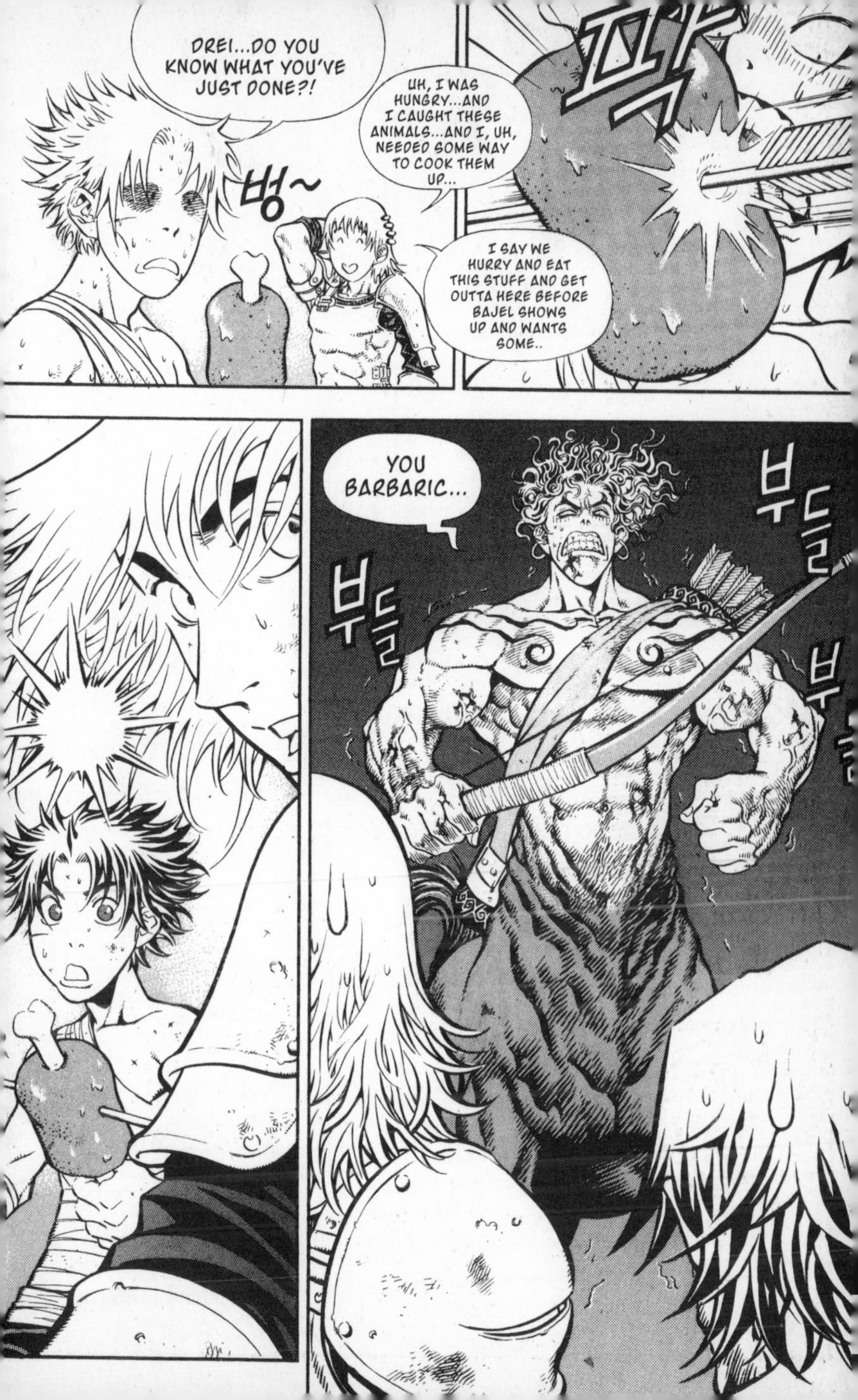
DREI...DO YOU KNOW WHAT YOU'VE JUST DONE?!
병~
UH, I WAS HUNGRY...AND I CAUGHT THESE ANIMALS...AND I, UH, NEEDED SOME WAY TO COOK THEM UP...
I SAY WE HURRY AND EAT THIS STUFF AND GET OUTTA HERE BEFORE BAJEL SHOWS UP AND WANTS SOME..
YOU BARBARIC...
부들
부들

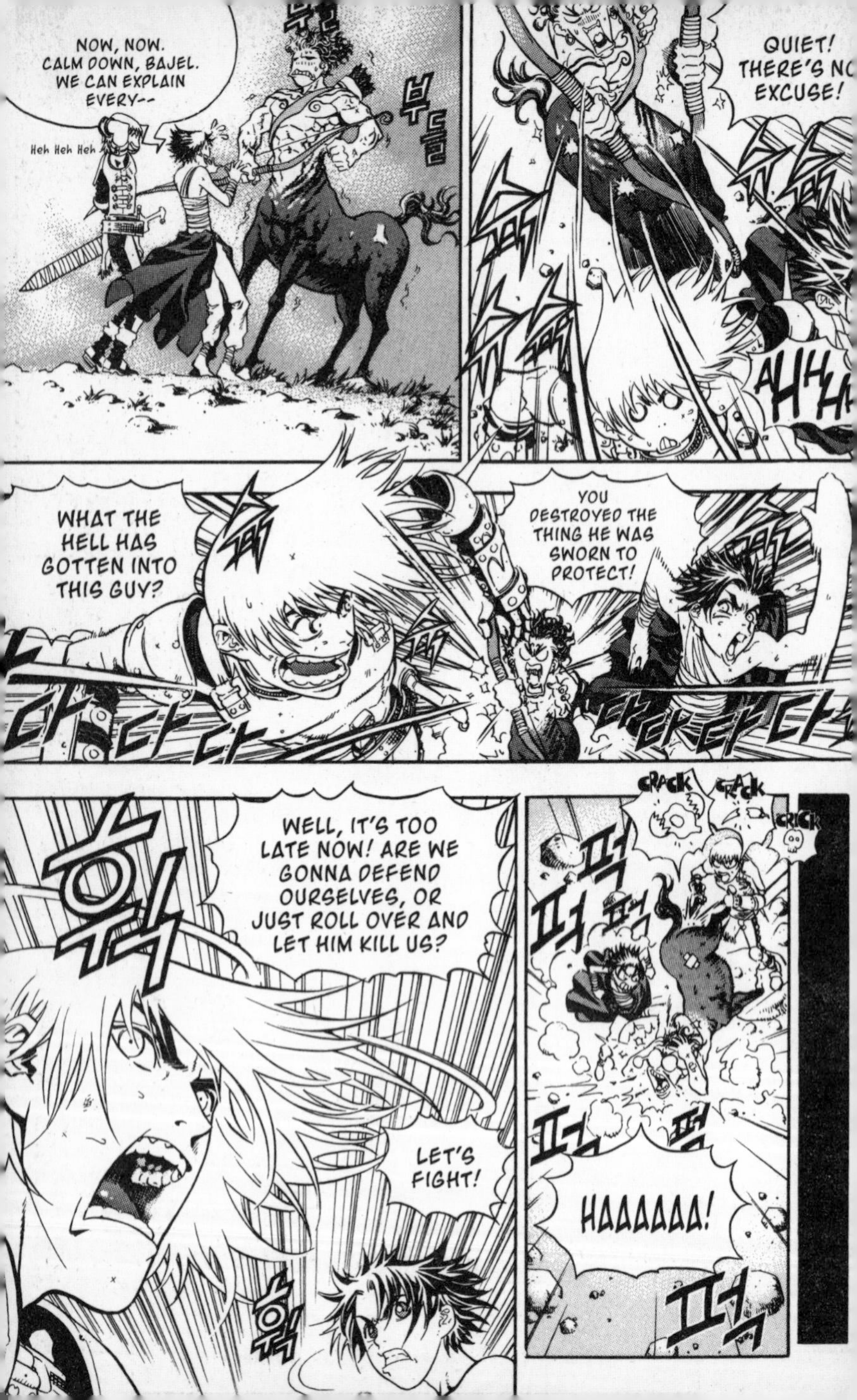
NOW, NOW. CALM DOWN, BAJEL. WE CAN EXPLAIN EVERY--
Heh Heh Heh
QUIET! THERE'S NO EXCUSE!
AHHH
WHAT THE HELL HAS GOTTEN INTO THIS GUY?
YOU DESTROYED THE THING HE WAS SWORN TO PROTECT!
WELL, IT'S TOO LATE NOW! ARE WE GONNA DEFEND OURSELVES, OR JUST ROLL OVER AND LET HIM KILL US?
LET'S FIGHT!
CRACK
CRACK
CRICK
HAAAAAA!

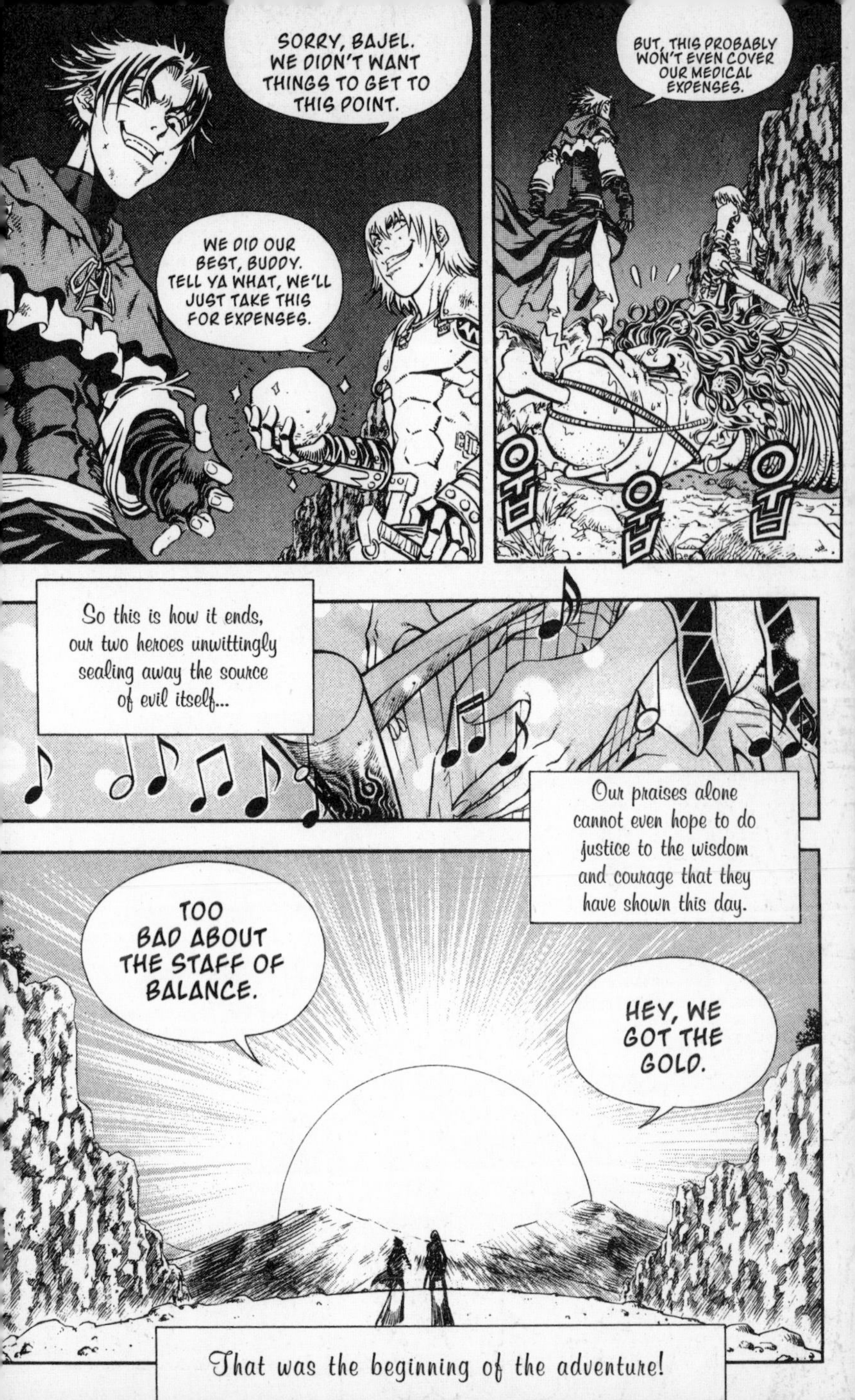
SORRY, BAJEL. WE DIDN'T WANT THINGS TO GET TO THIS POINT.
WE DID OUR BEST, BUDDY. TELL YA WHAT, WE'LL JUST TAKE THIS FOR EXPENSES.
BUT, THIS PROBABLY WON'T EVEN COVER OUR MEDICAL EXPENSES.
So this is how it ends, our two heroes unwittingly sealing away the source of evil itself...
Our praises alone cannot even hope to do justice to the wisdom and courage that they have shown this day.
TOO BAD ABOUT THE STAFF OF BALANCE.
HEY, WE GOT THE GOLD.
That was the beginning of the adventure!

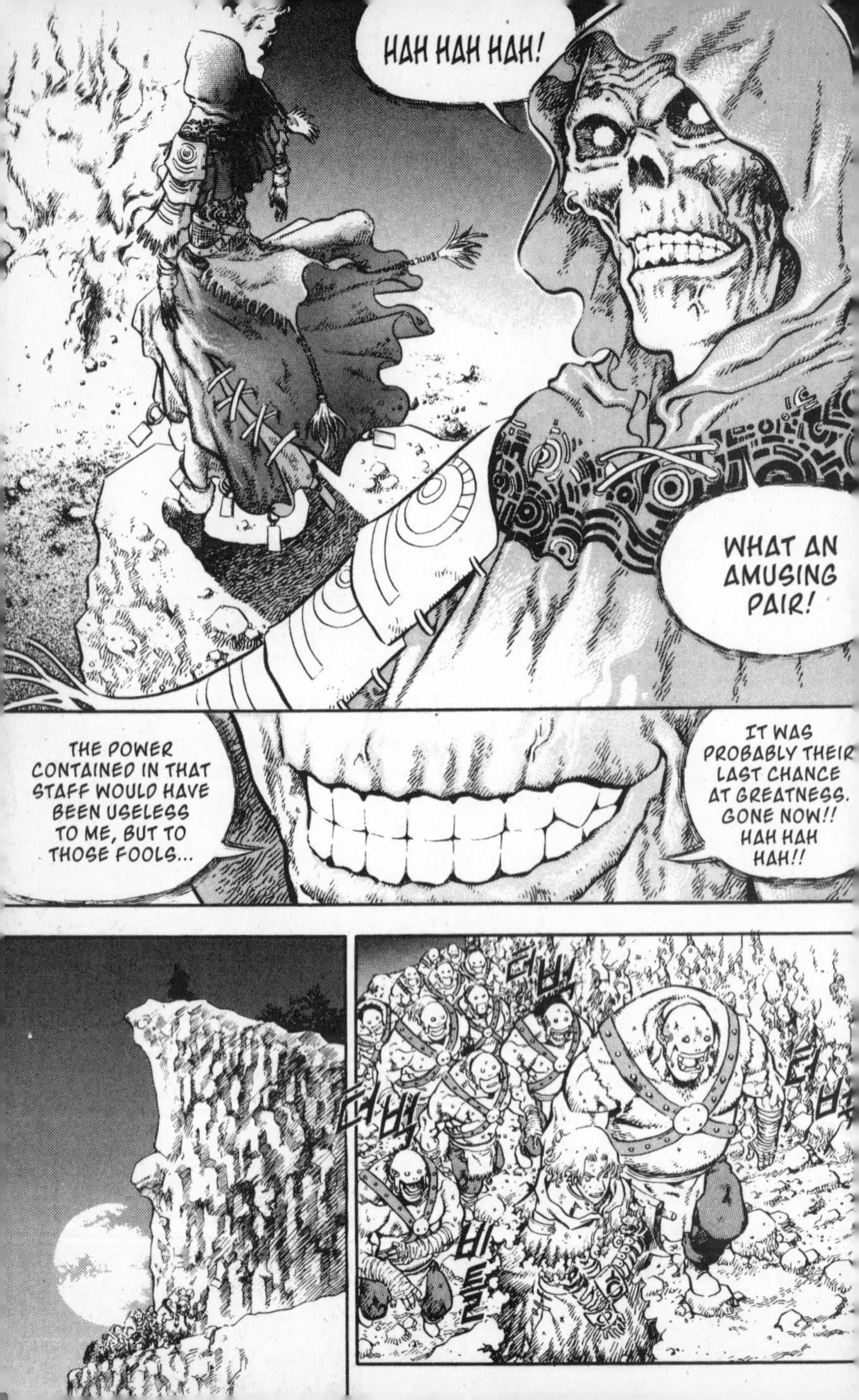
HAH HAH HAH!
WHAT AN AMUSING PAIR!
THE POWER CONTAINED IN THAT STAFF WOULD HAVE BEEN USELESS TO ME, BUT TO THOSE FOOLS...
IT WAS PROBABLY THEIR LAST CHANCE AT GREATNESS. GONE NOW!! HAH HAH HAH!!

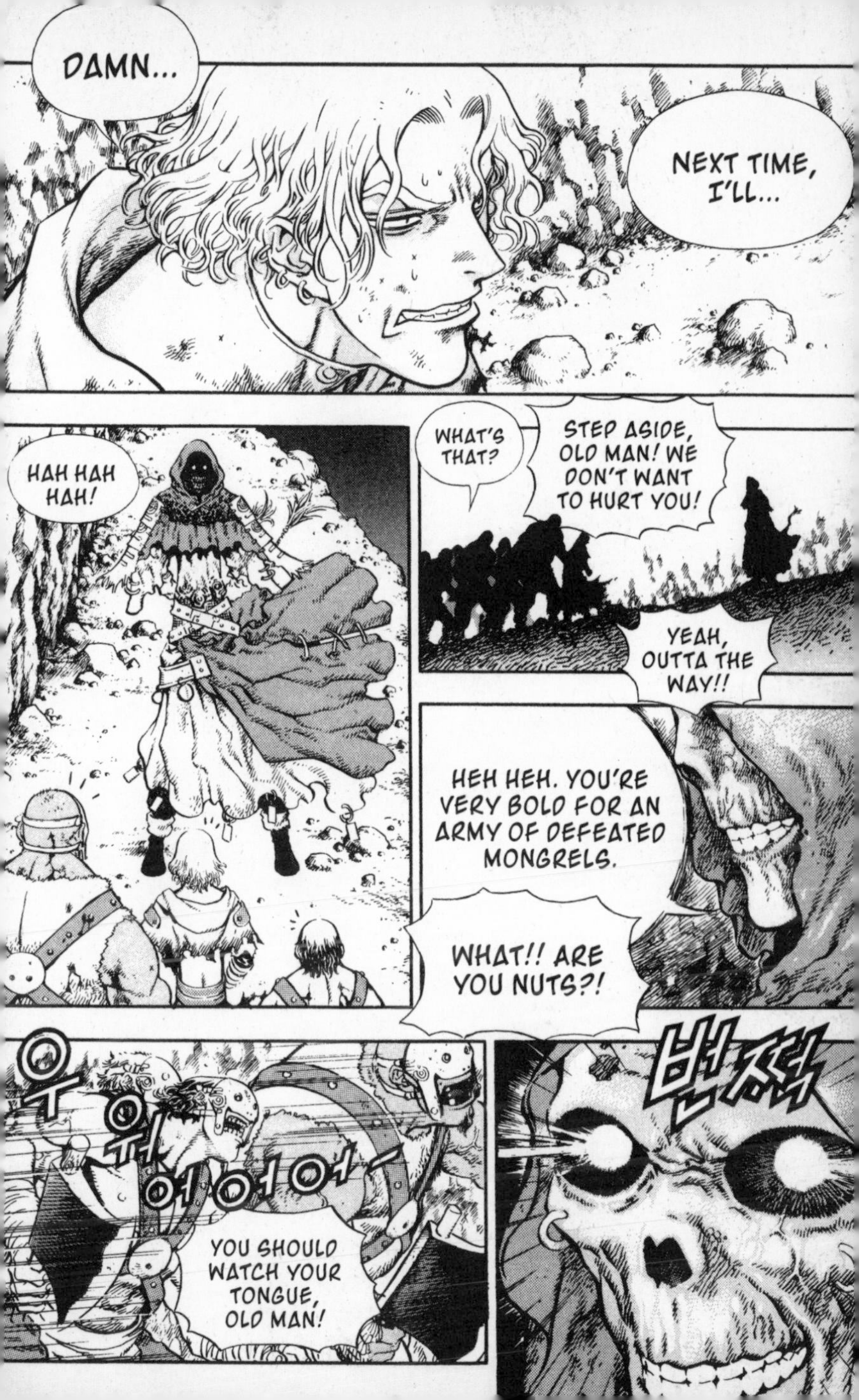
DAMN...
NEXT TIME, I'LL...
HAH HAH HAH!
WHAT'S THAT?
STEP ASIDE, OLD MAN! WE DON'T WANT TO HURT YOU!
YEAH, OUTTA THE WAY!!
HEH HEH. YOU'RE VERY BOLD FOR AN ARMY OF DEFEATED MONGRELS.
WHAT!! ARE YOU NUTS?!
우워어어어어—
YOU SHOULD WATCH YOUR TONGUE, OLD MAN!
번쩍

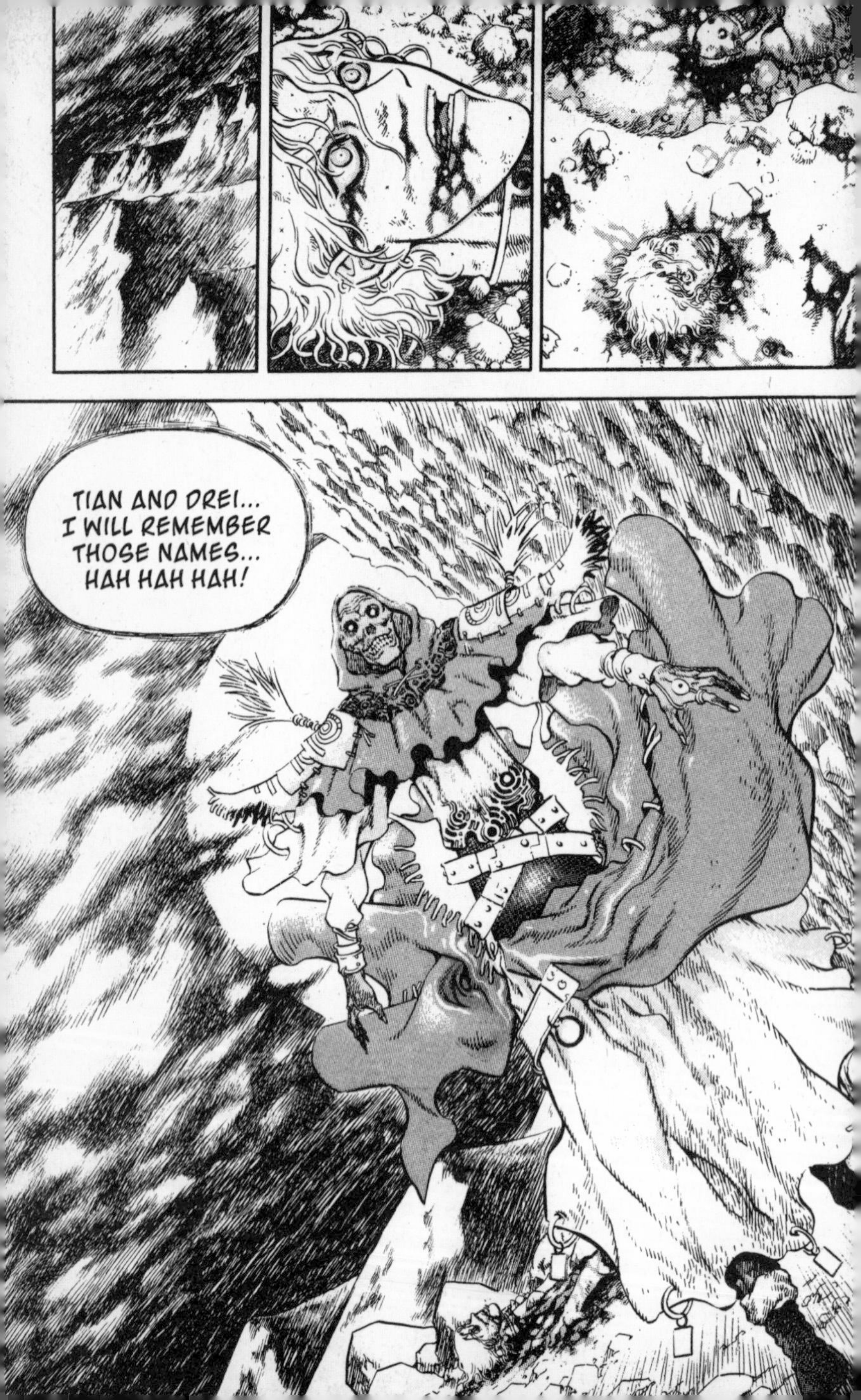
TIAN AND DREI...
I WILL REMEMBER
THOSE NAMES...
HAH HAH HAH!

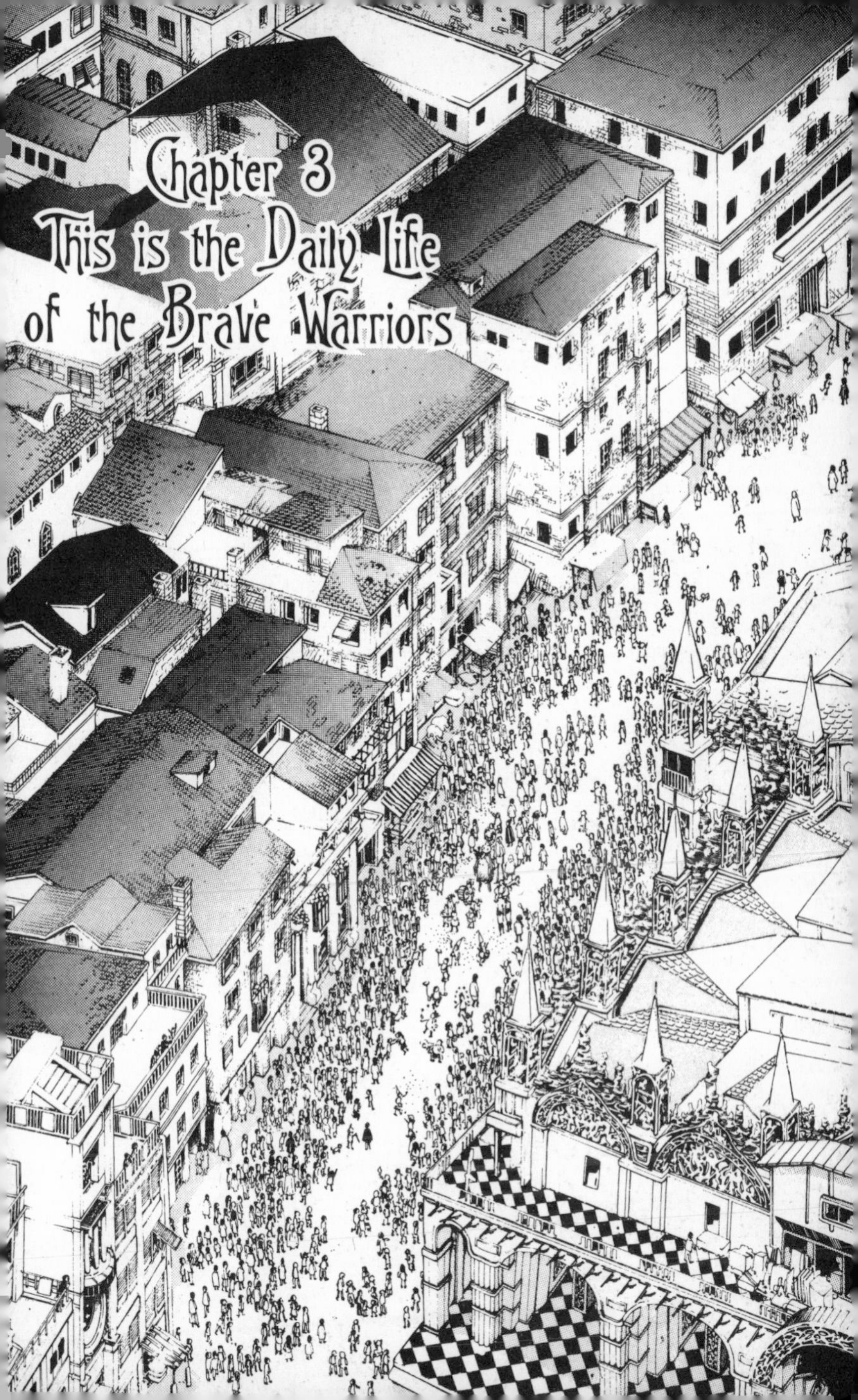
Chapter 3
This is the Daily Life
of the Brave Warriors

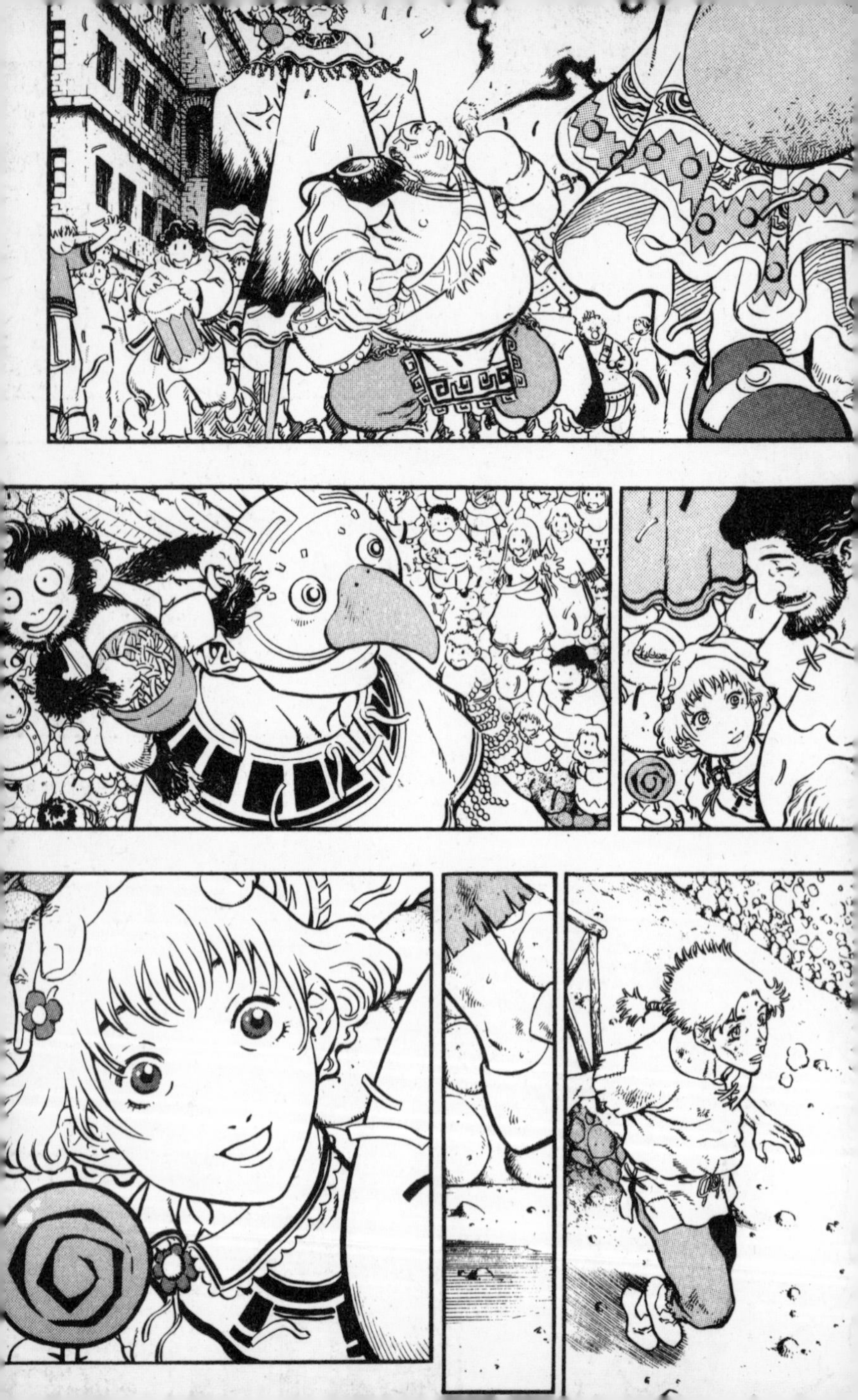

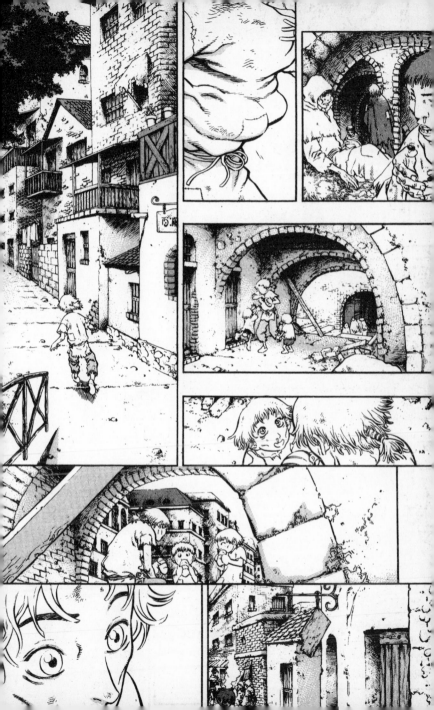

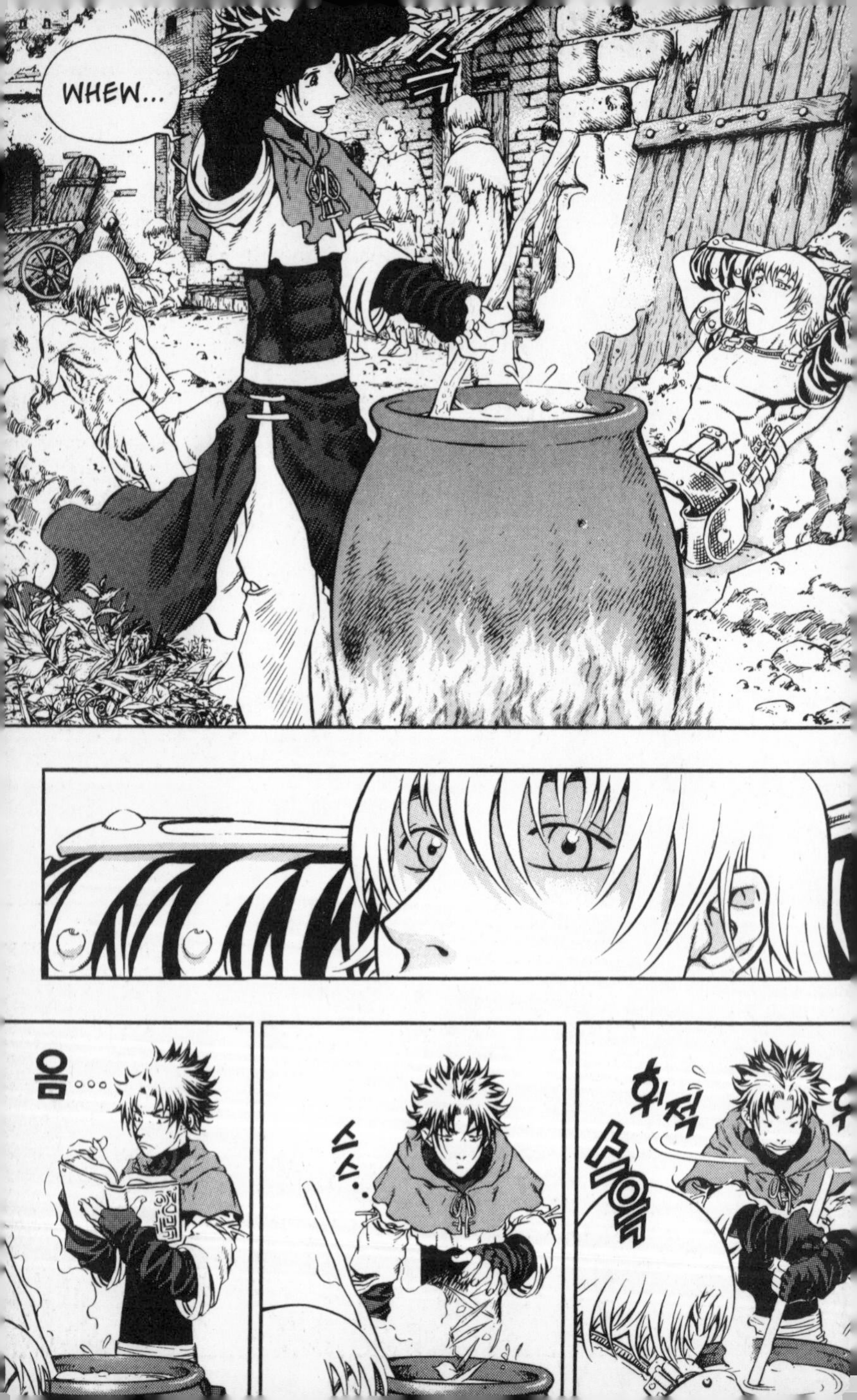
WHEW...
음...
휘적

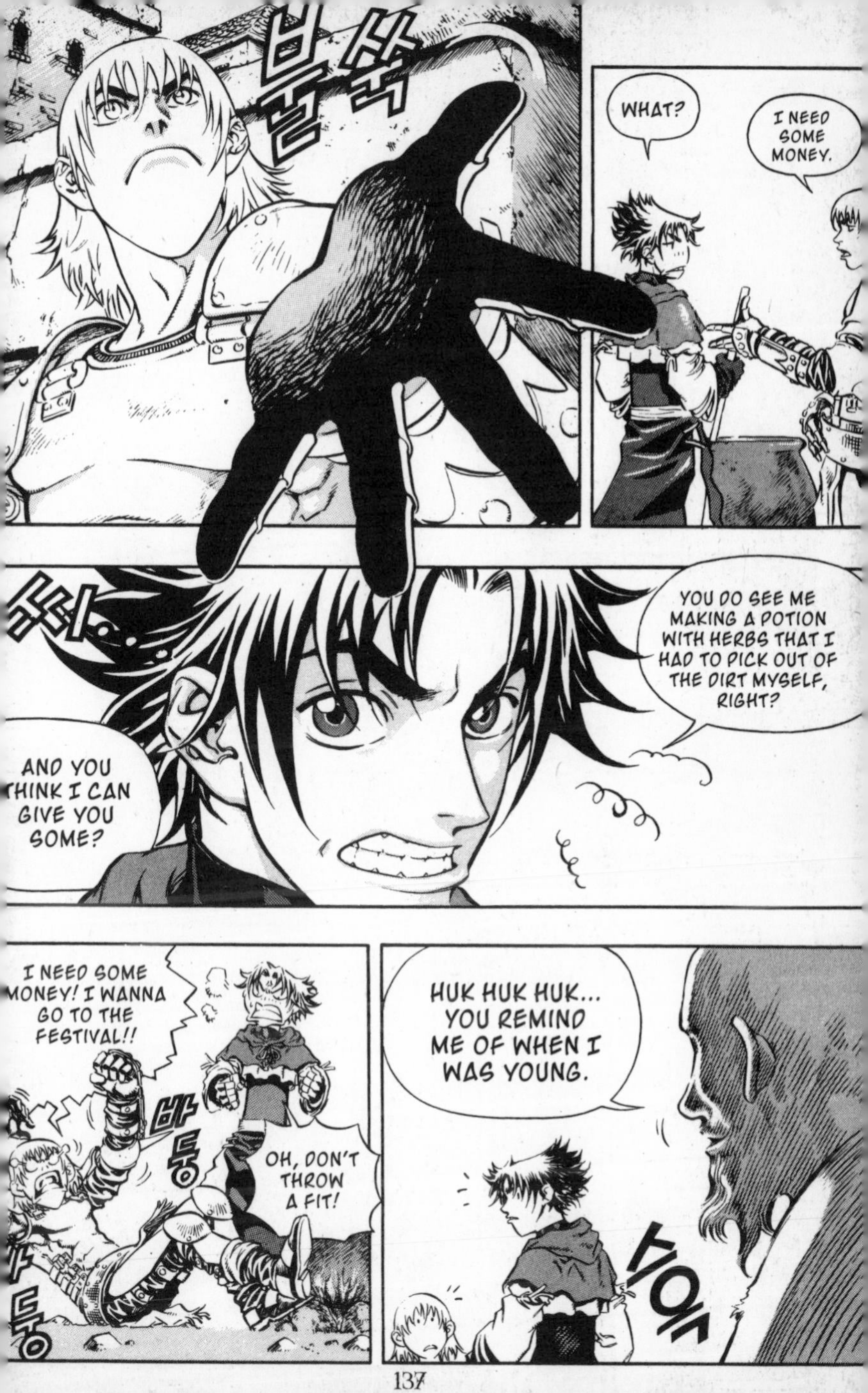
WHAT?
I NEED SOME MONEY.
YOU DO SEE ME MAKING A POTION WITH HERBS THAT I HAD TO PICK OUT OF THE DIRT MYSELF, RIGHT?
AND YOU THINK I CAN GIVE YOU SOME?
I NEED SOME MONEY! I WANNA GO TO THE FESTIVAL!!
OH, DON'T THROW A FIT!
HUK HUK HUK... YOU REMIND ME OF WHEN I WAS YOUNG.

HUK HUK HUK...

LOOKING INTO A DARK FUTURE.

TAKE THAT BACK, OLD MAN!

EEESHH...

I-I'M SORRY... PLEASE FORGIVE ME!

H-HERE! TAKE THIS! BREAD! IT LOOKS A LITTLE OLD, BUT I BOUGHT IT JUST THREE DAYS AGO.

Hmph!

Hmph! Hmph!

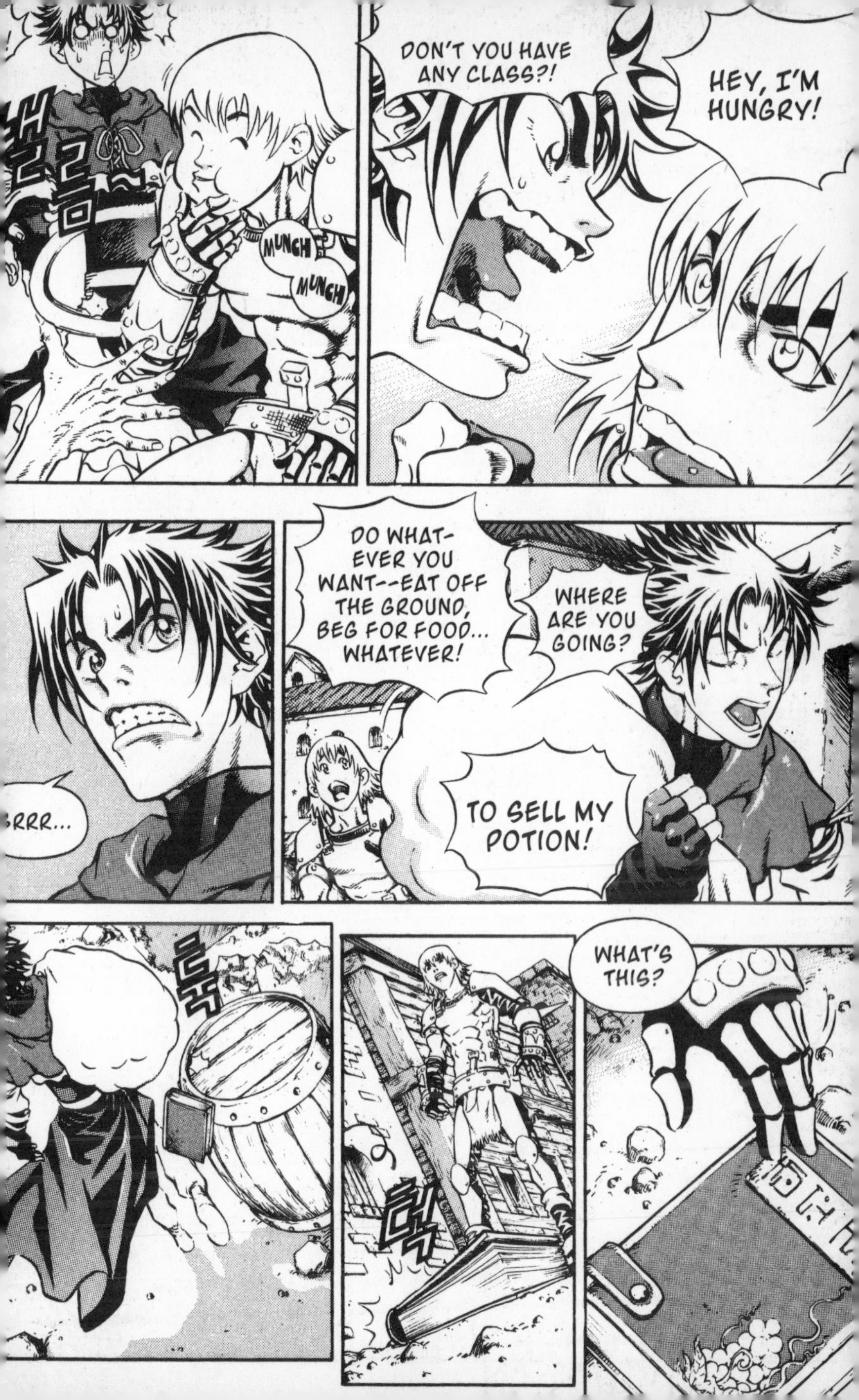
MUNCH
MUNCH
DON'T YOU HAVE ANY CLASS?!
HEY, I'M HUNGRY!
RRR...
DO WHAT-EVER YOU WANT--EAT OFF THE GROUND, BEG FOR FOOD... WHATEVER!
WHERE ARE YOU GOING?
TO SELL MY POTION!
WHAT'S THIS?

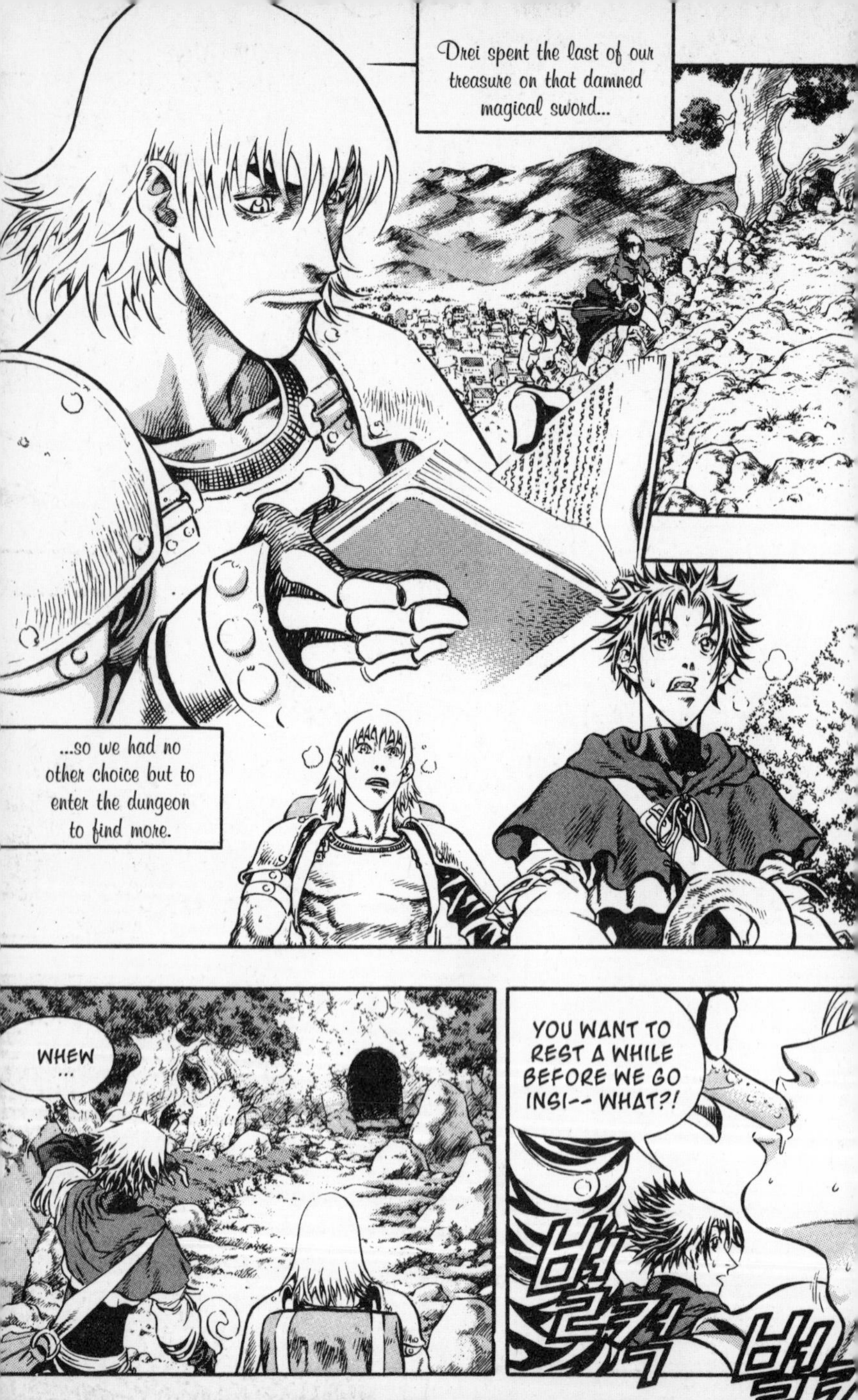
Drei spent the last of our treasure on that damned magical sword...
...so we had no other choice but to enter the dungeon to find more.
WHEW ...
YOU WANT TO REST A WHILE BEFORE WE GO INSI-- WHAT?!

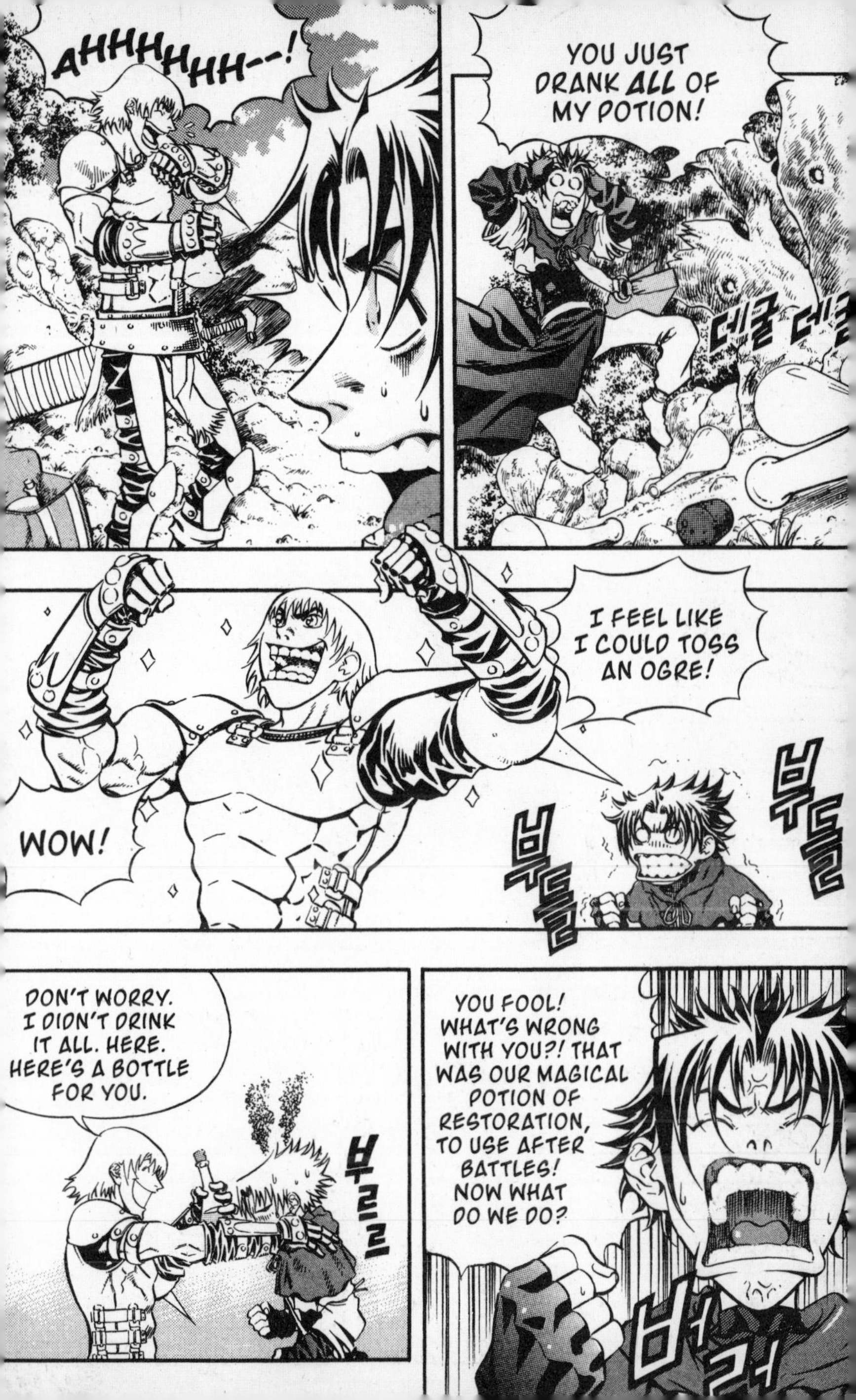
AHHHHHHH--!
YOU JUST DRANK ALL OF MY POTION!
I FEEL LIKE I COULD TOSS AN OGRE!
WOW!
부들
부들
DON'T WORRY. I DIDN'T DRINK IT ALL. HERE. HERE'S A BOTTLE FOR YOU.
YOU FOOL! WHAT'S WRONG WITH YOU?! THAT WAS OUR MAGICAL POTION OF RESTORATION, TO USE AFTER BATTLES! NOW WHAT DO WE DO?

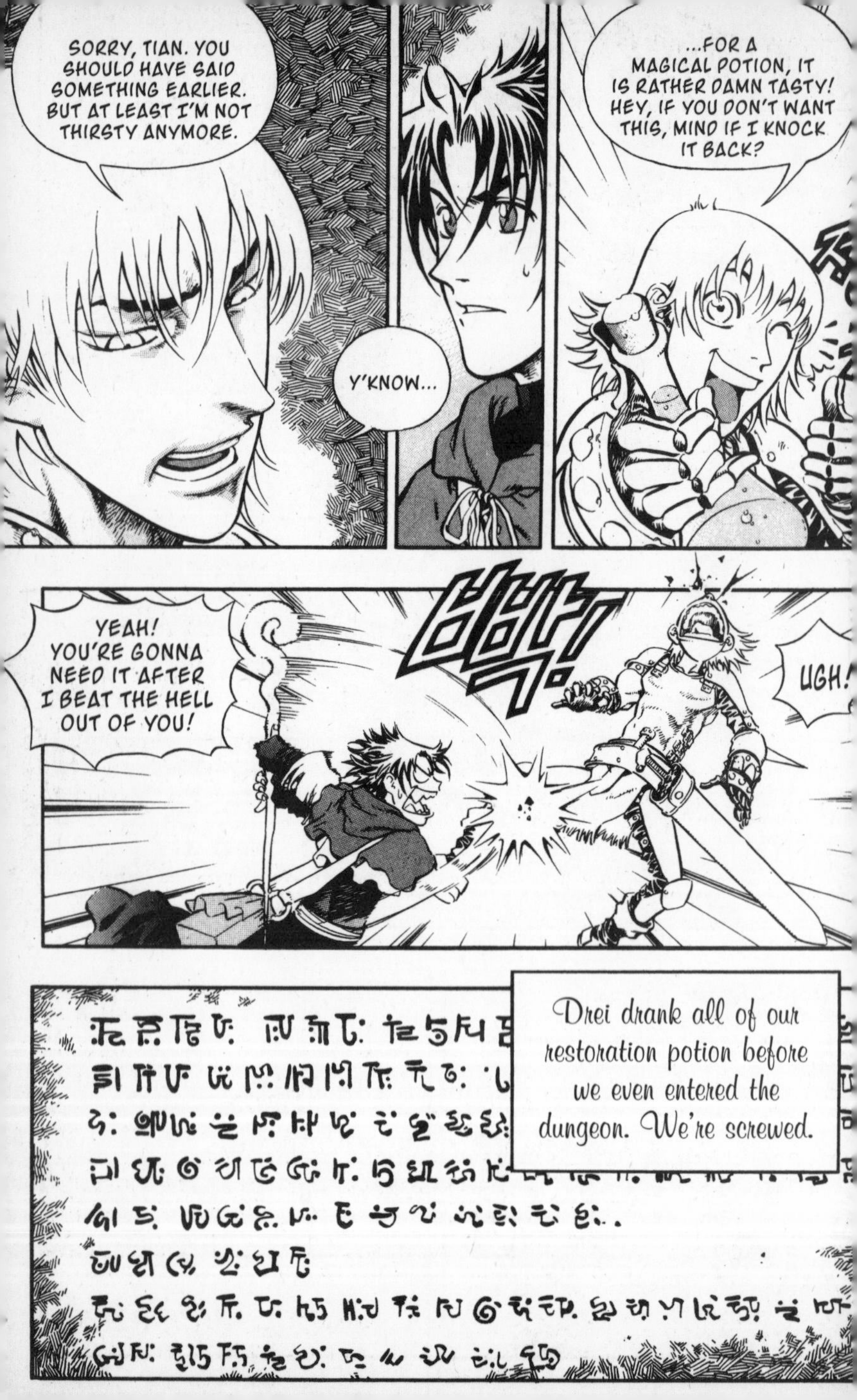
SORRY, TIAN. YOU SHOULD HAVE SAID SOMETHING EARLIER. BUT AT LEAST I'M NOT THIRSTY ANYMORE.
Y'KNOW...
...FOR A MAGICAL POTION, IT IS RATHER DAMN TASTY! HEY, IF YOU DON'T WANT THIS, MIND IF I KNOCK IT BACK?
YEAH! YOU'RE GONNA NEED IT AFTER I BEAT THE HELL OUT OF YOU!
UGH!
Drei drank all of our restoration potion before we even entered the dungeon. We're screwed.

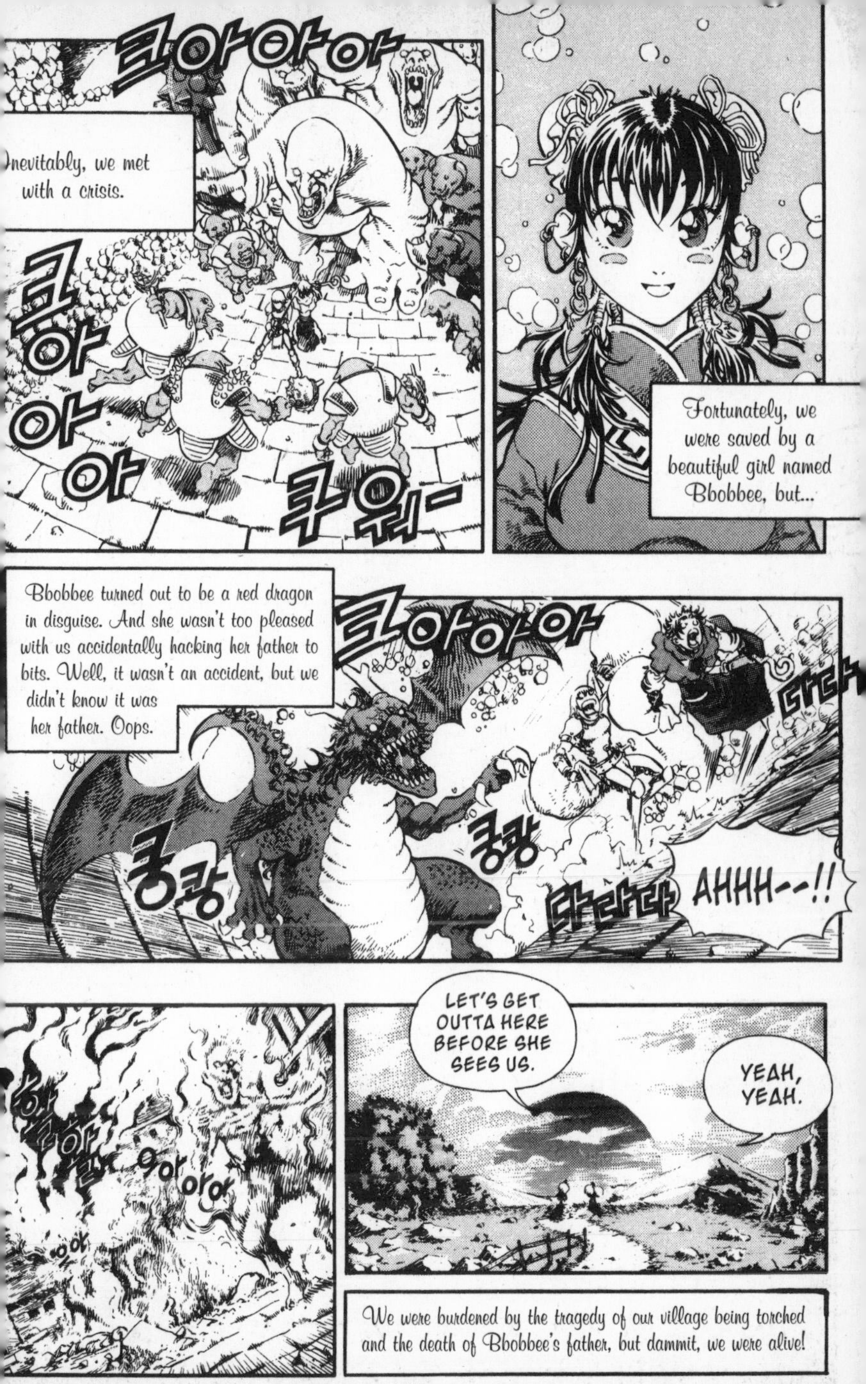
Inevitably, we met with a crisis.
쿠워-
Fortunately, we were saved by a beautiful girl named Bbobbee, but...
Bbobbee turned out to be a red dragon in disguise. And she wasn't too pleased with us accidentally hacking her father to bits. Well, it wasn't an accident, but we didn't know it was her father. Oops.
쿵쾅
쿵쾅
AHHH--!!
LET'S GET OUTTA HERE BEFORE SHE SEES US.
YEAH, YEAH.
We were burdened by the tragedy of our village being torched and the death of Bbobbee's father, but dammit, we were alive!

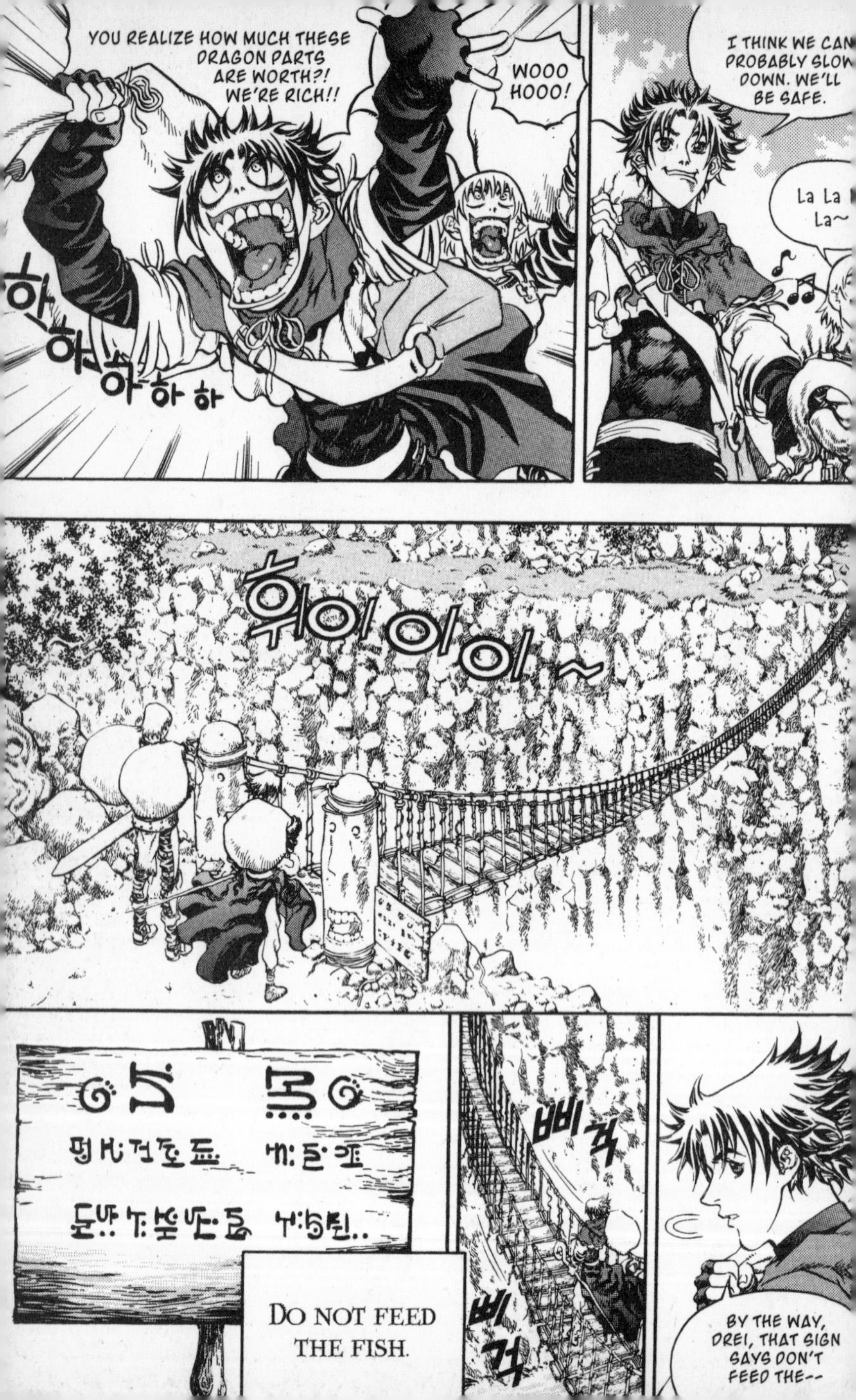
YOU REALIZE HOW MUCH THESE DRAGON PARTS ARE WORTH?! WE'RE RICH!!
WOOO HOOO!
하하하하하
I THINK WE CAN PROBABLY SLOW DOWN. WE'LL BE SAFE.
La La
La~
휘이이이~
DO NOT FEED THE FISH.
삐걱
삐걱
BY THE WAY, DREI, THAT SIGN SAYS DON'T FEED THE--

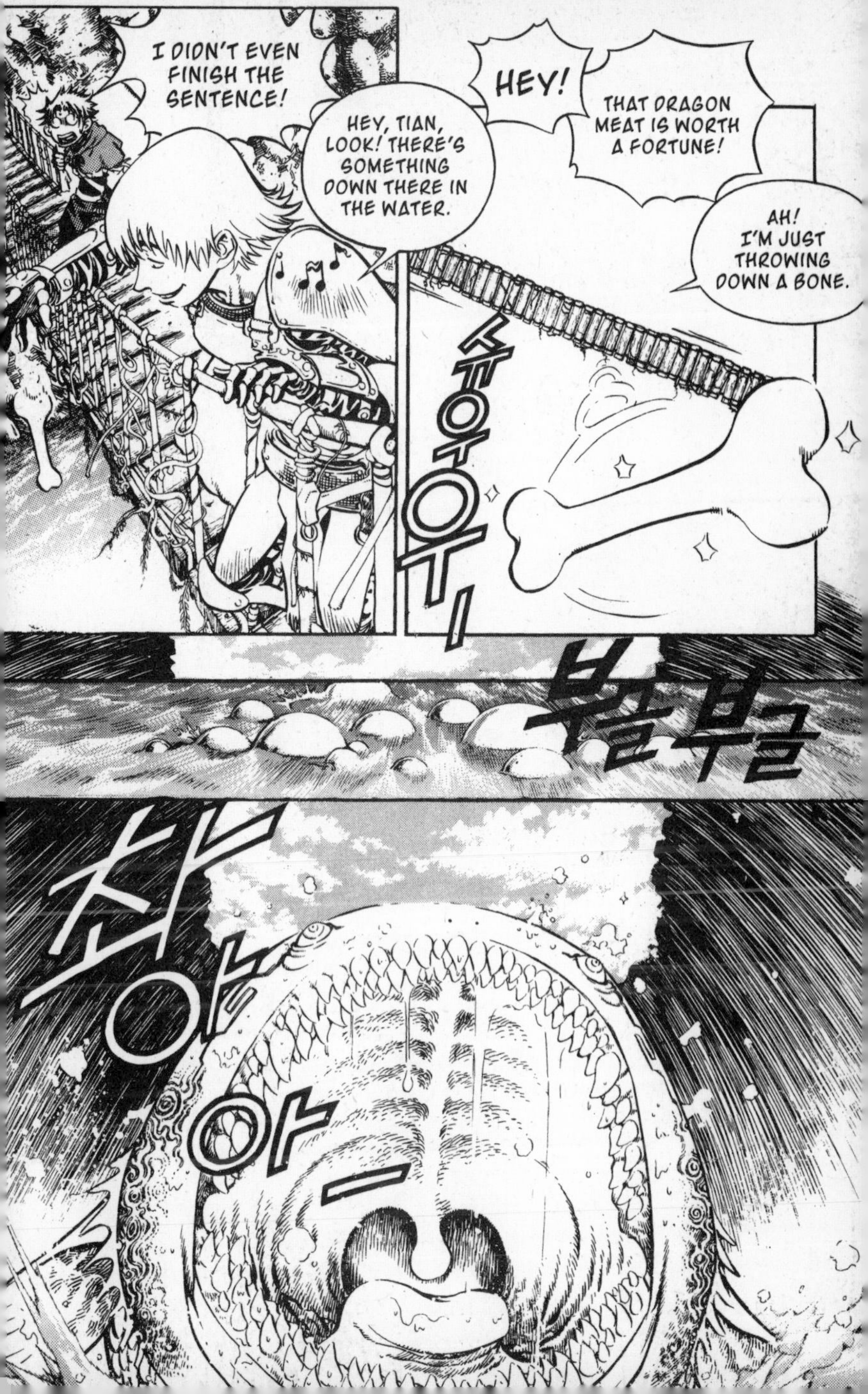
I DIDN'T EVEN FINISH THE SENTENCE!
HEY, TIAN, LOOK! THERE'S SOMETHING DOWN THERE IN THE WATER.
HEY!
THAT DRAGON MEAT IS WORTH A FORTUNE!
AH! I'M JUST THROWING DOWN A BONE.
부글부글

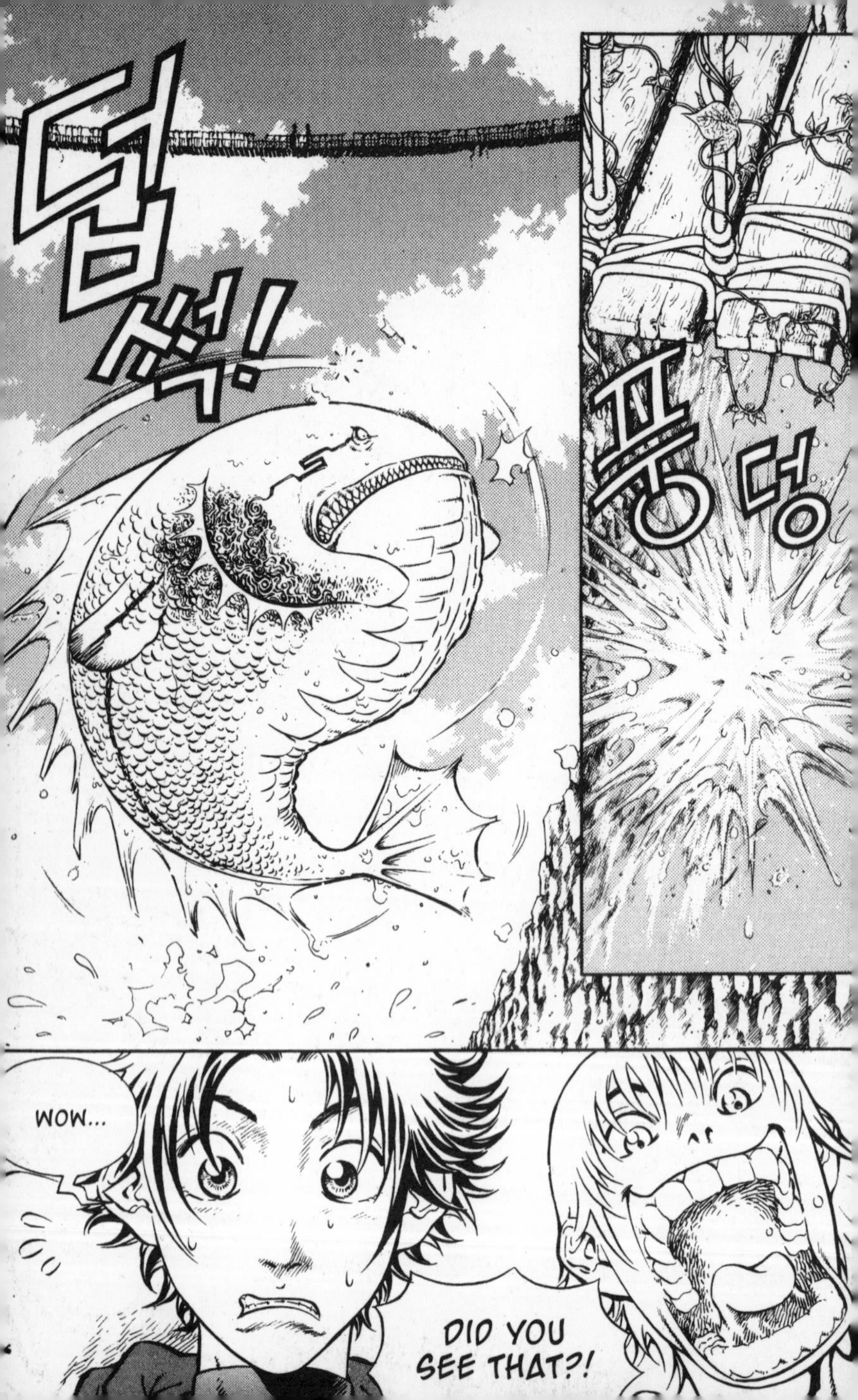

덥썩!
퐁덩
WOW...
DID YOU SEE THAT?!

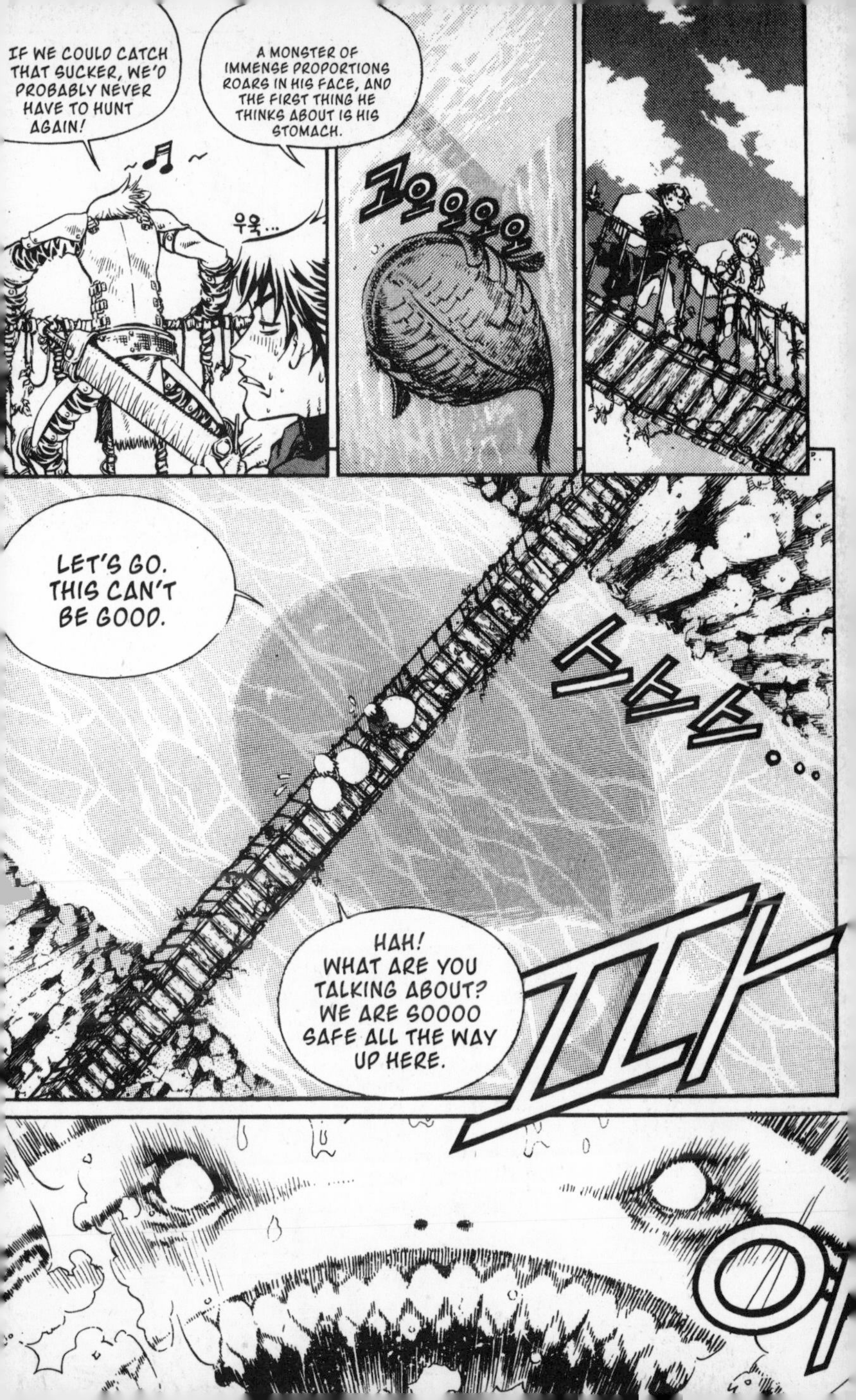
IF WE COULD CATCH THAT SUCKER, WE'D PROBABLY NEVER HAVE TO HUNT AGAIN!
A MONSTER OF IMMENSE PROPORTIONS ROARS IN HIS FACE, AND THE FIRST THING HE THINKS ABOUT IS HIS STOMACH.
우웃...
LET'S GO. THIS CAN'T BE GOOD.
HAH! WHAT ARE YOU TALKING ABOUT? WE ARE SOOOO SAFE ALL THE WAY UP HERE.

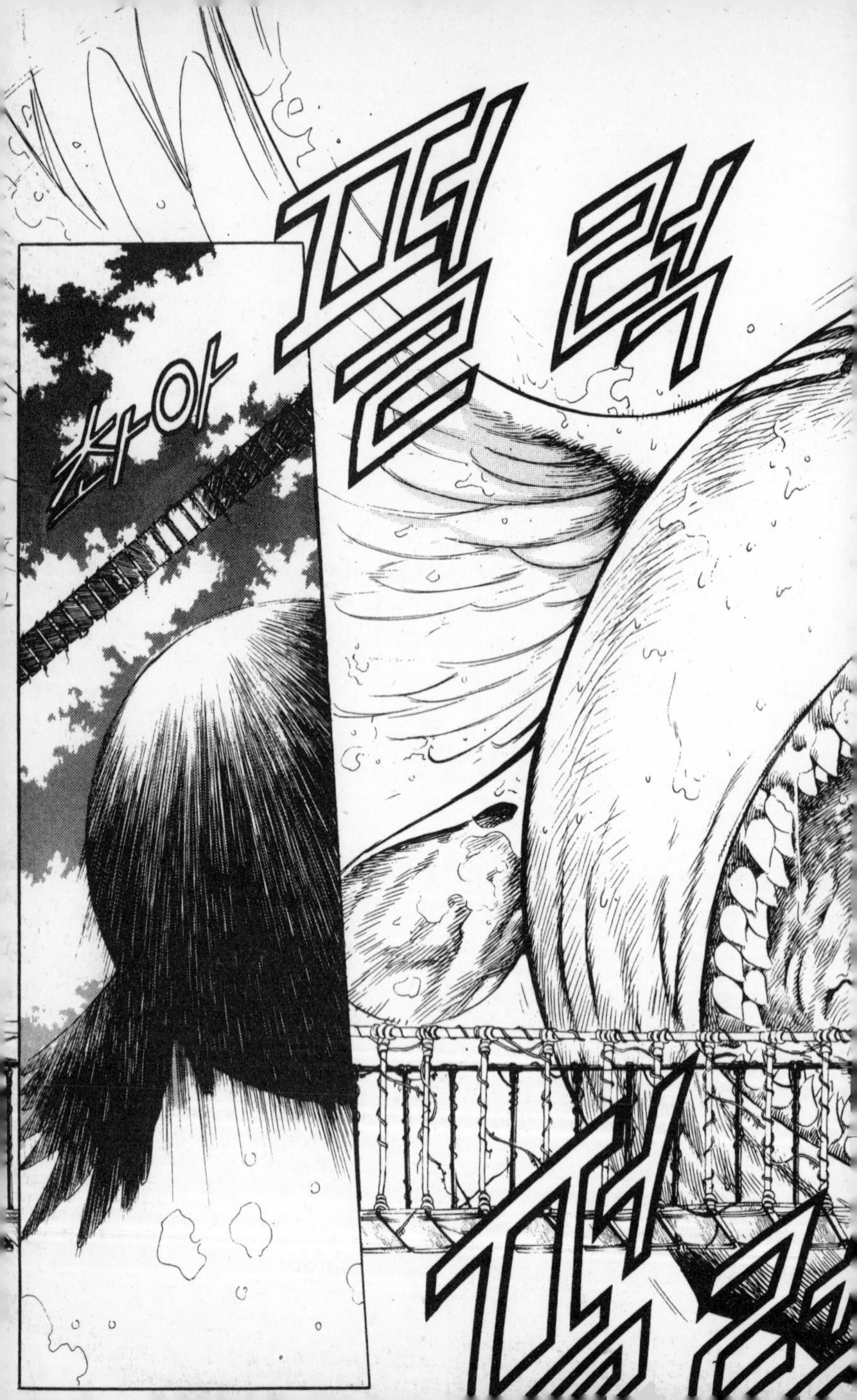

껄럭
촤아

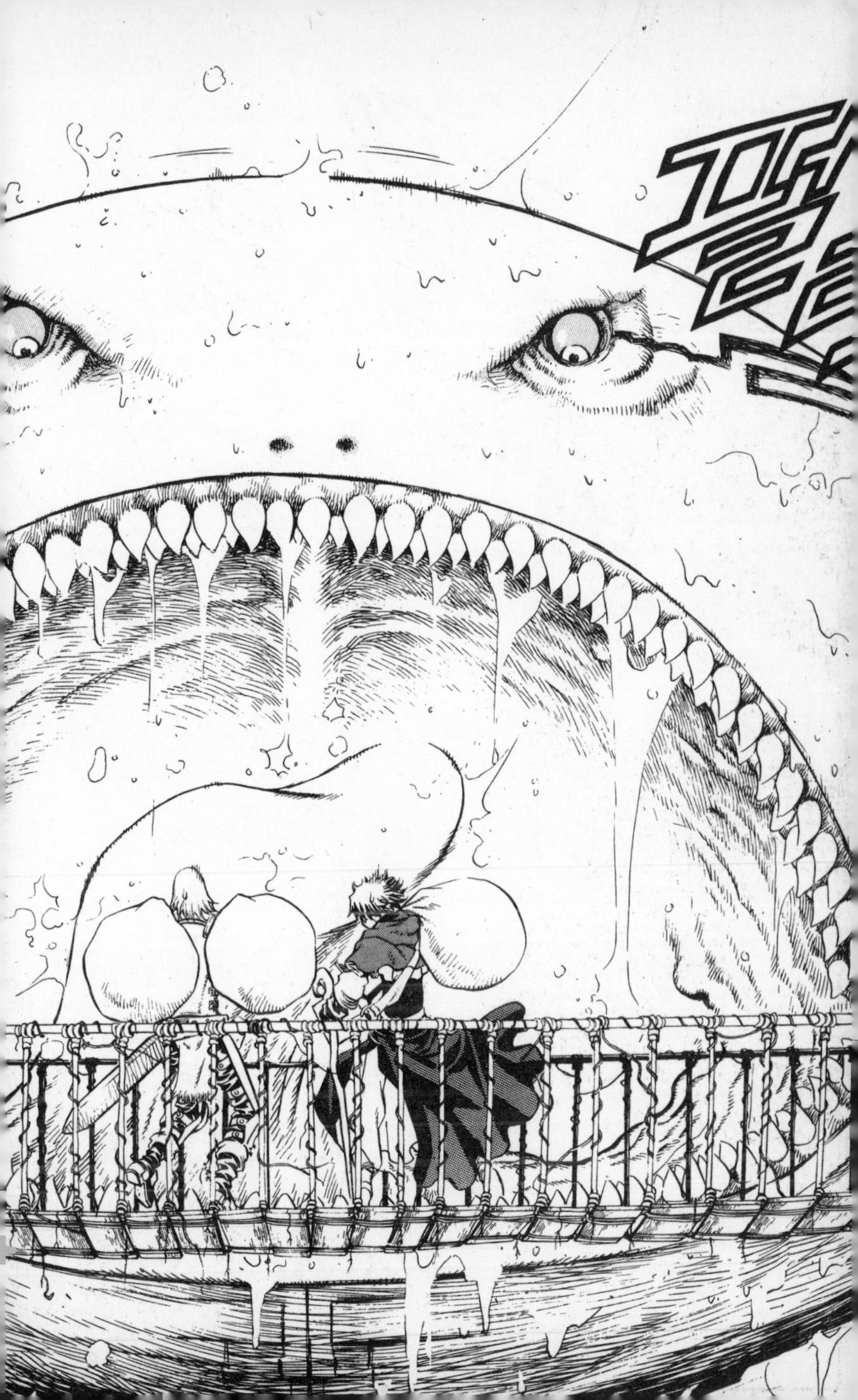

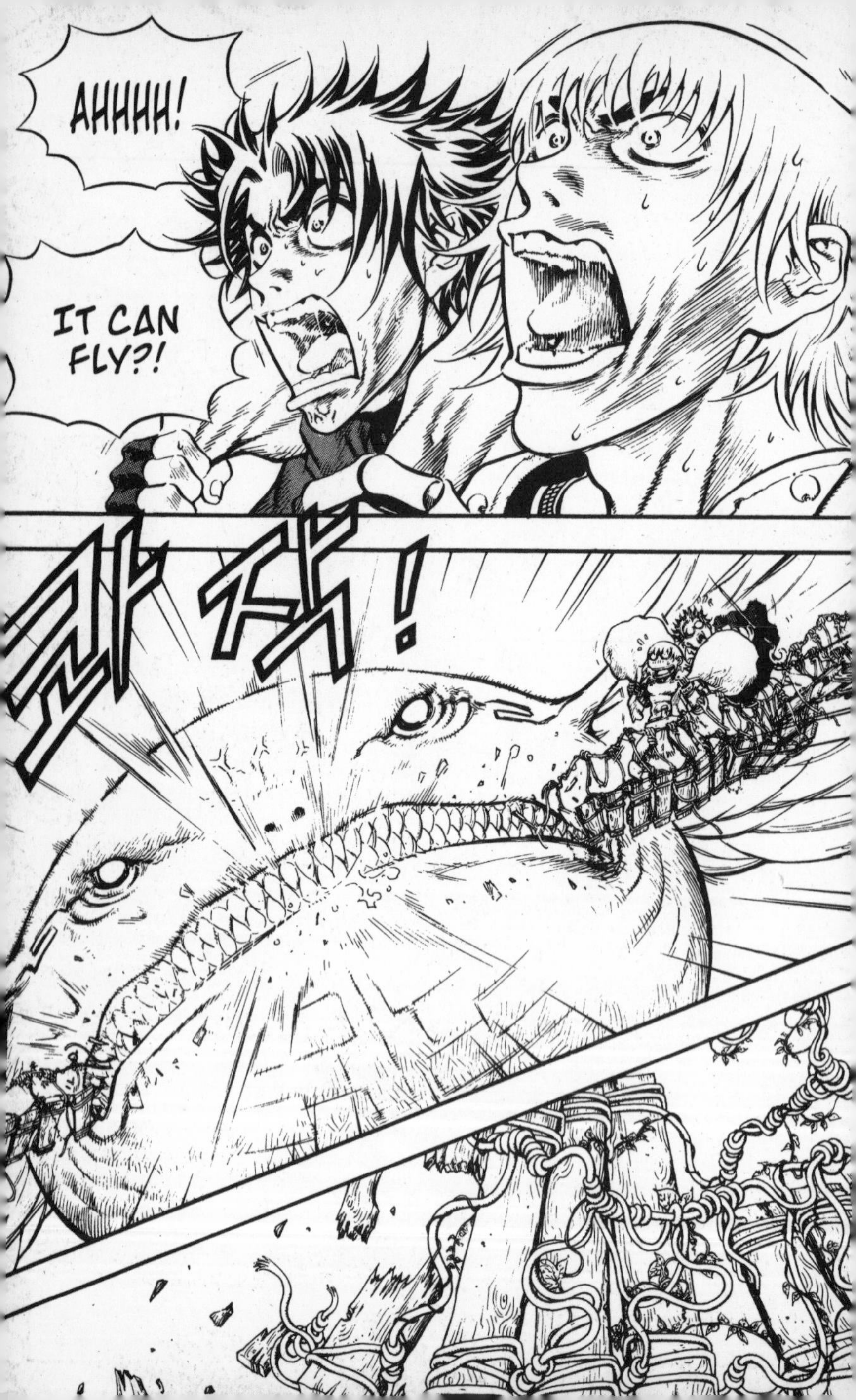
AHHHH!
IT CAN FLY?!

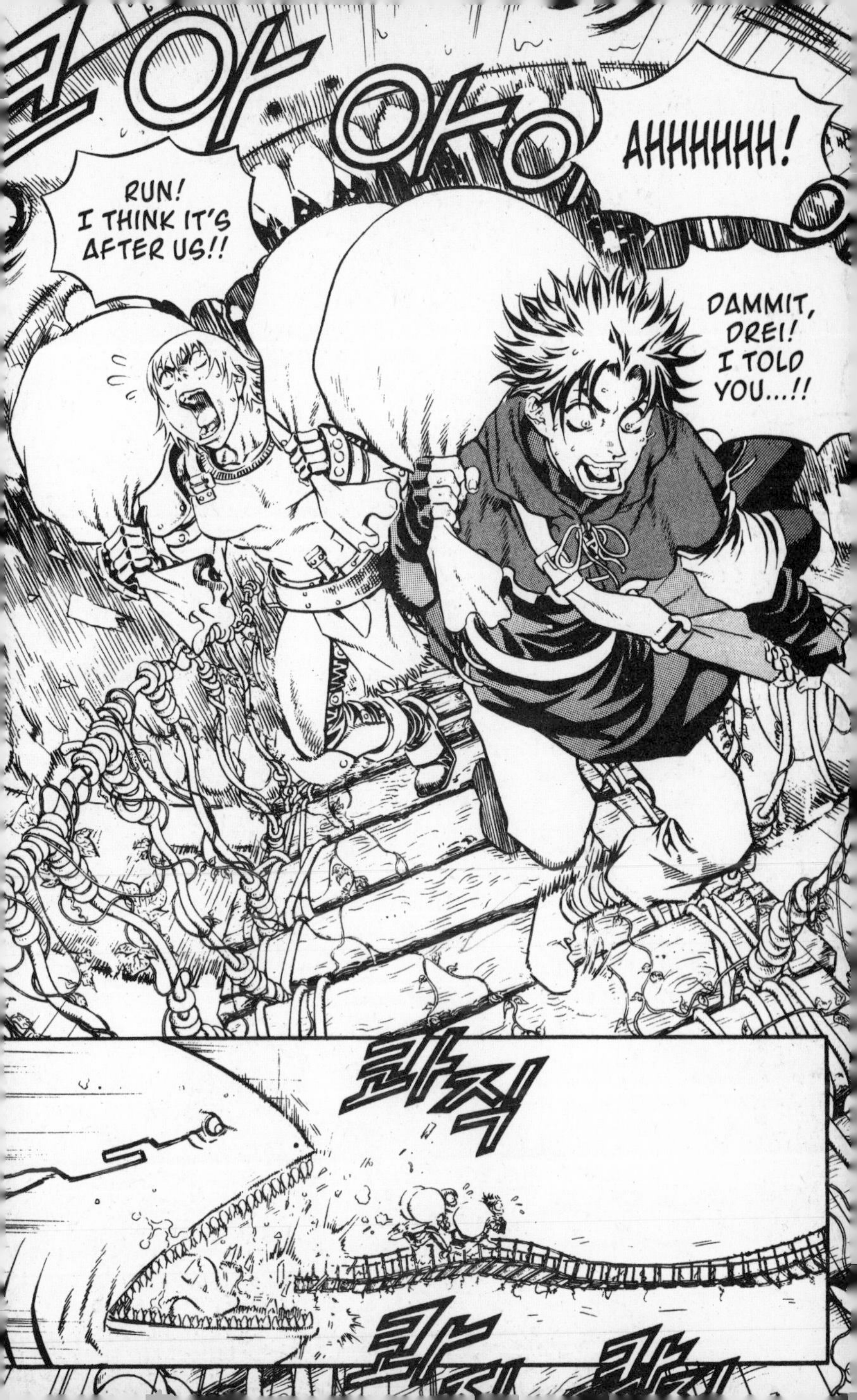
RUN! I THINK IT'S AFTER US!!
AHHHHHH!
DAMMIT, DREI! I TOLD YOU...!!

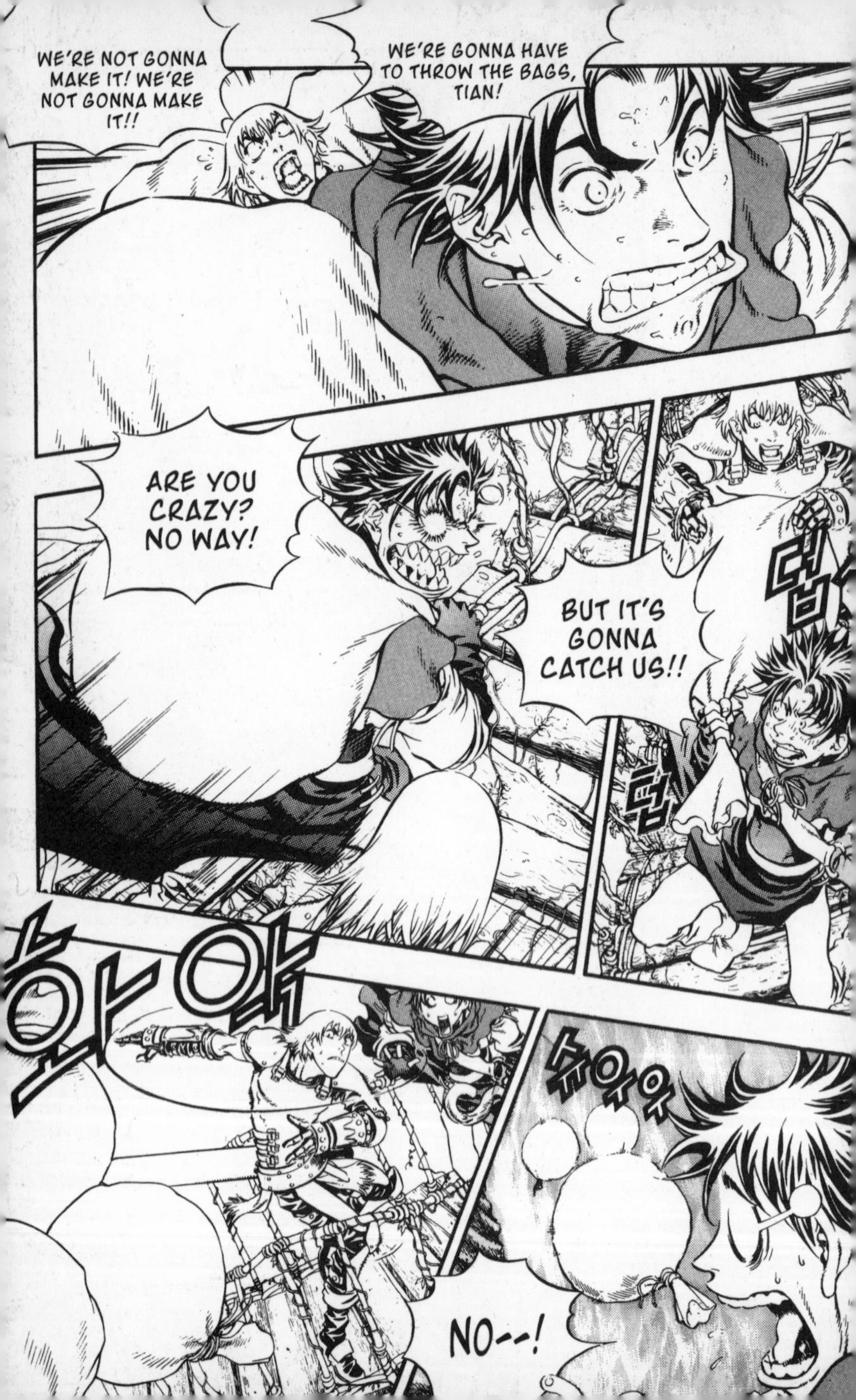
WE'RE NOT GONNA MAKE IT! WE'RE NOT GONNA MAKE IT!!
WE'RE GONNA HAVE TO THROW THE BAGS, TIAN!
ARE YOU CRAZY? NO WAY!
BUT IT'S GONNA CATCH US!!
NO--!

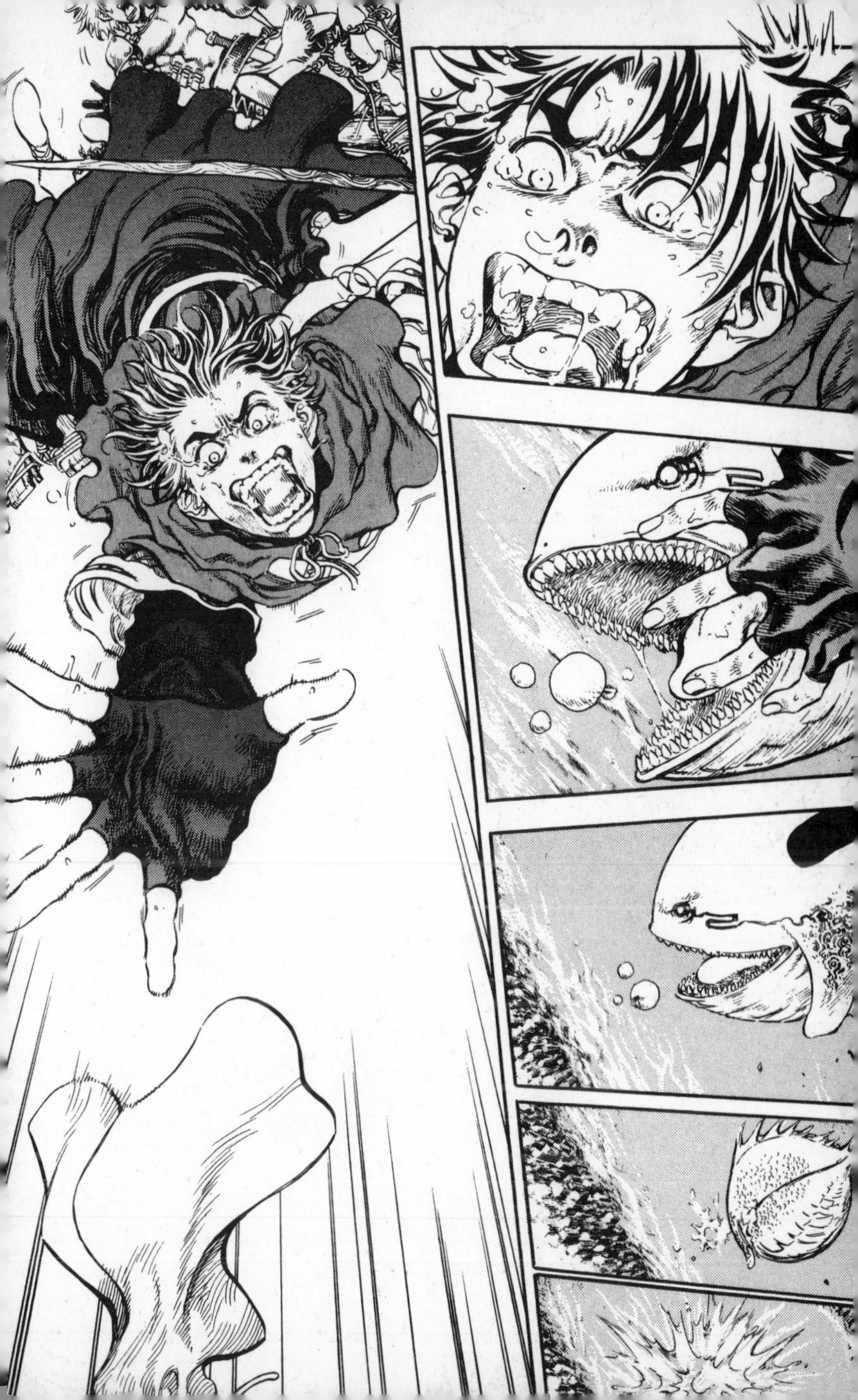

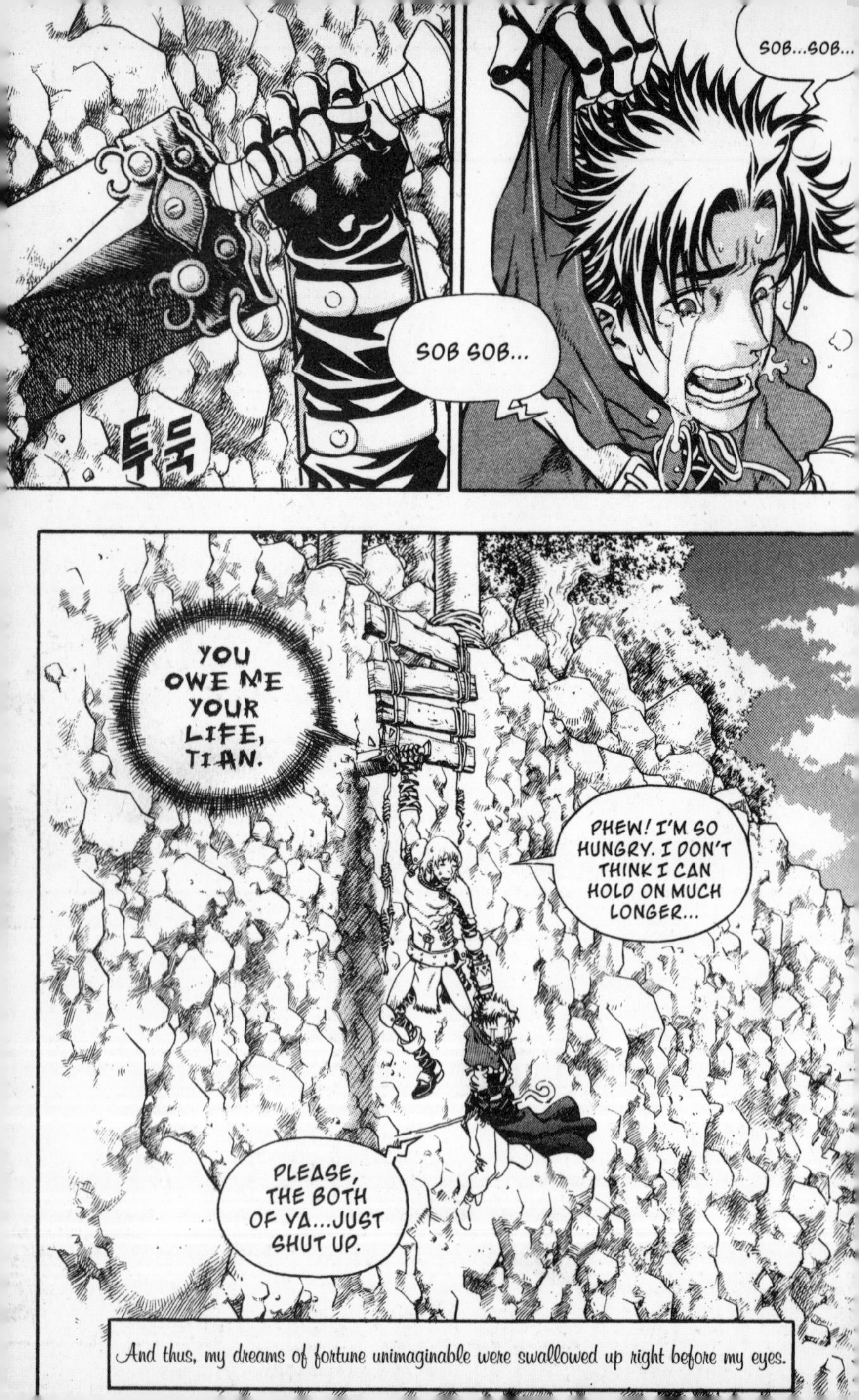
SOB...SOB...
SOB SOB...
투득
YOU OWE ME YOUR LIFE, TIAN.
PHEW! I'M SO HUNGRY. I DON'T THINK I CAN HOLD ON MUCH LONGER...
PLEASE, THE BOTH OF YA...JUST SHUT UP.
And thus, my dreams of fortune unimaginable were swallowed up right before my eyes.

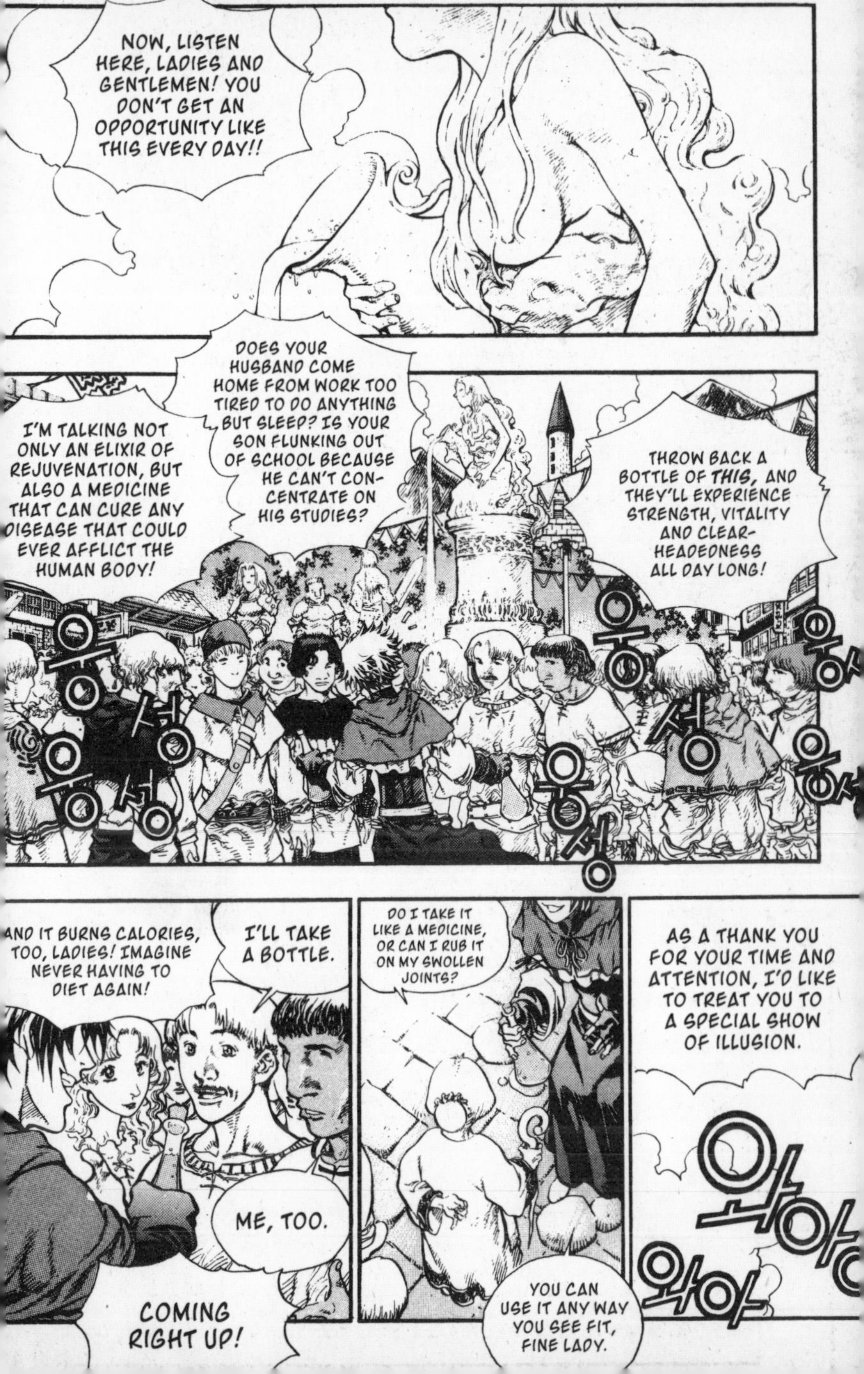
NOW, LISTEN HERE, LADIES AND GENTLEMEN! YOU DON'T GET AN OPPORTUNITY LIKE THIS EVERY DAY!!
I'M TALKING NOT ONLY AN ELIXIR OF REJUVENATION, BUT ALSO A MEDICINE THAT CAN CURE ANY DISEASE THAT COULD EVER AFFLICT THE HUMAN BODY!
DOES YOUR HUSBAND COME HOME FROM WORK TOO TIRED TO DO ANYTHING BUT SLEEP? IS YOUR SON FLUNKING OUT OF SCHOOL BECAUSE HE CAN'T CONCENTRATE ON HIS STUDIES?
THROW BACK A BOTTLE OF *THIS*, AND THEY'LL EXPERIENCE STRENGTH, VITALITY AND CLEAR-HEADEDNESS ALL DAY LONG!
웅성웅성
웅성웅성
AND IT BURNS CALORIES, TOO, LADIES! IMAGINE NEVER HAVING TO DIET AGAIN!
I'LL TAKE A BOTTLE.
ME, TOO.
COMING RIGHT UP!
DO I TAKE IT LIKE A MEDICINE, OR CAN I RUB IT ON MY SWOLLEN JOINTS?
YOU CAN USE IT ANY WAY YOU SEE FIT, FINE LADY.
AS A THANK YOU FOR YOUR TIME AND ATTENTION, I'D LIKE TO TREAT YOU TO A SPECIAL SHOW OF ILLUSION.
와아아
와아

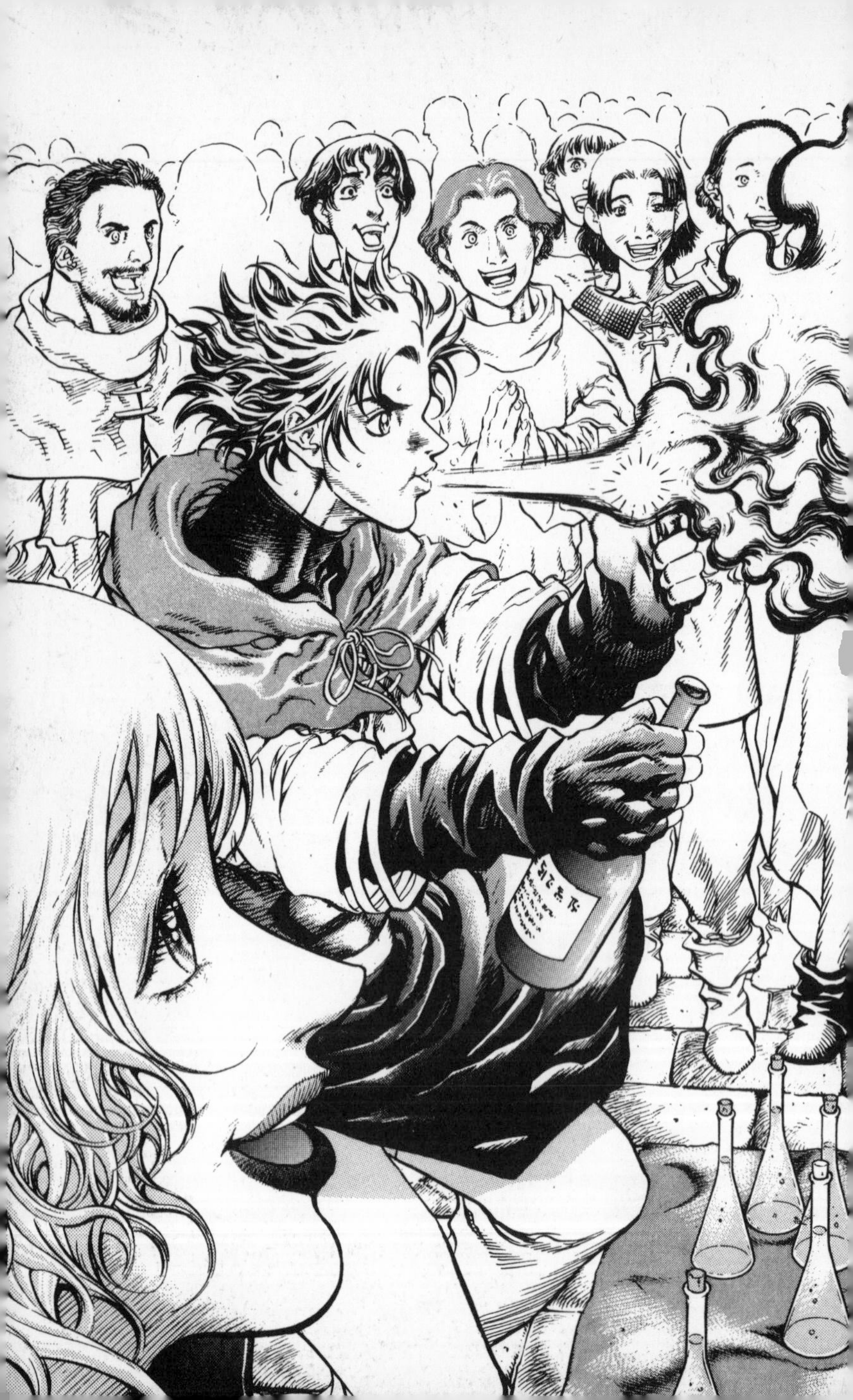

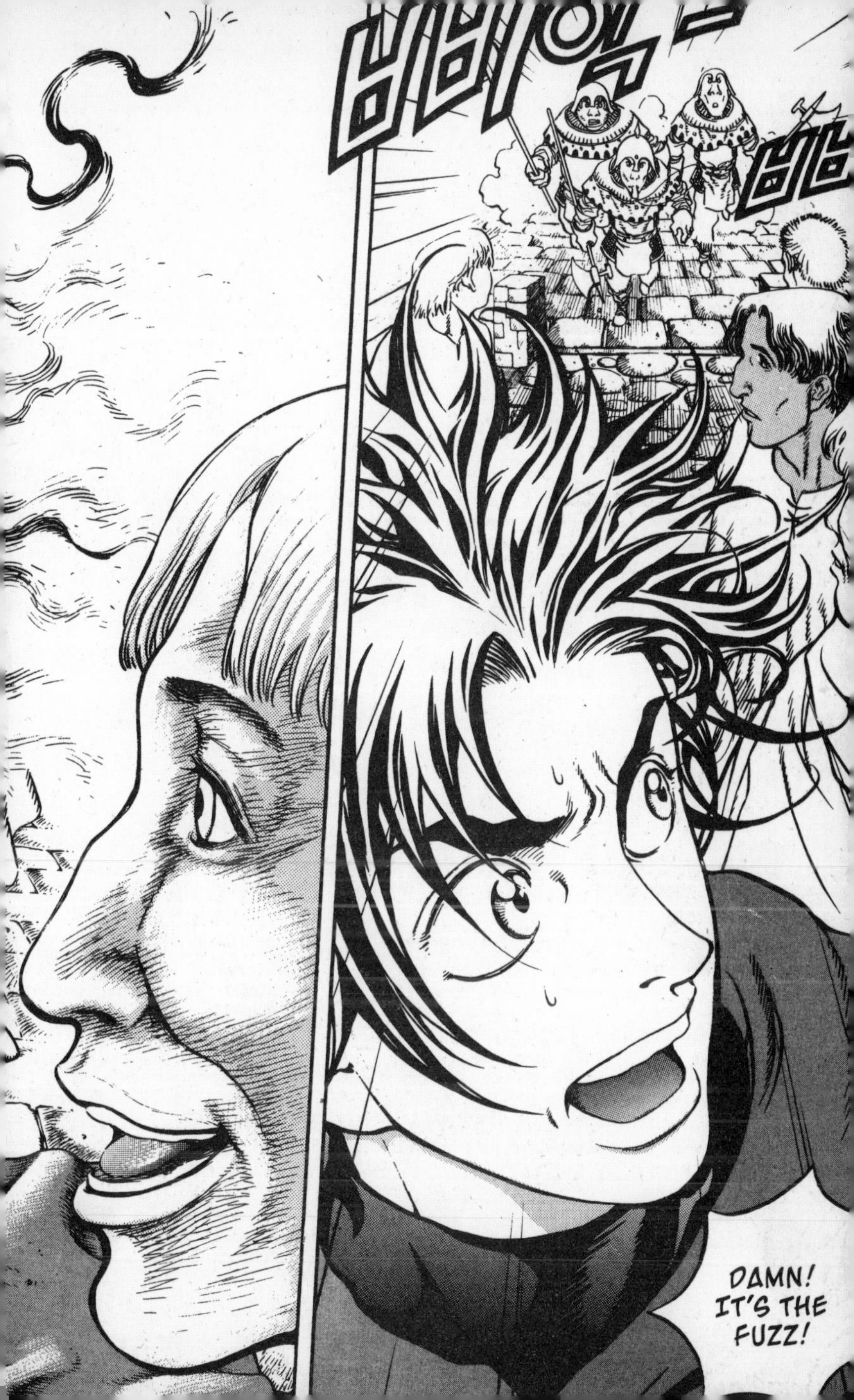
DAMN! IT'S THE FUZZ!

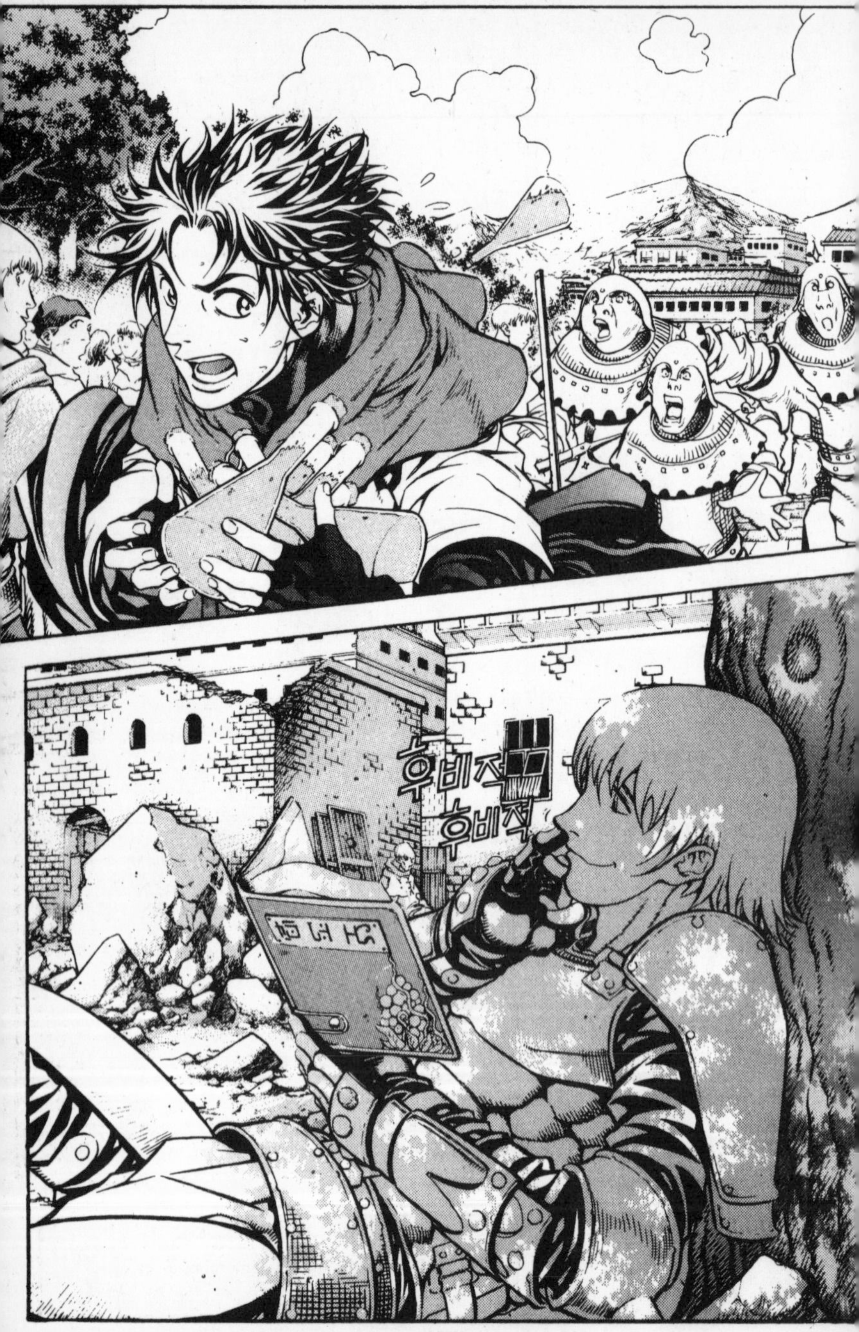
후비적
후비적

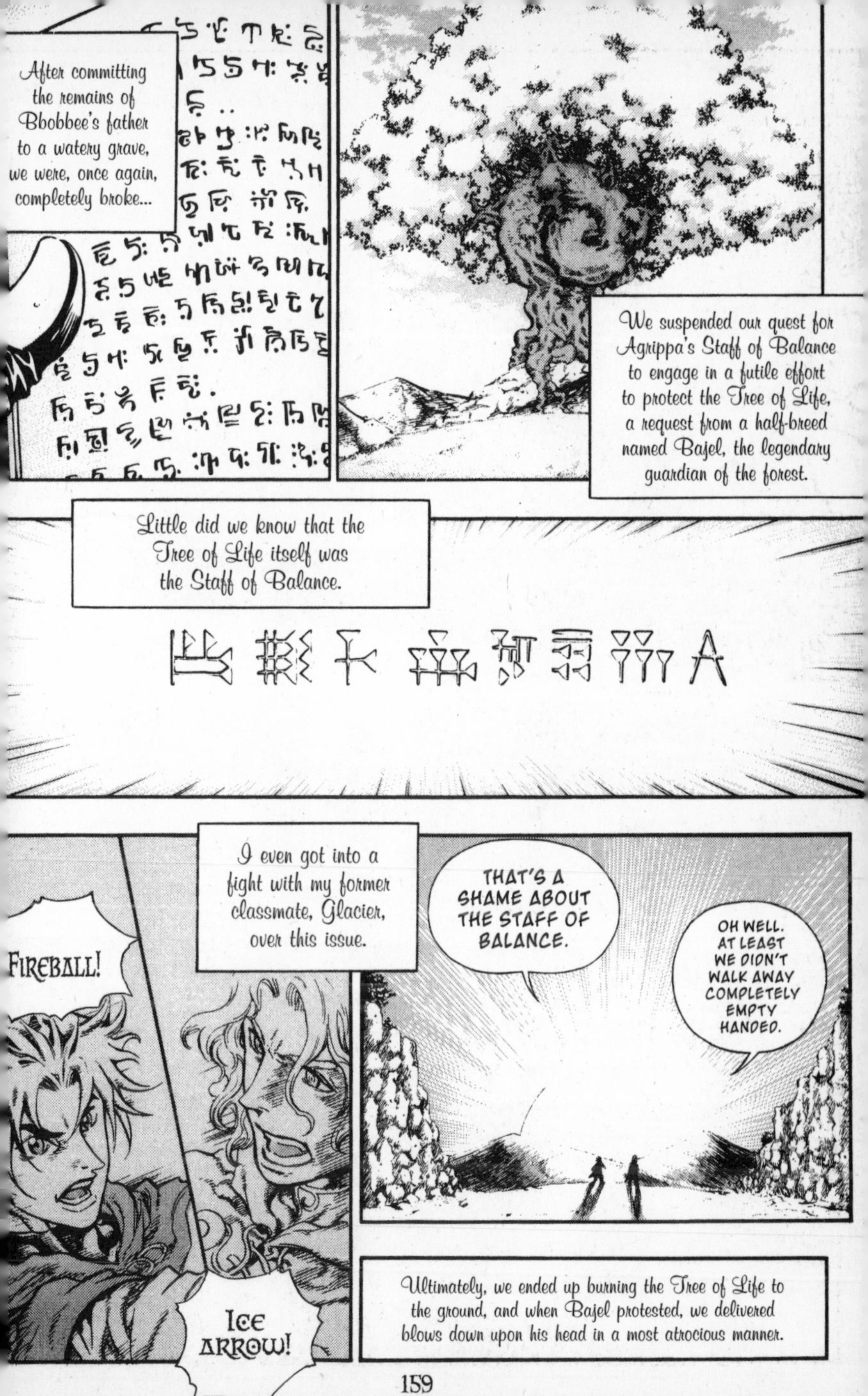
After committing the remains of Bbobbee's father to a watery grave, we were, once again, completely broke...
We suspended our quest for Agrippa's Staff of Balance to engage in a futile effort to protect the Tree of Life, a request from a half-breed named Bajel, the legendary guardian of the forest.
Little did we know that the Tree of Life itself was the Staff of Balance.
I even got into a fight with my former classmate, Glacier, over this issue.
FIREBALL!
ICE ARROW!
THAT'S A SHAME ABOUT THE STAFF OF BALANCE.
OH WELL. AT LEAST WE DIDN'T WALK AWAY COMPLETELY EMPTY HANDED.
Ultimately, we ended up burning the Tree of Life to the ground, and when Bajel protested, we delivered blows down upon his head in a most atrocious manner.

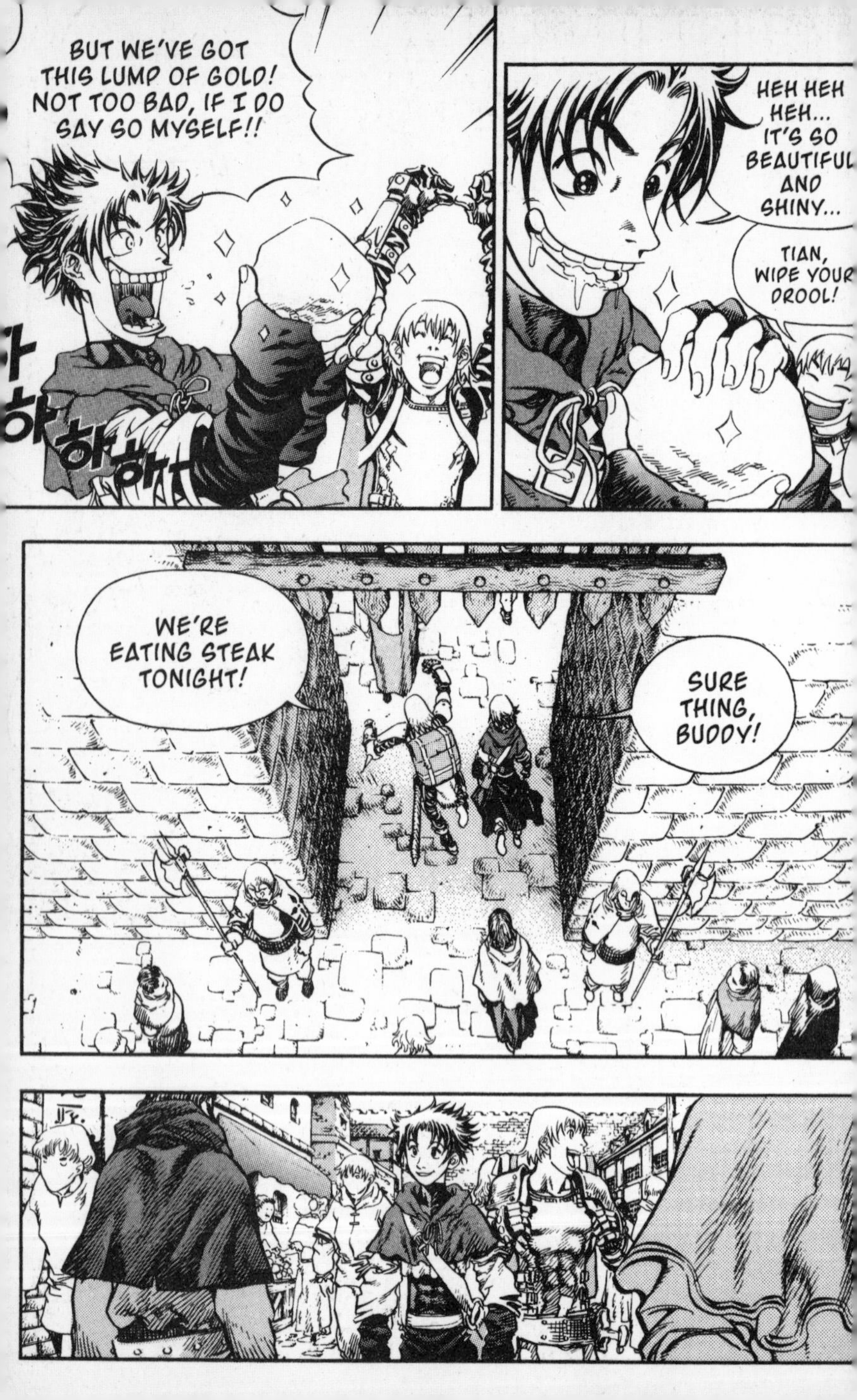

BUT WE'VE GOT THIS LUMP OF GOLD! NOT TOO BAD, IF I DO SAY SO MYSELF!!
하하하
HEH HEH HEH... IT'S SO BEAUTIFUL AND SHINY...
TIAN, WIPE YOUR DROOL!
WE'RE EATING STEAK TONIGHT!
SURE THING, BUDDY!

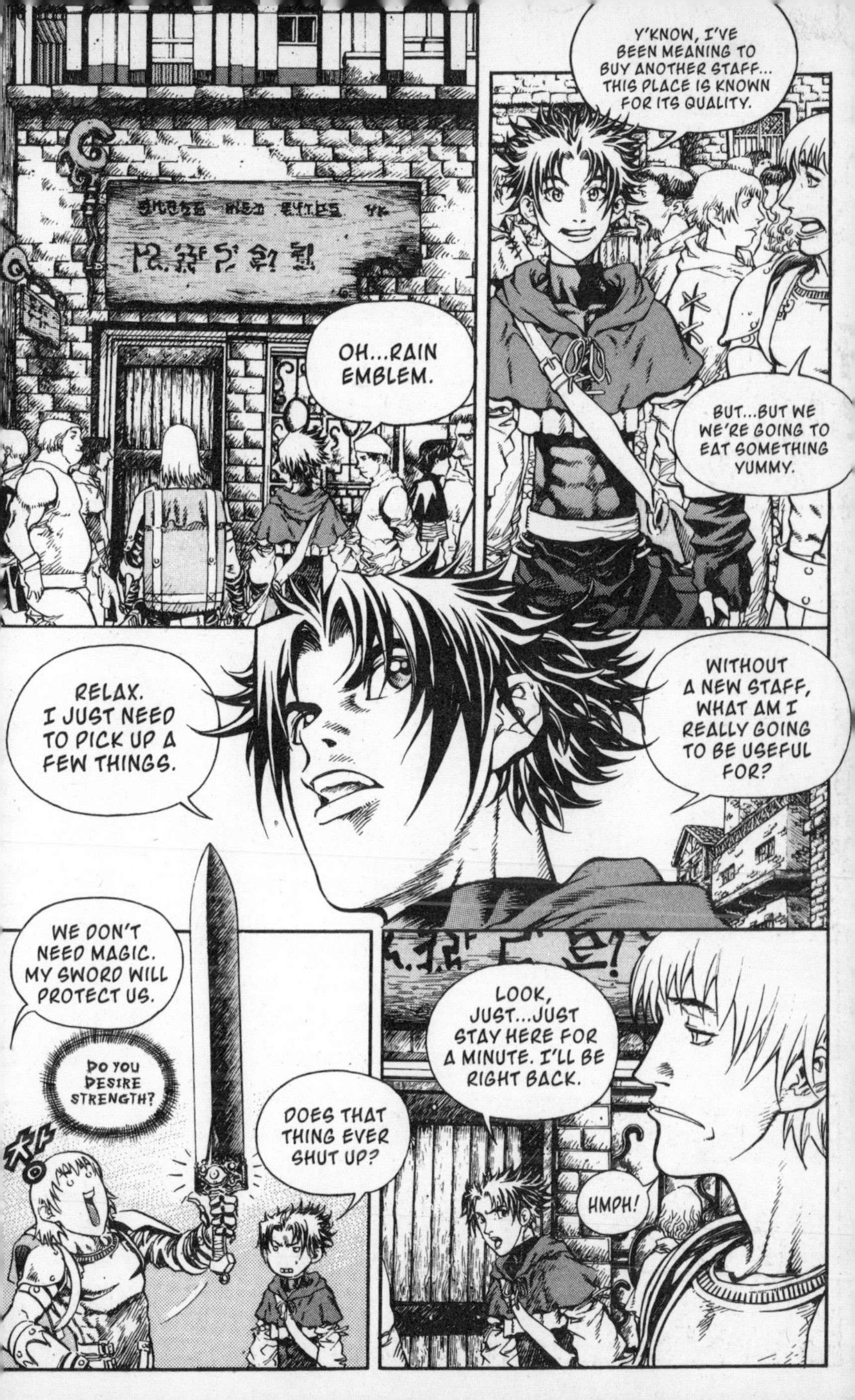

OH...RAIN EMBLEM.
Y'KNOW, I'VE BEEN MEANING TO BUY ANOTHER STAFF... THIS PLACE IS KNOWN FOR ITS QUALITY.
BUT...BUT WE WE'RE GOING TO EAT SOMETHING YUMMY.
RELAX. I JUST NEED TO PICK UP A FEW THINGS.
WITHOUT A NEW STAFF, WHAT AM I REALLY GOING TO BE USEFUL FOR?
WE DON'T NEED MAGIC. MY SWORD WILL PROTECT US.
DO YOU DESIRE STRENGTH?
DOES THAT THING EVER SHUT UP?
LOOK, JUST...JUST STAY HERE FOR A MINUTE. I'LL BE RIGHT BACK.
HMPH!

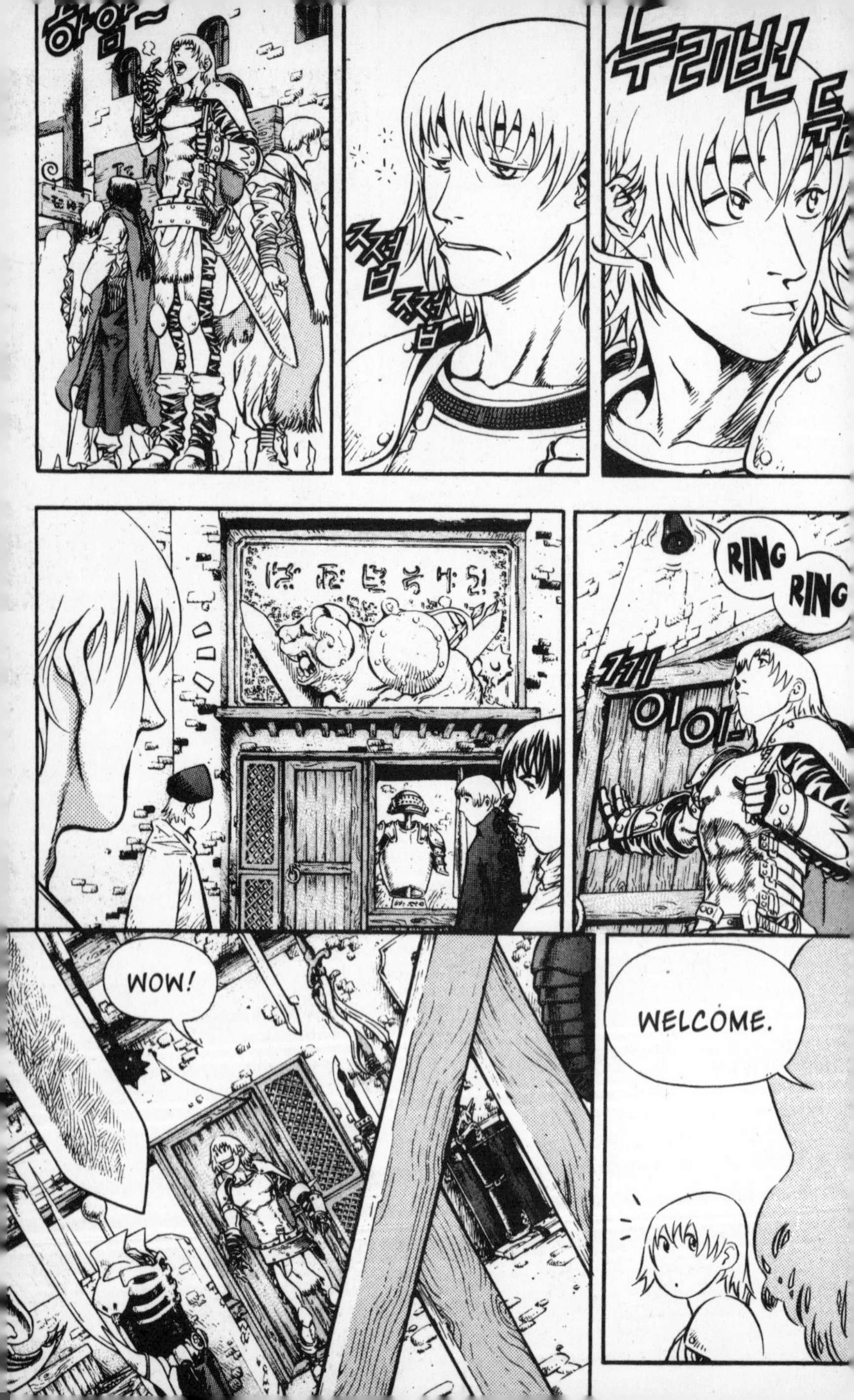
하암~
쩝
쩝
두리번 두
RING RING
끼이이-
WOW!
WELCOME.

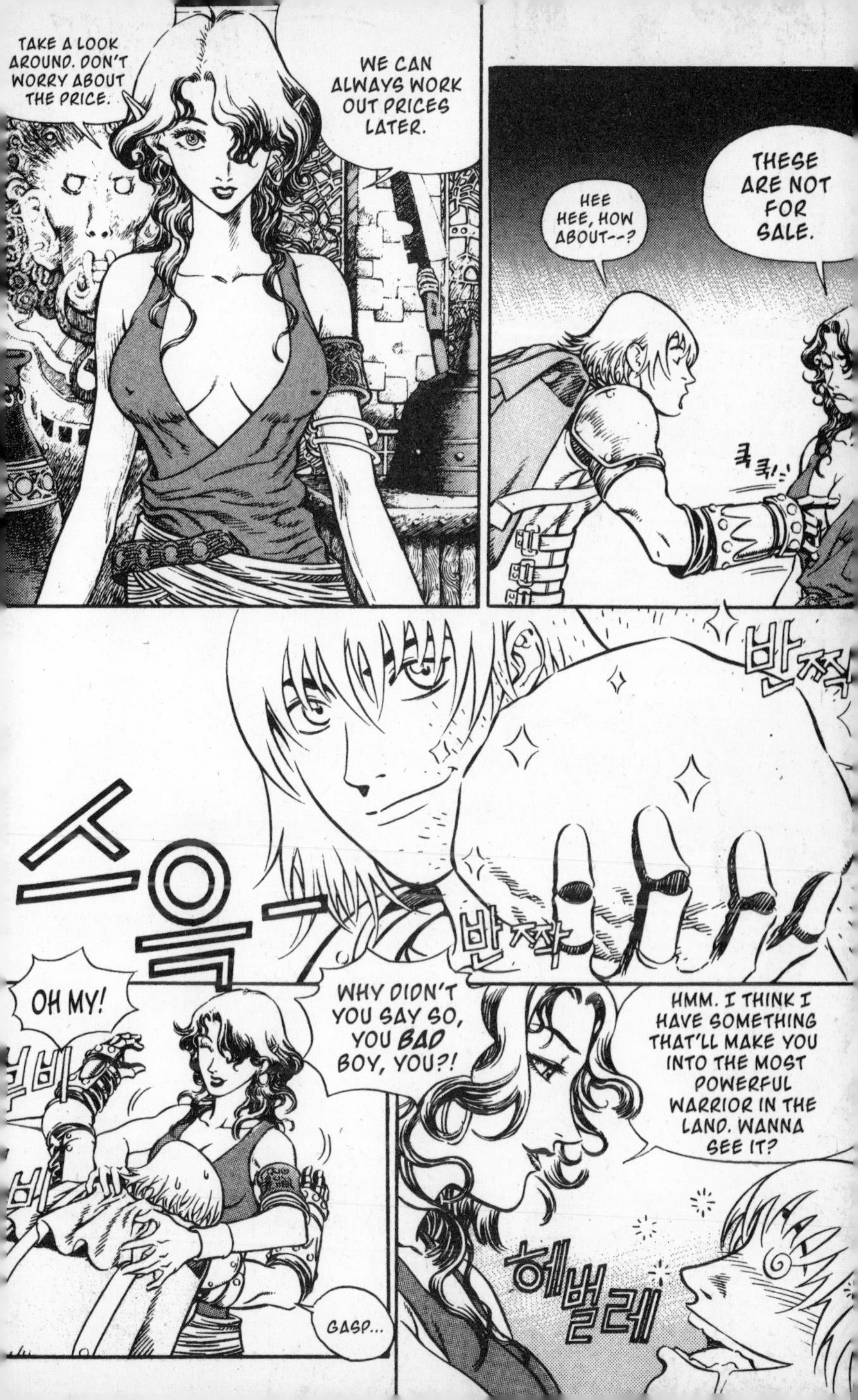
TAKE A LOOK AROUND. DON'T WORRY ABOUT THE PRICE.
WE CAN ALWAYS WORK OUT PRICES LATER.
HEE HEE, HOW ABOUT--?
THESE ARE NOT FOR SALE.
쿡 쿡!
스윽
반짝
반짝
OH MY!
WHY DIDN'T YOU SAY SO, YOU *BAD* BOY, YOU?!
GASP...
HMM. I THINK I HAVE SOMETHING THAT'LL MAKE YOU INTO THE MOST POWERFUL WARRIOR IN THE LAND. WANNA SEE IT?
헤벌레

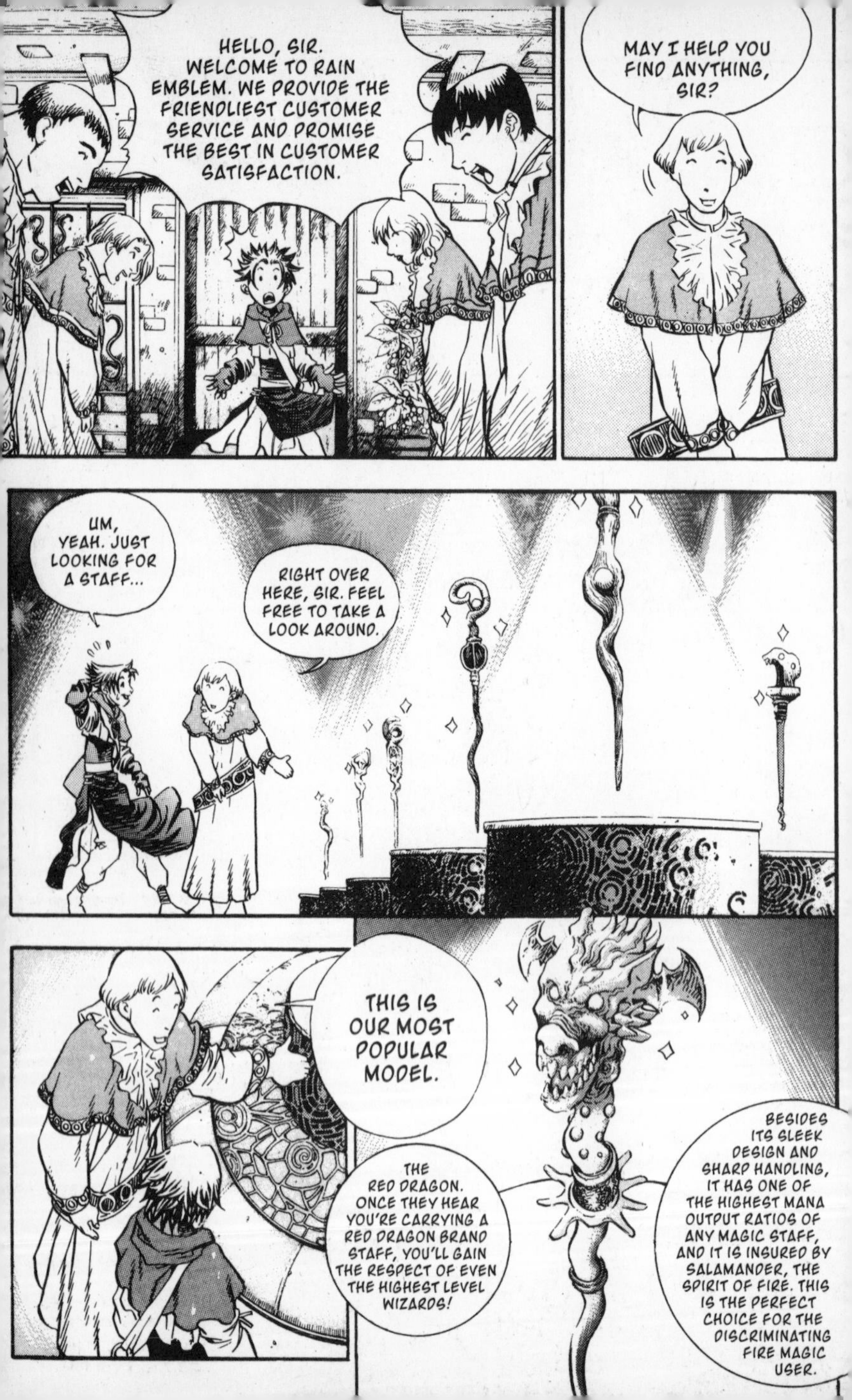
HELLO, SIR. WELCOME TO RAIN EMBLEM. WE PROVIDE THE FRIENDLIEST CUSTOMER SERVICE AND PROMISE THE BEST IN CUSTOMER SATISFACTION.
MAY I HELP YOU FIND ANYTHING, SIR?
UM, YEAH. JUST LOOKING FOR A STAFF...
RIGHT OVER HERE, SIR. FEEL FREE TO TAKE A LOOK AROUND.
THIS IS OUR MOST POPULAR MODEL.
THE RED DRAGON. ONCE THEY HEAR YOU'RE CARRYING A RED DRAGON BRAND STAFF, YOU'LL GAIN THE RESPECT OF EVEN THE HIGHEST LEVEL WIZARDS!
BESIDES ITS SLEEK DESIGN AND SHARP HANDLING, IT HAS ONE OF THE HIGHEST MANA OUTPUT RATIOS OF ANY MAGIC STAFF, AND IT IS INSURED BY SALAMANDER, THE SPIRIT OF FIRE. THIS IS THE PERFECT CHOICE FOR THE DISCRIMINATING FIRE MAGIC USER.

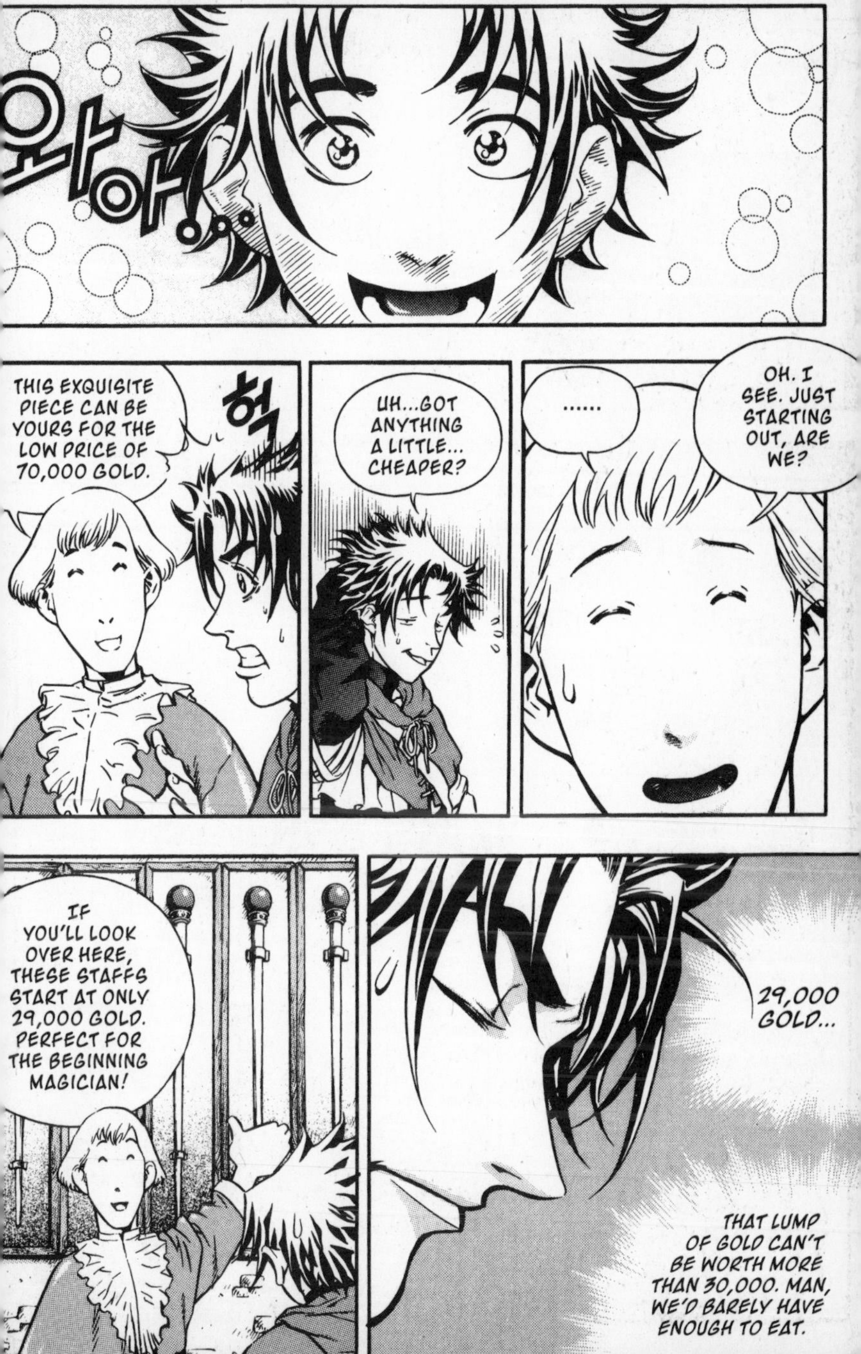
와아...
THIS EXQUISITE PIECE CAN BE YOURS FOR THE LOW PRICE OF 70,000 GOLD.
헉
UH...GOT ANYTHING A LITTLE... CHEAPER?
......
OH. I SEE. JUST STARTING OUT, ARE WE?
IF YOU'LL LOOK OVER HERE, THESE STAFFS START AT ONLY 29,000 GOLD. PERFECT FOR THE BEGINNING MAGICIAN!
29,000 GOLD...
THAT LUMP OF GOLD CAN'T BE WORTH MORE THAN 30,000. MAN, WE'D BARELY HAVE ENOUGH TO EAT.

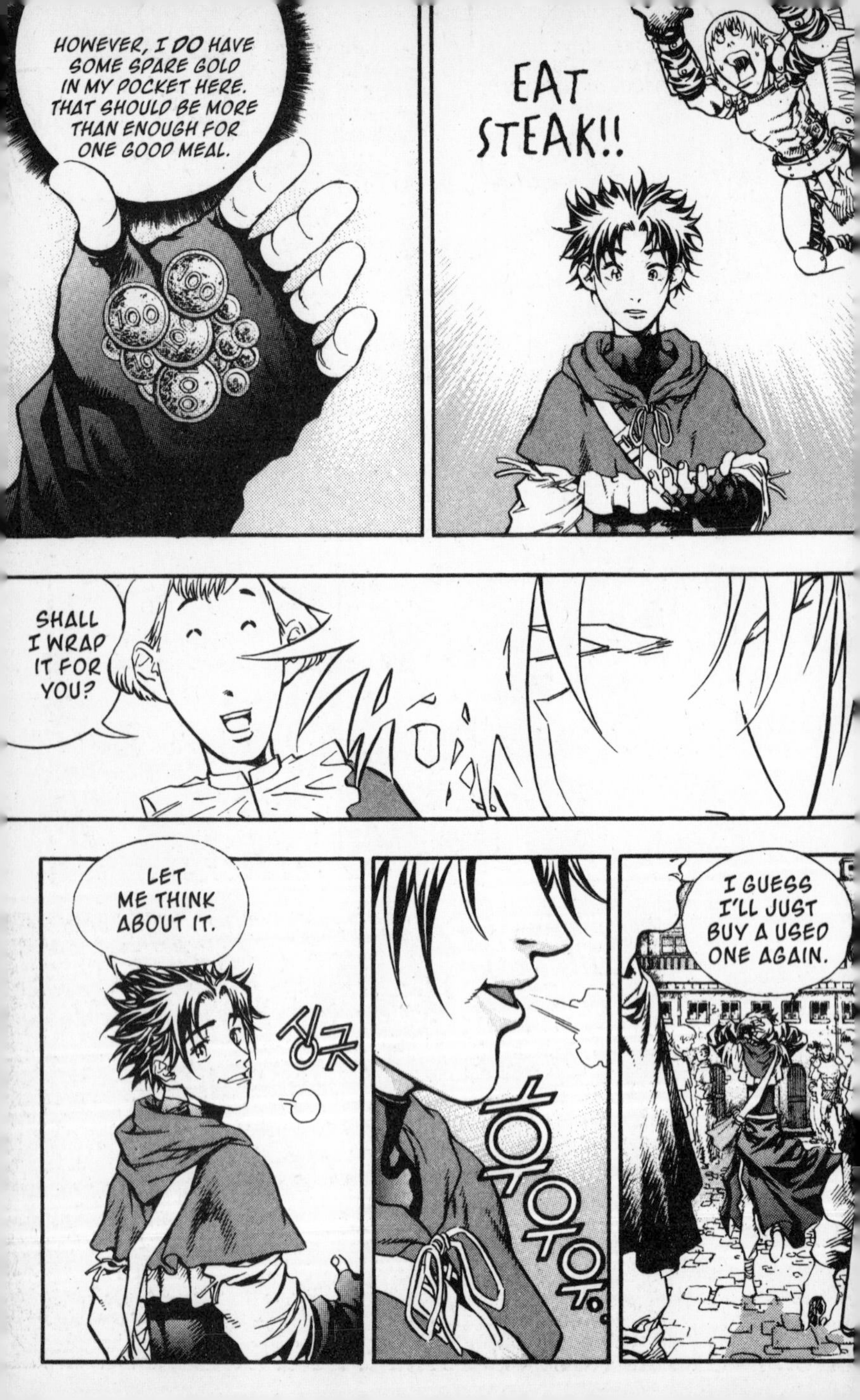
HOWEVER, I DO HAVE SOME SPARE GOLD IN MY POCKET HERE. THAT SHOULD BE MORE THAN ENOUGH FOR ONE GOOD MEAL.
EAT STEAK!!
SHALL I WRAP IT FOR YOU?
LET ME THINK ABOUT IT.
싱긋
후아아아아
I GUESS I'LL JUST BUY A USED ONE AGAIN.

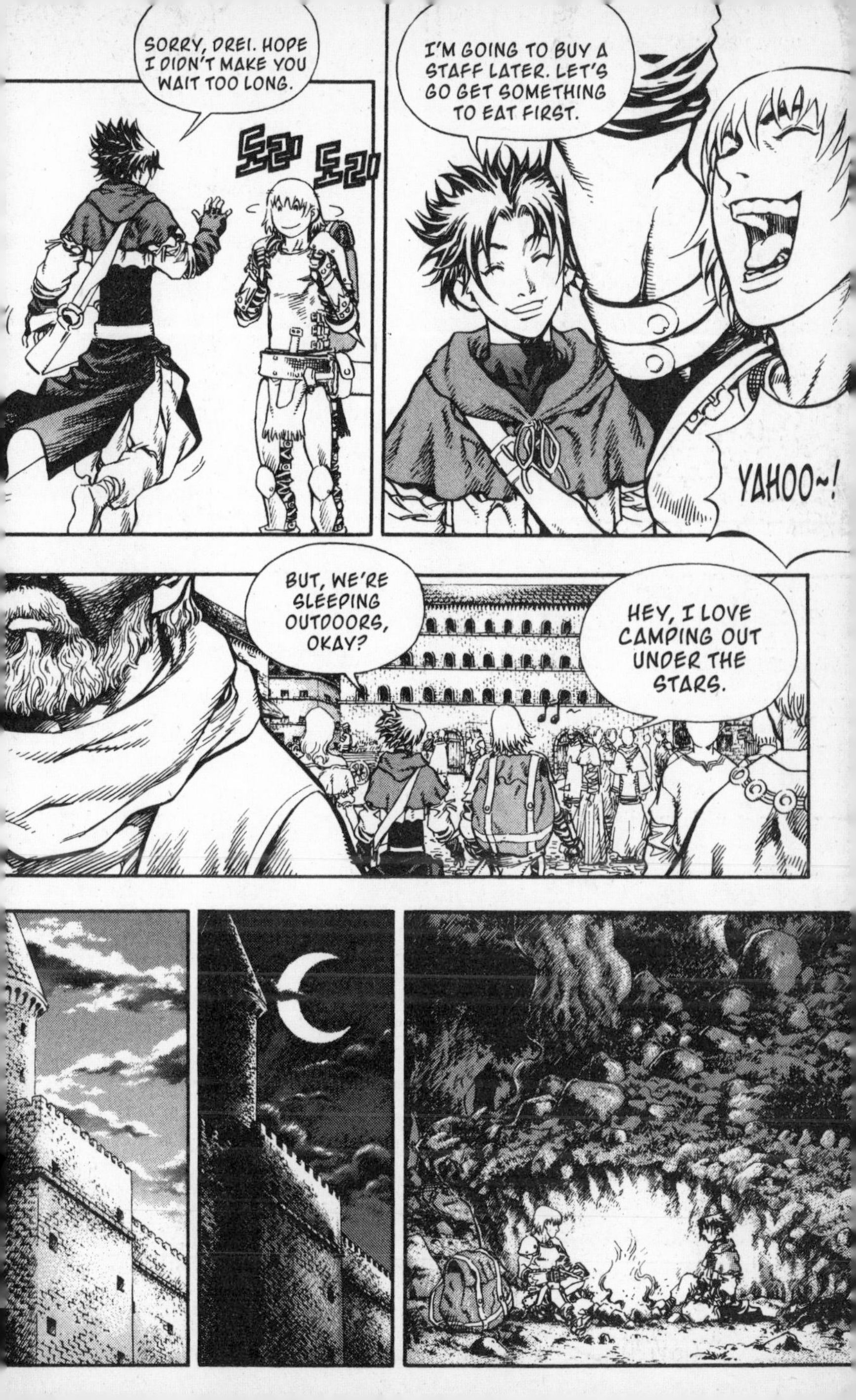
SORRY, DREI. HOPE I DIDN'T MAKE YOU WAIT TOO LONG.
I'M GOING TO BUY A STAFF LATER. LET'S GO GET SOMETHING TO EAT FIRST.
YAHOO~!
BUT, WE'RE SLEEPING OUTDOORS, OKAY?
HEY, I LOVE CAMPING OUT UNDER THE STARS.

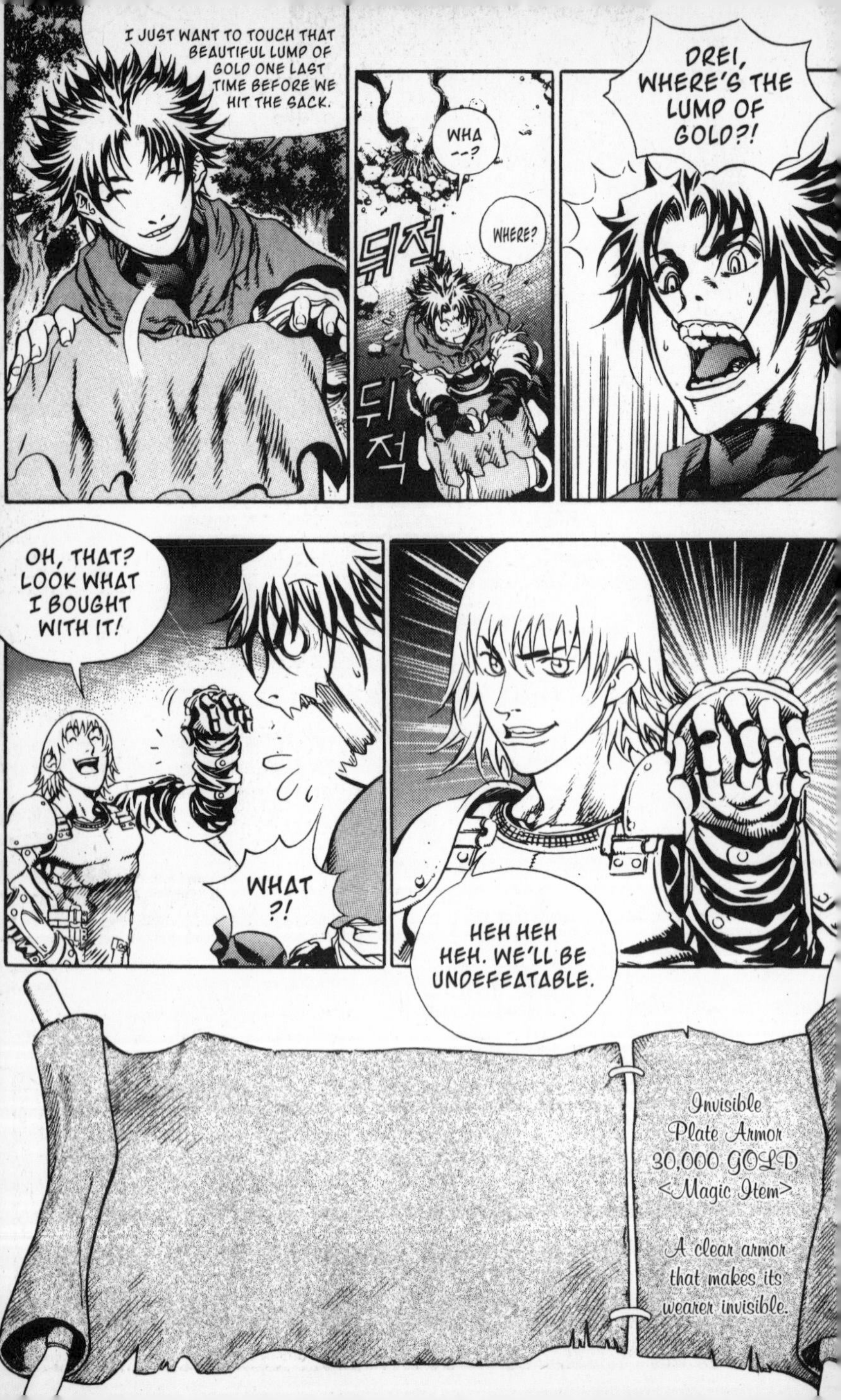

I JUST WANT TO TOUCH THAT BEAUTIFUL LUMP OF GOLD ONE LAST TIME BEFORE WE HIT THE SACK.
WHA --?
WHERE?
DREI, WHERE'S THE LUMP OF GOLD?!
OH, THAT? LOOK WHAT I BOUGHT WITH IT!
WHAT ?!
HEH HEH HEH. WE'LL BE UNDEFEATABLE.
Invisible Plate Armor
30,000 GOLD
<Magic Item>
A clear armor that makes its wearer invisible.

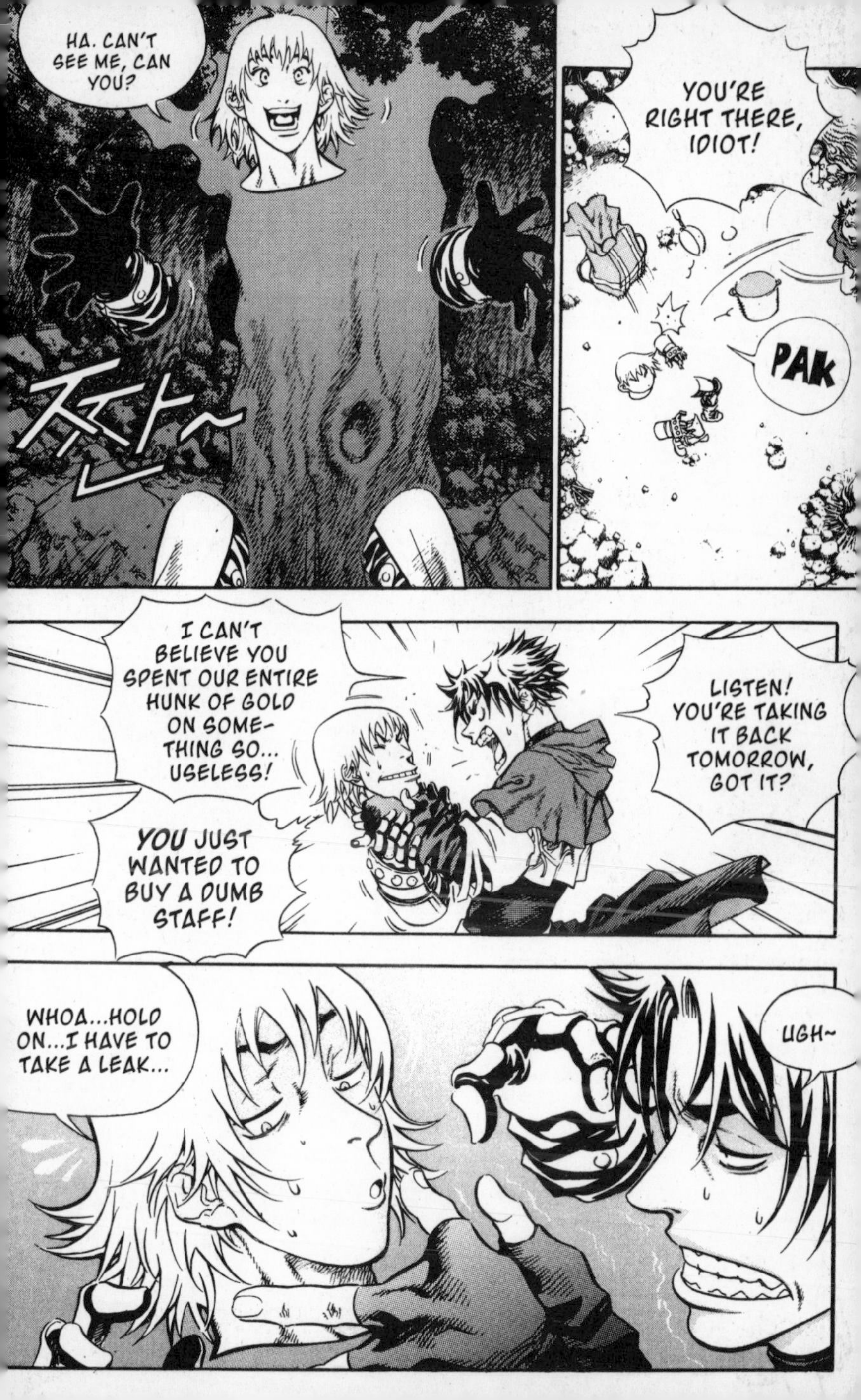
HA. CAN'T SEE ME, CAN YOU?
YOU'RE RIGHT THERE, IDIOT!
PAK
I CAN'T BELIEVE YOU SPENT OUR ENTIRE HUNK OF GOLD ON SOME-THING SO... USELESS!
LISTEN! YOU'RE TAKING IT BACK TOMORROW, GOT IT?
YOU JUST WANTED TO BUY A DUMB STAFF!
WHOA...HOLD ON...I HAVE TO TAKE A LEAK...
UGH~

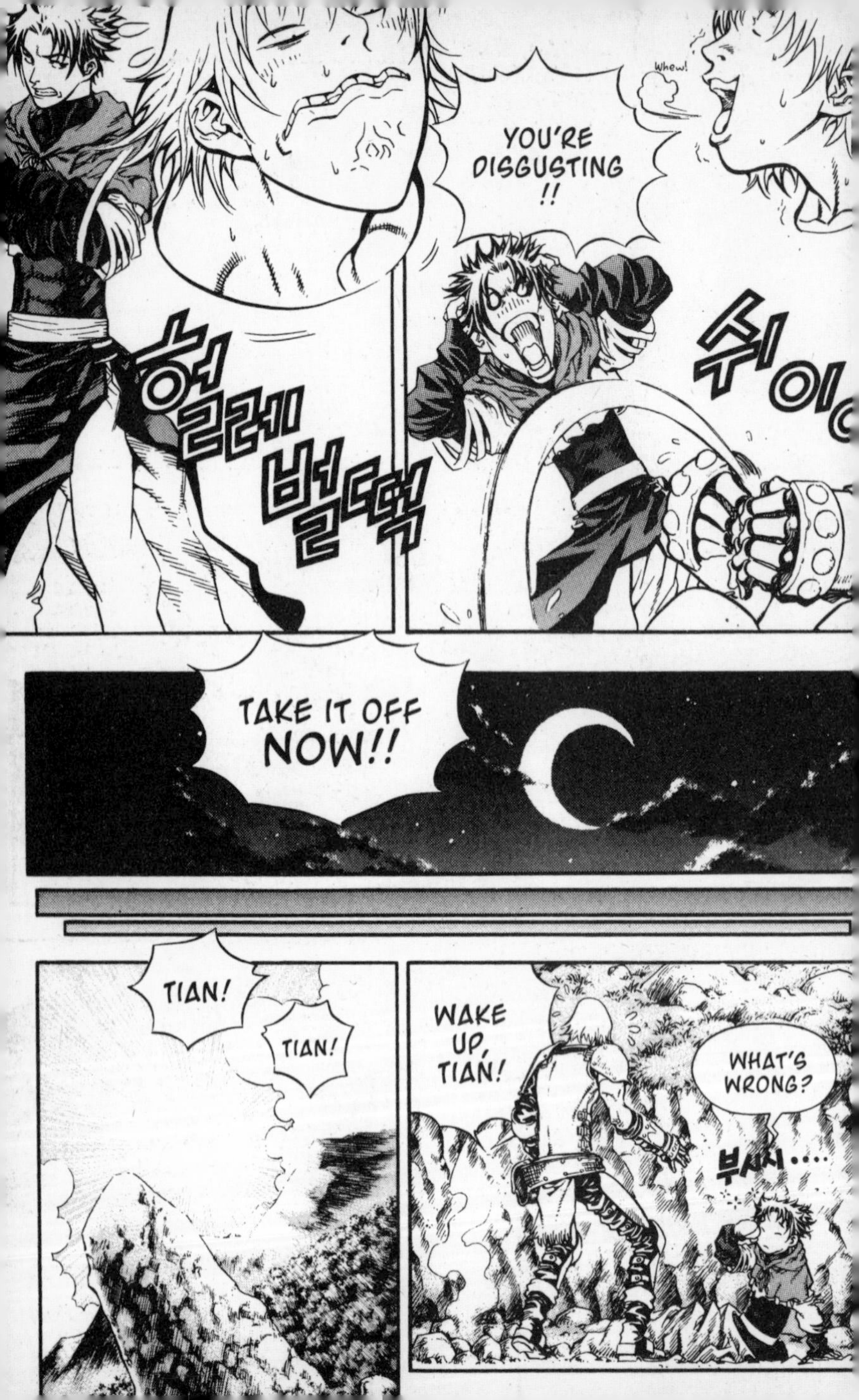
헐레벌떡
Whew!
YOU'RE DISGUSTING !!
쉬이
TAKE IT OFF NOW!!
TIAN!
TIAN!
WAKE UP, TIAN!
WHAT'S WRONG?
부시....

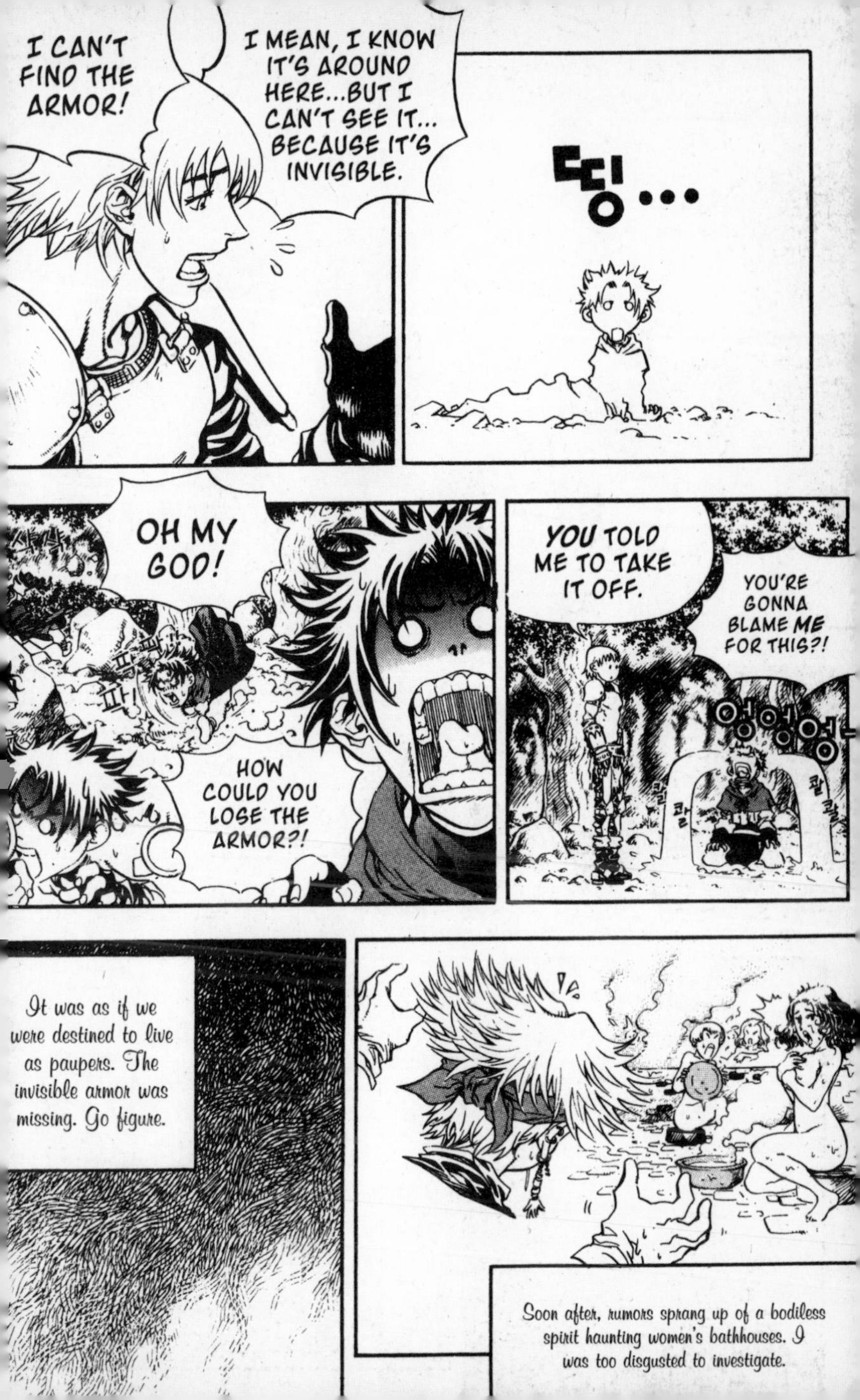
I CAN'T FIND THE ARMOR!
I MEAN, I KNOW IT'S AROUND HERE...BUT I CAN'T SEE IT... BECAUSE IT'S INVISIBLE.
띠잉...
OH MY GOD!
HOW COULD YOU LOSE THE ARMOR?!
YOU TOLD ME TO TAKE IT OFF.
YOU'RE GONNA BLAME ME FOR THIS?!
It was as if we were destined to live as paupers. The invisible armor was missing. Go figure.
Soon after, rumors sprang up of a bodiless spirit haunting women's bathhouses. I was too disgusted to investigate.

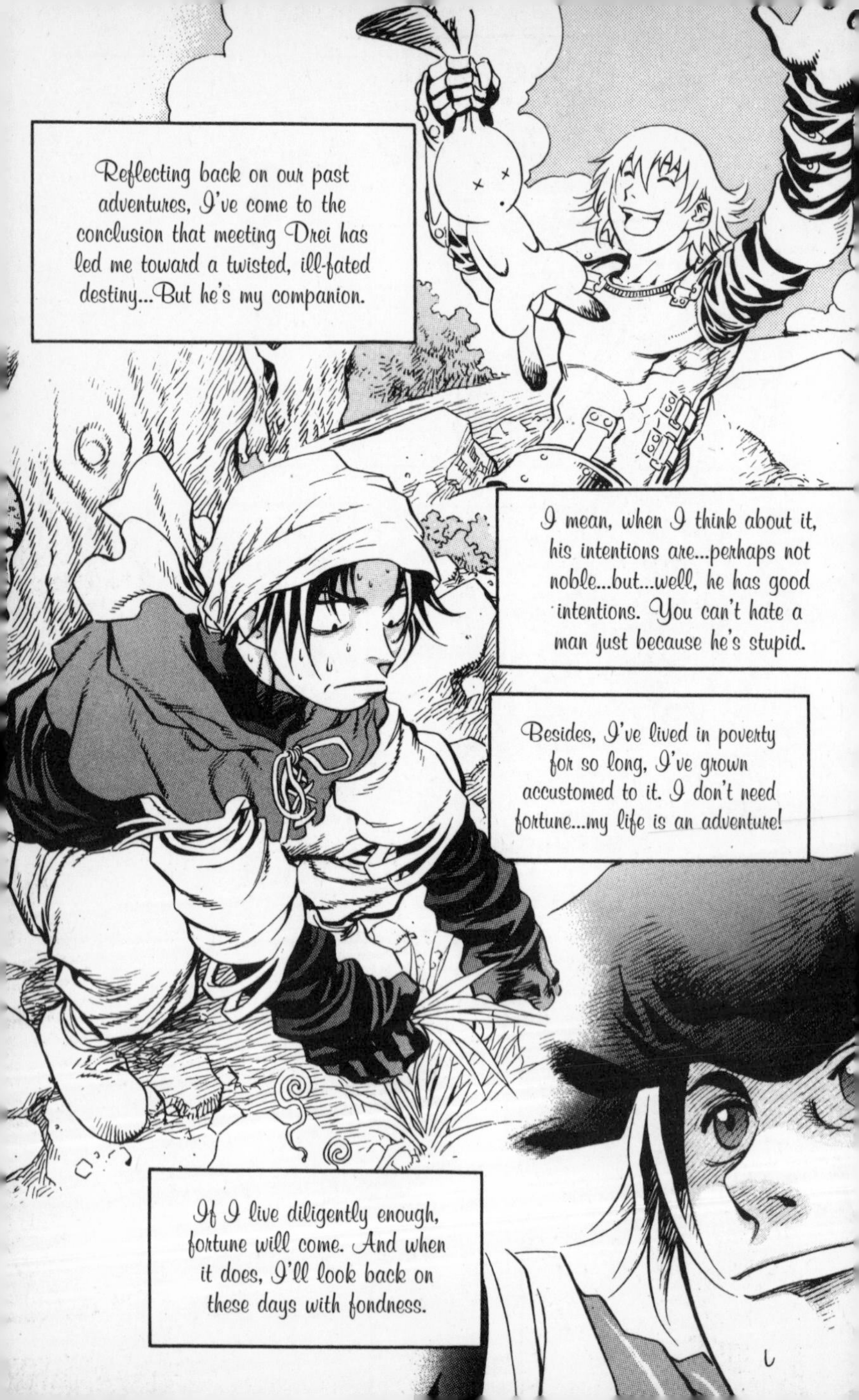
Reflecting back on our past adventures, I've come to the conclusion that meeting Drei has led me toward a twisted, ill-fated destiny...But he's my companion.
I mean, when I think about it, his intentions are...perhaps not noble...but...well, he has good intentions. You can't hate a man just because he's stupid.
Besides, I've lived in poverty for so long, I've grown accustomed to it. I don't need fortune...my life is an adventure!
If I live diligently enough, fortune will come. And when it does, I'll look back on these days with fondness.

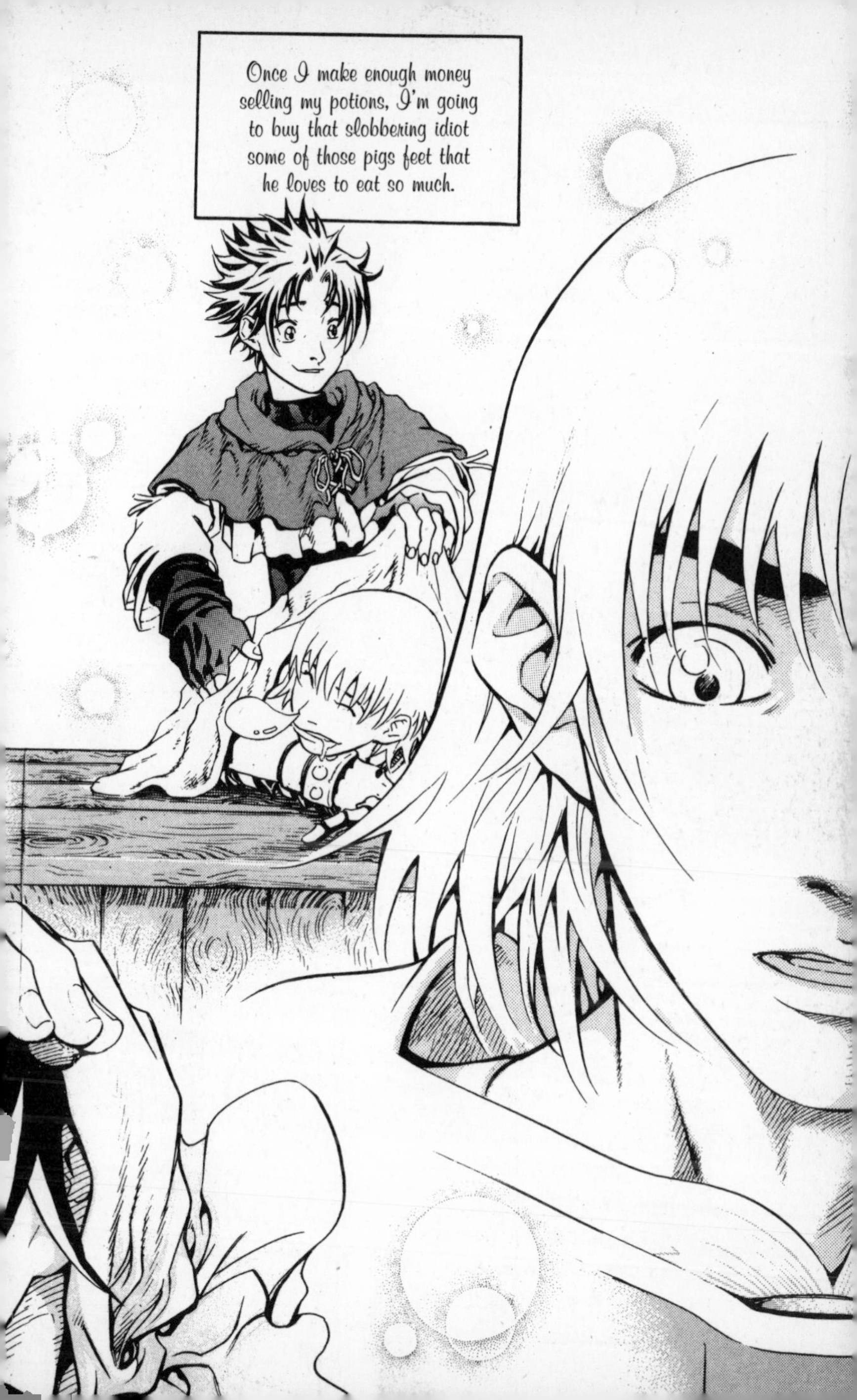
Once I make enough money selling my potions, I'm going to buy that slobbering idiot some of those pigs feet that he loves to eat so much.

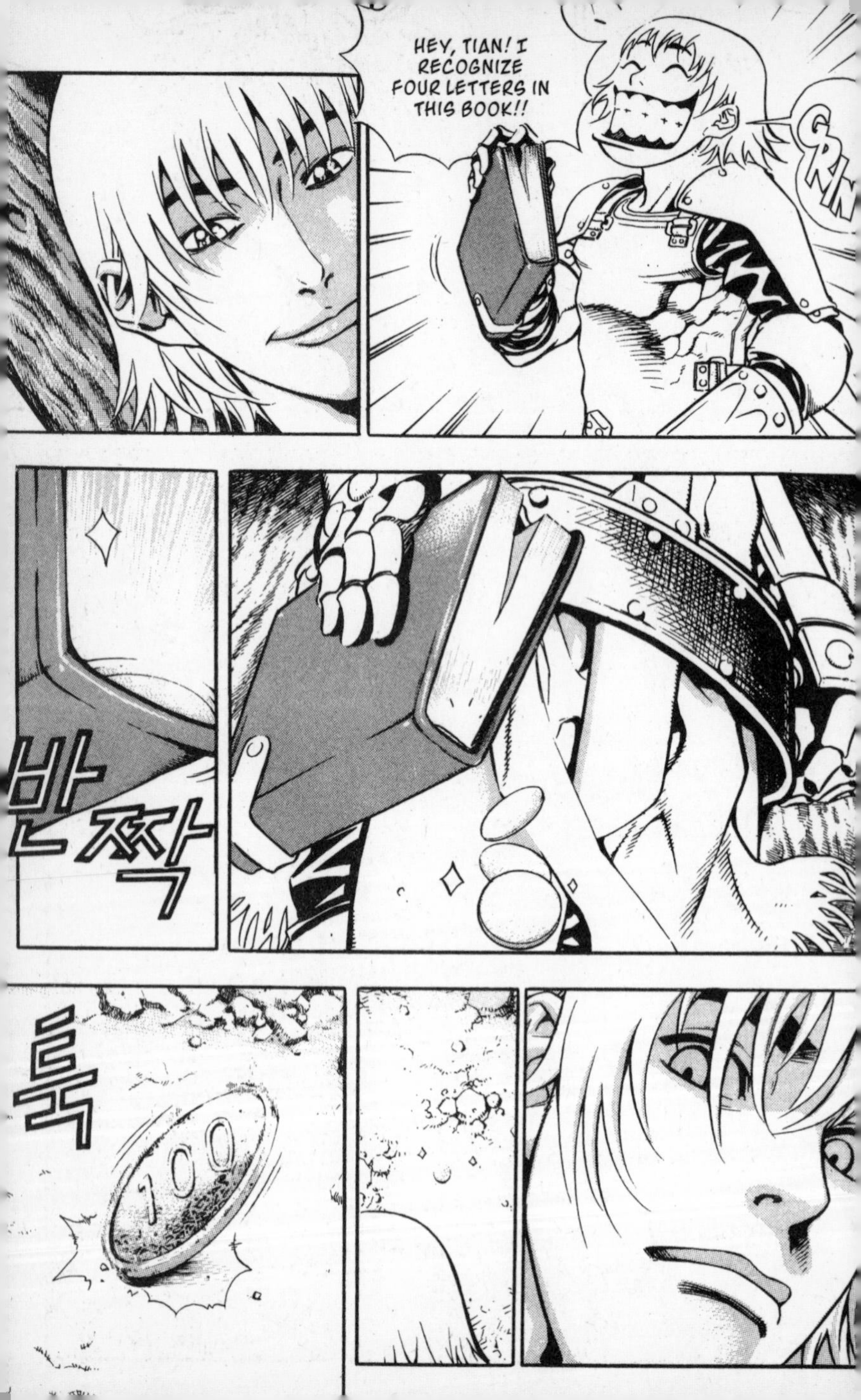
HEY, TIAN! I RECOGNIZE FOUR LETTERS IN THIS BOOK!!
GRIN
반짝
툭
100

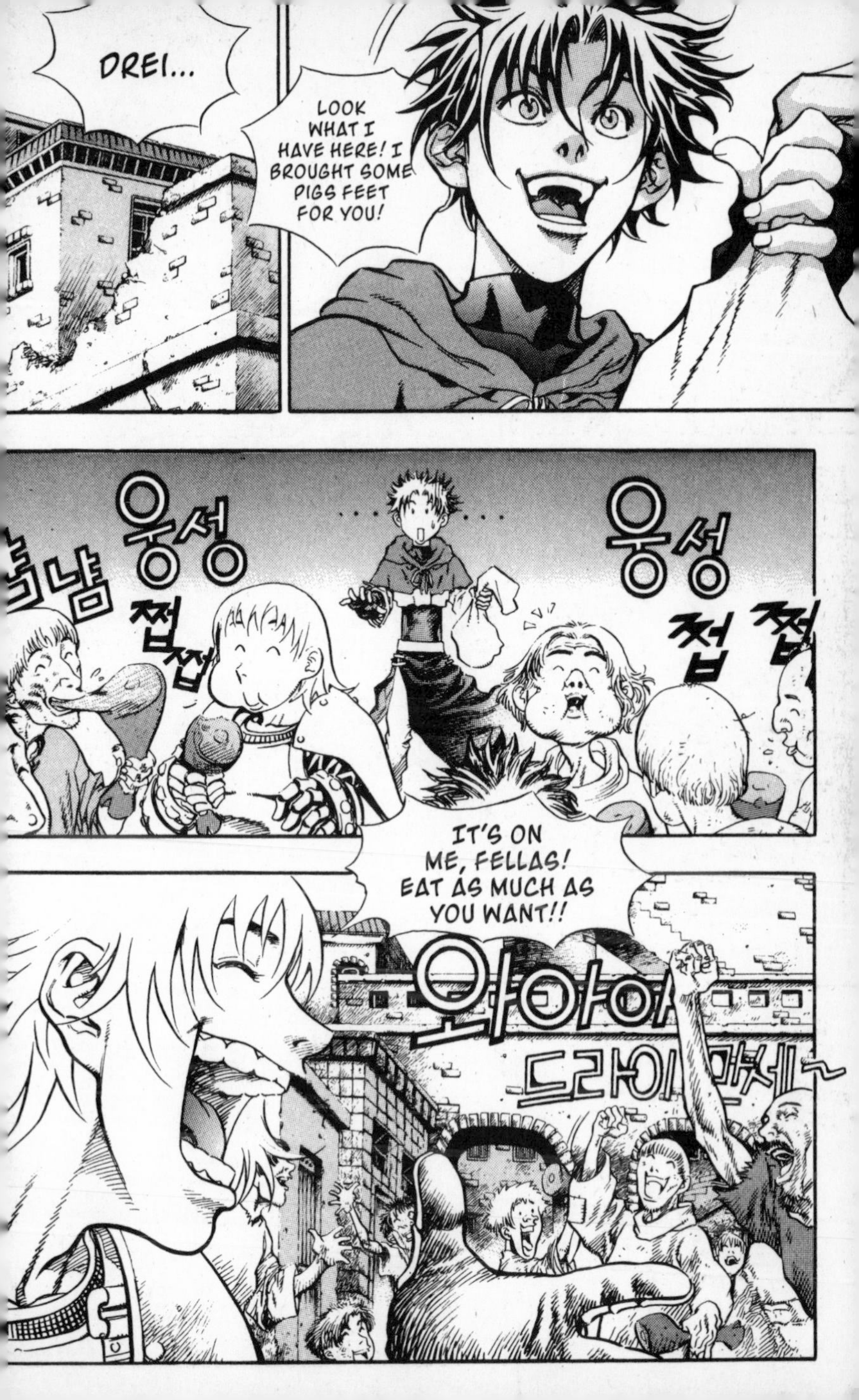
DREI...
LOOK WHAT I HAVE HERE! I BROUGHT SOME PIGS FEET FOR YOU!
웅성
쩝쩝
. . . .
웅성
쩝 쩝
IT'S ON ME, FELLAS! EAT AS MUCH AS YOU WANT!!
와아아
드라이 만세~

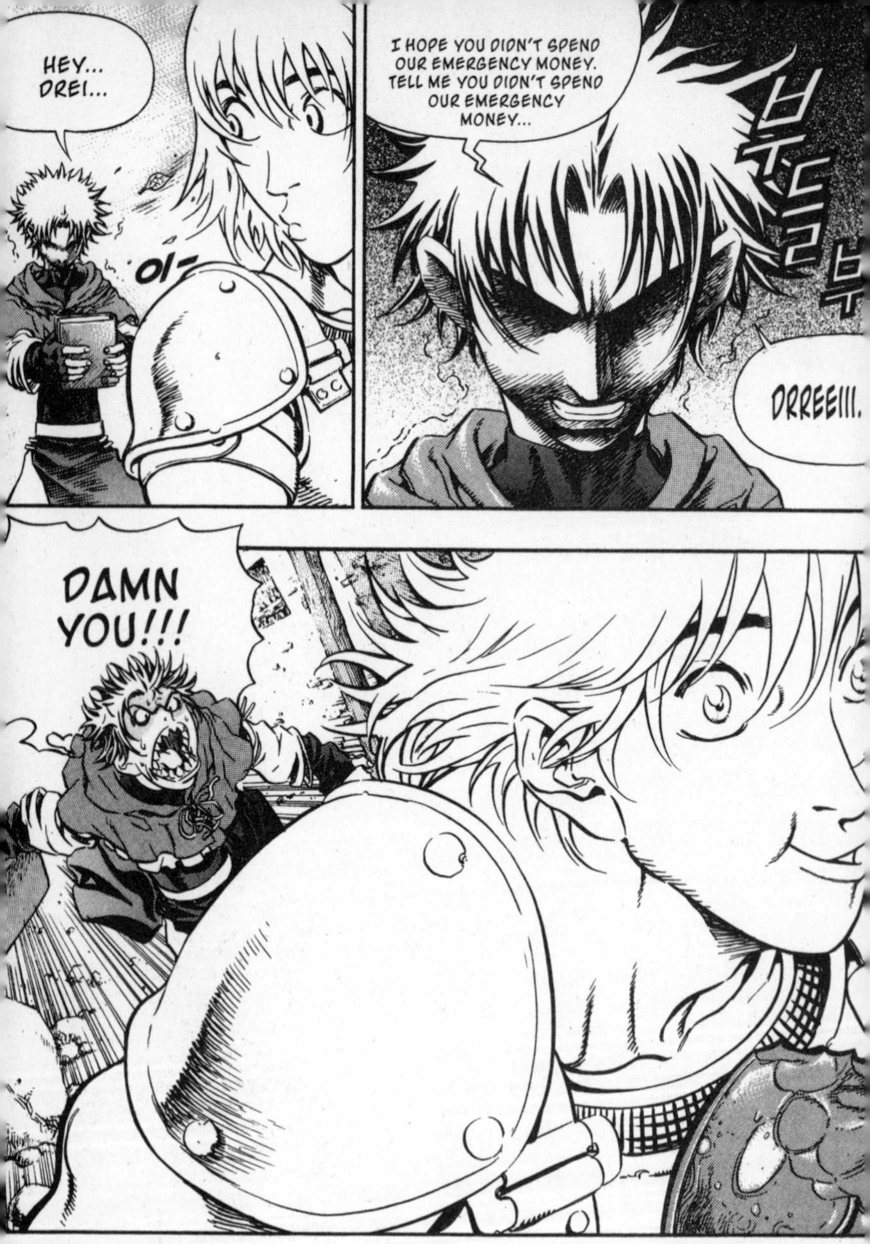
HEY... DREI...
I HOPE YOU DIDN'T SPEND OUR EMERGENCY MONEY. TELL ME YOU DIDN'T SPEND OUR EMERGENCY MONEY...
DRREEIII.
DAMN YOU!!!

That was another day in the life of the brave warriors!

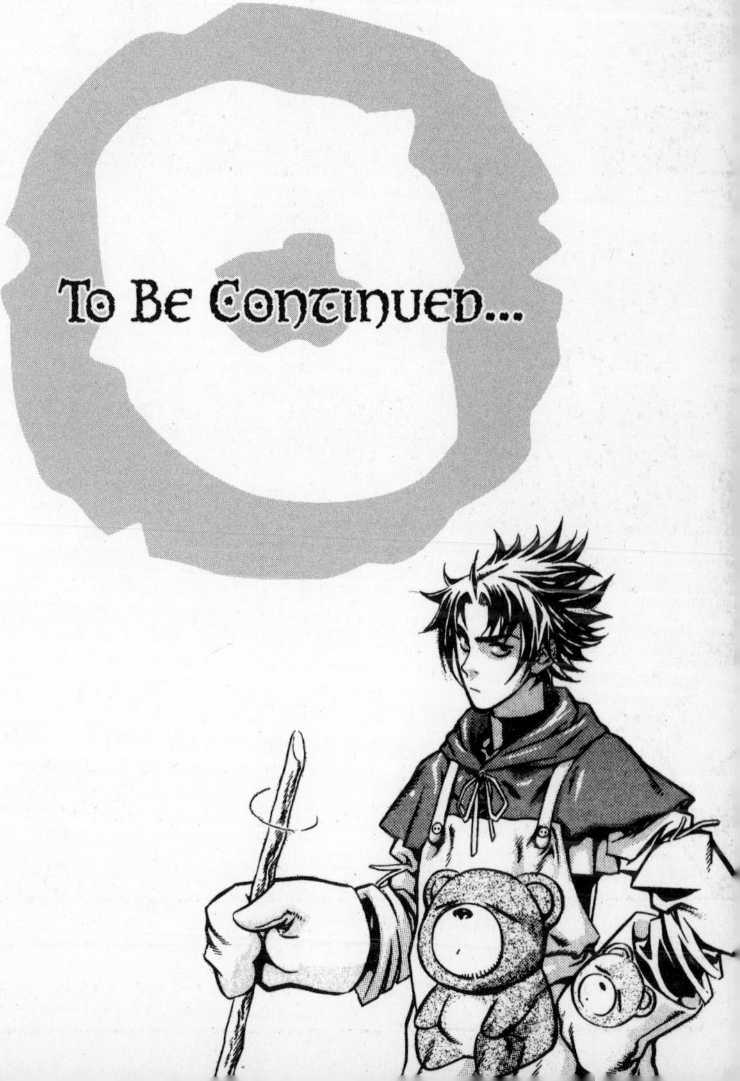
To Be Continued...

What Though Life Conspire To Cheat You
삶이 그대를 속일지라도

– Aleksandr Sergeyevich Pushkin –
푸슈킨

What though life conspire to cheat you,
삶이 그대를 속일지라도,
Do not sorrow or complain.
슬퍼하거나 노여워말라.
Lie still on the day of pain,
슬픈 날엔 참고 견뎌라,
And the day of joy will greet you.
이제 곧 기쁨의 나날이 오리니.

Hearts live in the coming day.
마음은 미래에 사는 것.
There's an end to passing sorrow.
현재는 한없이 우울한 것.
Suddenly all flies away,
모든 것이 하염없이 날아가버려도,
And delight returns tomorrow.
내일은 기쁨으로 돌아오리라.

Just like the world in which we are living, life itself can be a bit much to handle in the fantasy world of Tian and Drei.
It appears that this life cannot be lived with the innocent dreams and youthful vigor of the youngsters.
Tian and Drei are a depiction of our own selves: They work hard and diligently, only to repeat mistake after mistake and ruin their intricately laid important plans.
At times, we fall into despair because we are unable to carry on the burdens and the responsibilities that have been laid upon us, and there are times when we ignore them and run away.
However, if you have the strength remaining to stand up once again, clench your fists, and run towards tomorrow, then you have every right to be called a warrior.
Although life may conspire to cheat you, this world is also in dire need of a young warrior like yourself.

COUNTLESS CORPSES LITTER THE BATTLEFIELD,
THE GROUND DYED WITH THEIR BLOOD...
THE BATTLE WAS WAGED BETWEEN
AMERIA AND SOBEETROOK.

TIAN AND DREI ATTEMPT AN ESCAPE WITH A YOUNG
PRINCE WHO IS SUFFERING FROM AMNESIA.
AS THEIR PURSUERS APPROACH, TIAN MUST
TURN TO FACE THEM... AND THE TRUTH.

LAST FANTASY VOLUME 2
<THAT WAS THE TRAGEDY OF WAR!>
WE CALL THAT THE LAST FANTASY.

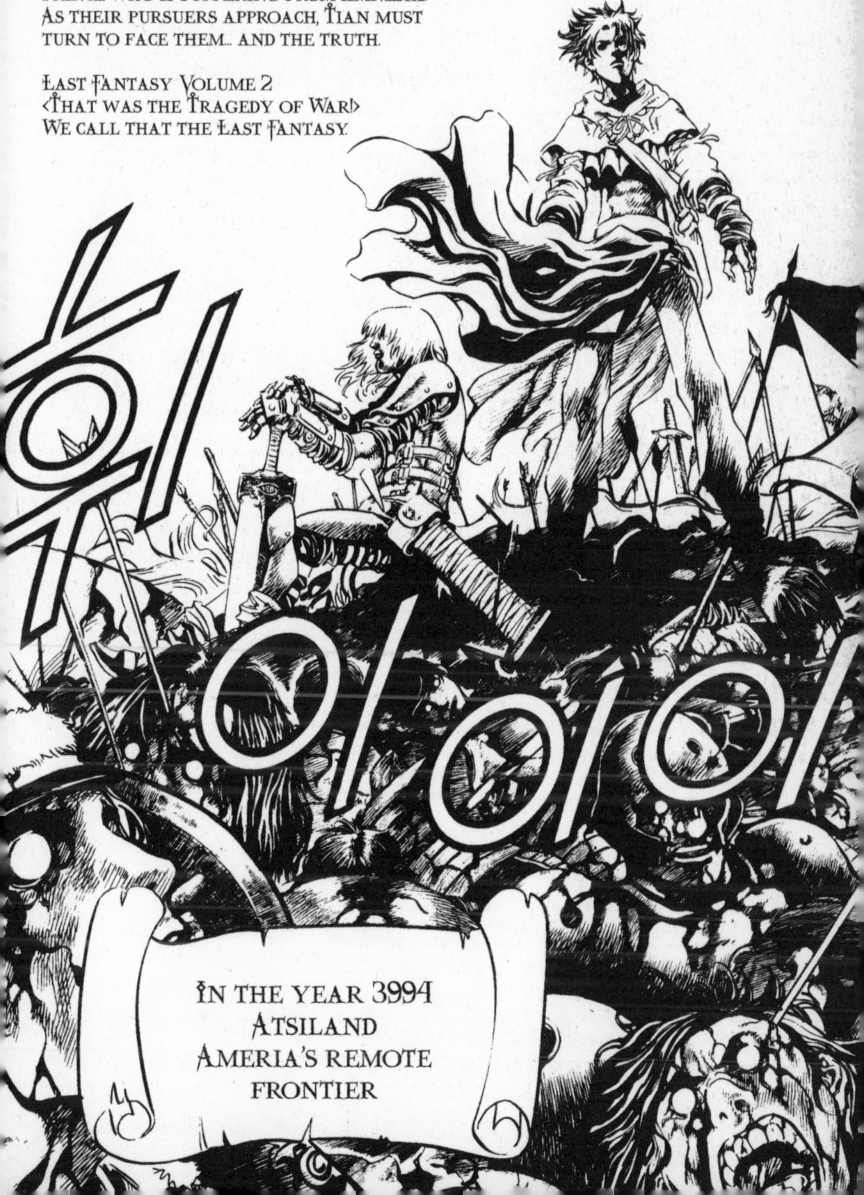
IN THE YEAR 3994
ATSILAND
AMERIA'S REMOTE
FRONTIER

‹The Makings of Last Fantasy›

● ●

Hello, this is the Writer Gang.
We hope that you've enjoyed reading the first volume of *Last Fantasy*.

The weakness that has been pointed out in a great majority of narratives that we have available to us in our country, including novels, plays, movies, animations and games, is the lack of plot and insufficient storyline. This is the case even for comic books—although there are a lot of cartoonists who are highly skilled in their art, lack of plot is a constant bugaboo.

Last Fantasy is the product of a plan to overcome the weaknesses that we see in so many storylines. There are three different writers working together on the story alone.

Although three people are working on the story, the pay for the manuscript isn't tripled, so there isn't much of a monetary advantage... ^^;
But we are facing this new challenge head-on! By combining all of our individual talents, we were able to create a story of higher caliber!
And we get to work with a great artist like Yong-Wan Kwon! The Writer Gang is greatly satisfied with this alone and are diligently putting our all into our work.

In the beginning, although it was agreed that our intention to combine all the talents of each individual writer was a good one, a lot of people expressed their apprehension that there would be a confusion of ideas with many different writers working collectively on one manga series. In other words, just as a ship with too many captains is bound to stray off course and instead end up in the mountains, a lot of concern was expressed for our endeavor as well.

—Don't you get into arguments because of difference of opinions?
—Don't you ever pass your work onto the other writers?

For all you curious readers and fellow writers, we now reveal the method that the members of the Writer Gang and Yong-Wan Kwon use to make this work!

PLANNING COMMITTEE MEETING: WRITER GANG

The planning committee meeting sets the basic construction for the story, and for this reason, all the members of the Writer Gang must attend. This is the fun part of the work. The things that we discuss during these meetings are...

—Countless ideas
—Goal of the current story in terms of the flow of the entire storyline
—General plot
—Items
—Introduction of new characters
—How many volumes will be written?

After a series of brainstormings, various stories plucked from our countless ideas are introduced into the general flow of the plot. There are so many stories that we are itching to write about, but in order to maintain the balance of the series as a whole, we have pushed back those stories until a later date.

SUMMARY OF IDEAS: WRITER GANG

For the most part, the person who has the most ideas during the planning committee meeting organizes and reports the ideas. It just happens that way. The things that are reported are...

—General plot of the episode
—Synopsis of each chapter
—Introduction of the groundwork and twists in the story

The report outline shows a general progression of the story. Simply put, it is a summary. However, if outsiders were to read it, they would not understand its content. The content is very complicated, and only those who have taken part in the meetings can understand the expressions that are used. At first glance, it may appear to be nothing more than doodles and chicken scratch. However, this is the important blueprint for the making of *Last Fantasy*.

SCENARIO: ANTI

#2. 산속(밤)
티안과 드라이는 야영을 하고있다.
진지한 표정으로 티안의 마법책을
읽는 척 하고 있는 드라이.
티안은 풀죽을 만들고 있는 중.
(곰돌이 앞치마는 아직 보이지 않음)
티안 : 글자도 모르면서 뭐해?
드라이 : 바보 취급하지마! 아는 글자가
3개나 된다구!
티안 : 그 정도면 충분히 바보야... (황당)

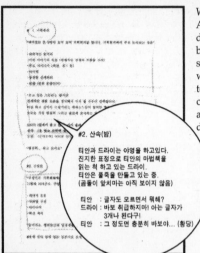

When a summary outline has been written, ANTI creates the scenario. In terms of details, this process can be seen as the beginning because the majority of the script and descriptions of the actions are written at this time. If any fun ideas come to mind, they are all written down without consideration of amount or volume. The amount will be taken into consideration during the coordinating stage.

Once the scenario is finished, it is printed so that the manuscript can undergo a rough sketch of the final product.

SCRIPTWRITING: JIN-SUK JEON

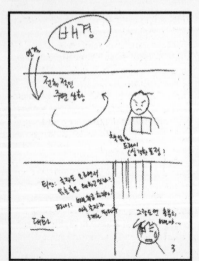

Based on the finished scenario, Jin-Suk Jeon creates a rough outline of the content of the story. The scenario largely stays the same. However, because the content of the story is being expressed through pictures, the scenes and the lines of the characters may be revised. This is when the distribution of the story content into different panels and the overall presentation is considered. This is a rough sketch without much feeling for the scene, especially because the only person who needs to be able to recognize certain parts of the sketch is Dong-Hyun Noh, who is responsible for the next step in the production process.

HEAD SCRIPTWRITER: NOH DONG HYUN

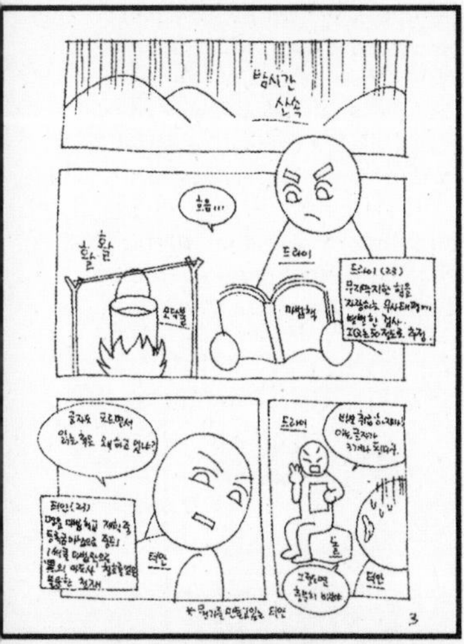
밤시간
산속

When the rough draft comes out, Dong-Hyun Noh, as the scriptwriter, cleans it up. There is a clear story that Yong-Wan Kwon wants to express. For this reason, the scene needs to be organized in a clear and clean manner. The other two members of the Writer Gang express their opinions, offer advice, and revise the final version of the characters and the script.

Although rare in occurrence, if all of a sudden, a better story comes to mind... then the work of the head scriptwriter is ineffective; everything starts from the beginning again. T.T

After ANTI checks the script one last time and the work is scanned and submitted to Yong-Wan Kwon, the work of the Writer Gang is concluded.

WORKING ON THE MANUSCRIPT: YONG-WAN KWON

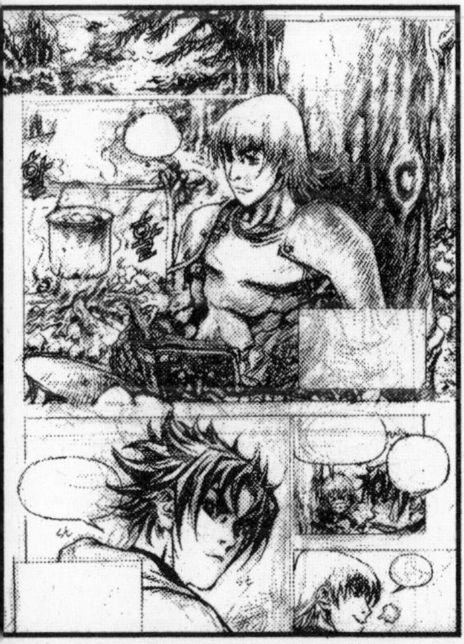

With the finalized copy that he receives from the Writer Gang, Yong-Wan Kwon begins to sketch the details of the pictures. On the document itself, he takes a blue colored pencil and draws a rough sketch and then he draws the subtle details onto the sketch with a pencil. The coordination of the Writer Gang produces a rough outline of the scenes in order to accurately tell the story, and once it passes through the hands of Yong-Wan Kwon, the manuscript is reproduced into an intense depiction of the scene. Yong-Wan Kwon puts in the same effort for the comical scenes as well, which is probably why *Last Fantasy* is even more entertaining and enjoyable. This is the very concept of *Last Fantasy*—the unbalanced combination of a comical story with serious pictures.

COMPLETION: THE FINAL TOUCHES

After Yong-Wan Kwon puts the finishing touches on the manuscript, two wonderful helpers, Sung-Hoon Jung and Yu-Sun Im, draw the background, and with that, the manuscript is completed. Completing the manuscript is no easy task because the Writer Gang has a lot of busy scenes like a crowded city street with a festival taking place, or a battlefield with a mountain of dead corpses. ^^;

After we submit the completed manuscript to the head editor, Sang-Won Song, he prints the script with the proper font type and size, then cuts and pastes them into each callout box. With that, the finished manuscript is sent to the printing company.

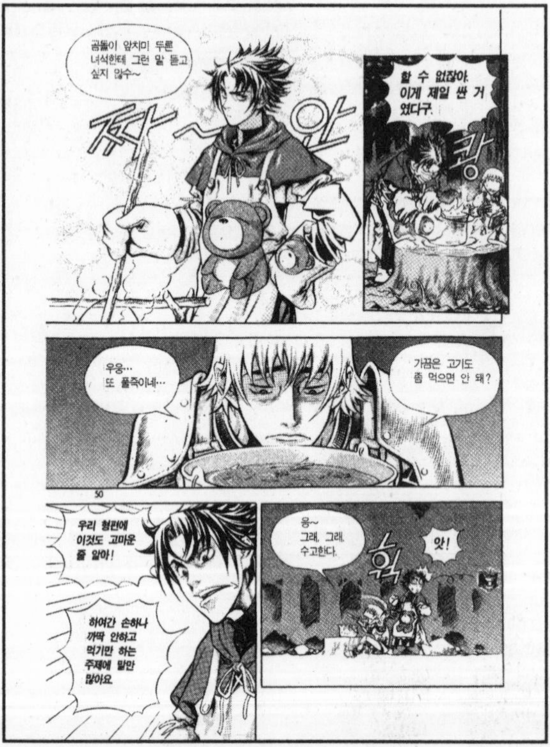
곰돌이 앞치마 두른 너석한테 그런 말 듣고 싶지 않수~
할 수 없잖아. 이게 제일 싼 거였다구.
우웅… 또 풀죽이네…
가끔은 고기도 좀 먹으면 안 돼?
50
우리 형편에 이것도 고마운 줄 알아!
하여간 손하나 까딱 안하고 먹기만 하는 주제에 말만 많아요
웅~ 그래, 그래. 수고한다.
앗!

As you can see, Last Fantasy is created through the collective effort of a lot of different people.

After four long months of preparation and revision, the first volume of *Last Fantasy* has been published. It took approximately one year to produce this book. Although the process itself was long and arduous, we believe that this is the very reason why we can all the more proudly present to you the final product of this book.

This was the first book that the Writer Gang worked on together. Of course, we hope that the results of this product may be favorable, but at the same time, whether this series is a success or not, the fact that we were able to collectively produce a joint project is reason enough to rejoice. There are times when we think that we should have made the story more entertaining, but for now, this was the best that we could produce. Of course, we will continue to make an effort to make each volume progressively more fun and entertaining.

In any case, we hope that many readers will read and enjoy Last Fantasy. However, this is not cause enough for us to want this book to only be borrowed, or scanned and distributed. For readers to buy the comic book is a rightful and natural desire of all cartoonists. Like all other things in this world, we cannot continue to produce these books without some financial incentive.

We hope that *Last Fantasy* would be a comic that is worthy of compensation of our efforts. If you feel that it does not have the value for you to spend your money, we ask you not to read it altogether. No cartoonist wants their work to be scanned and distributed, or merely borrowed, just for the sake of having a large following of readers, just as no one will offer their services without proper compensation for their work. The readers are the ones who construct the correct culture of the comic industry. If the market is crowded with self-consumption with no compensation, that market will have no choice but to close down. The comic industry is following after the path of Taiwanese comics and the Korean game industry, both of which crumbled, the former because of the formalized institution of lending, the latter because of the distribution of illegal copies.

This is not the case for only the books that the Writer Gang has written, or even just for Korean comic books. Buying comic books that you enjoy reading is a rightful part of enjoying this culture. Of course, if we were to say that we didn't wish our comic book to be included in the books that you enjoy, we would be lying. ^^;

Through the help of many people, we begin with this first book! We thank Yong-Wan Kwon for his illustrations, all of the assistants who helped with the entire process of production, and the editing committee. And of course we'd like to thank all the readers who used the little allowance that they have to buy this book.

To conclude... May this be the beginning that will be remembered as a legend in the years to come...

Writer Gang
www.creative-HON.com

LIFE
BY KEIKO SUENOBU

Ordinary high school teenagers...
Except that they're not.

LIFE™

© Keiko Suenobu

OT
OLDER TEEN
AGE 16+

Ayumu struggles with her studies, and the all-important high school entrance exams are approaching. Fortunately, she has help from her best bud Shii-chan, who is at the top of the class. But when the test results come back, the friends are surprised: Ayumu surpasses Shii-chan's scores and gets into the school of her choice—without Shii-chan! Losing her friend is so painful for Ayumu that she starts cutting herself to ease her sorrow. Finally, Ayumu seeks comfort in a new friend, Manami. But will Manami prove to be the friend that Ayumu truly needs? Or will Ayumu continue down a dark path?

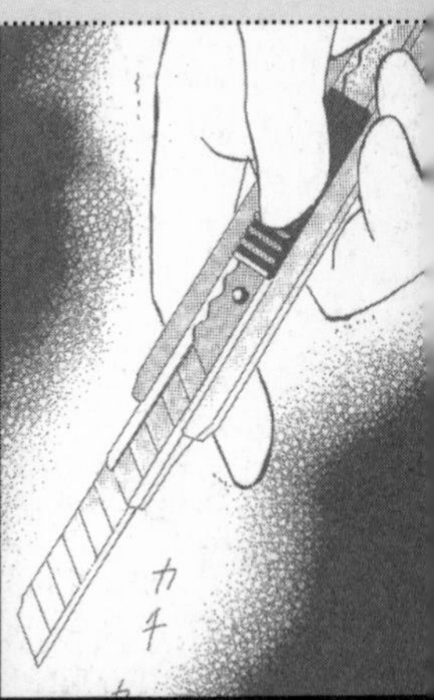
カチ

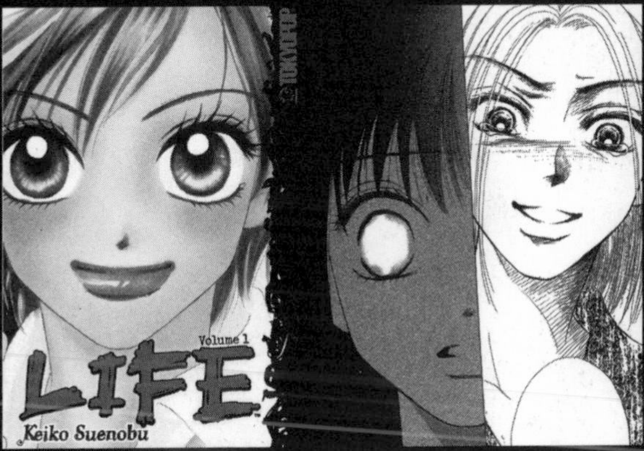
Volume 1
LIFE
Keiko Suenobu
TOKYOPOP

It's about real teenagers...

It's about real high school...

It's about real life.

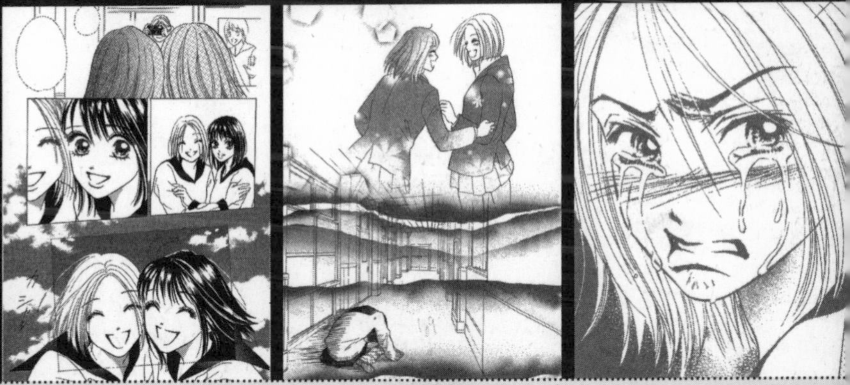

WWW.TOKYOPOP.COM/LIFE

BIZENGHAST

Dear Diary,
I'm starting to feel

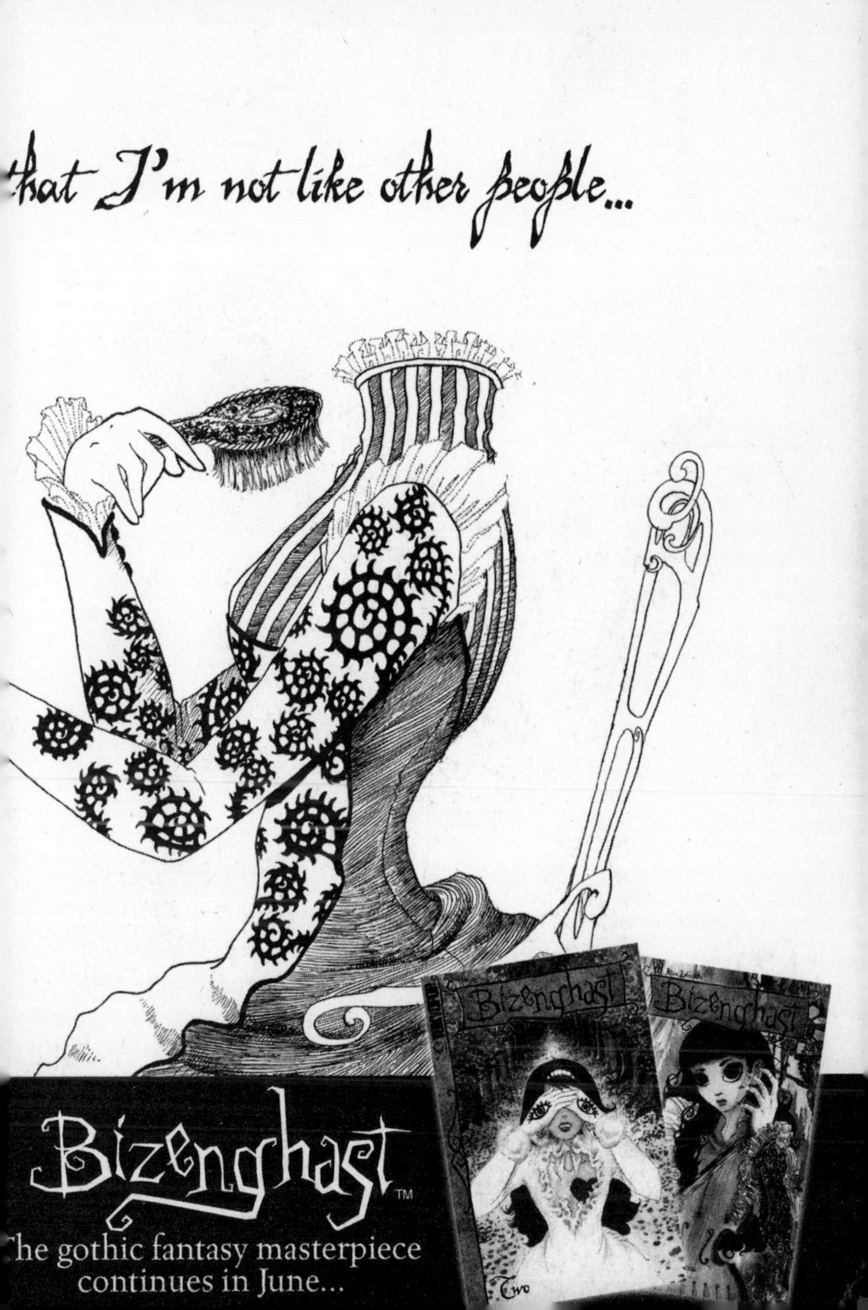

that I'm not like other people...
Bizenghast
Bizenghast
Two
Bizenghast™
The gothic fantasy masterpiece
continues in June...

POP FICTION

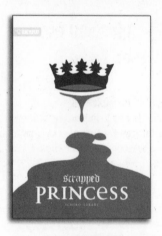